CONTENTS

Chapter 3: Ecotourism environments 60

WILEY AUSTRALIA TOURISM SERIES

ECOTOURISM

SECOND EDITION

DAVID WEAVER

WILEY

John Wiley & Sons Australia, Ltd

Second edition published 2008 by
John Wiley & Sons Australia, Ltd
42 McDougall Street, Milton Qld 4064

First edition published 2001

Typeset in 10.5/12 New Baskerville

National Library of Australia
Cataloguing-in-Publication data

Weaver, David, 1956– .
  Ecotourism.

  2nd ed.
  Bibliography.
  Includes index.
  ISBN 978 0 470 81304 1 (pbk.).

  1. Ecotourism. I. Title.

338.4791

Cover and internal design images:
© Digital Vision/Stephen Frink; © Corbis Corporation;
© Digital Stock/Corbis Corporation

Cartography by MAPgraphics Pty Ltd, Brisbane

Edited by Cathryn Game

10 9 8 7 6

PREFACE

It is now about 20 years since the term 'ecotourism' began to appear regularly in the English-language academic literature. Since that time, about 400 focused peer-reviewed academic articles and perhaps an equal number of book chapters and books have appeared on this topic, indicating ecotourism's migration from the margins to the mainstream of tourism research in Australia and elsewhere. Several trends are notable. First, its conceptual and practical boundaries are being continually expanded, as evidenced by the widespread recognition that ecotourism not only can occur as a form of mass tourism but also mostly does occur as such. Another manifestation of this expansion is the increasingly blurred line between ecotourism and cultural tourism, which was inspired in large part by the growing participation of indigenous communities, who have always regarded this distinction as a false dichotomy. This 'big tent' approach carries the danger that ecotourism will become diluted and ambiguous as a discrete form of tourism, but it also promises a bigger, more diverse and influential sector that can hold its own against other resource competitors and better reflects the realities of the evolving tourism sector. Another trend is the uneven distribution of research coverage. There have been extensive investigations of economic and environmental impact, community-based options, and the semantics and ethics of ecotourism, but relatively little consideration of critical topic areas such as the issue of greenwashing, the role of institutions, the impact of external environments, all aspects of the industry, and assessments and development of certification-based quality control mechanisms.

As ecotourism continues to mature as a subfield of tourism studies, these gaps will no doubt be filled, the establishment of the *Journal of Ecotourism* in 2002 being an excellent step towards the accommodation and collation of specialised research findings. However, the crucial contributions of other academic fields must also be recognised. Tourism students interested in ecological impact, for example, cannot progress in their understanding without access to the journal *Biological Conservation*, and the journal *Ecological Economics* is indispensable for those interested in economic impact. Such essential non-tourism journals are extensively utilised in this edition, which like its predecessor takes an interdisciplinary approach to the ecotourism phenomenon. Given the exponential increase in the amount of ecotourism research that has occurred since 2000, it should also be noted that the second edition represents an extensive rewrite of the first.

The biggest structural change is the division of the previous chapter 4, on impact, into two new chapters that respectively address first ecological, then economic and sociocultural impact. The extra space in each chapter accommodates not only the latest research outcomes but also greatly expanded text on the issue of potential solutions. In chapter 4 these focus on impact management strategies, such as zoning, site hardening and softening measures, visitor quotas and education. The subsequent chapter offers a new section focused on community-based ecotourism. As with the first edition, each chapter begins with a list of intended learning objectives that students should achieve as a result of reading and assimilating information presented in that particular chapter. The main body of every chapter, except chapter 1, continues to be supplemented by 'Practitioner's Perspective' and 'In the Field' boxed features focusing explicitly on 'real world' developments that illustrate concepts covered in the main text or point to new ideas and innovations that could have an important impact in the future. Concluding each chapter are questions, further reading references and a relevant case study that illustrates major concepts introduced in the chapter.

I am indebted to the ever-professional team at John Wiley & Sons Australia for facilitating the production of this new edition, and to Associate Publishing Editor Nina Crisp in particular for her patience and expertise in working with me through the chapters to obtain the highest quality outcomes. I wish to thank Cathryn Game for her editorial contribution to the new edition, and Susan Phillips for her excellent work on the supplements. I am also grateful to Pat Moody (former Dean of the College of Hospitality, Retail, and Sport Management at the University of South Carolina) and Charlie Partlow (Chair of the School of Hotel, Restaurant, and Tourism Management) for not just encouraging a culture of scholarship but also for being open to workload distributions that make possible a publication of this magnitude. Laura Lawton, as usual, provided constructive feedback and brought to my attention many of the sources cited herein. I also wish to thank the following reviewers who provided helpful suggestions that make this text so much stronger: Thomas Bauer, Hong Kong Polytechnic; Heather Zeppel, James Cook University; Narelle Beaumont, University of Southern Queensland; Trevor Thornton, Deakin University; Alcinda Trawen, Divine Word University; Chris Fanning, Flinders University; John Kennedy, Tai Poutini Polytechnic; Rik Thwaites, Charles Sturt University. Finally, I dedicate this book to my mother, Jarmila Weaver (1929–2006), who taught me that there are no limits on what we are capable of achieving in life.

David Weaver
August 2007

ACKNOWLEDGEMENTS ....

The author and publisher would like to thank the following copyright holders, organisations and individuals for their permission to reproduce copyright material in this book.

Images
• © Photodisc: **25** • MAPgraphics Pty Ltd, Brisbane: **72, 205, 247, 256, 276, 280, 281, 285, 290, 292, 294, 298** • Elsevier: **98** this article was published in *Annals of Tourism Research*, Volume 34, 4 issues, diagram of support for protected areas in Belize, adapted from © Elsevier • The International Ecotourism Society: **101** (graph) 'Relationship between visitation and resource impact as illustrated for six indicators of campsite condition', *Ecotourism: a guide for planners and managers*, vol. 2, p. 163 • © Ecotourism Australia: **173** • CABI: **198** Parker, S. 2001 'The Place of Ecotourism in Public Policy and Planning' in Weaver, D. B., *Encyclopedia of Ecotourism*, Wallingford, UK: CAB International, pp. 509–20 • Alison Allcock: **232** 'Diagram of national ecosystem strategy development process' in *Ecotourism*, p. 222. A. Allcock, 1999 • © Environmental Protection Agency: **250**.

Text
• Tourism Queensland: **57–9** Case Study: Identifying ecotourist markets for Australia. Statistics quoted from Tourism Queensland websites © Tourism Queensland http://www.tq.com.au/fms/tq_corporate/research/fact_sheets/the_german_ecotourism_market.pdf • © The World Conservation Union (IUCN): **66–7** • © World Wildlife Fund International: **112–15** • CABI: **167** from 'Potential ecotourism building types by category', table 33.1, from chapter titled 'Accommodations' by J. Gardner, p. 526 of the *Encylopedia of Ecotourism*, edited by David Weaver © CAB International 2001 • IAATO: **171** 'When in the Antarctic Treaty Area — Organisers and operators should ...' taken from webpage, http://www.iaato.org/guidelines.html • © Ecotourism Australia: **174, 222** • The International Ecotourism Society: **219** © TIES Mission and Vision Statement http://www.ecotourism.org/webmodules/webarticlesnet/templates/eco_template_ news.aspx?articleid=12&zoneid=25.

Every effort has been made to trace the ownership of copyright material. Information that will enable the publisher to rectify any error or omission in subsequent editions will be welcome. In such cases, please contact the Permissions Section of John Wiley & Sons Australia, Ltd who will arrange for the payment of the usual fee.

CHAPTER 1

Criteria
and context

LEARNING OBJECTIVES

After reading this chapter, you should be able to:

■ discuss the evolution of ecotourism through four tourism 'platforms'

■ evaluate the diversity of ecotourism definitions

■ describe and critically discuss the four core ecotourism criteria

■ explain the challenges associated with the concept of 'sustainability'

■ distinguish between minimalist and comprehensive ecotourism

■ describe the relationship between ecotourism and related activities such as nature-based tourism, wildlife tourism, adventure tourism, alternative tourism and sustainable tourism

■ explain how ecotourism is related to disassociated activities, such as 3S tourism and mass tourism.

The term **ecotourism** was unknown in the English language as recently as the mid-1980s. Yet, by the beginning of the 21st century, this form of recreational activity, which essentially involves the observation and appreciation of wildlife and other aspects of the natural environment while minimising the related ecological or sociocultural costs, had emerged as a major component of global tourism and an important focus for academics in the field of tourism studies. Many stakeholders, however, while enthusiastically embracing the concept of ecotourism as defined above, still do not really understand what it means: what activities qualify, who participates, where it occurs, what impact is acceptable, or how it can be optimally managed.

The goal of this textbook is to provide stakeholders, and interested university students in particular, with a balanced and comprehensive exposure to the growing knowledge base of ecotourism that will assist their ability to place in context, critically evaluate and effectively manage the sector. Towards this goal, chapter 1 introduces the concept of ecotourism first by tracing the origins of the term, then by presenting a selection of definitions as proposed by various researchers and organisations. Section 1.4 addresses the issue of definition in more detail by examining the criteria that are usually associated with ecotourism. From this discussion, the definition of ecotourism that is adopted for this textbook is presented along with a distinction between minimalist and comprehensive models of ecotourism. The relationship between ecotourism and other tourism-related terms that are commonly affiliated with ecotourism is considered in section 1.5, and this is followed by a discussion of the specific kinds of activity that constitute ecotourism. The final section presents a conceptual model that forms the philosophical basis of this text, and outlines the structure of the book.

1.2 EMERGENCE OF ECOTOURISM ······················

The word 'ecotourism' apparently first appeared in the English-language academic literature as a hyphenated term ('eco-tourism') in an article by Romeril (1985). However, the Mexican ecologist Hector Ceballos-Lascuraín used the Spanish word *ecoturismo* even earlier in the decade (Boo 1990), and the national forestry service in Canada was marketing the concept of an educational 'ecotour' along the Trans-Canada Highway as far back as 1973 (Canadian Forestry Service 1973, Fennell 2003). Intriguingly, Romeril used the word in reference to an earlier paper by Budowski (1976), which is often cited as one of the earliest references to the concept of ecotourism. In this article, Budowski recognised that the relationship between tourism and the natural environment tended to be one of conflict, but that the potential existed for a relationship based on symbiosis, or mutual benefit. His subsequent description of how this symbiotic type of tourism might function bears a close resemblance to contemporary ecotourism.

Ecotourism therefore existed as both a concept and a practice long before the coinage of the term in the mid-1980s. But the new term was quickly embraced by practitioners and academics as the preferred word for describing tourism that is focused on learning about the natural environment and sensitive to its well-being. Much of the credit for the dissemination of the term and the concept is due to Elizabeth Boo, whose seminal and widely circulated publication *Ecotourism: The Potentials and Pitfalls* (Boo 1990) contained a definition of ecotourism that was put forward by Ceballos-Lascuraín in the late 1980s. According to this definition, ecotourism is:

■ ... tourism that consists in traveling to relatively undisturbed or uncontaminated natural areas with the specific objective of studying, admiring and enjoying the scenery and its wild plants and animals, as well as any existing cultural manifestations (both past and present) found in these areas. (Ceballos-Lascuraín, in Boo 1990, p. 2.) ■

The word 'ecotourism' is an appealing label that has no doubt helped to galvanise interest in the concept of environmental tourism. However, the coining of the name and the dissemination of an appealing definition are not enough to explain the subsequent explosion in interest that has occurred in the tourism literature and in the industry. To account for this extraordinary degree of popularity, it is also necessary to consider the context in which ecotourism emerged.

■ *1.2.1* **Jafari's** *four platforms*

Jafari (1989, 2001) suggests that the tourism sector, and the field of tourism studies in particular, has advanced through four phases or 'platforms' since the end of World War II and the subsequent beginning of the modern **mass tourism** era (Weaver 2006). Although this evolution has been sequential, the boundaries between stages are transitional, and older platforms have retained and attracted supporters even after they have lost their dominance.

According to Jafari's model, the 1950s and 1960s were dominated by an **advocacy platform** wherein tourism was widely regarded as an ideal activity that resulted in many positive consequences for destinations and few negative consequences. Potential benefits include direct revenues and employment, indirect revenues and employment through the multiplier effect, stimulation of development in peripheral areas, promotion of cross-cultural understanding, and incentives to preserve a destination's culture and history. Proponents of this platform therefore believe that the growth of tourism should be encouraged and that governments should facilitate rather than impede or control this expansion.

By the early 1970s, at least in academia, the advocacy platform gave way to a **cautionary platform**, as the negative consequences of *laissez-faire* mass tourism growth became increasingly evident, especially in the less-developed countries of the so-called Third World (Wall & Mathieson 2005). This platform basically argues that tourism eventually results in net negative consequences for destinations *unless* careful regulations are put into place.

A central argument is that direct and indirect revenue flows in destinations with weak economies are substantially eroded by leakages related to high imports and the repatriation of multinational corporate profits. Cultural commodification and inter-cultural conflict are other problems attributed to mass tourism. Positioned therefore at the opposite end of the ideological continuum from the advocacy platform, the cautionary platform is represented by such classics as *Tourism: Blessing or Blight?* (Young 1973), *The Golden Hordes: International Tourism and the Pleasure Periphery* (Turner & Ash 1975) and the destination lifecycle model of Butler (1980). The latter, in particular, may be seen as the culmination of the cautionary platform, given its premise that continued uncontrolled tourism growth will sooner or later lead to the breaching of a destination's environmental, economic and sociocultural tolerance levels.

In Butler's well-known and widely tested S-shaped curve, a destination begins in the 'exploration' stage, which is characterised by a small visitor intake but no formal tourism system. Local responses to this incipient tourism flow inaugurate the 'involvement' stage, which soon progesses to 'development' and concomitant rapid growth as new markets take advantage of the opening of the destination. It is during the mature development phase that critical environmental and sociocultural thresholds are exeeded, leading to 'consolidation', 'stagnation' and eventually 'decline' if no remedial measures are taken. Conversely, if such measures are taken, the destination may experience 'rejuvenation'. The critical underlying assumption of Butler's model is that tourism carries the seeds of its own destruction unless carefully planned and managed (Weaver & Lawton 2006).

The **adaptancy platform** of the 1980s maintained the same left-wing ideological position as that of the cautionary platform, but was distinguished by its efforts to propose and implement tourism options that would supposedly be better suited to bringing about positive outcomes for destinations; that is, they are better 'adapted' to the conditions of a given place (e.g. Gonsalves 1987, Krippendorf 1984, Murphy 1985). These options were grouped under the banner of **alternative tourism**, in the specific sense that they were conceived as alternatives to the mass tourism that was allegedly harming less-developed regions. Typically, alternative and mass tourism are perceived by supporters of this platform as polarised **ideal types**, with the former being presented as 'good' tourism and the latter as 'bad' tourism.

Figure 1.1 depicts the contrasting characteristics that were commonly attributed to each ideal type. The early forms of alternative tourism identified under this label include home stays (i.e. staying in the homes of local residents), cultural villages, vacation farms and volunteer tourism (Dernoi 1981), all of which emphasised socially and culturally responsible outcomes but did not focus on benefits for the natural environment. In essence, ecotourism served to fill this void by emerging in the mid-1980s as a form of alternative tourism that emphasised the well-being of the natural environment while concurrently recognising the legitimate interests of host communities. Thus, ecotourism was generally regarded — and to a large extent is still perceived today — as a small-scale, locally controlled type of nature-based tourism that complements the local economy and blends into the local cultural landscape.

CHARACTERISTICS	MASS TOURISM	ALTERNATIVE TOURISM
Markets Segment	Psychocentric–midcentric	Allocentric–midcentric
Volume and mode	High; package tours	Low; individual arrangements
Seasonality	Distinct high and low seasons	No distinct seasonality
Origins	A few dominant markets	No dominant markets
Attractions Emphasis	Highly commercialised	Moderately commercialised
Character	Generic, 'contrived'	Area specific, 'authentic'
Orientation	Tourists only or mainly	Tourists and locals
Accommodation Size	Large scale	Small scale
Spatial pattern	Concentrated in 'tourist areas'	Dispersed throughout area
Density	High density	Low density
Architecture	'International' style; obtrusive, non-sympathetic	Vernacular style; unobtrusive, complementary
Ownership	Non-local, large corporations	Local, small businesses
Economic status Role of tourism	Dominates local economy	Complements existing activity
Linkages	Mainly external	Mainly internal
Leakages	Extensive	Minimal
Multiplier effect	Low	High
Regulation Control	Non-local private sector	Local 'community'
Amount	Minimal; to facilitate private sector	Extensive; to minimise local negative impact
Ideology	Free market forces	Public intervention
Emphasis	Economic growth, profits; sector-specific	Community stability and well-being; integrated, holistic
Time frame	Short term	Long term

■ **Figure 1.1** *The adaptancy platform: mass tourism and alternative tourism as ideal types*
Source: *Weaver & Lawton 2006.*

By the 1990s, there was growing realisation that alternative tourism could never be more than a partial and localised solution to the problems of tourism, which had by then clearly become a massive global industry. In addition, it became apparent that both alternative and mass tourism could generate both positive and negative consequences and therefore that the ideologically dogmatic platforms of the past were insufficient for dealing with the actual complexity of the sector. What was needed and what emerged, according to Jafari (1989, 2001), was a more objective and holistic approach that recognises the strengths and weaknesses of *all* types of tourism and utilises scientific knowledge to determine the best combination of tourism modes for each destination. Stimulating this new **knowledge-based platform** was the emergence of the sustainable development paradigm, which advocated a measured growth approach that takes into consideration a destination's environmental and sociocultural carrying capacity (see section 1.4.4). From an ecotourism perspective, a critical outcome has been the growing perception that this sector can legitimately occur as either alternative or mass tourism (see section 1.5.7).

1.3 DEFINITIONS

Since its inception, ecotourism has been defined in many different ways, ranging from the general and ambiguous to the specific and prescriptive. Descriptive (e.g. 'nature-based') and value-based (e.g. 'must be sustainable') components are also usually combined in the definition. Table 1.1 provides a chronological sample of the definitions proposed by a variety of ecotourism stakeholders since the late 1980s. This selection is intended to inform and illustrate the following discussion of ecotourism criteria, and does not include all published definitions. Those who wish to read more thorough accounts of ecotourism's definitional evolution should consult Björk (2000), Diamantis and Ladkin (1999a), Fennell (2003) and Page and Dowling (2002).

■ Table 1.1
Selected ecotourism definitions

SOURCE	DEFINITION
Valentine (1992)	Nature-based tourism that is ecologically sustainable and is based on relatively undisturbed natural areas, is non-damaging and non-degrading, contributes directly to the continued protection and management of protected areas, and is subject to an adequate and appropriate management regime
Scace, Grifone & Usher (1992, p. 14)	An enlightening nature-travel experience that contributes to conservation of the ecosystem while respecting the integrity of host communities
Ecotourism Society (in Lindberg & Hawkins 1993, p. 8)	Ecotourism is responsible travel to natural areas which conserves the environment and improves the welfare of local people.

(continued)

SOURCE	DEFINITION
J. Butler (in Scace 1993, p. 65)	• It must be consistent with a positive environmental ethic, fostering preferred behaviour. • It does not denigrate the environmental resource. There is no erosion of resource integrity. • It concentrates on intrinsic rather than extrinsic values. • It is biocentric rather than homocentric in philosophy, in that an ecotourist accepts nature largely on its own terms, rather than significantly transforming the environment for personal convenience. • Ecotourism must benefit the resource. The environment must experience a net benefit from the activity, although these are often spin-offs of social, economic, political or scientific benefits. • It is a first-hand experience with the natural environment. • There is in ecotourism an expectation of gratification measured in appreciation and education, not in thrill-seeking or physical achievement. • There are high cognitive (informative) and affective (emotional) dimensions to the experience, requiring a high level of preparation from both leaders and participants.
Allcock et al. (1994, p. 17) from the National Ecotourism Strategy of Australia	Nature-based tourism that involves education and interpretation of the natural environment and is managed to be ecologically sustainable. This definition recognises that 'natural environment' includes cultural components and that 'ecologically sustainable' involves an appropriate return to the local community and long-term conservation of the resource.
Goodwin (1996, p. 288)	Low-impact nature tourism which contributes to the maintenance of species and habitats either directly through a contribution to conservation and/or indirectly by providing revenue to the local community sufficient for local people to value, and therefore protect, their wildlife heritage area as a source of income.
Fennell (1999, p. 43)	A sustainable form of natural resource-based tourism that focuses primarily on experiencing and learning about nature, and is ethically managed to be low-impact, non-consumptive, and locally oriented (control, benefits and scale). It typically occurs in natural areas, and should contribute to the conservation or preservation of such areas. .
EAA (2000a)	Ecologically sustainable tourism, with a primary focus on experiencing natural areas, that fosters environmental and cultural understanding, appreciation and conservation
Blamey (2001)	Ecotourism is: • nature based • environmentally educated and • sustainably managed.

(continued)

SOURCE	DEFINITION
Quebec Declaration on Ecotourism 2001 (in Buckley 2003a, p. xiii)	Sustainable tourism that • contributes actively to the conservation of natural and cultural heritage • includes local and indigenous communities in its planning, development and operation and contributes to their well-being • interprets the natural and cultural heritage of the destination for visitors • lends itself better to independent travellers, as well as to organised tours for small groups.

1.4 CRITERIA

The above definitions illustrate the absence of any consensus on the precise meaning of ecotourism. However, Blamey (1997, 2001) is notable for distilling three core criteria of ecotourism that recur in other definitions; namely, a dominant nature-based element in the attractions, an educational or learning component and a requirement of 'sustainability'. The latter two components are value-based whereas the first is more descriptive. To these should be added another descriptive component; that is, the often overlooked but fundamental observation that ecotourism is a form of tourism. Beginning with the latter, each of these four criteria will now be considered in detail, as will the supplementary criterion of financial viability.

■ 1.4.1 Ecotourism *as a form of tourism*

Because ecotourism is a form of tourism, the **ecotourist** should meet the demand-side criteria that are normally used by the World Tourism Organization to define and differentiate tourists in general (WTO 2001). First, as depicted in figure 1.2, only certain travel purposes qualify as tourism. The most common of these are leisure/holidays, business, and visiting friends and relatives (VFR). Relatively minor purposes include pilgrimage, sport, health and education. Forms of travel that do not usually qualify as tourism include migration, military activity, commuting to work and refugee movements. Leisure/holidays and education are two qualifying categories that accommodate ecotourism.

Second, tourism involves a spatial component. Individuals who travel beyond their usual country of residence are designated as international tourists whereas those who travel within their usual country of residence are domestic tourists. Minimal distance thresholds are normally applied to distinguish domestic tourists from those engaged in localised travel. Such thresholds do not generally apply to international tourism, the act of crossing an international boundary being enough to warrant classification as an international tourist. Finally, tourists are further differentiated on the

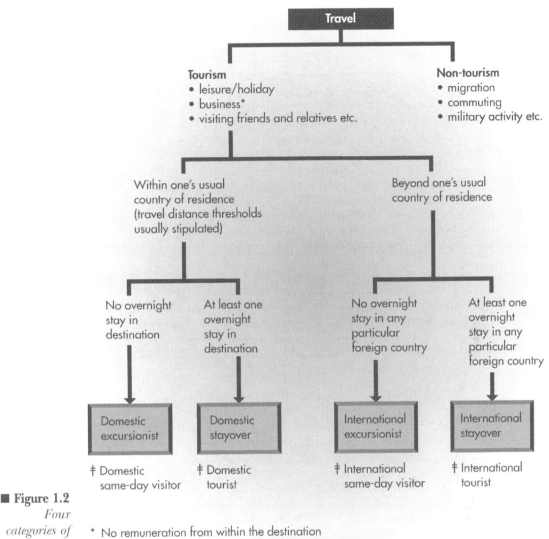

Travel

Tourism
- leisure/holiday
- business*
- visiting friends and relatives etc.

Non-tourism
- migration
- commuting
- military activity etc.

Within one's usual country of residence (travel distance thresholds usually stipulated)

Beyond one's usual country of residence

No overnight stay in destination

At least one overnight stay in destination

No overnight stay in any particular foreign country

At least one overnight stay in any particular foreign country

Domestic excursionist

Domestic stayover

International excursionist

International stayover

‡ Domestic same-day visitor

‡ Domestic tourist

‡ International same-day visitor

‡ International tourist

■ **Figure 1.2**
Four categories of tourist

* No remuneration from within the destination
‡ World Tourism Organization equivalents

basis of time. Persons spending at least one night in a particular destination are commonly referred to as 'stayovers' whereas those travelling to a destination without staying at least one night are designated as 'excursionists'.

Tourists — and hence ecotourists — can therefore be divided into four distinct categories on the basis of these spatial and temporal criteria (figure 1.2). **Domestic excursionists** travel to a destination within their usual country of residence that meets designated distance thresholds relative to their place of normal residence. However, unlike **domestic stayovers**, they do not spend at least one night in that location. In the case of Australia, domestic tourists are defined as persons who make a journey of at least 40 kilometres away from their residence that *must* involve at least one overnight stay. Technically, the category of domestic excursionist therefore does not apply to Australia (BTR 1998). An **international stayover** is someone who stays at least one night, but no more than 12 months, in a country that is not their usual country of residence whereas an **international excursionist** does not spend at least one night in this foreign country. Cruise-ship passengers in regions such as the Caribbean and the South Pacific are a common example of international excursionists.

From a supply-side perspective, the definitional issue of tourism is more flexible. Numerous operations or sites are designated as 'ecotourism' products and their visitors known as 'ecotourists', even though many of these visitors do not strictly meet the varying travel distance criteria used by each country to define domestic tourists. In such cases, to earn the ecotourism label, it is usually regarded as more important for the visitors and the product to fulfil the three criteria that follow. Still, the grouping of ecotourists into tourist categories is a useful exercise, because overnight visitors and international visitors often have different requirements and impact from those associated with domestic tourists. The presence of a 'tourist', moreover, implies the entry of new revenue into the destination.

■ 1.4.2 Basis *in nature*

Virtually all definitions of ecotourism refer to the natural environment, the prefix 'eco-' generally being taken to mean 'ecology' or 'ecosystem'. These references allude to the perception that ecotourism should be 'nature-based'; that is, its attractions should be based primarily on the natural environment or some element thereof. This latter clause recognises that ecotourism need not be based on a particular ecosystem or habitat (such as a rainforest or wetland), but may instead be focused on some specific component of that ecosystem. This indicates an 'elemental' as opposed to 'holistic' approach to the target product wherein the ecotourist is more interested in a certain rare or interesting species of flora or fauna than in the broader ecosystem in which that species occurs. Collectively described as **charismatic megafauna**, these attractive species include dolphins, polar bears, pandas, eagles, Bengal tigers and lions. Wildlife viewing in Kenya's Amboseli National Park in the late 1970s, for example, was focused on lions (accounting for 27–30 per cent of total visitor viewing time), cheetahs (12–15 per cent), elephants (13 per cent) and rhinoceroses (9 per cent) (as described by Henry 1980, in Roe, Leader-Williams & Dalal-Clayton 1997). Research by Kontoleon et al. (2002) reveals the importance of Sichuan's giant pandas to foreign tourists surveyed in Beijing. Mammals tend to be the most popular object of ecotourist attention, followed by birds and then reptiles and invertebrates (Newsome, Dowling & Moore 2005). In some destinations, **charismatic megaflora** such as redwood trees (California), rafflesia (Indonesia) or jarrah (Western Australia) underscore the ecotourism industry, while other locations are dependent on **charismatic megaliths** such as volcanoes, escarpments and caves.

From an ecosystems perspective, the holistic approach is preferable in that elements are not seen in isolation but rather as interdependent components of a single system. This subsequently is more conducive to quality learning and sustainability outcomes (see sections 1.4.3 and 1.4.4) and helps to explain why many definitions state that ecotourism should occur in a relatively undisturbed natural environment; that is, in a venue that provides exposure to an entire ecosystem. Nevertheless, the elemental approach is valid from a marketing point of view. Additional examples of such focused ecotourism attractions include the near-shore dolphin schools of Monkey Mia in Western Australia, the migrating polar bears in Churchill (Manitoba, Canada) and the monarch butterfly concentrations in the remnant upland fir forests of central Mexico. In such situations, however, managers should be responsive to the problems that may arise in maintaining a narrow product focus (see section 4.4.2). There are further implications in terms of venue. Wildlife normally is best observed in its natural habitat, but there are numerous examples of wildlife adaptation to modified non-captive environments, such as farmland and even urban structures, such as the downtown skyscrapers in the USA, where nesting peregrine falcons have been introduced (see section 3.5.2).

Associated cultural component

While the primary focus is on the natural environment, ecotourism definitions usually allow a secondary role for related cultural attractions, as indicated in the definition of Ceballos-Lascuraín (see section 1.2). This is a reasonable and desirable qualifier, because there is probably no completely undisturbed 'natural' environment. Virtually the entire surface of the Earth bears some evidence of human or 'cultural' intervention. To recognise and incorporate this cultural dimension, rather than dealing with only the non-human element, is to provide an even more holistic and realistic experience for ecotourists. Moreover, it is often extremely difficult to differentiate the 'cultural' and 'natural' components of a given landscape. Indigenous cultures that have coexisted with the natural environment for centuries or millennia illustrate this point, to the extent that they exist in symbiosis with that environment and have been responsible for many of the supposedly 'natural' attributes it contains. The apparent role of the Aboriginal people in introducing and disseminating the dingo (or wild dog) in Australia is but one example (Breiter 1996), as is the seamless interconnection between the Maori and the 'natural' features of New Zealand (see section 8.5). From a marketing standpoint, the incorporation of a cultural component, whether indigenous or non-indigenous, is a way of diversifying the product and, subsequently, the market base that may be attracted to that product.

■ *1.4.3* **Learning**

With regard to visitor motivation and the actual interaction between the visitor and the attraction, ecotourism definitions usually include an element of education, learning or appreciation about the natural attractions that form the basis of the ecotourism product. This learning dimension is both broad and subjective enough to include a diverse array of possible motivations and interactions. At one end of the motivational/interactive continuum, ecotourists may be involved in a formal educational process involving credit courses or dissertation research. This type of activity does not contravene the criteria discussed in section 1.4.1, because formal education qualifies as a purpose for tourism-related travel. Still along the more formal end of this continuum, some ecotourists prefer to receive a highly structured (but non-assessed) interpretation of the product, which may include some combination of live expert commentary, tape-recorded commentary and sophisticated signage along carefully designed interpretation trails. Towards the less formal end of the scale, ecotourists may rely on guidebooks in the absence of, or in preference to, these structured mediation opportunities.

On the informal side of the continuum, some ecotourists disregard all forms of external interpretation, preferring simply to observe and absorb the natural environment on their own terms and perhaps even at a subconscious level. In such cases, the educational component may be so subjective and obscure as to defy measurement, and is probably better described as an appreciative or spiritual experience rather than an educational one. At this point, the line between education/learning/ appreciation and their absence may also become so blurred that the learning criterion is no longer met.

Another dimension of learning is motivational, and considers the degree to which the ecotourist wants to be immersed in the product. At the 'shallow' end of this continuum, the participant is satisfied with superficial exposure and simple information that is entertaining. At the 'deep' end, a broader and deeper understanding is sought that may go well beyond the focal ecosystem or element by incorporating into product interpretation causal factors such as climate change and globalisation. This approach is evident, for example, in the well-known whale tours of Kaikoura, New Zealand (Curtin 2003), and in the dolphin program at Tangalooma in Queensland (Orams 1997). Several of the ecotourism definitions listed above are clearly positioned towards this pole. Scace, Grifone and Usher (1992) describe ecotourism as 'enlightening', and the Ecotourism Association of Australia (now **Ecotourism Australia**) (EAA 2000a) states that ecotourism 'fosters understanding'. James Butler (in Scace 1993) argues that ecotourism should promote 'preferred behaviour', suggesting a transformational element that, although not essential to the learning dimension, is desirable because it helps to realise sustainable outcomes relative to the product and to one's lifestyle more generally (see section 1.4.4; Kimmel 1999, Tisdell & Wilson 2001).

Interpretation

Because it goes beyond the simple conveyance of facts to reveal relationships and meaning (Knudson, Cable & Beck 1995), effective interpretation is critical to simultaneously achieving the diverse goals of entertainment as well as enlightenment and behaviour transformation. This is illustrated by the stromatolite colonies at Hamelin Pool Marine Nature Reserve (Shark Bay, Western Australia), which to the uninitiated are nothing more than heaps of slime. However, to the informed they are composed of rare primitive organisms that have remained unchanged since the first appearance of life on Earth. Effective interpretation conveys this in an interesting way while encouraging behaviour that minimises the negative impact of visitation. It is also often required to deal with sensitive or controversial situations such as the harvesting of polar bears and whales by indigenous communities (see section 5.4.3). In recognition of its importance for attaining visitor satisfaction, several Australian state governments have published interpretation self-help guidebooks for small businesses and communities involved in ecotourism (Department of Conservation 2000, Tourism Queensland 2000).

A distinction can be made between off-site and on-site interpretation. Before arriving at a destination, most ecotourists have already been exposed to product interpretation through guidebooks, brochures, the Internet, promotional videos and/or word of mouth. More rarely, the potential traveller may have had a virtual reality experience such as Antarctic Adventure in Hobart (Tourism Queensland 2000) or a mobile augmented reality (or MAR; see Weaver & Lawton 2006). Although neglected in the academic ecotourism literature, pre-experience interpretation is extremely important in so far as it influences the decision to visit particular destinations but not others. It also creates a set of images, standards and expectations that subsequently affects tourist behaviour. For example, a guidebook may give the impression that approaching a particular type of animal is acceptable when it may actually be prohibited. Appropriate messages and behaviour relevant to future travel can also be reinforced by the provision of post-experience interpretation (Forestell 1993), but this does not appear to be discussed in the ecotourism literature.

On-site interpretation sources include self-guided walks or car tours, guided walking tours and commentaries aboard safari vehicles, 'tundra buggies', cableways and submarines. Interpretation centres are both off-site and on-site in that they are located in or adjacent to a target habitat but maintain an internal artificial environment. Designed effectively, interpretation centres can provide a substitute for actual exposure to the attraction for large numbers of visitors and thereby contribute to a reduced negative impact on the environment. Each mode of interpretation differs in the way the learning experience is conveyed and received, but several basic principles should be borne in mind to increase the likelihood of attaining high levels of learning as well as satisfaction (Weiler & Ham 2001). Effective interpretation should:

- avoid a fact-oriented 'academic' instruction style, which tends to be boring and can alienate a non-captive audience that has no incentive to absorb such information
- be enjoyable for visitors and should therefore employ a conversational, enthusiastic and interesting style of presentation that might involve audience participation (Kimmel 1999)
- be made relevant through the use of references and analogies that are meaningful to the audience. Attention and satisfaction are almost guaranteed if focus is placed on things that listeners already regard as important

- be well organised and easy to follow, which means that an experience should convey no more than four or five main ideas that the participant will retain afterwards
- focus on themes rather than simple topics or subjects. Themes, from a deep learning perspective, should convey a sense of place unique to each particular site while simultaneously invoking universal environmental and cultural messages.

Of all the various sources of interpretation, skilled tour guides have the advantage of being able to continuously 'read' their audience as well as their surroundings in 'real time' and to adjust delivery content accordingly. They are also available to answer questions and may form emotional bonds with their audience. However, because resource limitations often restrict the extent to which tour guides can be provided at a site, it is also important for ecotourism managers to design and implement static forms of interpretation that facilitate visitor education by following the above principles to the greatest possible extent (see section 4.5.6).

■ *1.4.4* Sustainability

Most definitions hold that ecotourism should be minimally disruptive to the natural and cultural setting in which it occurs; that is, it should be 'sustainable'. This reference stems from the concept of **sustainable development**, which was defined and popularised by the Brundtland Report in the late 1980s as 'development that meets the needs of the present without compromising the ability of future generations to meet their own needs' (WCED 1987, p. 43). While this is a beguiling goal that has attracted widespread agreement, the following sections reveal the extent to which sustainable development has emerged as an 'essentially contested concept' (Hall 1998).

Weak and strong

This imperative of sustainability is closely linked to the knowledge-based platform in so far as it appears to accommodate both the sustaining of the environment (suggesting alternative tourism) as well as continued development (suggesting mass tourism). Some argue that this duality makes the idea of sustainable development contradictory, impractical and susceptible to appropriation by the supporters of those two different forms of tourism (Wheeller 1994). In contrast, many supporters of sustainability regard this flexibility as an asset, since it accommodates both development-focused sustainable mass tourism in areas already site-hardened to accommodate such activities and preservation-focused alternative tourism in culturally or ecologically sensitive environments. Hunter (1997), accordingly, regards sustainable development as an 'adaptive paradigm' that legitimises a weak or more **anthropocentric** (i.e. development-oriented) approach, *as well as* a strong or more **biocentric** (i.e. preservation-oriented) interpretation of **sustainable tourism**, depending on their appropriateness for a given setting. The beachfront and hinterland of Australia's Gold Coast respectively illustrate, at least in potential, these weak and strong manifestations of sustainable tourism (Weaver 2000a). Weak and strong impulses are also implicit in the above ecotourism definitions. Valentine (1992) and James Butler (in Scace 1993), for example, are clearly biocentric, whereas Ceballos-Lascuraín's early definition contains no sustainability imperative at all.

Environmental and sociocultural

Another area of contention in the definitions is the inclusion of environmental as well as sociocultural dimensions of sustainability. Scace, Grifone and Usher (1992), for example, say that ecotourism must respect 'the integrity of host communities', while the Ecotourism Society (in Lindberg & Hawkins 1993) states that ecotourism should 'improve the welfare of local people'. Similarly, Fennell (1999) holds that ecotourism should be 'locally oriented' in terms of benefits to destination residents. This inclusion of sociocultural sustainability is warranted, not only for ethical reasons but also because this is more likely to foster the levels of community support for ecotourism that are necessary to adequately protect the local natural resource base on which the sector relies (see section 5.3.2).

However, this also potentially provides a basis for conflict. It is fashionable to argue that the sustainability of the natural environment and local community are interdependent, but which should take priority if an apparent conflict does emerge is not clear. This could, for example, involve the wish of a local indigenous community to expand its slash-and-burn agriculture into a virgin rainforest where ecotourism has already been introduced, or to increase its revenues (and therefore presumably its economic wellbeing) by dramatically escalating the number of ecotourists allowed into that environment. An even more confounding issue, however, is determining which individuals legitimately constitute the 'local community' and who decides what is in its best interests, assuming that a consensus on this can be reached (see section 5.5).

Status quo and enhancement

An important issue in ecotourism and sustainable development in general is whether the objective is to maintain the *status quo*, as implied by the word 'sustainability', or to improve this existing situation. The former scenario, which can be referred to as **status quo sustainability**, is justified in situations where levels of environmental integrity are such that they do not need to be changed. However, in areas where the environment has been seriously compromised, an **enhancement sustainability** approach would seem to be more responsible. This approach is evident in James Butler's assertion (in Scace 1993) that the 'environment must experience a net benefit' as a result of ecotourism (see table 1.1). Ways of achieving this range from the direct participation of ecotourists in afforestation projects, research projects and policing to the donation of monies to environmental programs on or off site (see section 4.3.1). Should such an approach be adopted, a further consideration is whether it is just the site of the product that should be enhanced or Planet Earth as a whole. The latter approach is demonstrated by the accommodation facility owner who pays a voluntary 'carbon tax' to offset the fossil fuel emissions caused by visitors travelling to the site, or who achieves this same effect by planting an equivalent number of trees.

Monitoring and implementation issues

Regardless of which sustainability model is adopted, ecotourism operations and products need to be periodically assessed to determine in some objective way whether they actually *are* 'sustainable'. However, as discussed by Weaver (2006), this objective is complicated by an array of challenges associated with the inherent complexity of ecotourism and tourism more generally. For example:

- To what extent should operators be responsible for the indirect and induced effects of ecotourism, as for example the new homes that are built in a rainforest to house workers hired by a lodging facility?
- For how far away and for how long into the future should these effects be considered? The negative impact of a toxic substance leak, for example, may ultimately be felt 100 kilometres away and six months later.
- Cause-and-effect relationships are often unpredictable, so how can one be assured that an operation appearing to be sustainable is actually so? For example, animals not apparently bothered by the presence of ecotourists may actually be experiencing levels of stress that interfere with basic survival activities. An apparently sustainable rate of activity growth might reach an unanticipated point where an 'avalanche effect' is triggered; that is, one small increment of growth results in disproportionate change to the system, as when one extra snowflake results in the critical mass that triggers an avalanche.
- There is no consensus as to which **indicators** or combination of indicators are the most appropriate for measuring sustainability in the ecotourism sector, especially given that each site is unique. Moreover, for similar reasons, little is known about the **benchmark** and **threshold** values of these variables that indicate an appropriate level of tourism activity.
- The sustainability of an ecotourism operation is effectively irrelevant if external forces such as climate change and hurricanes, over which operators exert no control, threaten to undermine the integrity of the surrounding ecosystem (see chapter 7).
- Sustainability is a long-term prospect, but the financial and political realities that underlie budget allocations for the costly process of sustainability monitoring are inherently short term.

Sustainability — imperative or appearance?

Given all of these problems, it is impossible to say *beyond any doubt* that a particular ecotourism operation or activity is environmentally or socioculturally sustainable, unless one is satisfied with a sustainability approach so weak as to be effectively meaningless. To insist that a product *must* be sustainable to qualify as ecotourism (as many definitions do) is therefore unrealistic. More reasonable is the expectation that ecotourism operate in accordance with sustainability **best practice** and that every effort be made to monitor impact and redress in a timely manner any inadvertent negative impact that comes to light.

■ *1.4.5* **Financial** *viability*

Some ecotourism operations are managed on a non-profit basis, and financial viability therefore is not one of the core criteria included in this section. However, in practical terms, most operations will go out of business if they are not financially sustainable, and this is therefore a legitimate supplementary criterion that is usually absent from ecotourism definitions. It imposes realism into the management process, for example, by dictating the degree to which an operator can implement effective but very costly modes of interpretation and environmental mitigation. In addition, this consideration focuses on the importance of customer satisfaction as a means of ensuring revenue flow through repeat patronage and positive word-of-mouth advertising.

■ *1.4.6* **Textbook** *definition of ecotourism*

Based on the above discussion of criteria, the following definition of ecotourism is proposed for this textbook:

> ■ Ecotourism is a form of tourism that fosters learning experiences and appreciation of the natural environment, or some component thereof, within its associated cultural context. It is managed in accordance with industry best practice to attain environmentally and socioculturally sustainable outcomes as well as financial viability. ■

The following elements are incorporated into this definition:
* Ecotourism is a form of tourism (criterion 1).
* Attractions are primarily nature-based, but can include associated cultural resources and influences (criterion 2).
* Educational and learning outcomes are fostered (criterion 3).
* It is managed so that environmental and sociocultural sustainability outcomes are more likely to be achieved (criterion 4).
* The importance of an operation's financial sustainability is recognised (see chapter 6).

■ *1.4.7* **Minimalist** *and comprehensive ecotourism*

Within the parameters of this definition, two distinctive modes of ecotourism are detectable (Weaver 2005a). As an ideal type (i.e. as an undistorted model against which real-life situations can be compared), **minimalist ecotourism** involves shallow or superficial learning opportunities in conjunction with specific charismatic wildlife and sustainability objectives that are *status quo*-oriented and focused on a particular site. **Comprehensive ecotourism**, in contrast, is focused on entire ecosystems and encourages deep learning opportunities as well as behaviour transformation. An 'enhancement sustainability' approach is adopted that seeks to restore these ecosystems and the environment of Planet Earth in general, as well as the welfare of local communities and humanity as a whole. Financial sustainability and high levels of customer satisfaction are important components of both models. Although it might appear logical to align the minimalist and comprehensive models respectively with the weak and strong approach towards sustainability (see section 1.4.4), the possibilities and benefits of applying the comprehensive model to weak as well as strong sustainability situations must be considered (see chapter 2).

1.5 ECOTOURISM IN THE CONTEXT OF OTHER TOURISM TYPES

Since its emergence in the mid-1980s, ecotourism has co-evolved with a number of related activities, including nature-based tourism, wildlife tourism, sustainable tourism, adventure tourism and alternative tourism. All of these terms, to a greater or lesser extent, have been used as synonyms for ecotourism. This is unfortunate, because such careless misuse of the terminology increases confusion and misunderstanding. The purpose of this section is to examine the relationship between ecotourism and these additional terms. As well, this section considers the link between ecotourism and several types of tourism that are usually disassociated completely with ecotourism, including 3S tourism (sea, sand, sun tourism) and mass tourism. The relationship with cultural tourism, consumptive tourism, non-consumptive tourism and various hybrid activities is also investigated.

■ 1.5.1 Nature-based *tourism*

Nature-based tourism is any type of tourism that relies on attractions directly related to the natural environment. Accordingly, ecotourism is a subset of nature-based tourism (Fennell 1999), allowing for the supplementary portion of ecotourism that focuses on the cultural attributes of a destination and the cultural influences on the natural environment (see figure 1.3). Other categories of nature-based tourism include 3S tourism, adventure tourism, wildlife tourism, captive tourism (i.e. zoological parks, botanical gardens, aquariums and aviaries), extractive tourism (e.g. hunting and fishing) and some types of health tourism. Unlike ecotourism, none of these is explicitly required to have a learning component or a mandate to be managed with sustainability objectives in mind.

■ **Figure 1.3**
Ecotourism and nature-based tourism

■ 1.5.2 Wildlife *tourism*

Wildlife tourism is a rapidly evolving subset of nature-based tourism that Higginbottom (2004) characterises as being based on encounters with non-domesticated animals in non-captive and captive settings. This captive element, along with the inclusion of non-consumptive (i.e. observation and study) as well as consumptive (i.e. hunting and fishing) activities, suggests that ecotourism accounts for only a relatively small component of all wildlife tourism (see figure 1.4). Moreover, not all ecotourism is wildlife tourism, given the small portion of the former that focuses on geological and other non-wildlife attractions (see section 1.6). The relationship, in summary, is similar to the one ecotourism enjoys with nature-based tourism (see figure 1.3).

■ **Figure 1.4**
*Ecotourism
and wildlife
tourism*

■ 1.5.3 Cultural *tourism*

Ecotourism contains a cultural component in its attraction base (see section 1.4.2), but is seldom equated with cultural tourism. This is because a **cultural tourism** product should place its primary emphasis on the cultural component, whereas this element is secondary in ecotourism. Recognising this secondary cultural aspect and situations in which the boundary between the cultural and natural environment is hazy (as in the case of many indigenous cultures), the relationship between ecotourism and cultural tourism can be depicted as overlapping circles (see figure 1.5). At the Angkor Khmer temples complex in Cambodia, for example, a visitor who is interested in mainly the architecture and design of the site would be considered a cultural tourist, whereas someone who is more interested in the jungle's reclamation of the site would appropriately be classified as an ecotourist. In the overlap cases where the nature-based and cultural impulses of the tourist are amalgamated, a hybrid designation may be warranted (see section 1.5.4).

■ **Figure 1.5**
*Ecotourism
and cultural
tourism*

■ *1.5.4* **Adventure** *tourism*

To qualify as **adventure tourism**, an activity or product generally incorporates three components:
- an element of *risk*
- higher levels of *physical exertion*
- use of *specialised skills* to participate successfully and safely in the activity (Buckley 2006, Weaver 2001a).

Some forms of ecotourism (especially those that occur in a wilderness or marine environment) meet these requirements and hence qualify as adventure tourism. However, for several reasons, most adventure tourism does not qualify as ecotourism. First, adventure tourism attractions are not always nature-based, as indicated by the popularity of off-beat travel guides such as Fielding's *The World's Most Dangerous Places*, which features destinations beset by civil war and other conflict. Second, as with nature-based and wildlife tourism in general, adventure tourism has no inherent requirement of sustainability, although many adventure tourism businesses operate in a sustainable way. The third and arguably most important distinction between adventure tourism and ecotourism concerns the nature of the interaction between the participant and the attraction. While ecotourists seek a learning/educational experience, adventure tourists primarily desire an environment that facilitates the risk, challenge and physical exertion that they seek. Steep mountain slopes and white water are valued as venues more for the thrills and challenges that they offer than for the opportunities they provide for studying nature in such specialised settings.

Figure 1.6 shows ecotourism's overlapping relationship with adventure tourism, which is similar to its link with cultural tourism except that the extent of the overlap is not as great. This is because only a small portion of all ecotourism activity entails the level of risk, exertion and skill that characterises adventure tourism, even after allowing for the fact that perceptions of physical challenge are subjective (see chapter 2). A mundane experience for a seasoned sea kayaker, for example, may be a highly challenging adventure for a person with physical disabilities.

■ **Figure 1.6**
*Ecotourism
and
adventure
tourism*

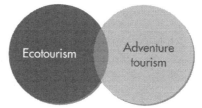

■ *1.5.5* **Hybrids**

Although it is convenient to segment tourism activity into neatly discrete categories, the differences in numerous instances are too subtle to make meaningful distinctions. A visitor to the Angkor Khmer temples complex, as suggested earlier, may be equally and simultaneously interested in the architecture, the ecology of the encroaching jungle and the thrill of exploring the ruins. Hybrid forms of tourism deal with such complex and multifaceted situations. An example of a hybrid is **trekking**, an activity (commonly associated with Nepal and northern Thailand) that combines elements of adventure tourism, cultural tourism and ecotourism (Weaver 1998). More recently, Fennell (1999) coined the acronym **ACE tourism** to describe amalgams such as trekking that combine these three elements of adventure, culture and ecotourism. Fennell (1999) incorporates an element of flexibility into his model by suggesting that the relative contribution of each to any particular tourism product at any given time can vary depending on its setting, market, underlying philosophy and actual practice. Similarly, Buckley (2000) employs the term **NEAT** to describe the combination of nature-based, ecotourism and adventure tourism. While deliberately excluding 3S tourism (i.e. sea, sand, sun tourism), Buckley notes the potential for NEAT to function as an add-on to the latter.

In addition to the issue of blurred boundaries, the rationale for coining such hybrid terms is that they represent a means of branding a diversified and potentially more attractive tourism product to the market. A related advantage is the possibility of creating synergies and combining the best characteristics of each so that the participant is offered mentally and physically challenging experiences in a sustainable 'nature/culture' package. However, such a strategy also carries the risk of product dilution, whereby the core strengths of each product are weakened and the identity of the target market becomes less clear.

■ 1.5.6 3S *(sea, sand, sun) tourism*

With its reliance on sea, sand and sun, **3S tourism** clearly fits under the category of nature-based tourism (see section 1.5.1). However, because 3S tourism is often associated with large-scale and mass resort tourism (see section 1.5.7), the link with ecotourism is not often made. Yet there are numerous situations (see section 7.2.1) in which the two activities exist in a complementary relationship and some activities seem to qualify as both ecotourism and 3S tourism. This is particularly true for the group of related marine activities that includes scuba diving, skindiving, snorkelling and submarine tours (Garrod & Wilson 2003). All of these pursuits are typically associated with 3S tourism. However, providing that they are carried out in a sustainable way, there is no reason why they should not be described as examples of ecotourism when the main intent is to appreciate and learn about the marine environment. Strengthening this argument is the trend in underwater sport away from spearfishing towards the passive viewing of marine fauna in such countries as Australia (Davis, Banks & Davey 1996).

■ 1.5.7 **Alternative** *tourism and mass tourism*

As discussed in section 1.2, ecotourism has its origins in the paradigm of alternative tourism, and has typically if implicitly (being rarely mentioned in any of the definitions) been seen as its nature-based variant. From this adaptancy platform perspective, ecotourism and mass tourism are mutually exclusive. Yet, with the emergence of the supposedly more scientific and objective knowledge-based platform in the 1990s, it has become necessary to reassess the relationship between ecotourism and mass tourism. This is because the knowledge-based platform disassociates the scale of tourism from its value; that is, no longer is alternative or small-scale tourism considered to be inherently 'good' or large-scale tourism considered inherently 'bad'. Weaver and Lawton (2006), for example, cite several potential disadvantages of alternative tourism, including:

• its status as an elite Eurocentric model often imposed on the less-developed countries
• its role in potentially strengthening the control of the existing local elite (i.e. locals who occupy a privileged position in the community)
• its modest economic returns
• its inadequacies, in terms of its economies of scale, for allowing operators to implement sophisticated sustainability practices
• its fostering of a more intrusive and hence potentially disruptive level of contact between host and guest
• its perception as an activity that it is accessible only to elite tourists
• its inadvertent role in opening an area to less benign forms of tourism such as conventional mass tourism.

Clarke (1997) and Weaver (2006), moreover, describe ways in which mass tourism is actually better positioned than small-scale tourism to realise sustainable practices. These include the availability of economies of scale that generate substantial revenue and justify expensive **site-hardening** measures (i.e. measures that increase the carrying capacity of a site — see section 4.5.3) and profitable recycling and co-generation initiatives (see section 6.3.1).

From this new perspective, there is no inherent reason for ecotourism not also being a form of mass tourism as long as it adheres to the basic criteria described in section 1.4. It is not impossible to visualise a sophisticated nature-based interpretation centre and surrounding 'high-tech' trails that are capable of supporting and educating a large number of visitors in an environmentally sustainable and profitable way. As will become clear in subsequent chapters, much if not most ecotourism may *already* qualify as mass tourism. Figure 1.7 reflects this argument by depicting ecotourism as a sector that straddles the boundary between alternative and mass tourism, with most of it being contained within the latter. The use of a single large circle to encompass both forms of tourism is intended to represent extremes of a continuum rather than completely separate categories. The dotted line shows that the boundary between the two is unclear and transitional. Nevertheless, the relationship between mass tourism and ecotourism is still a matter of controversy, not all ecotourism theorists or researchers adhering to the views expressed herein (see, for example, Boyd 2000, Diamantis & Ladkin 1999a and Jaakson 1997).

Alternative tourism

Mass tourism

Ecotourism

■ **Figure 1.7**
Ecotourism, alternative tourism and mass tourism

■ *1.5.8* **Sustainable** *tourism*

Ecotourism is a subset of sustainable tourism, given that sustainability-focused management is one of the core criteria discussed earlier. Figure 1.8 can therefore be modified to include an area of sustainable tourism that at least theoretically accounts for all ecotourism, most (but not all) of alternative tourism and a substantial portion (but probably still a minority) of mass tourism. This structure reflects the tendency of the knowledge-based platform to view both alternative and mass tourism as either sustainable or unsustainable, depending on the circumstances that pertain to a particular destination.

All tourism

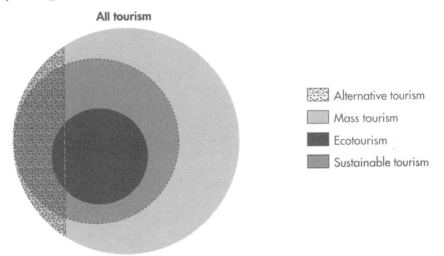

Alternative tourism

Mass tourism

Ecotourism

Sustainable tourism

■ **Figure 1.8**
Ecotourism and sustainable tourism

■ *1.5.9* **Consumptive** *and non-consumptive tourism*

The tourism and outdoor recreation literature often makes a distinction between consumptive and non-consumptive tourism. **Consumptive tourism** is usually perceived as involving tangible *products* extracted from the natural environment, and is associated with hunting and fishing (except arguably for catch-and-release angling). In contrast, **non-consumptive tourism** is seen as providing intangible *experiences*, such as those offered by birdwatching and other forms of wildlife or nature observation (Valentine & Birtles 2004). Hence ecotourism unequivocally is a non-consumptive form of tourism.

Such generalisations, however, must be qualified. First, all forms of tourism involve both a consumptive and non-consumptive element. The aesthetic experience of being outdoors (i.e. a 'non-consumptive' experience), for example, is an integral aspect of most hunting and fishing, while ecotourists consume products such as food and fossil fuels as part of their supposedly 'non-consumptive' experience. Moreover, the maintenance of bird checklists may be regarded as a symbolic form of consumption or trophy collection. Second, there is no basis for supposing that non-consumptive tourism is somehow better or more sustainable than consumptive tourism, as is often assumed. Wildlife observation, for example, is often stressful for the animals in question (see section 4.4.1), while hunting can be a useful mechanism for eradicating feral wildlife or keeping other species in balance (see section 7.2.2). Given these ambiguities, this text avoids the terms 'consumptive' and 'non-consumptive' in reference to ecotourism or any other form of tourism. The term **extractive tourism** is used as a substitute for consumptive tourism in its literal sense.

1.6 TYPES OF ECOTOURISM ACTIVITY

Activities that fall under the ecotourism umbrella are listed in figure 1.9, which allows comparison with other specific nature-based activities, including those that overlap with ecotourism. Overlap also occurs within the ecotourism category, nature observation and nature photography, for example, often being linked. Furthermore, **leaf-peeping**, birdwatching and **whale-watching** are subsets of nature observation, yet they have evolved as distinctive enough products to warrant their status as separate pursuits. Whale-watching (which for the sake of convenience includes other **cetaceans**, such as dolphins and porpoises), in turn, can be divided into separate subcategories, of which each has its own marketing and management implications (Orams 1999). Onshore whale-watching from coastal cliffs, for example, has little if any impact on cetaceans, while interactive whale-watching (which is also a form of adventure tourism) may have a profound impact that requires stringent restrictions on the number of participants and types of interaction to be sustainable (see section 8.2). Similar differentiation is also occurring in the birdwatching category as its continuing growth leads to specialised modes of observation. For example, some sites focus on the night-time viewing of nocturnal birds such as owls, in which case special care must be taken to manage the use of flashlights and avoid the disruption of sleeping day-active birds. Other specific management considerations apply to the observation of bird migrations. **Celestial ecotourism** is a preliminary term encompassing a variety of activities (e.g. stargazing and northern lights viewing) associated with the observation of daytime and night-time skies.

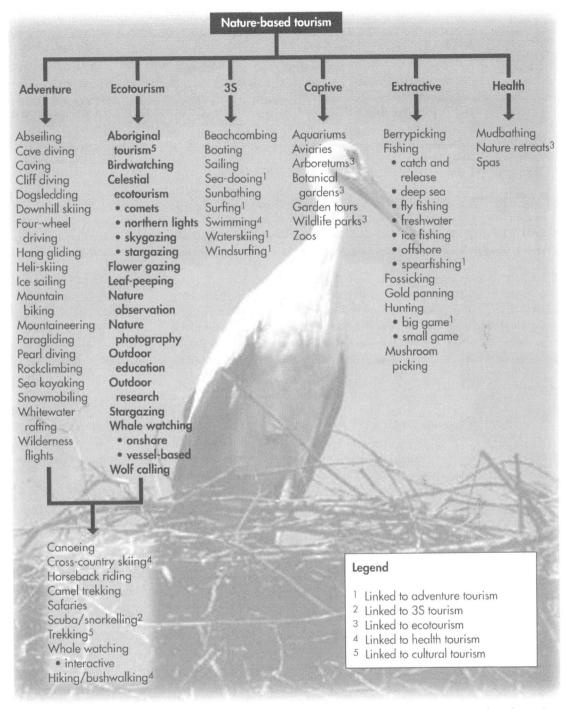

Nature-based tourism

Adventure

Abseiling
Cave diving
Caving
Cliff diving
Dogsledding
Downhill skiing
Four-wheel
  driving
Hang gliding
Heli-skiing
Ice sailing
Mountain
  biking
Mountaineering
Paragliding
Pearl diving
Rockclimbing
Sea kayaking
Snowmobiling
Whitewater
  rafting
Wilderness
  flights

Ecotourism

**Aboriginal
  tourism[5]**
Birdwatching
**Celestial
  ecotourism**
  • **comets**
  • **northern lights**
  • **skygazing**
  • **stargazing**
Flower gazing
Leaf-peeping
**Nature
  observation**
**Nature
  photography**
**Outdoor
  education**
**Outdoor
  research**
Stargazing
Whale watching
  • **onshore**
  • **vessel-based**
Wolf calling

3S

Beachcombing
Boating
Sailing
Sea-dooing[1]
Sunbathing
Surfing[1]
Swimming[4]
Waterskiing[1]
Windsurfing[1]

Captive

Aquariums
Aviaries
Arboretums[3]
Botanical
  gardens[3]
Garden tours
Wildlife parks[3]
Zoos

Extractive

Berrypicking
Fishing
  • catch and
    release
  • deep sea
  • fly fishing
  • freshwater
  • ice fishing
  • offshore
  • spearfishing[1]
Fossicking
Gold panning
Hunting
  • big game[1]
  • small game
Mushroom
  picking

Health

Mudbathing
Nature retreats[3]
Spas

Canoeing
Cross-country skiing[4]
Horseback riding
Camel trekking
Safaries
Scuba/snorkelling[2]
Trekking[5]
Whale watching
  • interactive
Hiking/bushwalking[4]

Legend

[1] Linked to adventure tourism
[2] Linked to 3S tourism
[3] Linked to ecotourism
[4] Linked to health tourism
[5] Linked to cultural tourism

■ **Figure 1.9** *Ecotourism activities in the context of nature-based tourism*
Source: *adapted from Weaver, Faulkner & Lawton, 1999.*

Aboriginal (or indigenous) tourism is included as a form of ecotourism because of the links between indigenous cultures and the natural environment (see section 1.4). Activities that involve captive flora and fauna are not normally associated with ecotourism, although in many cases the freedom afforded to animals by wildlife parks and botanical gardens is comparable to that which is available in national parks or other protected areas. Associated activities in such situations may be ecotourism-related. The broader issue as to whether 'captive' and 'non-captive' forms of tourism are converging is an intriguing area that requires further investigation.

1.7 TEXTBOOK PRINCIPLES AND STRUCTURE

Philosophically, while adhering to a core set of defining criteria, this textbook assumes that legitimate forms of ecotourism can include a wide variety of settings and, under the right circumstances, can and should involve high visitation levels. It also assumes that ecotourism products should always strive in the long term towards the comprehensive model and that the issue of financial viability must always be taken into account if the sector is expected to thrive.

Figure 1.10 depicts an idealised chain reaction of what this book hopes to achieve in terms of sector development, wherein effective opportunities for learning combine with environmentally and socioculturally sustainable management strategies to produce satisfied customers and communities, as well as healthy ecosystems. These in turn result in financially viable operators and a thriving ecotourism sector that is capable of resisting the negative effects of hostile external environments. Reinforcement occurs because of the growing ability and willingness of the industry to reinvest in the product, so that the learning opportunities and management strategies are constantly improved and shifted increasingly in the direction of comprehensive ecotourism.

Structurally, this textbook consists of 10 chapters. Following the introduction to criteria and context provided in this chapter, chapter 2 examines the demand or market component of ecotourism and its emergence as part of the broader trend of environmentalism. Chapter 3 shifts the focus to the supply or product component by examining public and private protected areas. The environmental impact of ecotourism, and strategies to minimise its negative effects and maximise its positive effects, are discussed in chapter 4, while chapter 5 similarly considers its sociocultural and economic impact. Chapter 6 addresses relevant management and business issues from the perspective of both the public and private sectors. Significant external environments, such as agriculture and forestry, are examined in chapter 7, while chapter 8 focuses on the organisational and institutional framework within which successful ecotourism management takes place. In chapter 9, content and themes from the earlier chapters are integrated into four special contexts: whale-watching, small islands, polar regions and indigenous people. Finally, chapter 10 examines the status of contemporary ecotourism by world region.

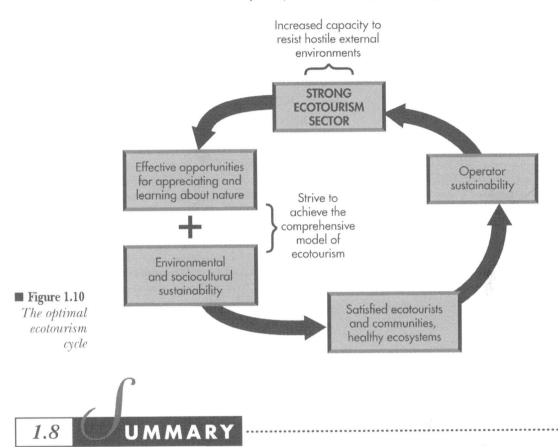

■ **Figure 1.10**
The optimal ecotourism cycle

1.8 SUMMARY

The term 'ecotourism' first appeared in the mid-1980s in association with an 'adaptancy platform' that regarded it as a form of alternative tourism. As such, it was contrasted with a mass tourism model perceived to be inherently unsustainable. However, with the appearance of a more balanced and objective 'knowledge-based platform', there is a growing tendency to recognise the legitimacy of ecotourism in both an alternative *and* mass tourism guise. While diverse ecotourism definitions have been proposed since its inception, a consensus is emerging around four core criteria. First, ecotourism is a form of tourism, and relevant criteria should therefore dictate who is an 'ecotourist'. Second, ecotourism attractions are based primarily on the natural environment or some constituent element, as well as affiliated cultural attributes. Third, ecotourism is learning-focused through effective interpretation. Finally, ecotourism must be managed in concert with sustainability-related best practice so as to minimise its negative impact and maximise its positive impact. Although not strictly a core criterion, ecotourism should also be financially viable. Further analysis of these criteria gives rise to minimalist and comprehensive dimensions of ecotourism, with the latter involving charismatic megafauna, shallow learning and status quo sustainability. In contrast, the latter focuses on ecosystems, promotes deep learning and strives to enhance the environmental and sociocultural well-being of destinations.

Having established a reasonable working definition of ecotourism, we can assess its relationship with other forms of tourism. Essentially, ecotourism is a subset of sustainable tourism and nature-based tourism that overlaps with other sectors that are primarily nature-based, such as adventure tourism, wildlife tourism and 3S tourism. Ecotourism also overlaps with cultural tourism, given its secondary cultural component. Where hybrid forms of tourism have emerged, such terms as trekking, ACE tourism and NEAT have been coined to describe the resulting amalgam. By way of reiteration, ecotourism can be a form of either alternative or mass tourism, as long as the core criteria are met. Although ecotourism is often associated with non-consumptive tourism, this term (along with 'consumptive') is avoided because it has inherent ambiguities. Although ecotourism therefore overlaps with other forms of tourism, a growing array of activities and subactivities situate comfortably under this umbrella. The aspiration of this textbook, ultimately, is to promote a thriving ecotourism sector that can resist negative external influences and evolve into a comprehensive model that enhances the environmental and sociocultural wellbeing of destinations.

QUESTIONS

1 (a) How do the advocacy and knowledge-based platforms, respectively, perceive ecotourism?
   (b) Which platform is more legitimate in terms of its perception, and why?

2 (a) What are the advantages and disadvantages of including the cultural attributes of a destination in the ecotourism product?
   (b) To what extent should cultural attributes be included in the ecotourism product?

3 (a) Why is it problematic to insist that an ecotourism product must be sustainable?
   (b) How can this problem be overcome?

4 (a) Under what circumstances is it appropriate, respectively, to advocate a strong or weak approach to sustainability?
   (b) What strengths and weaknesses are associated with each approach?

5 To what extent should financial viability be taken into account when trying to attain ecotourism that is environmentally and socioculturally sustainable?

6 What are the benefits and challenges to destinations of adopting, respectively, a minimalist and comprehensive approach to ecotourism?

7 (a) What are the relative advantages of developing and marketing a tourism product as a hybrid (such as trekking or ACE tourism) rather than as ecotourism?
(b) What disadvantages are associated with this strategy?

8 (a) Why is it appropriate to refer to ecotourism as both a 'consumptive' *and* 'non-consumptive' form of tourism?
(b) What are the implications of these characteristics for the sustainability of ecotourism?

FURTHER READING

Blamey, RK 2001, 'Principles of ecotourism', in DB Weaver (ed.), *Encyclopedia of Ecotourism*, CABI, Wallingford, UK, pp. 5–22. In this chapter, Blamey provides a thoughtful and detailed discussion of the three core criteria (i.e. nature-based attractions, learning and sustainability) that comprise ecotourism.

Buckley, R 2000, 'Neat trends: Current issues in nature, eco- and adventure tourism', *International Journal of Tourism Research* 2: 1–8. In this article Buckley describes his rationale for coining the term NEAT to describe a hybrid form of tourism that includes ecotourism, adventure tourism and cultural tourism. The implications of this tourism sector are also discussed.

Fennell, D 2003, *Ecotourism: An Introduction*, 2nd edn, Routledge, London. This excellent ecotourism text provides a detailed discussion of ecotourism's evolution and its diverse array of definitions. The relationship of ecotourism to other forms of tourism is also examined.

Weaver, D 2005, 'Comprehensive and minimalist dimensions of ecotourism', *Annals of Tourism Research* 32: 439–55. The concepts of comprehensive and minimalist ecotourism are described, along with the importance of fostering a comprehensive model that encompasses hard as well as soft ecotourism (see chapter 2).

—— **2006, *Sustainable Tourism: Theory and Practice*, Elsevier Butterworth-Heinemann, Oxford.** Critical topics addressed in this book include problems of sustainability and its application to alternative tourism as well as the conventional mass tourism sector. Issues of quality control and destination/visitor management are also considered. The final chapter applies these concepts to ecotourism.

2 Emerging *markets*

LEARNING OBJECTIVES

After reading this chapter, you should be able to:

- explain the concept of a paradigm and a paradigm shift

- differentiate the dominant Western environmental paradigm from the green paradigm

- assess the evidence for the existence of a shift to the green paradigm

- contextualise ecotourism within the green paradigm and the debate over a paradigm shift

- discuss the motivation, behaviour, geographic origins, gender, age, education and income of emerging ecotourist markets

- distinguish soft ecotourists from hard ecotourists and assess the implications of each for product development and management, including the application of a comprehensive tourism model

- critically analyse the size and growth rate of the ecotourist market.

As discussed in chapter 1, our understanding of ecotourism is growing with regard to its defining criteria and relationship to other forms of tourism. Furthermore, the 'platforms' of Jafari (1989), which indicate changing attitudes towards tourism and development in general since the 1950s, provide a valuable framework for placing the evolution of ecotourism in context. These platforms are, however, a reflection of broader social trends towards a heightened sense of environmental awareness, and it is necessary to understand and evaluate these trends to attain a greater appreciation for ecotourism as a significant social phenomenon that is generating its own markets and products. The first section of this chapter considers the evidence for a fundamental shift in the world view of society as the underlying reason for the emergence of ecotourism and ecotourists. Section 2.3 then examines the phenomenon of the environmentally conscientious consumer as evidence of such a market shift. The market segmentation of environmental travellers and ecotourists is considered in section 2.4, which focuses on segmentation variables, such as motivation, attitudes, behaviour, age, gender, education and income. Finally, to gauge the actual importance of the phenomenon, section 2.5 critically considers the size and growth of ecotourism and ecotourist markets.

2.2

A PARADIGM SHIFT?

In any sphere of activity, managers must ascertain whether identifiable trends are the product of mainly internal factors or whether they are the result of larger-scale social forces. If the latter is true, the trends are not as likely to be restricted in either time or space and are probably long-term developments that the manager must take very seriously. All those involved with ecotourism should therefore consider whether this phenomenon is just a temporary fad (having been around only since the late 1980s) or a major development in tourism that is indicative of broader changes in society as a whole. The answer to this question determines, for example, whether a destination or resort manager should place a high priority on developing ecotourism products and on identifying and attracting the ecotourist market. To help address this question, it is useful to introduce the concepts of **paradigm** and **paradigm shift**.

■ 2.2.1 Paradigms *and paradigm shifts*

In its broadest sense, a paradigm is a collective world view, or 'the entire constellation of beliefs, values, techniques, and so on shared by the members of a given community' (Kuhn 1970, p. 175). According to the theory developed by Thomas Kuhn, these social paradigms experience a lifecycle. Initially, an established paradigm dominates a society until it is no longer able to explain or accommodate evidence that contradicts its core premises. At this point, a new paradigm, which appears to resolve these contradictions, gradually emerges and displaces the existing paradigm, in the process retaining complementary or at least non-contradictory elements of the old paradigm. This displacement, which is a transitional process that may occur over decades or even centuries, is known as a paradigm shift. Its specific relevance to ecotourism is considered in section 2.2.5.

Paradigm shift is illustrated by the dominance in Europe of a theocentric (religion-centred) world view following the collapse of the ancient Roman Empire. In the late 1400s and early 1500s, this paradigm was challenged by evidence contradicting the accepted assertion that the world was flat and located at the centre of the universe. As evidence mounted, the 'scientific paradigm' gradually developed and emerged as the dominant European paradigm, where it has remained since, having retained many aspects of Christian dogma while rejecting others. Knill (1991) and others contend that the scientific paradigm is currently being challenged in a similar way, as described below.

■ 2.2.2 Dominant *Western environmental paradigm*

The essence of the scientific paradigm is an atomic or mechanistic view of the universe in which everything can be broken down into component parts to expose the underlying order of reality. It is through the objective and rigorous application of scientific method that this exposure occurs. Knill (1991) uses the term **dominant Western environmental paradigm** to describe the scientific paradigm as it pertains to its perception of the relationship between humans and the natural environment. This perception includes the anthropocentric belief that humans are separate from and superior to the natural environment, which has status only as a 'resource' or commodity available for exploitation through technology. It has no intrinsic worth. Further, 'progress' is a continuous linear process, and there is effectively no limit to what can be achieved and what problems can be solved through the application of the scientific method and its associated technology. This **technological utopianism** (i.e. the idea that technology can lead to an ideal world, or Utopia) is illustrated by the fuel sequence, wherein the exhaustion of accessible wood and whale oil in the late 19th century led to the exploitation of fossil fuels. In turn, the depletion of commercially viable coal and oil deposits in the early 21st century is creating opportunities for the development of new 'alternative' geothermal, wind and solar energy resources. *Laissez-faire* capitalism — an unconstrained marketplace — is the ideal ideological context because it provides scientists and entrepreneurs with financial incentives to develop new products and technology that respond to given resource deficiencies and 'improve' quality of life for ever-expanding markets.

As a compelling amalgam of technological utopianism, capitalism and ostensibly democratic political institutions, the dominant Western environmental paradigm has become pervasive throughout Western society and, in its basic form, has been unconsciously taken for granted by the vast majority of its people. (The socialist version, emphasising state intervention, does not contend seriously at the present time with its capitalist rival.)

Contradictions and anomalies

Throughout the 20th century, the voices of dissent against the dominant Western environmental paradigm and its attendant assumptions increased from a whisper to a shout as the contradictions and anomalies in that paradigm have become increasingly evident. An examination of these contradictions and the responses they have elicited raise the possibility that a paradigm shift is again occurring. Within science itself, the orderly and mechanistic view of the universe has been challenged by quantum physics, which has found that 'reality' at the subatomic scale is chaotic and influenced by the act of observation itself (thereby raising questions about the assumption of objectivity) (Capra 1982, Faulkner & Russell 2003).

More tangible and disturbing anomalies are evident beyond the arcane world of quantum physics. Classic Western economics has long assumed the benefits of continuous linear growth, or 'progress', which is made possible by exploiting the world's natural capital at ever-increasing levels, but fails to take into account the ecological or socioeconomic consequences of this exploitation. Water, air and biodiversity are regarded as external factors whose critical role in maintaining human life is not usually factored into the calculations of economic production. This occurs in part because the role they play is extremely difficult to quantify, but also because of the anthropocentrism that regards them as inherently exploitable commodities. In this view, a sand dune or mangrove is economically 'worthless' until available for development, even though it protects the inshore against a cyclone that could cause catastrophic damage. In the early 21st century, the spectre of accelerated anthropogenic (human-induced) climate change has provided a focus for critical assessment of capitalist orthodoxy (Flannery 2006), as have the unanticipated problems associated with atomic energy, genetically modified foods ('frankenfoods'), ozone-depleting chlorofluorocarbons (CFCs) and antibiotics, which are giving rise to drug-resistant forms of bacteria.

Conventional mass tourism

While not as ominous in its implications as atomic meltdowns, rising sea levels or super-viruses, the relentless expansion of mass tourism is one of the sector-specific contradictions of the dominant Western environmental paradigm and its affiliated advocacy platform. The contradictory element in this mode of tourism, specifically, is embodied in Butler's (1980) assertion that the deterioration of the destination's physical and sociocultural environment is the logical culmination of an unregulated destination life-cycle sequence (see section 1.2.1); that is, the very fact that many tourists are attracted to pristine and scenic environments creates levels of visitation stress that eventually undermine this attractiveness. The theory of paradigm shift, accordingly, would suggest that sustainable tourism and ecotourism have been widely adopted because of their promise to resolve this inherent contradiction of conventional mass tourism by focusing on the core principle of ecological and sociocultural sustainability (see section 2.2.5).

◼ 2.2.3 The *environmental movement*

Concerns about the theocentric paradigm were expressed centuries before any serious challenge was mounted by science and, similarly, the roots of resistance to the dominant Western environmental paradigm may be traced to the early 1800s and earlier. Initially, these were little more than lone voices sounded by such pioneers as Thomas Malthus, an Englishman who argued that humans tend to reproduce beyond the carrying capacity of the natural environment, and Henry David Thoreau, an American naturalist and writer who advocated harmony with nature. However, they were significant in that they gradually gave rise to an increasingly influential **environmental movement** that is now articulating its own all-embracing paradigm as a challenge to conventional science. Among the early manifestations of the movement, although often anthropocentrically and commercially motivated, was the drive to create national parks during the late 1800s in such countries as Australia, the USA and Canada.

From this time until the mid-1900s, there was continuous tension between two main schools of the movement. On one hand, resource *conservationists* such as Gifford Pinchot (chief forester in the USA in the early 1900s under President Theodore Roosevelt) adopted a more anthropocentric and utilitarian approach towards the environment, believing that resources should be saved or 'conserved' for future use. Conversely, resource *preservationists*, such as John Muir (a major force behind the establishment of Yosemite National Park and founder of the Sierra Club, an influential international environmental organisation), were more biocentric and argued that resources should be saved *from* future use (Cutter & Renwick 2003).

In Australia, the **bushwalker movement** of the early 1900s, consisting of largely urban, middle-class individuals organised into walking clubs, was instrumental in having national parks and other protected areas established, such as Cradle Mountain in Tasmania, or on the outskirts of expanding major cities, such as Sydney (Hutton & Connors 1999).

Contemporary activism

During the latter half of the 20th century, the environmental movement expanded beyond a mainly elite professional and academic base to incorporate a substantial segment of the general public. Television and other mass media, through such popular telegenic environmentalists as Jacques Cousteau and David Suzuki, have played a critical role by exposing to a mass audience such environmental issues as climate change, ozone depletion, pesticide contamination, overpopulation and deforestation. Concurrently, environmental conscientiousness was raised through a sequence of high-profile environmentally themed books. An early example is Rachel Carson's (1962) classic *Silent Spring*, which exposed the environmental damage caused by the pesticide DDT. Other influential publications include *Limits to*

Growth (Meadows et al. 1972), *Small is Beautiful* (Schumacher 1973), *Gaia: A New Look at Life on Earth* (Lovelock 1979), the Brundtland Report, which popularised the notion of sustainable development (WCED 1987), and *Rebels Against the Future* (Sale 1996).

The impact of these trends and publications, in turn, was amplified by a series of high-profile environmental disasters, including the 1979 Three Mile Island (USA) and 1981 Chernobyl (Soviet Union) nuclear reactor accidents, the 1984 chemical factory leak in Bhopal (India), and several major oil spills. In Australia, considerable attention was focused on plans for large-scale oil drilling on the Great Barrier Reef, sand mining and logging activity on Fraser Island, the logging of native forests in New South Wales and Tasmania, plans to dam the Franklin River in Tasmania, and uranium mining in Kakadu National Park. Regional issues, such as the massive forest fires that devastated the island of Borneo during the 1980s and 1990s, also provided focus for the Australian movement while concurrently giving impetus to the emergence of a more influential environmentalism movement in South-East Asia and other parts of the developing world (Hirsch & Warren 1998).

Governments worldwide responded to the publicity and growing public concerns by placing the environment on the international agenda through such events as the 1991 Earth Summit held in Rio de Janeiro (Brazil), which was attended by 180 heads of state and resulted in the **Agenda 21** blueprint for sustainable development across an array of sectors. The 2002 Earth Summit, held in Johannesburg, illustrates the extent to which the momentum of contemporary environmentalism has been carried into the 21st century as a major and increasingly mainstream social and political phenomenon.

■ 2.2.4 Green *paradigm*

The critical question is whether the developments described above — that is, the identification of serious contradictions in the dominant Western environmental paradigm, the escalation of concern for the environment and the increasingly effective mobilisation of pro-environment sentiment through the environmental movement — indicate the occurrence of a paradigm shift. Although such questions can be answered definitively only with the benefit of hindsight, many scholars argue in the affirmative and have attempted to characterise this alleged new force. Descriptive terms that have been proposed include the 'new environmental paradigm', 'new ecological paradigm' (e.g. Dunlap et al. 2000) and **green paradigm** (Knill 1991). The latter term is used in this text, since the adjective 'green' has come to symbolise a group of ideas that expresses a generic concern for environmental sustainability.

The green paradigm is still in its infancy and incorporates contributions from a diverse array of perspectives (e.g. deep ecology, ecofeminism, paganism) in the broader environmental movement. However, despite this fragmentation, common themes are emerging that allow the broad contours of this evolving paradigm to be discerned. Figure 2.1 depicts major characteristics of the mainly anthropocentric dominant Western environmental paradigm and the mainly biocentric green paradigm as contrasting ideal types. The latter, for example, regards humanity as a part *of* nature (not apart *from* nature), dependent on the rest of the environment for its survival. Notions of subjectivity, integration and holism consequently replace the emphasis on objectivity and reductionism, and an element of chaos and unpredictability is accommodated. It seeks steady state dynamics rather than linear growth and adopts a communal approach that emphasises the collective well-being over profit and survival of the strongest (i.e. social Darwinism).

■ **Figure 2.1**
The dominant Western environmental paradigm and the green paradigm as ideal types
Source: *Weaver & Lawton 2006.*

Dominant Western environmental paradigm
Humans are apart from nature
Humans are superior to nature
Reality is objective
Reality can be compartmentalised
The future is predictable
The universe has order
The importance of rationality and reason
Hierarchical structures
Competitive structures
Emphasis on the individual
Facilitation through capitalism
Linear progress and growth
Use of hard technology
Patriarchal and male

Green paradigm
Humans are part of nature
Humans and nature are equal
Reality is subjective
Reality is integrated and holistic
The future is unpredictable
The universe is chaotic
The importance of intuition
Consensus-based structures
Cooperative structures
Emphasis on the communal
Facilitation through socialism
Maintenance of a steady state
Use of soft technology
Matriarchal and female

The presentation of ideal types is a useful device for contrasting dominant and emerging paradigms. However, as stated above, paradigm clashes in reality are highly complex processes in which the new paradigm adopts ideas extensively from the old paradigm and vice versa. The newly dominant paradigm, in many ways, is therefore a synthesis of the old and new world views. Scientific thought, for example, did not lead to the elimination of Christianity, and the notion of being apart from and superior to nature can be regarded as a retained Judeo-Christian idea linked to some interpretations of the Old Testament. Similarly, the green paradigm does not discard science and capitalism, but rather selectively incorporates those elements that help to attain and affirm its own world view. Thus, it rejects **hard technology** such as nuclear energy and genetic modification, but accommodates computer technology and other scientific methods that assist the development of **soft technology**, such as solar-powered water heaters and micro-hydroelectric dams (see, for example, Hazeltine & Bull 2003). As discussed in section 1.4.4, the concept of sustainable development is itself indicative of a synthesis. With regard to ideology, the concept of 'democratic capitalism' (Novak 1982) is one attempt to bring the prevalent ideology more into line with the green paradigm.

These apparent syntheses, however, may also be interpreted more cynically as attempts by the old paradigm to prolong its dominance in the early phases of the shift by selectively incorporating popular impulses of the new paradigm that do not contradict its *own* basic belief system (Kuhn 1970). This is one criticism that is sometimes directed against both sustainable development and sustainable tourism as well as against the argument that ecotourism can exist as a form of mass tourism (see section 1.5.7).

■ 2.2.5 Ecotourism *in the context of paradigm shift*

Whether ecotourism is part of a paradigm shift or just a fad is crucial to stakeholders, since each scenario implies the logic of dramatically different managerial and planning responses. This chapter presents evidence for the emergence of a green paradigm, but it is still too early to answer this question definitively, given parallel evidence for the dominant Western environmental paradigm's continued dominance. Nevertheless, there is little doubt that ecotourism is linked to the green paradigm through its learning and sustainability impulses, just as conventional mass tourism is related to the dominant Western environmental paradigm. Having introduced ecotourism (see chapter 1), the tourism platforms (see section 1.2.1) and the concept of paradigms and paradigm shifts (see section 2.2.1), it is now possible to speculate more formally on their interrelationships. Figure 2.2 models these linkages by beginning with the large-scale or 'macro' process of assumed paradigm shift (column 1), then associates these competing paradigms with the applicable tourism platforms, or medium-scale sector-specific 'meta' processes (column 2). Columns 3 and 4, respectively, depict the meta-structures (i.e. tourism-related structures) and small-scale 'micro' structures (i.e. ecotourism-related structures) that have emerged or are emerging from these processes.

The first phase (roughly from the 1950s to 1970s) is characterised by the supremacy of the dominant Western environmental paradigm and the associated advocacy platform, which supports *sustained* (as opposed to sustainable) mass tourism. Ecotourism exists only as an unarticulated and fringe subsector. In the second phase, the emerging green paradigm in the 1970s gives rise to the cautionary platform and its rejection of mass tourism as an unsustainable activity (i.e. *unsustainable mass tourism*). The status of ecotourism remains unchanged. Phase 3, in the 1980s, is still influenced by the green paradigm and involves the formalisation of ecotourism during the adaptancy platform under the guise of *alternative tourism*. As such, it retains the status of a fringe activity. In the fourth and current phase, the knowledge-based platform and its ideal of *sustainable tourism* reflect the apparent synthesis of ideas from both the dominant Western environmental paradigm and the green paradigm. Thus, ecotourism can be small-scale or large-scale in magnitude and thus is invariably removed from or incorporated in the tourism mainstream. Accordingly, it can be either community- or corporate-based (see chapters 5 and 6) and is sensitive to being not just environmentally and socioculturally sustainable but also financially viable (see section 1.4.5). To meet these objectives, ecotourism must be attentive to local sensitivities as well as sophisticated management strategies that employ cutting-edge scientific developments (see chapter 4).

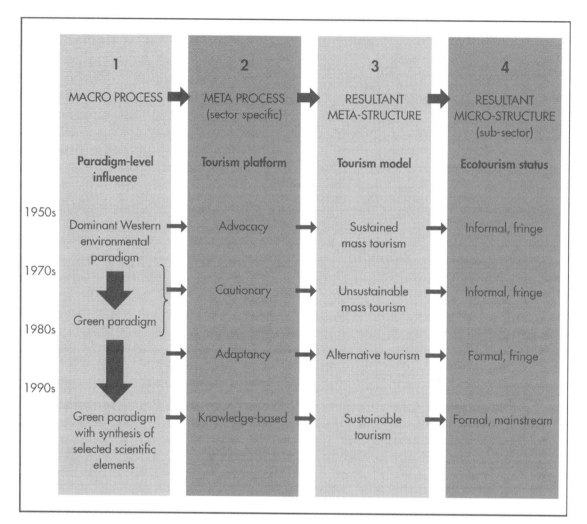

	1	2	3	4
	MACRO PROCESS	META PROCESS (sector specific)	RESULTANT META-STRUCTURE	RESULTANT MICRO-STRUCTURE (sub-sector)
	Paradigm-level influence	**Tourism platform**	**Tourism model**	**Ecotourism status**
1950s	Dominant Western environmental paradigm	Advocacy	Sustained mass tourism	Informal, fringe
1970s		Cautionary	Unsustainable mass tourism	Informal, fringe
1980s	Green paradigm			
		Adaptancy	Alternative tourism	Formal, fringe
1990s	Green paradigm with synthesis of selected scientific elements	Knowledge-based	Sustainable tourism	Formal, mainstream

■ **Figure 2.2**

Evolution of ecotourism in the context of the paradigm shift

GREEN CONSUMERS AND TRAVELLERS

Although the debate over a contemporary paradigm shift is intriguing in its own right, stakeholders must inform their product development and management strategies with tangible information about relevant social trends such as the emergence of a **green consumer** market and, more specific to tourism, the **green traveller** market and the ecotourist.

■ *2.3.1* The *green consumer*

There has been much speculation since the 1980s about the emergence of the green consumer in Western societies, fuelled by empirical evidence that indicates heightened environmental concern and the growth of environmentally friendly attitudes among the general public. The extremely influential US market serves to illustrate this trend. According to a 2006 Los Angeles Times/Bloomberg poll, 73 per cent of a sample of adults (n = 1478) believed that global warming is a 'serious problem', while 57 per cent agreed that 'improving the environment' should take priority over 'economic growth' in instances of conflict between the two. Sixty-two per cent thought that the US government was not doing enough to protect the natural environment (PollingReport.com 2006). Expenditure and investment trends further indicate a strong environmental impulse that was largely non-existent before the 1980s (Mercer 2000). Organic products, for example, have increased as a percentage of total US food sales from 0.8 per cent in 1997 (US$3.6 billion) to 1.9 per cent in 2003 (US$10.4 billion) (Organic Trade Association 2006). In 1985 their value was a negligible $178 million (Ottman 1998). A similar trajectory is evident in socially responsible investments (SRI), which increased from under US$40 billion in 1984 to US$2.3 trillion in 2005, or about 10 per cent of all assets under professional management (Social Investment Forum 2006).

Such outcomes, which lend support to the contention for a paradigm shift, have also been obtained from surveys in Western Europe, Canada and Australia. For example, an Angus Reid poll in November 2006 revealed 'protecting the environment' to be the single biggest issue that Australians felt needed to be addressed by world leaders. Twenty-two per cent of surveyed adults gave this response, followed by 'eliminating extreme poverty and hunger' (19 per cent) and 'closing the gap between rich and poor countries' and 'the war on terrorism' (9 per cent each) (Angus Reid Global Monitor 2006). Yet other data show that this high level of apparent commitment is superficial and unstable, and does not necessarily translate into a consistent pattern of pro-environmental behaviour. This ambiguity is apparent in the above-cited poll, which also found that just 44 per cent of American adults rated global warming as an important issue that would influence whom they vote for in upcoming congressional elections. A Harris poll in 2005 found that just 12 per cent of American adults considered themselves to be 'active environmentalists', whereas another 58 per cent were 'sympathetic to environmental concerns'. Twenty-four per cent were neutral, and four per cent were unsympathetic.

Some of the evidence actually indicates a reversal of the green trend. In a 1989 Gallup/CNN/USA Today poll, 76 per cent of American adults described themselves as 'environmentalists'. Subsequent polling in 1995 and 1999 yielded responses of 63 per cent and 50 per cent, respectively (PollingReport.com 2006). Similarly, 35 per cent of British consumers in 1989 rated the environment as the country's single most important issue.

By 1992, this figure declined to 11 per cent and then again to 3 per cent by 1996. In that year, concerns over the environment were superseded by worries of a more immediate and visceral nature concerning unemployment (44 per cent listing it as the country's most important issue) and health (34 per cent) (Diamantis & Ladkin 1999b). The attacks of 11 September 2001 and subsequent incidents and threats of terrorism have had a similar effect of peripheralising environment issues in the public mind.

Consumer clusters

At the risk of oversimplification, it can be argued that Western societies in the early 21st century are divided into three basic groups, although the boundaries between them are not rigid (see figure 2.3). About one in four adults are basically 'non-environmentalists' who do not consider environmental issues to be important either from a policy perspective or in terms of their personal consumer behaviour. A study by Ray and Anderson (2000) identified these individuals as 'traditionalists' whose attitudes and behaviour adhere closely to the dominant Western environmental paradigm. At the other end of the bell curve, a similar proportion of American adults, described in the same study as 'cultural creatives', are committed to the environment and engage in substantial 'green' consumption and behaviour on a daily basis. They tend to believe that fundamental change at an institutional, social and technological level is necessary to ensure a sustainable future for the world. Overrepresented in this group are females, urban professionals, higher income earners and holders of university degrees.

The remaining fifty per cent display an ambivalence arising from their comfort in accommodating ideas from both paradigms. These are the individuals who tend to express sympathy with environmental causes, but generally engage in green behaviour only if it is convenient; that is, equally or less expensive than the alternatives and as easy or easier of access. They are also more likely to harbour suspicions that 'green' products are a marketing ploy, are of lower quality than conventional goods or are overpriced (Diamantis & Ladkin 1999b). These opportunistic green consumers, or **veneer environmentalists**, tend to vacillate between higher and lower states of green awareness and consumption, depending on personal circumstances as well as broader economic and geopolitical circumstances. As of 2007, fears of terrorism pulled them towards the non-environmentalist pole while concerns over escalating petrol prices simultaneously pulled them towards the environmentalist pole. Thus, while just roughly a quarter of adults adhere *strongly* to the green paradigm, three in four identify at least to some extent with environmentalism. Ray and Anderson (2000) further emphasise that the traditionals are declining rapidly as a portion of the population while the cultural creatives are expanding rapidly, in part through 'recruitment' from the veneer environmentalists. Future expansion of pro-environmental sentiments is also suggested by especially strong support among younger adults.

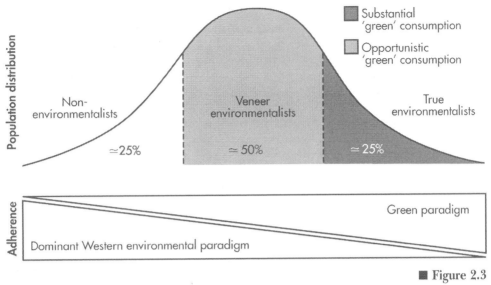

■ **Figure 2.3**

Environmentalism-related population clusters in Western society

Geographically, adherence to the green paradigm is approximately related to a country's stage of economic development, with highly developed, 'post-industrial' societies having the highest inclination and pre-industrial or industrialising societies having the lowest. The bell curve depicted in figure 2.3 is most likely to be encountered in the USA and such similar countries as Canada, Australia, New Zealand and the UK, and the highest levels of environmentalism are found in Scandinavia and Germany. In the USA, prosperous 'blue' (i.e. socially and politically liberal) states such as California and Connecticut display higher levels of adherence than less prosperous 'red' (i.e. socially and politically conservative) states such as Mississippi or Kansas. Environmentalism is also less evident in southern and Eastern Europe, as well as in non-Western developed countries such as Japan, Taiwan and South Korea. Even more incipient are the less-developed countries, although surveyed adults in the latter are more likely to be greatly concerned over the condition of the environment (Leiserowitz, Kates & Parris 2005), indicating potential for the green paradigm to make inroads. In 2007 and 2008, the hosting of the summer Olympics by Beijing forced China to confront its environmental problems.

■ 2.3.2 The *green traveller and travel industry*

The trends described in section 2.3.1 are mirrored in the travel and hospitality sectors, with strong environmental attitudes, if not necessarily behaviour, being evident among both travellers and related businesses (Weaver 2006). A comprehensive study of American adult travellers in 2003, for example, found that for 74 per cent of those surveyed, it was important that their travel did not damage the natural environment. However, only 38 per cent would pay more to use a travel company that tries to protect and preserve the natural environment of their target destinations, and 40 per cent expressed an interest in helping to protect and preserve the environment if those efforts could be fitted conveniently into their existing lifestyle (TIA 2003). These results are similar to those obtained in a survey of British package tourists (MORI 2000). In the American sample, a hard core of 11 per cent indicated that the environment is their primary consideration in selecting travel companies (TIA 2003). The researchers involved in this study argue that about a third of American travellers can be described as environmentally and socioculturally conscientious **geotourists** who seek unique and authentic experiences that emphasise a destination's sense of place.

Green attitudes and practices have also become entrenched in the mainstream of the tourism and hospitality industry (Diamantis & Ladkin 1999b, Weaver 2006). Most large corporations, along with global and regional organisations such as PATA (Pacific Asia Travel Association) and the World Tourism Organization, openly espouse a green agenda. High-profile documents that support this directive include *Agenda 21 for the Travel and Tourism Industry* (WTO 1997), which outlines 12 principles for sustainable tourism, and the *Global Code of Ethics for Tourism* (WTO 2006b). The *Blueprint for New Tourism*, released by the World Travel and Tourism Council (WTTC 2003), is notable because of the latter's status as the premier global interest group for the private sector tourism industry. Many hospitality and tourism trade magazines now include an environmental column or feature, and a specialised publication, the *Green Hotelier*, is available as part of the International Hotels Environment Initiative (IHEI) that emerged from Agenda 21. Other major sector-specific initiatives include the Tour Operators Initiative for Sustainable Tourism Development and the Cruise Industry Waste Management Practices and Procedures program (Weaver 2006). Worthy of mention in terms of quality control initiatives is **Green Globe**, a membership-based organisation mandated to attain sustainable outcomes for the tourism and hospitality industry worldwide through adherence of members (mostly hotels) to sustainability-related indicators. Initially conceived in 1994 as a self-regulated system without specific goals, Green Globe has now moved towards a full certification system supported by independent monitoring (Griffin & DeLacey 2002).

Such developments suggest an increasing compatibility between conventional mass tourism and ecotourism. However, considerable scepticism surrounds the supposed green trend in the tourism industry, which some regard as a cynical exercise in greenwashing and hollow rhetoric (Mowforth & Munt 1998), as per the theory that old paradigms actively seek to incorporate popular and complementary elements of arising new paradigms in order to perpetuate their dominance. A less conspiratorial and more charitable view holds that although significant positive shifts in behaviour have occurred, these have been simply opportunistic, pragmatic or instrumental, involving such practices as recycling, community outreach and energy use reduction that are profitable as well as useful for publicity and marketing purposes. Concurrently, there is virtually no evidence that the industry is moving fundamentally away from its traditional anthropocentric emphasis on profitability and growth (Holden 2003). Ultimately, it may simply be that the contemporary tourism industry is reacting to the veneer environmentalist norms of society and the travelling public in particular, with its own version of veneer environmentalism (Weaver 2006). Should society at some point in the future shift at the grassroots to a more biocentric environmentalism, then one may expect industry to follow suit in the interests of its own survival, even at the risk of compromising its own core ideological assumptions.

2.4 ECOTOURIST MARKET

Ecotourists may be defined as those who fulfil the criteria outlined in section 1.4 (i.e. tourists seeking nature-based learning experiences and behaving as much as possible in an environmentally and socioculturally sustainable manner), and as such they constitute a subset of the green traveller market. Buckley (2003b), furthermore, regards the ecotourist as a type of geotourist. However, as with green travel in general, ecotourists are not a homogeneous market but display a range of motivation, behaviour and other characteristics that entail variable levels of anthropocentrism and biocentrism. **Market segmentation** is the process whereby a market such as ecotourists is divided into distinctive subcomponents or **market segments** (whose members share common traits) so that appropriate and cost-effective 'target' marketing, product development and management strategies can be formulated for each. Through market segmentation, marketing and management efforts can be focused in the most efficient way to serve existing customers, to attract new customers who are similar to existing clientele and to identify underrepresented markets for potential recruitment (Bécherel 1999, Weaver & Lawton 2006). With regard to ecotourism, market segmentation can be conducted at two levels. The first is to determine how ecotourists differ from consumers and tourists in general and the second is to identify distinctive ecotourist subgroups. Several standard criteria are used in market segmentation, including motivation, attitude and behaviour, geographic location and demographics.

◼ 2.4.1 Motivation, *attitude and behaviour*

Motivation, attitude and behaviour are often considered separately, but are combined here because (a) motivation and attitude influence behaviour and (b) together they comprise the underlying dynamics of the 'hard' to 'soft' spectrum described below. The idea of such a continuum is implicit in the array of definitions provided in table 1.1, which range from very rigid and prescriptive (i.e. hard) to more liberal (i.e. soft), and is also evident in the tourism literature (see below).

⌀ Hard ecotourists

The **hard ecotourist** ideal type is associated with a strongly biocentric attitude that entails a deep commitment to environmental issues, a belief that one's activities should enhance the resource base, and a desire for a deep and meaningful interaction with the natural environment (see figure 2.4). As such, hard ecotourists are found at the more extreme environmentalist end of the population bell curve (see figure 2.3). These motivation and attitudes give rise to a preference for physically active and challenging experiences that involve close personal contact with nature and do not require on-site services or facilities. In terms of trip characteristics, hard ecotourists prefer as much as possible making their own travel arrangements, small group travel, and specialised trips that require enough time to reach the relatively undisturbed natural venues that they prefer. A 'strong sustainability' philosophy underlies such hard ecotourism venues and activities. Volunteer activity constitutes a distinctive form of hard ecotourism that is closely aligned with comprehensive ecotourism (see 'In the Field: Volunteer tourism').

■ **Figure 2.4**
Characteristics of the hard and soft ecotourists as ideal types
Source: *adapted from Weaver & Lawton 2002.*

HARD (active, deep)	SOFT (passive, shallow)
← *the ecotourism spectrum* →	
Strong environmental commitment	Moderate or superficial environmental commitment
Enhancive sustainability	Steady state sustainability
Specialised trips	Multi-purpose trips
Long trips	Short trips
Small groups	Larger groups
Physically active	Physically passive
Physical challenge	Physical comfort
No services expected	Services expected
Deep interaction with nature	Shallow interaction with nature
Emphasis on personal experience	Emphasis on mediation
Make own travel arrangements	Rely on travel agents and tour operators

Soft ecotourists

Soft ecotourists display significant anthropocentric tendencies and hence tend to be dominated by the veneer environmentalist segment of figure 2.3. Their commitment to environmental issues is not as deep as that of hard ecotourists, their attitudes are more suggestive of steady state rather than enhancive sustainability, and their desired level of engagement with the natural environment is relatively shallow, suggesting an alignment with minimalist ecotourism. The preferred experience of a soft ecotourist is physically less taxing and supported by accommodation, eating and toilet facilities, parking lots and other services. Large group travel is common, and soft ecotourists do not mind being in company of other soft ecotourists, as they have a much higher crowding threshold than hard ecotourists. The soft ecotourist typically engages in ecotourism as one component of a multi-purpose trip, thereby producing short duration experiences that are often on a day-only basis. To the extent that they seek involvement and learning experiences associated with nature, soft ecotourists are alleged to prefer mediation, whether through guided tours, interpretation trails, or interpretive centres. The soft ecotourist is also more likely to have travel arrangements made formally through travel agencies and tour operators. In essence, soft ecotourists are mass tourists who enjoy tangential contact with the natural environment often as a diversion from beach-based or other conventional forms of tourist activity (see section 7.2). All these traits indicate also that a 'weak sustainability' approach is commonly encountered in soft ecotourism venues and activities.

IN THE FIELD

Volunteer tourism

The term **volunteer tourism** (or 'voluntourism') encompasses a variety of activities in which participating tourists receive no financial compensation in return for engaging in organised activities that are environmentally and/or socioculturally beneficial to the host destination. Participants normally pay their full expenses, and related activities are usually carried out under the auspices of non-profit organisations. Volunteer tourism qualifies as a form of alternative tourism (Weaver 2006) and as hard ecotourism when the focus is on nature-based venues and activities. Examples include the Earthwatch Institute, which in Australia has had volunteers participating in projects such as the study of flying fox numbers and their diet in Kakadu National Park (Northern Territory) and examining the effects of honey bees on native bee species on Kangaroo Island (South Australia) (Weiler & Richins 1995). Self-explanatory is the Gibbon Rehabilitation Project in Thailand (Broad 2003), while the Volunteer for Nature program in Canada is focused on small project biodiversity protection in Ontario (Halpenny & Caissie 2003).

The volunteer activity in Costa Rica's Santa Elena Rainforest Reserve, coordinated by Canadian-based Youth Challenge International, has been the subject of particular academic scrutiny. Wearing (2001) describes how the project helped to protect a threatened area of rainforest, raised local awareness about conservation and encouraged follow-up projects by other non-profit organisations. As such, and because it increased the environmental and social awareness of the participants, this initiative illustrates the concept of comprehensive ecotourism with its emphasis on transformative behaviour and net benefits to local communities. Even so, volunteer tourism should not be perceived uncritically. Potential problems derive from the egotistical motivations of some participants (e.g. adventure and résumé enhancement), the possibility of insufficient training of participants, rapid turnaround of volunteers, the intrusion of volunteer tourists into the local community, and increasing corporatisation of the sector as sponsoring organisations become larger and more business-like in their operation.

Variations in the hard–soft spectrum

The idea of a hard–soft ecotourism continuum was first proposed by Laarman and Durst (1987) and has since received substantial support in the literature as an essential framework (e.g. Lindberg 1991, Orams 2001a, Pearce & Moscardo 1994, Weaver & Lawton 2002, Weiler & Richins 1995). The need to understand this continuum cannot be overstated, since the motivation and experiential preferences of different ecotourist types will influence the type of ecotourism product that is sought and, hence, the clientele that is attracted to a particular business or destination. In the ecotourism literature, intermediate categories are commonly recognised (see figure 2.5). The Queensland Ecotourism Plan (Queensland 1997), for example, identifies 'small group' ecotourists as a market situated between 'self-reliant' and 'popular' ecotourists. This particular typology, however, is not supported in the plan by any empirical evidence and, therefore, like the hard–soft continuum, in general should be treated as speculative.

Source	Hard			Soft
Conceptual				
Laarman & Durst (1987)	Hard			Soft
Lindberg (1991)	Hard-core	Dedicated	Mainstream	Casual
Queensland (1997)	Self-reliant ecotourism		Small group ecotourism	Popular ecotourism
Empirical Pearce & Moscardo (1994)	Nature experience & appreciation 24%	Get away, relax with nature 66%		Novelty sun-seekers* 10%
	(based on a sample of 545 general travellers passing through Cardwell, northern Qld.)			
Chapman (1995)	Nature involvement 54%	Personal development 19%	Laid-back 19%	Social activity 8%
	(based on a sample of 507 users of NSW state forests during time of participation)			
Palacio & McCool (1997)	Ecotourists 18%	Nature escapists 22%	Comfortable naturalists 33%	Passive players* 27%
	(based on a sample of 207 travellers through Belize's international airport)			
Diamantis (1999b)	Frequent 60%		Occasional 40%	
	(based on a sample of 1760 UK residents from databases of ecotourism-related tour operators and organisations)			
Weaver & Lawton (2001)	Harder 34%	Structured 40%		Softer 27%
	(based on a sample of 1180 overnight patrons of two ecolodges in Lamington National Park, southeastern Qld.)			

■ **Figure 2.5** *Ecotourist typologies*
Source: *adapted from Weaver & Lawton 2001.*
* Many 'novelty sun-seekers' and 'passive players' fall outside the continuum.

In contrast to these non-empirical typologies, Pearce and Moscardo (1994) surveyed a sample of drivers passing through the northern Queensland town of Cardwell and found that two-thirds could be described as members of a soft 'get-away, relax-with-nature' group. Conversely, about a quarter of the sample displayed hard ecotourism tendencies while the rest were 'novelty sun-seekers'. The idea of a continuum is evident in this and all the other empirical studies listed in figure 2.6, yet the specific outcomes are quite variable in terms of group characteristics and representation as a proportion of total sample. This may be owing in part to data collection procedures, but is more likely to be due to the variable nature both of the survey instruments and the targeted population in each study. In the case of Pearce and Moscardo (1994) and Palacio and McCool (1997), the sample consisted of individuals in transit who may or may not have experienced, or were intending to experience, an ecotourism product. Many 'novelty sun-seekers' and 'passive players' therefore fall outside the continuum. Diamantis (1999), in contrast, derived his sample from persons on the database of ecotourism tour operators and organisations, although nothing more is revealed about the nature of the products that they had used or when this use occurred.

Chapman (1995) and Weaver and Lawton (2002) take a different approach by sampling known users of a particular nature-based product. In the former case, visitors to a New South Wales state forest were sampled, while the latter study focused on overnight patrons of two ecotourism lodges in the Gold Coast hinterland. This study identified the dualistic **structured ecotourist**, who behaves like a hard ecotourist when interacting with nature (i.e. prefers long walks in a challenging physical setting) but resembles a soft ecotourist in their preference for comfortable overnight accommodation and good food (i.e. they are hard on the outside, soft on the inside). Such case studies are useful because of their empiricism, but what is required now is the standardised application of a single motivational–behavioural survey across an array of ecotourism destinations and products to see whether any universal model of the hard–soft continuum emerges. A potential complication is the possibility that a given individual may behave as a hard ecotourist on one particular trip and as a soft ecotourist on another. This raises the question of whether ecotourism classifications should be based on individuals or products, or a combination of both.

■ 2.4.2 Geography

Place of residence is one of the most widely used and readily available criteria for the segmentation of tourist markets, and it can be considered at various scales. The highest level of geographical segmentation is the distinction between the developed and developing worlds. Evidence from a variety of destinations suggests that the vast majority of ecotourists reside in the developed regions, yet they dominate the ecotourism market in most of the developing world. Advanced levels of economic development in regions of the developed world produce the high amounts of discretionary income and time that facilitate tourism activity (Weaver & Lawton 2006). At the same time the rapid diffusion of the green paradigm in those societies channels an increasing portion of tourism-related travel into ecotourism-related activities.

Country-based segmentation, which is the next scale of geographic engagement, supports this developed world/developing world dichotomy. On the basis of extensive examination of anecdotal information, Eagles and Higgins (1998) regard the most important ecotourist markets, in order of size, to be the USA, the UK, Germany, Canada, France, Australia, the Netherlands, Sweden, Austria, New Zealand, Norway and Denmark (see the case study 'Identifying ecotourist markets for Australia in the United States, United Kingdom and Germany' at the end of this chapter). If accurate, the broader regional pattern can then be refined as a northern European – 'New World Anglo' connection. The Japanese ecotourism market is also apparently becoming more significant, although Eagles and Higgins (1998) speculate that the motivations of this market may be based on more of an 'aesthetic appreciation rather than ecological understanding' of nature-based attractions (see 'Practitioner's perspective: An East Asian model of ecotourism?').

The International Visitor Survey, published by Tourism Research Council New Zealand (2006), provides detailed coverage of major inbound markets to New Zealand in terms of specific activities undertaken and attractions visited. It therefore offers exceptional insight into the tendency of various nationalities to engage in ecotourism-related activity. Table 2.1 compares six of New Zealand's largest inbound markets against five selected ecotourism activities. Residents of Germany display the greatest tendency to engage in ecotourism and residents of China the least. Japan shows the most internal variation, with high proclivity for visiting glow worm caves and bushwalking but low proclivity for glacier walks, whale-watching and penguin-viewing. The finding of relatively low proclivity for Australians across all five activities is interesting given the country's reputation as an ecotourism leader. However, it could simply be that Australians are more likely to engage in ecotourism domestically and favour New Zealand for other types of activity. Understanding the relative tendencies of various inbound markets to participate in ecotourism, however, provides only part of the story. In absolute numbers, the 74 442 Australians who participated in a half-day bush walk in New Zealand during 2005 far outnumbered the 26 265 Germans who did the same. A similar discrepancy between relative and absolute participation is evident between the Germans and British in both whale-watching and penguin-viewing. Hence, for marketing and management purposes, protected area managers need to understand the markets that produce *more* ecotourists as well as the markets that are *more likely* to produce ecotourists.

Further geographic segmentation can be made at an intra-national scale. Not all people from Germany or Canada, for example, display an equal inclination to engage in ecotourism activities. A particularly useful distinction can be made between urban and rural areas. 'Pushed out' by higher incomes and the pressures of urban living, city dwellers, and especially those living in large metropolitan areas, are more likely than their rural counterparts to pursue ecotourism-related activities in the countryside. Rural residents, in contrast, are more likely to engage in hunting and fishing in those same rural environments (US Department of the Interior 2002).

■ Table 2.1 *Participation in ecotourism-related activity by New Zealand inbound markets, 2005*

COUNTRY	TOTAL VISITORS	HALF-DAY BUSH WALK	GLACIER WALK	GLOW WORM CAVES	WHALE-WATCHING	PENGUIN-VIEWING
Germany	52 904	49.6% = 26 265	34.6% = 18 310	23.9% = 12 651	20.8% = 10 983	18.0% = 9 520
UK	279 952	24.4% = 56 292	22.3% = 68 809	18.5% = 51 972	11.8% = 36 079	8.8% = 22 516
Japan	145 953	23.7% = 34 570	4.9% = 7 137	31.3% = 45 635	3.8% = 5 531	2.6% = 3 781
USA	192 720	17.7% = 34 066	12.2% = 23 411	18.6% = 35 938	3.1% = 6 031	6.4% = 12 304
Australia	797 885	9.3% = 74 442	8.5% = 67 676	9.8% = 78 084	1.9% = 15 393	1.4% = 11 174
China	83 609	3.5% = 2 936	3.5% = 2 928	11.8% = 9 878	1.1% = 943	3.7% = 3 106

Source: *adapted from International Visitor Survey 2005, Tourism Research Council New Zealand 2006.*

*P*RACTITIONER'S PERSPECTIVE

An East Asian model of ecotourism?

Several studies have considered the participation of East Asian markets such as Taiwan in ecotourism as it is defined in Western terms (Kerstetter, Hou & Lin 2004, Tao, Eagles & Smith 2004). There is growing evidence, however, that East Asian markets such as Japan, South Korea, Taiwan and China practise a culturally distinct form of ecotourism. For example, Japanese visitors to New Zealand are the most likely of six selected major markets to visit glow worm caves but among the least likely to view whales or penguins (table 2.1). On the basis of an analysis of Internet material and other sources relating to East Asian protected areas, Weaver (2002a) characterises East Asia as a 'blossom and waterfall' ecotourism region in which vegetation and geology, along with certain kinds of microfauna, tend to take priority as attractions over large wildlife. This contrasts with the more Western-oriented 'rainforest and reef' region that covers South-East Asia.

For protected area managers in such countries as Australia and Canada, where East Asian inbound markets are critical, this suggests that visitor satisfaction may depend on emphasising a different kind of natural attraction mix than is usually associated with ecotourism. Equally important from an interpretation perspective is a learning dimension skewed towards aesthetic appreciation and embracing the spiritual and philosophical impulses of Buddhist, Taoist and Shinto belief systems. The inherent respect for nature in these systems may facilitate efforts by managers to achieve environmentally sustainable outcomes. Also intriguing is a tolerance for large group dynamics, wherein many East

(continued)

Asian protected areas apparently accommodate very large numbers of visitors with minimal problems of social conflict or misbehaviour.

The desirability of identifying and catering to this East Asian model is underscored by the magnitude of that market, with protected areas in Japan alone experiencing more than 300 million visits per year, versus about 60 million in the US national park system (Weaver 2002a). More generally, it may be time to enrich and revitalise the global ecotourism sector, with its deep Western roots, through exposure to its East Asian variant, just as Western society more broadly has been enriched during the past half-century by its exposure to East Asian philosophy and cuisine.

■ 2.4.3 Sociodemographic *criteria*

Sociodemographic segmentation involves differentiation on the basis of population statistics. Commonly employed criteria include gender, age, education, income and employment.

Gender

Two main observations are pertinent with respect to the relationship between gender and ecotourism. The first concerns the increasing 'feminisation' of the sector. Most (although not all) ecotourist surveys conducted in the early 1990s or earlier revealed a pattern of disproportionately high male representation. For example, Kellert (1985) found in the early 1980s that 73 per cent of committed birdwatchers were male, and males accounted for 55 per cent of sampled Canadian ecotourists travelling in Costa Rica in the late 1980s (Fennell & Smale 1992). The opposite tendency has been observed since the mid-1990s. For example, Diamantis (1999) found that females accounted for 57 per cent of occasional and 54 per cent of frequent ecotourists in the United Kingdom. Similarly, females accounted for 62 per cent of respondents to the 1999 survey of ecotourism lodge customers in Queensland's Lamington National Park (Weaver & Lawton 2002) and, notably, 73 per cent of the cluster with the highest biocentric tendencies (Weaver 2002b). A comprehensive study of major markets in the USA and Europe by the World Tourism Organization (2002) concluded that females were more likely to participate in ecotourism than males, although an analysis of birdwatcher survey results in the USA identified no statistically significant differences in participation rates on the basis of gender (Eubanks, Stoll & Ditton 2004).

There are several possible explanations for this apparent pattern of feminisation. As discussed below, ecotourism participation is correlated with tertiary education qualifications, and females are disproportionately represented among university students in the major market countries. Some studies support the hypothesis that females tend to be more biocentric than males (Vaske et al. 2001), as demonstrated by the above

Lamington results and a study of Earthwatch Australia in which 69 per cent of participants were female (Weiler & Richins 1995). Not all ecotourism-related activities, however, have the same gender balance. According to the Ecotourism Supplementary Survey of Australia's International Visitor Survey, inbound female tourists were more likely to undertake guided and unguided walks of less than two hours in Australia, whereas males had a greater propensity to engage in whale-watching and longer non-guided walks (Blamey & Hatch 1998). Other studies have found higher male representation in adventurous and physically demanding activities, as well as in some forms of birdwatching. Hvenegaard and Dearden (1998), for example, found that males accounted for two-thirds of birdwatching ecotourists in Thailand's Doi Inthanon National Park. The contrast with the other birder surveys cited above may be owing to the exotic and relatively more physically taxing venue of the Thailand study. Clearly, further empirical research is required to better identify variations in participation by gender across the full array of ecotourism activities and venues.

Age

Like gender, variable results have been reported with respect to the age of ecotourists. Hvenegaard and Dearden (1998) found that birdwatching ecotourists and general ecotourists were older (average of 40.2 and 37.0 years respectively) than general tourists (33.8 years) in the Doi Inthanon study. However, the Ecotourism Supplementary Survey in Australia found that just under half of all inbound visitors to Australia in the 20–29 age bracket were 'nature tourists', compared with less than a third of individuals in the over-50 age bracket (Blamey & Hatch 1998). The apparent discrepancies, again, are most likely due to differences in the target population. The birders in the Doi Inthanon study are proven ecotourists who had arranged their travel through ecotour companies and organisations, whereas the Australian study solicited a cross-section of all inbound tourists, which indicated simply that a high proportion of younger tourists are nature-seeking backpackers. The Australian study does not reveal anything about the age distribution of inbound ecotourists as a group. According to Wight (2001), soft ecotourists tend to be younger than hard ecotourists, and this is supported by Diamantis (1999), who found that more than half of 'occasional' (i.e. softer) ecotourists in the UK were in the 17–34 age group, compared with a third of 'frequent' (i.e. harder) ecotourists.

With respect to activity, Wight (1996) cites a Tourism Canada survey of adventure tourism and ecotourism operators from the early 1990s in which older adults dominated wildlife-watching while younger clients, not surprisingly, were dominant in more physically demanding activities such as scuba diving and cross-country skiing. Eight birder surveys in the USA, for example, yielded average ages ranging from 51 to 61 years (Eubanks, Stoll & Ditton 2004). The Lamington National Park study (Weaver & Lawton 2002), in which the average age of sampled patrons was over 50 years, indicates that relatively remote ecotourism lodges also tend to appeal to the older adult market segment, perhaps because the latter is better able to afford the premium rates that such facilities command. The future of such products appears promising, given the continuing ageing trend that is occurring in the major ecotourist market countries due to rising life expectancies and low fertility rates (Anderson & Hussey 2000).

Education, income and occupation

The empirical ecotourism research shows a consistent pattern with respect to education, with ecotourists having higher educational qualifications than other consumers (Hvenegaard & Dearden 1998, World Tourism Organization 2002). Diamantis (1999) found that 60 per cent of British ecotourists possessed tertiary qualifications, while more than 55 per cent of respondents in the Lamington National Park study (Weaver & Lawton 2002) held an undergraduate or postgraduate university degree. Almost 75 per cent of birdwatching ecotourists in the Doi Inthanon study (Thailand) had at least an undergraduate degree (Hvenegaard & Dearden 1998) while the participants in the US birder study stated that they had completed, on average, 17 years of formal education (Eubanks, Stoll & Ditton 2004).

Ecotourism is also closely linked to higher income levels (World Tourism Organization 2002). For example, visitor clusters linked closely to ecotourism in the Doi Inthanon study (Hvenegaard & Dearden 1998) had higher incomes than general tourists or trekkers. A study of the US ecotourist market by Tourism Queensland (2006a) found that 52 per cent had an annual household income above US$60,000. Special caution should be exercised, however, when examining the correlation between income and the inclination to engage in ecotourism. While higher discretionary incomes are necessary to reach some of the more exotic ecotourism destinations and products, higher income levels among ecotourists also reflect the high salaries earned by individuals with advanced educational qualifications.

2.5 SIZE OF THE ECOTOURIST MARKET

Recent ecotourism-related publications are notable for providing nothing more than a vague indication of the size of the global ecotourism market. This is sensible, given that there is no universally accepted definition of ecotourism and no protocol in place for collecting such data at an international level. One can, however, examine supply-side surrogate data, such as visits to higher-order protected areas in individual countries, then interpret and extrapolate from it with caution. In the case of Australia, we may start with the observation that 39 per cent of visitors from the top five inbound markets visited a national or state park in 2004. It must be then noted that not all of these visits to protected areas were for ecotourism-related purposes (see chapter 3), while some ecotourism activities, such as whale-watching (undertaken by 7 per cent of visitors), occur mostly outside protected areas (Tourism Research Australia 2005). Furthermore, visits to protected areas for most inbound visitors constitute just one minor component of their Australian trip. It may therefore be ventured that soft ecotourists comprise around 30 per cent of visitation to Australia (at least for these five main markets), although a majority would earn this label simply by merit of just one or two casual visits to a protected area near a large urban area. A similar line of reasoning probably underlies an estimate by the World Tourism Organization that ecotourism accounts for around 20 per cent of the global tourism market (or 150 million international stayover tourists) (in Wight 2001). At the other end of the spectrum, no more than two per cent of total visitors to Australia, or 100 000, would qualify even generously as hard ecotourists, this being the proportion of visitors in the 1996 Ecotourism Supplementary Survey who listed visiting natural areas as their most important reason for coming to Australia (Blamey & Hatch 1998).

On the domestic side, intermediate outcomes have been obtained from the 2001 National Survey of Fishing, Hunting and Wildlife-Associated Recreation in the US, which found that 10 per cent of American adults (about 21 million persons in 2001) travelled away from their homes for the specific purpose of watching wildlife (US Department of the Interior 2002). However, because this survey employed a minimum travel threshold of just one mile away from one's home, the *ecotourist* proportion of this total is likely to be around five per cent, assuming that all of these participants attempted to behave in a sustainable manner during their wildlife encounters.

■ 2.5.1 Growth *of ecotourism*

As with size, and for similar reasons, attempts to gauge the growth of ecotourism are fraught with hazard. Weaver (1998) cites anecdotal information from the late 1980s that showed some specialised ecotour operations expanding their customer base at an annual rate of 15–25 per cent. This remarkable expansion is actually nothing extraordinary given the relatively small customer base numbers at that time, wherein even a modest increase in the actual customer base will translate into very high relative growth. Such anecdotal statistics therefore are not inherently problematic. However, they become so when they are carelessly and inappropriately extrapolated to the ill-defined ecotourism sector as a whole, which has been done frequently by vested interest groups and even in refereed academic journal articles that cite these groups. Related claims that ecotourism is the fastest growing sector of the tourism industry are equally sensationalist and baseless.

Although no doubt certain protected areas and activities do continue to demonstrate an exceptionally high rate of growth, macro statistics paint a more ambiguous picture. Longitudinal studies of this topic that involve Australian or New Zealanders are lacking, but a comprehensive survey of participation in various recreational activities conducted among US adults over the period 1982–83 to 1994–95 did reveal an impressive 155 per cent growth in birdwatching. This compares with 15 per cent growth in the US population as a whole over that period (Cordell, Lewis & McDonald 1995). Subsequent surveys, however, show a decrease in US birdwatching participation. The Outdoor Industry Foundation (2005), for example, notes a 17 per cent decline (from 18.3 to 15.1 million) between 2001 and 2004 in the number of American adults who reporting travelling at least a quarter of a mile on a birdwatching excursion. The 2001 National Survey of Fishing, Hunting and Wildlife-Associated Recreation corroborates this trend, reporting that participation in birdwatching at least one mile from home declined 27 per cent between 1991 and 2001, from 30.0 million to 21.8 million adults (US Department of the Interior 2002). These findings, indicating a period of rapid growth for American birdwatching in the 1980s followed by consolidation and readjustment, seem to provide a more realistic assessment of ecotourism's pattern of growth over the past two decades.

2.6 SUMMARY

Growing evidence suggests that the dominant Western environmental paradigm is being challenged by a green paradigm, although it is debatable whether this indicates an actual paradigm shift. The evolution of ecotourism through four tourism platforms (see figure 2.2) could indicate such a transformation, with the most recent stage suggesting a synthesis of the two paradigms in concert with the concept of 'sustainable development'. The same trend is apparent in the broader 'greening' of the general consumer and traveller markets, although much of this apparent transformation is superficial and indicative of veneer environmentalism. Many consumers profess to have environmentalist sympathies, but except for approximately a quarter with clear environmentalist tendencies, do not translate these sympathies into a consistent pattern of pro-environmental behaviour. Similar ambivalence is evident in the tourism and hospitality industry, and it may be argued that veneer environmentalism in the latter is a response to these veneer environmentalist consumer tendencies.

Such gradations in commitment to the environment are apparent when the ecotourist market is segmented into such categories as motivation, attitude and behaviour. What results is a small and highly committed group of hard ecotourists at one end of a continuum, and a much larger and more superficial group of soft ecotourists at the other end, who in many ways resemble (and may actually be) conventional mass tourists. Segmentation on the basis of geographical criteria reveals that most ecotourists reside in urban areas in the more economically developed countries of Europe, North America and Oceania, although the emergence of a distinct East Asian ecotourist market also needs to be considered. Sociodemographically, trends towards feminisation and ageing are evident, although gender and age profiles vary significantly by activity. A profile of high educational attainment and higher than average incomes is more consistent across the market.

Calculating the size of the ecotourism market is problematic due to the lack of a clear definition or data-gathering protocol, although a generous estimate would be that around 20 per cent of international tourism is ecotourism-related, most of it soft. Estimates of ecotourism growth rates are also problematic because of the tendency to extrapolate high growth rates from anecdotal evidence to the sector as a whole. Indicative data, however, suggest a period of rapid growth in the 1980s followed by consolidation.

QUESTIONS

1. (a) To what extent is contemporary ecotourism a synthesis of the dominant Western environmental paradigm and the green paradigm?
   (b) What does this say about the argument that Western society is currently experiencing a paradigm shift?
   (c) What are the implications of this synthesis for attaining management outcomes that are environmentally and socioculturally sustainable?

2. (a) Why is it important for ecotourism managers and marketers to undertake market segmentation?
   (b) Is there such a thing as a 'typical' ecotourist that emerges from such an exercise?
   (c) What is the value in constructing a profile of the typical ecotourist?
   (d) Do you think that most ecotourists are self-aware that they are ecotourists?

3. (a) How do hard and soft ecotourists fit within the population bell curve of environmental attitudes (figure 2.3)?
   (b) How do these soft and hard dimensions align with the minimalist and comprehensive dimensions discussed in chapter 1?
   (c) Can soft ecotourists be compatible with comprehensive ecotourism modes of interpretation and product presentation?

4. (a) What is a 'structured ecotourist'?
   (b) What are the implications of the structured ecotourist market for managers of protected areas and nature lodges?

5. (a) Why is it important for venue managers to identify both the relative and the absolute ecotourism participation levels of inbound markets?
   (b) How do German and Australian visitors to New Zealand differ in this regard?

6. (a) What factors might account for the apparent trend of feminisation in ecotourism?
   (b) What are the implications of this trend for the ecotourism industry?

7 (a) Why do ecotourist markets display a consistent pattern of high educational attainment, high incomes and strong occupational representation from the professions?

(b) Given these characteristics, what kind of marketing strategies would be effective in promoting ecotourism products?

8 (a) Why is it extremely difficult to measure the size and growth of the ecotourism market?

(b) What could be done to produce an accurate estimate of this market at a global scale?

FURTHER READING

Flannery, T 2006, *The Weather Makers: How Man is Changing the Climate and What It Means for Life on Earth*, Atlantic Monthly Press, New York. The author discusses the causes and implications of climate change, which is a prominent issue of discourse in the clash between the dominant Western environmental paradigm and the green paradigm.

Hutton, D & Connors, L 1999, *A History of the Australian Environmental Movement*, Cambridge University Press, Cambridge. This text provides a detailed and up-to-date chronicle of the environmental movement in Australia. Of particular interest are the sections that deal with the role of bushwalkers in developing the country's protected area system.

Wearing, S 2001, *Volunteer Tourism: Experiences that Make a Difference*, CABI, Wallingford, UK. A thorough ethnographic analysis of the volunteer ecotourism experience is provided, using Youth Conservation International's rainforest preservation project in Costa Rica as a case study.

Weaver, D 2002a, 'Asian ecotourism: Patterns and themes', *Tourism Geographies* 4: 153–72. The author raises the possibility of a distinctive East Asian model of ecotourism, which is described as the 'blossom and waterfall' region.

Weaver, D & Lawton, L 2002, 'Overnight ecotourist market segmentation in the Gold Coast hinterland of Australia', *Journal of Travel Research* 40: 270–80. This is an example of an empirical study that reveals soft and hard ecotourism impulses while also identifying a 'structured ecotourist' hybrid that combines hard and soft tendencies.

Wight, P 2001, 'Ecotourists: Not a homogeneous market segment', in DB Weaver (ed.), *Encyclopedia of Ecotourism*, CABI, Wallingford, UK, pp. 37–62. The ecotourist market is examined in a detailed, up-to-date and comprehensive way by Wight, who shows how ecotourists differ not only from tourists in general but among themselves as well.

Identifying ecotourist markets
for Australia in the USA, UK and Germany

Ecotourist markets are not homogeneous, and country of origin has proven to be an especially useful criterion for differentiating motivations and activities. In 2004, the Destination Australia Marketing Alliance (DAMA), a coalition of Australian state and federal tourism offices seeking to maximise the potential of inbound tourism, commissioned market analyses for several major countries of origin. About a thousand adults in each country were randomly selected and profiled, then specialised markets such as ecotourists were isolated and subjected to further analysis. Three of the countries — the UK, the USA and Germany — are especially important to Australia in terms of their ecotourism proclivities and offer an interesting study in comparative characteristics (Tourism Queensland 2006a, 2006b, 2006c). The initial stage of the research required DAMA to identify the 'ecotourist' market segment. It was decided to include individuals from the main surveys who met the following three criteria (percentage of adults from each market responding affirmatively are listed after each criterion):

1 During their most recent long-haul trip, they must have participated in at least one of the following:
   • saw wildlife in its natural surroundings (Germans 27, British 39, Americans 27)
   • stayed in the wilderness (Germans 11, British 10, Americans 5)
   • visited a rainforest or jungle (Germans 7, British 10, Americans 10)
   • visited national parks (Germans 21, British 28, Americans 26).

2 In general, they look for at least one of the following in their long-haul travel:
   • visiting an environmental or ecological site (Germans 47, British 49, Americans 36)
   • seeing wildlife in its natural habitat (Germans 73, British 62, Americans 43)
   • walking in untouched countryside and natural environments (Germans 79, British 65, Americans 38).

3 They sometimes plan their long-haul holidays around at least one of the following:
   • bird or animal watching (Germans 24, British 11, Americans 12)
   • camping (Germans 5, British 11, Americans 14)

(continued)

- nature, ecological, environmental or wilderness activities (Germans 31, British 22, Americans 29)
- walking, hiking, bushwalking, rainforest walking or rambling (Germans 56, British 21, Americans 20).

Within these parameters, 33 per cent of the Germans qualified as 'ecotourists', compared with 26 per cent of the British and 20 per cent of the Americans. More specifically, the responses to the criteria (see above) reveal the Germans as having the greatest proclivity to engage in walking activities and wildlife viewing, although these proclivities were not necessarily exercised in their most recent long-haul trip. Americans, in contrast, had the lowest tendencies in this regard. Since it is common for trips involving ecotourism trips to include other kinds of activity, the survey also asked the ecotourists to list which other pursuits they typically considered when planning their long-haul travel. For the Germans, food and wine (85 per cent) and photography (72 per cent) were the two main non-ecotourism-specific motives, whereas food and wine (55 per cent) and shopping (35 per cent) were most important for British ecotourists. Americans preferred history or visiting historical sites (79 per cent) and sightseeing tours (62 per cent).

To get ideas for their long-haul travel, German ecotourists rely mainly on word-of-mouth from friends and relatives (49 per cent) and travel agents (39 per cent), whereas British ecotourists most frequently cite television travel programs (43 per cent) and word-of-mouth (37 per cent). Americans appear to be the most active information seekers, relying equally on word-of-mouth and magazines (57 per cent each). Americans are also more reliant on the Internet to research destinations (55 per cent) compared with the British (44 per cent) and the Germans (below 26 per cent). In their most recent long-haul travel, 44 per cent of Germans travelled with one other person, compared with 50 per cent of British ecotourists and 35 per cent of American ecotourists. This reflects the fact that a large majority of respondents in all countries did not have children under the age of 16 residing in their household. Sixteen per cent of Americans travelled in groups of five or more other persons, which was a far higher rate than the other two markets. The British were most likely to have stayed in luxury accommodation (31 per cent) and alternative tourism accommodation (22 per cent) during that trip, compared with the Americans (27 and 17 per cent respectively) and the Germans (26 and 13 per cent respectively).

Eighty-four, 71 and 76 per cent of Germans, British and Americans, respectively, have never been to Australia, although in each case it is the top long-haul destination that they have seriously considered visiting (at levels of 36, 39 and 54 per cent respectively). In all cases, the image of Australia as an ecotourist destination is extremely positive. For example, agreement with the statement 'Australia has a huge variety of unique wildlife and habitats' was 95, 97 and 92 per cent respectively for each of the three markets, and 88, 86 and 87 per cent respectively for the statement 'Australia has so many extremes of landscape all in one place'. However, the statement 'Australia has fabulous beaches' yielded a more diverse response pattern of 83, 97 and 73 per cent, indicating that beaches are not equally important to all inbound tourist markets.

Demographically, the German market was divided equally between males and females, but the British sample was skewed towards males (53 per cent male), whereas the American sample was skewed towards females (57 per cent female). All markets had average ages in the forties and high levels of education, and 50 per cent of Americans, 36 per cent of British and 26 per cent of Germans had a tertiary degree.

Source:

*Tourism Queensland 2006a, 'The United States ecotourism market', www.tq.com.au
Tourism Queensland 2006b, 'The German ecotourism market', www.tq.com.au.
Tourism Queensland 2006c, 'The United Kingdom ecotourism market', www.tq.com.au.*

Questions

1 (a) What are the strengths and weaknesses of the DAMA 'ecotourist' definition?

    (b) If you could redesign the original survey, what changes would you make to this definition?

2 (a) Which of the three markets appears to have the highest 'social' proclivity?

    (b) How might this proclivity both positively and negatively affect the management of ecotourism venues?

3 (a) On the basis of the results presented above, what would be the ideal two-week Australian itinerary for each of the three markets?

    (b) How would you publicise each of these itineraries?

3 Ecotourism *environments*

After reading this chapter, you should be able to:

- explain why protected areas are becoming increasingly important as venues for ecotourism-related activities

- describe the IUCN classification system for protected areas

- match the relative compatibility of each IUCN protected area category with both hard and soft ecotourism

- discuss the advantages and disadvantages of private protected areas as a distinctive and increasingly important type of ecotourism venue

- describe and account for the uneven spatial and temporal distribution of ecotourism in country-wide protected area systems and in individual protected areas

- assess the potential of modified environments, including wastelands and urban areas, to accommodate ecotourism.

*I*NTRODUCTION ....

Ecotourism is associated with the emergence of a green paradigm, although the differentiation between hard and soft ecotourists suggests that elements of the dominant Western environmental paradigm still strongly influence the market side of the sector. Hard and soft ecotourists also differ in the type of experiences and venues that they seek, which has important implications from a product development and management perspective. This chapter focuses on ecotourism environments and in particular on protected areas, which account for most ecotourism activity because of the formal environmental protection that they provide. Public protected areas and their importance as ecotourism settings are discussed in section 3.2. The suitability of various protected area categories to accommodate different forms of ecotourism is also considered along with the phenomenon of marine protected areas. Section 3.3 examines ecotourism in the context of the rapidly expanding network of private protected areas and emphasises how these are distinct from but potentially complementary to public systems. The spatial distribution of ecotourism in and among public and private protected areas is discussed in section 3.4, which informs the discussion of protected area management in chapter 4. The final section of this chapter examines the potential of highly modified spaces, whether protected or not, to support ecotourism activity. These settings include agricultural land, urban space, artificial wetlands and reefs, and wasteland.

*P*UBLIC PROTECTED AREAS ....

The World Conservation Union (or IUCN) (in Earthtrends 2006) defines a **protected area** as:

> ■ ... an area of land and/or sea especially dedicated to the protection and maintenance of biological diversity, and of natural and associated cultural resources, and managed through legal or other effective means. ■

A public protected area is managed by a public authority such as a federal or state government department, in contrast with private protected areas, which are controlled by private sector interests or non-government organisations (NGOs) (see section 3.3). Protected areas in their modern form were first established in the 1870s and are a product of the environmental movement (see section 2.2.3), although commercial considerations were also instrumental in the early establishment of parks in such countries as the USA and Canada (Butler & Boyd 2000). By 2004, there were worldwide about 100 000 public terrestrial protected areas of at least a thousand hectares, covering 1.5 billion hectares in total, or 6.1 per cent of the world's land surface (Earthtrends 2006).

The actual proportion of area officially protected varies widely between countries. As shown in table 3.1, countries with the highest proportion of land in protected areas are mid-sized or smaller countries broadly distributed among the major world regions. By contrast, countries with the lowest percentage of protected land are concentrated in the Middle East and North Africa. Australia, the USA and Canada occupy an intermediate position, having 6.7 per cent, 8.4 per cent and 5.3 per cent of their territory, respectively, occupied by public protected areas (Earthtrends 2006). However, given the size of these countries, their actual area occupied by protected areas is immense compared with most of the countries occupying the top 20 positions in relative terms.

Table 3.2 lists the top 20 countries by actual amount of land in protected areas as of 2005. Four countries (Botswana, Mongolia, Tanzania and Venezuela) appear in both tables, revealing large protected area systems in both absolute and relative terms. The high status of Brazil, Colombia, Venezuela, Peru and Bolivia in table 3.2 indicates the trans-boundary Amazonian region as perhaps the world's greatest concentration of protected areas. Such statistics and patterns are significant to ecotourism given the close association between this sector and public protected areas, but it must also be emphasised that many protected areas, especially in the developing world, are **paper parks** in which applicable regulations are not adequately enforced (see the case study at the end of this chapter).

■ **Table 3.1** *Countries with the highest and lowest proportion of land in protected areas, 2005*

TOP 20 COUNTRIES	PERCENTAGE PROTECTED	BOTTOM 20 COUNTRIES	PERCENTAGE PROTECTED
Venezuela	34.2	Gambia	0.0
Bhutan	29.6	Guinea-Bissau	0.0
Germany	29.3	Iraq	0.0
Switzerland	28.7	Kuwait	0.0
Belize	28.6	Papua New Guinea	0.0
Austria	28.0	United Arab Emirates	0.0
New Zealand	24.0	Yemen	0.0
Dominican Republic	22.9	El Salvador	0.1
Denmark	21.8	Libya	0.1
Cambodia	20.5	Oman	0.1
Israel	18.4	Guinea	0.2
Tajikistan	18.3	Lesotho	0.2
Botswana	18.1	Mauritania	0.2

(continued)

■ Table 3.1 *continued*

TOP 20 COUNTRIES	PERCENTAGE PROTECTED	BOTTOM 20 COUNTRIES	PERCENTAGE PROTECTED
Equatorial Guinea	16.8	Solomon Islands	0.2
United Kingdom	15.3	Tunisia	0.2
Tanzania	14.6	Uruguay	0.2
Slovenia	14.4	Afghanistan	0.3
Congo	14.1	Haiti	0.3
Mongolia	13.5	Myanmar (Burma)	0.3
Thailand	12.7	Somalia	0.3

Includes categories I–VI protected areas and equivalent not classified by the IUCN.
Excludes very small countries and countries for which no data has been reported.

Source: *Earthtrends 2006.*

■ Table 3.2 *Countries with the largest amount of protected land, 2005*

TOP COUNTRIES	AREA[1]	TOP COUNTRIES	AREA[1]
Brazil	153 256	Zambia	31 225
US	149 009	Indonesia	25 992
Russia	128 699	Mongolia	21 791
China	110 067	Peru	21 608
Colombia	82 528	Bolivia	21 101
Saudi Arabia	81 914	Congo, Dem.	19 443
Australia	74 531	Ethiopia	18 620
Venezuela	64 438	Botswana	17 491
Canada	62 875	Argentina	17 448
Tanzania	37 428	India	15 628

[1](× 1000 hectares)
Includes categories I–VI protected areas and equivalent not classified by the IUCN.
Excludes very small countries and countries for which no data has been reported.

Source: *Earthtrends 2006.*

◼ 3.2.1 Importance *of public protected areas as ecotourism venues*

The literature shows that public protected areas are the overwhelmingly dominant setting for ecotourism-related activity throughout the world. This is apparent both in the growing number of academic publications that focus specifically on ecotourism in such environments (e.g. Butler & Boyd 2000, Eagles & McCool 2002, Newsome, Moore & Dowling 2002) and in their almost universal use as case studies for the supply-side, ecotourism-related research published in refereed journals. One reason, as outlined above, is the dramatic expansion in the number and acreage of protected areas during the past century. Several additional factors are outlined below.

Natural environments

Depending on their designation (see section 3.2.2), most protected areas are more or less oriented towards the protection of relatively undisturbed natural environments and biodiversity. They therefore provide a suitable physical setting for ecotourism in light of the nature-based criterion discussed in chapter 1 (see section 1.4.2). Protected area status, moreover, is often granted to an area on the basis of exceptional natural qualities or strategic location that adds to its value as an ecotourism venue. Some protected areas, for instance, are well known because of their charismatic megafauna or megaflora. Examples include Sichuan's Giant Panda sanctuaries, the iguanas and turtles of the Galapagos National Park (Ecuador) and the giant redwoods of California's Redwood National Park (USA). Other protected areas, such as Grand Canyon National Park (USA), Uluru (Australia) and the Gunung Mulu cave system in Malaysian Borneo, are best known for their charismatic megaliths. Other parks are characterised by outstanding scenery or the preservation of remnant natural habitat.

High public profile

Some protected areas have attained a high enough profile to be considered a primary or iconic tourist attraction in their country or region. Among these tourism icons are Yosemite, Grand Canyon and Yellowstone national parks in the USA, Canada's Banff and Jasper national parks, Kruger National Park in South Africa and Tanzania's Serengeti National Wildlife Reserve. Australian examples include Uluru National Park, Kakadu National Park, Blue Mountains National Park and the Great Barrier Reef Marine Park. As iconic attractions, these particular sites are preferred or 'must see' destinations for large numbers of visitors. On a broader scale, designation of an area as an internationally recognised **World Heritage Site** also confers status and market visibility on selected protected areas (Harrison & Hitchcock 2004). There is evidence that conferral of such status results in increased visitation levels, at least from international tourists, as reported by Buckley (2004a), who compared visitation levels in six Australian World Heritage sites for which a sufficient time series of data was available (Fraser Island, Kakadu, Uluru, south-west Tasmania, Shark Bay and the Great Barrier Reef) with a control group of non-WHS protected areas.

Structural suitability to ecotourism

The mandate of most high-order nature-based protected areas includes recreational activities, such as ecotourism, that focus on the appreciation of the natural environment (see below). World Heritage designation, for example, requires that adequate site interpretation be made available (Shackley 1998), thereby facilitating the education and learning criterion of ecotourism. In Queensland, preservation of the natural environment is the primary purpose of national parks, but 'nature-based recreational use is encouraged, where possible' (Queensland Parks and Wildlife Service 2004). A concomitant advantage for ecotourism in such high-order protected areas is the exclusion of most hunting and fishing as well as motorised off-road recreational vehicles.

Investment in infrastructure and services

As public spaces that are intended to provide recreational and educational opportunities, public protected areas receive varying levels of investment in infrastructure and services. These typically include walking trails, parking areas, toilet facilities, campgrounds and equipment rental sites. Interpretation centres and restaurants may also be provided. Many of these services can be provided at little or no cost, thereby encouraging high levels of visitation.

Convergence between protected and natural landscapes

Although the growth in the number and cumulative size of protected areas during the past century has been impressive, this increase has been far exceeded by the pace at which remaining natural environments are being destroyed and degraded. For example, only about half of the world's original forest remains, and most of this destruction has occurred during the 20th century (World Resources Institute 2005). If this trend continues, it is not inconceivable that natural habitat one day will occur only in protected areas, suggesting that most conventional ecotourism will also occur only in such locations.

■ 3.2.2 IUCN *categories and ecotourism compatibility*

The extent to which the above factors apply to any particular protected area depends primarily on the latter's designation. Not all protected areas are equally compatible with all types of ecotourism. Until recently, any attempt to systematically analyse protected areas for ecotourism compatibility was hindered by the proliferation of protected area designations, since any political jurisdiction can establish whatever classification structure it deems appropriate. Green and Paine (1997) calculated that during the mid-1990s, there were at least 1388 different categories of 'protected area' worldwide. Adding to the confusion is the plethora of meanings possible for a single designation such as 'national park', 'wildlife reserve' or state forest'. A 'national park' in the USA or Australia, for example, usually preserves relatively undisturbed natural environments, whereas the same term in the United Kingdom describes an extensively modified landscape that is protected for its cultural as well as ecological merit.

The World Conservation Union (IUCN) has responded by devising a simplified protected area classification scheme comprising just six basic categories (see table 3.3). The logic of this **IUCN classification system**, which is now widely accepted as the international standard for protected areas, is that the lower the designated number of a site, the lower the amount of environmental modification and human intervention that is acceptable. Thus, category I describes wilderness areas reserved for scientific and research purposes or 'primitive' recreation, while category V describes areas, such as the United Kingdom national parks, where the cultural and natural environment exist in a complementary relationship. Category VI departs somewhat from the logic in that it involves a 'natural' area that is available for the sustainable extraction of resources. The term **national park** is applied to any highly protected, relatively undisturbed (i.e. category II) area, regardless of the official designation given to it by a particular government. For example, Kenya's Masai Mara National Reserve and New South Wales' Lord Howe Island Permanent Park Preserve (Australia) are both classified as 'national parks' under the IUCN system because they meet category II criteria (WCPA 2006). Table 3.4 assists in the interpretation of table 3.3 by depicting for each IUCN designation the level of priority assigned to various management objectives.

■ **Table 3.3** *IUCN (World Conservation Union) protected area categories*

CATEGORY	DESIGNATION, NUMBER AND AREA (2003)	DESCRIPTION
Ia	**Strict Nature Reserve** 4731: 103.4 million ha	Area of land and/or sea possessing some outstanding or representative ecosystems, geological or physiological features and/or species, available primarily for scientific research and/or environmental monitoring
Ib	**Wilderness Area** 1302: 101.6 million ha	Large area of unmodified or slightly modified land and/or sea, retaining its natural character and influence, without permanent or significant habitation, which is protected and managed so as to preserve its natural condition
II	**National Park** 3881: 441.3 million ha	Natural area of land and/or sea, designated to (a) protect the ecological integrity of one or more ecosystems for present and future generations, (b) exclude exploitation or occupation inimical to the purposes of designation of the area and (c) provide a foundation for spiritual, scientific, educational, recreational and visitor opportunities, all of which must be environmentally and culturally compatible

(continued)

CATEGORY	DESIGNATION, NUMBER AND AREA (2003)	DESCRIPTION
III	**Natural Monument** 19 833: 27.5 million ha	Area containing one, or more, specific natural or natural/cultural feature which is of outstanding or unique value because of its inherent rarity, representative or aesthetic qualities or cultural significance
IV	**Habitat/Species Management Area** 27 641: 302.3 million ha	Area of land and/or sea subject to active intervention for management purposes so as to ensure the maintenance of habitats and/or to meet the requirements of specific species
V	**Protected Landscape/ Seascape** 6555: 105.6 million ha	Area of land, with coast and sea as appropriate, where the interaction of people and nature over time has produced an area of distinct character with significant aesthetic, ecological and/or cultural value and often with high biological diversity. Safeguarding the integrity of this traditional interaction is vital to the protection, maintenance and evolution of such an area.
VI	**Managed Resource Protected Area** 4123: 437.7 million ha	Area containing predominantly unmodified natural systems, managed to ensure long-term protection and maintenance of biological diversity, while providing at the same time a sustainable flow of natural products and services to meet community needs

Source: *IUCN 2003.*

■ Table 3.4 *Management objectives by IUCN protected area category*

MANAGEMENT OBJECTIVE	Ia	Ib	II	III	IV	V	VI
Scientific research	1	3	2	2	2	2	3
Wilderness protection	2	1	2	3	3	—	2
Preservation of species and genetic diversity	1	2	1	1	1	2	1
Maintenance of environmental services	2	1	1	—	1	2	1
Protection of specific natural or cultural features	—	—	2	1	3	1	3
Tourism and recreation	—	2	1	1	3	1	3
Education	—	—	2	2	2	2	3
Sustainable use of resources from natural ecosystems	—	3	3	—	2	2	1
Maintenance of cultural or traditional attributes	—	—	—	—	—	1	2

1 Primary objective
2 Secondary objective
3 Potentially applicable objective — not applicable.

Source: *WCPA 2006.*

Since the establishment of this system, the World Conservation Union has examined the regulations that pertain to every public protected area and has assigned each of them to the category that best matches those regulations. As a result, it is now much simpler to assess the basic compatibility of ecotourism with any individual protected area, although in each case specific details are required for management and product development purposes. This is especially important given that designation is based on the official or *de jure* status of an area, rather than the extent to which the regulations are actually enforced (i.e. the *de facto* situation). The paper park syndrome, for example, is not taken into account. With this proviso, the status of ecotourism in each type of designation will now be investigated.

Category I

Category Ia and Ib areas offer the highest possible level of environmental protection within the IUCN system. Strict prohibitions on human activity and concomitant restrictions on the establishment of services or infrastructure mean that such areas are not suitable for soft ecotourism or most other forms of tourism. Allowance is made in Strict Nature Reserves (category Ia) only for hard ecotourism that involves scientific research or related activities. Groups generally allowed access include volunteer-based non-profit organisations (see section 2.4.1) and university and government researchers. Wilderness Areas (category Ib), as a secondary management objective, allow access to very small numbers of hard ecotourists and adventure tourists who engage in activities that do not rely on permanent *in situ* facilities, such as bushwalking, wildlife observation and primitive camping.

Categories II and III

From an ecotourism perspective, categories II and III are by far the most important protected area designations because they accommodate both environmental preservation and compatible forms of recreation as primary management objectives. This recreational component, which can include soft and hard manifestations of ecotourism, is becoming more important as protected area managers grow increasingly dependent on visitor-based revenues (see section 3.5). Internal zoning is usually the mechanism through which diverse activities, such as interpretation centres (soft ecotourism) and wilderness bushwalking (hard ecotourism), are accommodated (see section 4.5.2). At the same time, many other types of tourism are permissible as long as they do not conflict with the primary goal of environmental preservation. The structural difference between categories II and III is normally one of degree. Category II protects the broader integrity of one or more ecosystems, and category III (natural monuments) protects specific features of merit.

Visitor patterns in national parks

Category II protected areas, or 'national parks', are the workhorse of the ecotourism sector, as a whole accommodating very large visitor numbers. The US National Park Service, for example, recorded more than 65 million recreational visits to the nature-based portion of its national park system (which conforms to IUCN category II) in 2005 (NPS 2006c). The adjacent Canadian national park system (excluding historical parks) received more than 11 million person-visits during 2004–05 (Parks Canada 2006). In Australia, the national parks of Victoria alone accommodated an estimated 28.6 million visits in 2004–05 (Parks Victoria 2006), which is explained by the proximity of high-profile and accessible national parks to major urban concentrations. A similar pattern is found in New South Wales and Queensland.

National park visitors, however, are not all ecotourists, although they are often all regarded as such. Figure 3.1 proposes that ecotourists account for a majority of visitors to the global system of category II national parks, although the proportions will vary between individual parks. In terms of overall person-visits, soft ecotourists comprise the overwhelming majority of the ecotourist component — engaging in casual nature observation and learning often as just being one aspect of their park visit — while hard ecotourists constitute a fringe element. However, if recalibrated in terms of *visitor-days*, then hard ecotourists become a much higher proportion of the total due to their tendency for longer stays. Other tourists, such as those in the adventure, cultural and 3S categories, constitute a minority, although the quantification of this component is impeded by the indistinct boundaries that often exist between these groups and ecotourists (see chapter 1). The final group is of comparable size and consists of local residents who are excluded from the ecotourism category because they do not meet the applicable travel distance thresholds that define the domestic tourist. Nevertheless, many visitors in this category are indistinguishable from ecotourists in their motivation and behaviour.

■ **Figure 3.1**
Types and approximate proportions of visitors to categories II and III protected areas
Source:
adapted from Lawton 2001.

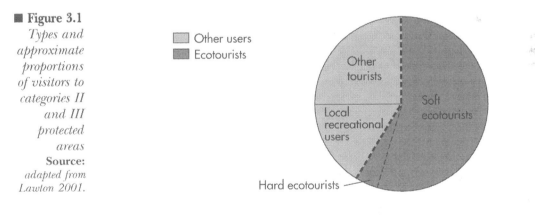

☐ Other users
■ Ecotourists

Other tourists

Local recreational users

Soft ecotourists

Hard ecotourists

Categories IV, V and VI

The lower IUCN categories involve landscapes and seascapes that have been extensively altered by human activities, are actively managed to achieve stipulated conservation objectives and/or are used for the sustainable extraction of renewable resources. Their potential for hard ecotourism is therefore limited. Yet, although not having the same high profile as national parks, they have a very high potential for soft ecotourism for the following reasons:

- Modified landscapes often provide a good array of services for visitors.
- Many of these areas are managed specifically to accommodate a large number and diversity of visitors, although the potential presence of hunters and motorised recreational vehicle users may deter many ecotourists.
- Being protected areas, in theory they are safeguarded in the long term from alterations and activities that are incompatible with their designation and dissuasive to ecotourism.
- At the same time, their modified state means that they are not as sensitive to the negative impact of ecotourism as relatively undisturbed natural habitat.
- The strong cultural presence may be attractive to ecotourists seeking diverse stimulation and interpretation of settings where the natural and cultural environments interact in a variety of ways.
- These three categories cumulatively occupy a large amount of territory, accounting as of 2003 for about 60 per cent of the global system of protected areas (see table 3.3).
- Modified spaces can accommodate a diverse array of wild flora and fauna and therefore provide high-quality ecotourism experiences (see section 3.5).

The 10 national parks of England and Wales, which host about 40 million visitors annually, are an important example of a lower-order protected area system providing soft ecotourism opportunities (Parker & Ravenscroft 2000). In many destinations, lower-order protected areas serve as protective transitional spaces or **buffer zones** between higher-order protected areas and unprotected areas. Examples include Forest Reserves (category IV) adjacent to national parks in Australia and National Forests (category VI) adjacent to national parks in the USA.

■ 3.2.3 **Marine** *protected areas*

A global system of **marine protected areas (MPAs)** is gradually being established, although its development has been much slower than its terrestrial counterpart. There were about 3500 MPAs as of 2004, occupying only a minuscule portion of the world's marine space (Earthtrends 2006). Their suitability for ecotourism is influenced by a number of factors. First, the marine environment both supports and transports life, rendering it particularly difficult to 'fence off' a given portion for preservation and management purposes. At the same time, this unstable environment is extremely vulnerable to disruptive external forces such as oil spills, land-based agricultural and mining run-off and sedimentation, cruise ship activity, military exercises and over-fishing (see chapter 6). Geopolitics associated with the Law of the Sea (a United Nations convention that establishes rules governing all uses of oceans and their resources) are also potentially problematic, especially in regard to the issue of establishing international MPAs in the high seas where most of the world's saltwater space is found (see 'In the Field: Establishing a whale sanctuary in the South Pacific'). Moreover, countries with coastlines have full jurisdiction over only their territorial waters (which extend 12 miles from shore), but not over their exclusive economic zones (which extend for an additional 188 miles). In scientific terms, relatively little is known about the ecology and carrying capacity of marine environments, and management is further complicated by the 'invisibility' factor of activities that cannot be easily monitored from above the surface (e.g. diving and observational submarines).

The primary reason for the establishment of MPAs is to protect local marine resources and to maintain marine biodiversity. However, the need to both promote and control tourism is widely recognised as an important secondary consideration, given the rapid growth in boating, scuba diving, snorkelling, submarine-based observation and whale-watching (see section 8.2) and the opportunities and threats that these can cumulatively generate. The relationship between MPAs and tourism is especially relevant to Australia, which exercises primary control over a marine area of 11 000 000 km^2 (compared with 7 700 000 km^2 of land area) and contains about a third of the world's MPAs. These areas protect about five per cent of Australia's marine space, although most of this, as well as a disproportionate share of the country's marine-based tourism industry, is accounted for by just one entity, the Great Barrier Reef Marine Park.

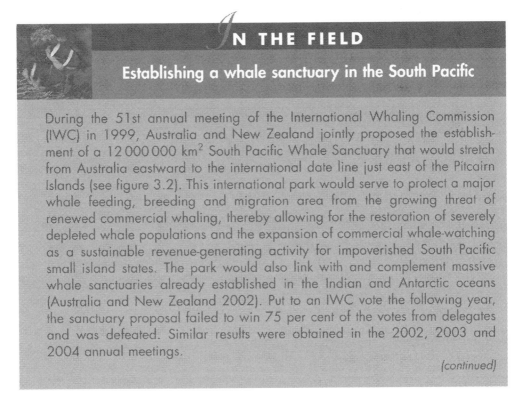

IN THE FIELD

Establishing a whale sanctuary in the South Pacific

During the 51st annual meeting of the International Whaling Commission (IWC) in 1999, Australia and New Zealand jointly proposed the establishment of a 12 000 000 km^2 South Pacific Whale Sanctuary that would stretch from Australia eastward to the international date line just east of the Pitcairn Islands (see figure 3.2). This international park would serve to protect a major whale feeding, breeding and migration area from the growing threat of renewed commercial whaling, thereby allowing for the restoration of severely depleted whale populations and the expansion of commercial whale-watching as a sustainable revenue-generating activity for impoverished South Pacific small island states. The park would also link with and complement massive whale sanctuaries already established in the Indian and Antarctic oceans (Australia and New Zealand 2002). Put to an IWC vote the following year, the sanctuary proposal failed to win 75 per cent of the votes from delegates and was defeated. Similar results were obtained in the 2002, 2003 and 2004 annual meetings.

(continued)

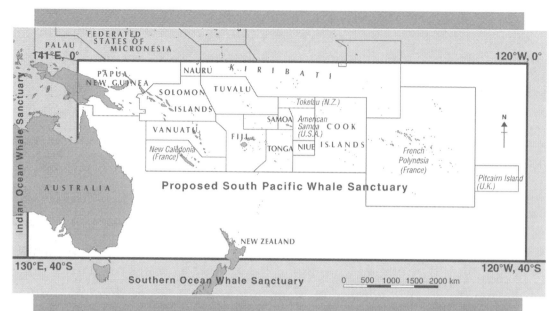

Figure 3.2

Spatial dimensions of proposed South Pacific Whale Sanctuary

Supporters attribute the consecutive defeats to small member states in the Caribbean and elsewhere that voted with the government of Japan in exchange for favourable foreign aid concessions from the latter, which argues that some whale species have recovered sufficiently to justify the restoration of commercial whaling in the region. Currently, Japan and a few other countries (notably Norway and Iceland) are allowed a limited harvest of whales under international law for purposes of 'scientific research'. Ominously, attempts to establish the South Pacific Whale Sanctuary have been accompanied by Japan's attempts to abolish the Southern Ocean Whale Sanctuary, which was established in 1994 to protect Antarctic whale habitat. Such efforts, however, have also failed to achieve 75 per cent approval, thereby creating a stalemate between the anti- and pro-whaling factions of the IWC. To break this stalemate, Australia and New Zealand joined most South Pacific countries in 2003 to announce that their collective Exclusive Economic Zones (EEZ) would henceforth be off-limits to commercial whaling, thereby effectively circumventing the IWC and creating in all but name the regional whale sanctuary that is desired by most countries in the region. Critics, however, point out that the effectiveness of such entities is reduced by their failure to prohibit other anthropogenic threats to whales, such as seismic surveying, exploration drilling, commercial shipping and extraction of minerals, as well as unrestricted whale-watching (TerraNature 2005).

Non-government involvement in protected areas can occur in several ways. One controversial aspect is the leasing or privatisation of various services in public protected areas. Food and rental services as well as management and policing are functions that are sometimes conceded to the private sector. Another possibility is the retention of private property rights in publicly protected areas, as is the practice in the national parks of England and Wales (Parker & Ravenscroft 2000). A more fundamental mode of private sector involvement is the non-government ownership of protected areas. Numerous stakeholders are potentially included under this umbrella, including small property holders, corporations, non-governmental organisations (for example, the Nature Conservancy and Ducks Unlimited), community associations and indigenous groups.

Given the complexity of stakeholder and ownership options involved in protected areas, it is sometimes not possible to designate a protected area as a clearly 'public' or 'private' entity, particularly when they involve indigenous or local community participation. Rather, it is more useful to think of protected areas as being situated on a spectrum that ranges from purely 'public' to entirely 'private'. One increasingly common way of compromising between the desire to establish a public protected area and the desire to maintain private property rights is to negotiate a **purchase of development rights (PDR) agreement** (often called 'conservation easements' in the USA) in which a landowner is paid in return for agreeing to permanently restrict the types of activity that are allowed on their property (Wright & Skaggs 2002). Essentially, this fee represents the difference between the market value of the land (typically determined by what is permitted under existing zoning bylaws) and its value as a property with permanent restrictions in place. For example, a property that has a market value of $1 million as a housing subdivision but $200 000 as an undeveloped wetland would merit a one-time payment of $800 000 to the landowner, who would retain ownership but have no legal right to develop the wetland, which becomes in effect a private protected area. The funds to effect such an agreement may be raised through special taxes levied by a municipality for that purpose, or from non-governmental organisations such as the Nature Conservancy whose goal is to protect natural habitat without necessarily having to expend funds on acquiring land or subsequently on managing and maintaining that land. Landowners typically enter into such agreements because of their desire to both own and protect their land, and for these individuals ecotourism may offer a complementary means of earning revenue from their property without violating the terms of the PDR agreement. Areas most likely to be targeted for PDR agreements include buffer zones around higher-order protected areas, remnant natural habitats in rural agricultural areas, and space around rapidly growing cities where there is a desire to slow or halt the process of urban sprawl by establishing a green belt.

■ *3.3.1* **Reasons** *for establishment*

Little is known about the number and extent of private protected areas, due to their diverse ownership, their exclusion from the IUCN classification protocol and, in many cases, their lack of any other formal status. Langholz and Brandon (2001) argue that private protected areas are expanding at a rapid rate nevertheless. One reason given for this growth is the inability of governments to meet both public and conservation needs through their own protected area systems. These systems, among other problems, are too small, inadequately funded and, in some developing countries, hindered by corruption and mismanagement (Langholz et al. 2000; see also the case study at the end of this chapter). Such problems, however, are not exclusive to the less-developed world. High-profile systems such as the US National Park Service have also been subject to severe budget cutbacks since the 1980s (Nelson 2000).

Concurrently, the growth of the private protected area network has been stimulated by growing public interest in environmentalism (see chapter 2) and by the subsequent desire to become directly involved in the preservation of the world's rapidly depleting biodiversity. This is especially apparent in situations where the government role in achieving such objectives is perceived as being inadequate. In some cases, this involvement has been aided and abetted by the government itself for ideological reasons, or simply as an expedient method of relieving pressure on and augmenting the public protected area system. For example, the formation of private reserves as buffer zones to core public protected areas is encouraged by the Costa Rican government (Weaver 1998). In becoming involved with such initiatives, the non-government sector has the advantage of not being bound by government restrictions on entry fees, management strategies, or the allocation of revenue, although they may be subject to other legislation and regulations pertaining to the natural environment.

The opportunity to generate profits and/or to provide economic diversification and local control for destination communities is an important if not dominant incentive for the establishment of private protected areas in some areas. For example, half the respondents in a survey of 68 Costa Rican owners of private protected areas listed profit or financial gain as a primary reason for their involvement (Langholz et al. 2000). However, three-quarters of respondents also cited the importance of leaving an environmental inheritance to their children, which suggests that the biocentric motivation cited earlier may be at least as important as financial considerations. In many instances, economic benefits from private protected areas are derived from activities other than tourism, such as the identification and collection of flora with pharmaceutical potential and the harvesting of wild foodstuffs. On the tourism side, there is considerable regional interest in such activities as big game hunting, which is the emphasis of Zimbabwe's **CAMPFIRE** program and similar initiatives in other parts of sub-Saharan Africa (see section 7.2.2). However, considerably more attention is being focused on the economic potential of ecotourism, which is now well established in many private protected areas.

■ *3.3.2* Ecotourism *in private protected areas*

Ecotourism is a significant activity in an increasing number of private protected areas. For example, a survey of 32 private reserves in Latin America and sub-Saharan Africa (Langholz 1996) found that on average, two-thirds of all reserve operating income was obtained from tourism, compared with 40 per cent in 1989. The level of reliance, however, was unequally distributed, nearly half indicating a dependency rate of 90 per cent or higher. Only one reserve responded that tourism was not important as a source of income. Because of tourism, the fiscal viability of the sampled reserves had improved, but they were becoming increasingly dependent on this form of funding, which could result in management practices oriented more towards visitor satisfaction and visitation increase than environmental preservation. The popularity of private protected areas in general has been increased by the experience of several high-profile sites. Arguably, the best-known example is Costa Rica's Monteverde Cloud Forest Reserve. Visitation to this site, which is leased by the local Monteverde community to the Tropical Science Centre (a Costa Rica-based environmental NGO) increased from 471 in 1974 to approximately 50 000 per year during the late 1990s (Honey 1999). Annual revenues by 1994 were estimated to be greater than the receipts obtained from the entire Costa Rican national park system. A portion of these funds, along with donations and other revenue, has been used to expand and manage the reserve.

Costa Rica is something of a stronghold for private protected areas, also hosting other well-known sites such as Rara Avis (which focuses on scientific visits), La Selva Biological Station and the Santa Elena Cloud Forest Reserve (Honey 1999). Belize is also acquiring a similar reputation thanks to such initiatives as the Community Baboon Sanctuary, which is often touted as a model of cooperation between community and industry (Horwich & Lyon 1999). Although important as ecotourism sites in their own right, these high-profile examples also contribute to the diffusion of the ecotourism concept through the publicity they receive and by serving as prototypes for the successful implementation of private protected areas elsewhere in Central America.

■ *3.3.3* Problems

The status of private protected areas as a venue for ecotourism is increasing, and this is drawing attention to a number of potential problems aside from tourism dependency. One of these is instability, since tenure arrangements, ownership and land use objectives (except perhaps in the case of PDR agreements) can all be changed impulsively at the discretion of private owners. Such decisions may be precipitated, for example, by a decline in tourism revenue or by more lucrative offers from developers. Where economic benefits are the primary motivator for their establishment, the profit motive can easily take priority over conservation objectives, leading to unsustainable increases in visitation levels or the introduction of incompatible services and facilities. There is also a possibility that private sites will enter into a competitive relationship with the public system. This could potentially dissuade governments from injecting much-needed funds into the public system if private operations are better able to meet desired recreational and conservation objectives.

3.4 DISTRIBUTION OF ECOTOURISM IN PROTECTED AREAS

Ecotourism is commonly associated with the stereotype of a small group of hikers interfacing with nature deep in a pristine natural area. However, this image is misleading and holds true only if the definition is restricted to hard ecotourism. Soft ecotourism, in contrast, is characterised by spatial and (to a lesser extent) temporal concentration, both among and in protected areas. These tendencies have positive as well as negative implications for managing the impact of ecotourism (see chapters 4 and 5).

■ 3.4.1 Distribution *among protected areas*

In most countries, a small proportion of parks accounts for most protected area visitation. This is especially true for soft ecotourists since their visitation is effectively confined to the minority of parks that are both accessible and provide a high level of services and facilities. In contrast, hard ecotourists are more evenly distributed among the entities in a park system since they are not similarly dependent on these services and facilities and actually seek more remote locales. Data from the Canadian system of 38 national parks illustrates this skewed pattern of distribution, with the four most visited accounting for more than half of all person-visits in 2004–05 (see table 3.5). The top two entities (Banff and Jasper) and six of the top 10 are concentrated in the southern Rocky Mountains, which is Canada's major non-urban destination for leisure-oriented inbound visitors. The US pattern is similar, with the top 10 National Parks (of 57 in total) accounting for 56 per cent of all visitors (NPS 2006c). Seven of these top 10 parks are located in the western states but are not as concentrated as their Canadian western counterparts. Visitation in Costa Rica and Kenya, two popular ecotourism destinations in the less-developed world, are also skewed, with the most visited parks being located either close to the major urban gateways or coastal mass tourism resorts that provide most of their soft tourism clientele (Weaver 1998) (see section 5.2.2).

■ 3.4.2 Distribution *in protected areas*

An even higher level of spatial concentration characterises the distribution of ecotourism in individual parks, the more visited units generally having higher levels of concentration. Such parks adhere to variations of the '95–5' rule, wherein the vast majority (e.g. 95 per cent) of all visits tend to be confined to only a very small proportion (e.g. 5 per cent) of the protected area.

■ Table 3.5 *2004–05 person-visits to Canadian national parks*

NATIONAL PARK	PERSON-VISITS 2004–05	PERCENTAGE OF TOTAL	CUMULATIVE PERCENTAGE
Banff	3 139 934	27.0	27.0
Jasper	1 180 153	10.1	37.1
Prince Edward Island	887 471	7.6	44.7
Pacific Rim	794 608	6.8	51.5
Mount Revelstoke–Glacier	591 280	5.1	56.6
Yoho	576 413	5.0	61.6
Saguenay–St Lawrence	438 117	3.8	65.4
Kootenay	420 721	3.6	69.0
Waterton Lakes	366 431	3.1	72.1
Fathom Five	360 858	3.1	75.2
Cape Breton Highlands	327 082	2.8	78.0
Fundy	290 754	2.5	80.5
Point Pelee	272 006	2.3	82.8
Terra Nova	259 079	2.2	85.0
Riding Mountain	245 565	2.1	87.1
Kouchibouguac	227 105	1.9	89.0
Prince Albert	221 006	1.9	90.9
La Mauricie	184 083	1.6	92.5
Elk Island	171 447	1.5	94.0
Bruce Peninsula	167 391	1.5	95.5
Forillon	149 610	1.3	96.8
Gros Morne	118 071	1.1	97.9
St Lawrence Islands	50 453	0.4	98.3
Kejimkujik	49 551	0.4	98.7
Kluane	45 491	0.4	99.1
Georgian Bay Islands	41 886	0.4	99.5
Mingan Archipelago	32 535	0.3	99.8
Pukaskwa	7 250	–	99.8
Grasslands	5 905	–	99.8
Gwaii Haanas	2 056	–	99.9
Wood Buffalo	1 226	–	99.9
Wapusk	1 135	–	99.9
Nahanni	885	–	99.9
Sirmilik	608	–	99.9
Auyuittuq	200	–	99.9
Ivvavik	187	–	99.9
Quttinirpaaq	149	–	99.9
Aulavik	48	–	100.00
Total	11 628 750		

Source: *Parks Canada 2006.*

These concentrations occur in three types of area:

1. heavily developed sites, or **sacrificial space**, where large numbers of soft ecotourists congregate to access a concentration of services, facilities and attractions
2. the immediate hinterland of these sites, where short-distance walking trails, canopy boardwalks, scenic outlooks and other facilities are made available
3. transportation corridors and other access roads.

In contrast, hard ecotourists, along with pure adventure tourists, are the '5 per cent' who venture into the non-serviced '95 per cent' of the park.

This pattern is so common among the world's high-profile category II destinations that it may be considered universal. Almost all tourism activity in Canada's Banff National Park, for example, occurs in the narrow Bow Valley Corridor between the Banff town site and Lake Louise, an area that accounts for only 3–4 per cent of the total park area (Dearden 2000). About 90 per cent of visitation in Grand Canyon National Park in Arizona (USA) occurs at and near the South Rim visitors' centre. According to Honey (1999), the managers of Monteverde Cloud Forest Reserve in Costa Rica limit most tourist activity to a network of trail corridors that occupy about 2 per cent of the park. The vast majority of visitors to Lamington National Park in the Gold Coast hinterland (Australia) concentrate at the trail heads adjacent to the Binna Burra and O'Reilly's ecolodges. In Australia the trend is not restricted to land-based entities. It is estimated that 95 per cent of all tourism activity in the Great Barrier Reef Marine Park occurs offshore from Cairns and the Whitsundays in an area that comprises no more than 1–2 per cent of the entire protected area (GBRMPA 2000).

In many instances, spatial concentration is reinforced by seasonal concentration. Few visitors go to higher latitude parks during the winter season (except where winter sporting opportunities are available) or to subtropical parks during the rainy season. In Yellowstone National Park (USA), almost 70 per cent of all visitations occur during the summer months of June, July and August (NPS 2006c). Only about 10 per cent of visitation to Kakadu National Park (Australia) occurs between November and March (Breiter 1996). During 'high season', higher tourist concentrations are often experienced on public holidays and weekends, during which almost all outdoor activity is confined to daylight hours. In Monteverde Cloud Forest Reserve in Costa Rica, visitors tend to begin their day at about the same time of 8 a.m., thereby contributing to problems of congestion in areas of spatial concentration (Honey 1999).

3.5 MODIFIED SPACES

Virtually all ecotourism case studies in the literature focus on relatively undisturbed environments and especially those in higher-order protected areas such as national parks. Yet, because ecotourism attractions can be based on the natural environment 'or some element thereof' (section 1.4.2), opportunities are created to provide ecotourism experiences in extensively modified venues that provide habitats for specific kinds of adaptable flora and fauna. Moreover, modified spaces enrich the learning experience because they reflect a more complex array of interactions between humans and the natural environment. Other reasons for considering them as potential ecotourism settings include the fact that they occupy a very large and expanding portion of the world's land area and, therefore, in theory offer an enormous capacity to accommodate the growing demand for ecotourism. At the same time, they divert pressure away from vulnerable natural environments (Lawton & Weaver 2001). Because they have already been significantly altered from their natural state by human activity, these spaces in addition are often resilient to high levels of tourism-related activity. The question of ecological carrying capacity, therefore, is not as contentious an issue (although it may be replaced by heightened sociocultural concerns). This is not to suggest that the preservation of remaining natural habitat is any less of an imperative, or that ecotourism is somehow compatible with the removal and replacement of such environments. To the contrary, Lawton and Weaver (2001) argue that ecotourism provides an incentive for enhancing the capacity of modified spaces to accommodate wildlife and associated native habitat through strategies that partially or fully rehabilitate those spaces.

It is difficult to estimate the amount of ecotourism that is currently supported by extensively modified attraction spaces, because they have rarely been studied as ecotourism settings and consist mostly of unprotected private or communal lands that are not monitored to determine the amount and type of visitation they receive. Furthermore, because there are few mechanisms in place to increase the probability that visitation is both sustainable and learning-oriented, it is difficult to determine whether on-site activities meet these ecotourism criteria. The following discussion therefore focuses more on the potential of various modified environments, including agricultural areas, cities, artificial wetlands, artificial reefs and degraded spaces to provide ecotourism opportunities.

■ 3.5.1 Agricultural *land*

Food-producing lands occupy about half of the world's land surface (World Resources Institute 2005) and include an array of extensively as well as moderately modified environments, each of which has its own implications for ecotourism. Approximately 10 per cent of the world's land area is occupied by field crops, orchards, plantations, market gardens, paddies, vineyards and the like (i.e. field and tree crops). Such land uses represent an extreme form of environmental modification, but they are still capable of supporting significant wildlife populations under certain conditions. These include proximity to remnant or extensive natural spaces, the presence of hedgerows and other planted wooded areas, crop diversity, the absence or minimal use of toxic pesticides and herbicides, and the implementation of pro-wildlife management strategies by owners. A good example of farmland–ecotourism compatibility occurs in long-established cacao and nutmeg plantations, which often appear undifferentiated from a natural forest because of the high canopy trees that are maintained to provide shade for the sensitive tree crops. As a result, the success of well-known Caribbean ecotourism locations such as the Asa Wright Nature Centre in Trinidad can be attributed more to the presence of wildlife-friendly working plantations than to the presence of natural forests. Examples of opportunistic exploitation by wildlife in other farmland settings include stubble feeding by ungulates and migratory waterfowl in North America. In the latter case, grazing flocks of 50 000 or more snow geese or other waterfowl are one of the major ecotourism attractions of the Canadian prairie region. To be exploited as an ecotourism opportunity, however, the cooperation of relevant land-owning farmers and other wildlife stakeholders, including recreational hunters, is a critical factor (see section 7.3.1). Indeed, the utilisation of any unprotected and highly modified space for ecotourism implies that ecotourism operations need to interact and cooperate with a variety of external environments (see chapter 7).

Wildlife is also attracted to grazing lands, which may closely resemble natural habitat in grassland and savanna settings that have not been seriously affected by desertification. In the early 1990s, at any given time, an estimated 65–80 per cent of Kenya's wild animals were located beyond Kenya's protected areas (JICA 1994), occupying land used mainly for commercial or subsistence grazing. Such situations raise even more issues about the possibilities for the coexistence of agriculture and ecotourism. An interesting connection between modified spaces and lower-order protected areas exists where public or private grasslands are managed to preserve aspects of their biodiversity as well as to provide grazing opportunities for local farmers and ranchers. In many parts of the North American prairie region, it is not uncommon to see native ungulates such as antelope and mule deer grazing in the company of cattle or other domesticated livestock.

Finally, areas used for shifting cultivation have a great deal of ecotourism potential. When practised in a sustainable way, shifting cultivation involves the cyclic clearance of secondary forest in order to plant a variety of subsistence crops over a period of several years. When the fertility of the soil begins to decline, this land is abandoned and allowed to revert to forest, which is cleared again when soil fertility is restored 30 or 40 years after its initial clearance. Landscapes dominated by shifting cultivation tend to display remarkable biodiversity and multiple ecological niches, from mature secondary forest to land that is newly cleared (often through burning), thereby providing excellent habitat for a wide array of wildlife. Furthermore, these lands contain dense networks of footpaths that could readily be used by ecotourists.

■ 3.5.2 Urban *space*

Urban areas do not initially appear to offer any opportunities for ecotourism. Yet the relationship is not as improbable as it seems. On the supply side, many cities, and particularly those in the more-developed but less densely populated countries (e.g. USA, Australia, Canada), are dominated by green space. The more extensive urban green spaces, such as municipal parks, cemeteries and golf courses, offer excellent and diverse wildlife habitat, especially if such measures as green space corridors are implemented to encourage the presence of wild flora and fauna (Weaver 2005b). Urban areas also often contain remnant natural spaces that harbour wildlife, as illustrated by Doctors Gully in Darwin, Northern Territory (Australia) and by large protected areas that are now surrounded by urban development in major cities such as Sydney and Melbourne. Another facilitating factor in some areas is the 'oasis effect', wherein the mature, diverse and well-watered greenery of a city attracts wildlife from a surrounding intensively cultivated rural area lacking these same advantages. The extreme example of wildlife 'synurbisation' (or the adjustment of wildlife to urban environments), however, is the successful introduction of peregrine falcons to inner-city high rises in some North American and European cities (Luniak 2004).

On the demand side, urban areas already attract large international and domestic tourist populations for whom non-captive urban wildlife is readily accessible and potentially an interesting distraction from conventional urban attractions. Yet there are few high-profile non-captive wildlife attractions in urban areas, and rarely are these marketed under the banner of ecotourism. One example of such a product is the Congress Street Bridge in Austin, Texas, which harbours a seasonal colony of 1.5 million Mexican free-tailed bats. Each year this site attracts around 100 000 visitors, who congregate in the evenings to watch the bats leave the bridge to feed (Bat Conservation International 2006).

■ 3.5.3 Artificial *wetlands*

Whether urban or rural, artificial wetlands often attract an enormous variety of wildlife and may eventually resemble a natural, undisturbed habitat in their complexity. An urban example is the Hornsby Bend settling lagoon in Austin, Texas (USA), where 118 bird species have been recorded (Bonta 1997). An Australian counterpart is the Wetlands Centre near Newcastle, which is a former rubbish tip and rugby oval that has been restored to a natural wetland, attracting 25 000 recreational visitors in 2005 (Hunter Wetlands Centre 2006). Rural-based examples in Australia include the Serendip Sanctuary in Victoria and Fogg Dam in the Northern Territory, where a reservoir created to establish a rice-growing project in the 1950s (which was aborted) now hosts an extensive array of native flora and fauna. Visitors apparently do not differentiate Fogg Dam from truly 'natural' sites, 94 per cent of sampled visitors declaring that their experience at this site constituted 'ecotourism' due to the proliferation and variety of wildlife they encountered (Ryan, Hughes & Chirgwin 2000). This finding provides encouragement to those seeking to foster ecotourism in altered environments.

■ 3.5.4 Artificial *reefs*

Lawton and Weaver (2001) classify **artificial reefs** as either unintentional or intentional. Unintentional artificial reefs consist of shipwrecks as well as other solid materials that are lost or discarded through accident, natural disaster or dumping. Accordingly, reefs that develop at such sites are randomly distributed, and the colonisation process is usually preceded or accompanied by damage to the marine environment by spent fuel and other contaminants. In contrast, intentional artificial reefs are usually established in a methodical manner with respect to positioning and contaminant removal. This type of artificial reef was originally conceived as a way of improving habitat for commercial fish populations, but has more recently become popular for the ecotourism opportunities that they provide.

One of the most active programs occurs off the Israeli port city of Eilat, on the Gulf of Aqaba, where surplus aircraft and dead coral heads are being submerged to deflect diving pressure from nearby natural reefs. The Atlantis Waikiki artificial reef off Honolulu is especially interesting as a large-scale, soft ecotourism venture. The 1.85-hectare site, which consists of a sunken oiler, concrete terrace reefs and surplus aircraft, is used for Atlantis submarine tours, which have attracted more than 10 million passengers since the mid-1980s (Atlantis Adventure 2006). Also of interest is the patented Reef Ball, a squat concrete dome covered with holes and ranging in size from a basketball to a car, which is very quickly colonised by marine life. The Reef Ball Foundation as of 2006 was involved in 3000 projects in 70 countries (Reef Ball Foundation 2006).

■ 3.5.5 Wasteland

Even the most modified or degraded sites apparently have ecotourism potential, as illustrated by the Hornsby Bend sewage lagoon (see section 3.5.3). Another example related to waste disposal is Toronto's Leslie Street Spit in Canada, which extends into Lake Ontario and consists of detritus from urban construction projects that has been dumped over many decades. Now the subject of rehabilitation, the area is very important as a stopover for migratory waterfowl (at least 290 species of birds have been observed) and is a living laboratory for the study of plant succession. Current management plans for the site include organised bus tours, the establishment of observation blinds and the production of educational brochures (Leslie Street Spit 2001).

Sites devastated by war, mining, deforestation, storage of contaminated materials, overgrazing or other human factors also deserve consideration (see 'Practitioner's perspective: Chernobyl as ecotourism paradise?' opposite). One factor is the ability of devastated sites to provide habitat for wildlife, as demonstrated by some abandoned quarries and mine tailing areas, especially given that these areas are often considered worthless for any other purpose. Ecotourism is being proposed as a viable use for large Department of Energy waste sites in the USA that have been placed on the National Priorities List for clean-up, such as the Savannah River Site in

South Carolina. This 803 km² area includes extensive natural buffer zones and disposal sites that have remained undisturbed since World War II but, because of low-level contamination, are deemed unsuitable for agriculture or urbanisation. Similarly, the Idaho National Engineering and Environmental Laboratory waste site contains some of the only remaining shrub-steppe habitat in the USA (Burger 2000).

A second consideration concerns situations where landscape restoration is actively practised. While the desired end result may be the creation of an ecotourism-sustaining landscape, the process of rehabilitation itself can be developed as a learning-based ecotourism experience. **Restoration ecotourism**, as with the Leslie Street Spit in Canada, appears to be one of the objectives of Costa Rica's Guanacaste National Park, which consists of highly degraded deciduous forest and former ranch lands that are gradually being returned to their natural state. One of the most bizarre examples of devastated space utilisation for ecotourism is Sarigua National Park in Panama, an 8000-hectare, high-order protected area. Ecotourists are attracted to this park's desert-like landscape and its unusual plants and animals, which occur nowhere else in the country. Yet, far from being a rare ecological anomaly, Sarigua is no more than an extreme case of desertification that resulted from overgrazing and deforestation (Navarro 1998). Such examples, and all the other instances of ecotourism occurring in modified spaces, serve to challenge conventional thinking as to what constitutes an appropriate ecotourism venue.

PRACTITIONER'S PERSPECTIVE

Chernobyl as ecotourism paradise?

The Ukrainian town of Chernobyl is indelibly etched into the public consciousness as the site of the world's worst nuclear disaster, having produced among other consequences the legacy of a strict exclusion zone of 2826 km² in which human activity continues to be severely curtailed more than two decades after the infamous meltdown. One consequence that was wholly unanticipated, however, is Chernobyl's status as an emerging wildlife haven. The absence of a significant human presence over such a large area for such a long period has resulted in the creation of a quasi-wilderness forest and grassland environment that contains plants and animals of exceptional rarity. These include Przewalski horses, black storks and white-tailed eagles, which are repopulating the zone along with wolves and wild boar. More than 270 bird species have been recorded, including 31 listed as internationally endangered and 180 that are nesting in the area (Stewart 2006).

(continued)

The unusual Chernobyl habitat has begun to attract media attention and interest from hard ecotourists, forcing authorities to consider whether to accommodate this unexpected demand and to what extent. 'Safaris' already offered by a handful of specialised tour operators require participants to don nuclear protection suits, stay only for a severely restricted period and avoid 'hotspots' where radiation readings are especially dangerous. Still, there is no precedent that would allow the zone's managers to stipulate temporal or spatial thresholds that minimise risks to visiting ecotourists. There is also the risk that further opening to tourism would help to create a false sense of normalcy, when in fact the zone's plant and animal life remains highly contaminated. Yet even the United Nations has supported the establishment of an ecotourism industry at Chernobyl, despite the reservations of many displaced local residents who regard it as an inappropriate form of exploitation, and other Ukrainians who are uncomfortable with the thought of this site potentially becoming the country's iconic ecotourist attraction (Wall 2004). A related question is whether the exclusion zone should be designated as a protected area and whether it would be appropriate to have it operated and managed under international auspices, given the dubious 'heritage' that it has bequeathed to all humanity.

3.6 SUMMARY

Public protected areas, both land- and marine-based, and those designated as category II and III in particular, are the most important ecotourism venues by far, given that they not only preserve outstanding natural environments but also allow for the provision of compatible recreational activities such as ecotourism. Such entities, along with their lower-order counterparts, have proliferated during the past hundred years and are now being augmented by a growing number of marine protected areas and private protected areas. The growing popularity of private entities is based on their profit-generating potential, the broadening of interest in environmental issues, their relative freedom from legislative and other constraints, and the perception that the public systems are increasingly incapable of fulfilling their preservation and recreation mandates. In most protected area systems, soft ecotourist visitation is concentrated in a small number of high-profile, heavily serviced and accessible parks. These parks in turn are individually characterised by marked spatial and temporal concentrations of visitation, which have both positive and negative management implications. Using extensively modified spaces for ecotourism is one way of relieving pressure on high-profile protected areas, although this is seldom considered in the literature or by practitioners. Agricultural land, urban areas, artificial wetlands, artificial reefs and wasteland all have potential to accommodate ecotourism, including restoration ecotourism, in a way that could greatly expand the spatial scope of the sector.

QUESTIONS

1 (a) What is the rationale for the development of the IUCN protected area classification system?
   (b) How can this system assist managers of ecotourism-related products in both the public and private sector?

2 (a) Why are category II protected areas in particular dominant as ecotourism venues?
   (b) What factors will determine whether this dominance intensifies or weakens in the future?

3 (a) Can all visitors who use protected areas for recreational purposes be classified as ecotourists?
   (b) Is it desirable or ethical for protected area managers to ensure that ecotourists account for a majority of their visitors?

4 (a) To what extent are the more modified protected areas of categories IV, V and VI compatible with both hard and soft ecotourism?
   (b) What are the positive and negative implications for hard and soft ecotourism of its taking place in these lower-order protected areas?

5 Why is such a small portion of the sea designated as marine protected areas?

6 (a) What factors account for the growth of private protected areas?
   (b) Why can lands subject to purchase of development rights agreements be considered private protected areas?

7 (a) How is ecotourism distributed in protected area systems and in individual protected areas?
   (b) What factors account for these patterns?
   (c) What are the management implications of these patterns?

8 (a) What arguments can be made for the use of extensively modified environments as ecotourism venues?
   (b) What are the potential drawbacks and opportunities of utilising modified areas in this way?
   (c) Is restoration ecotourism an idea that is likely appeal to a significant portion of the ecotourist market?

Butler, RW & Boyd, SW (eds) 2000, *Tourism and National Parks: Issues and Implications*, **John Wiley & Sons, Chichester, UK.** This 19-chapter edited book covers an array of topics associated with tourism and protected areas, including history, settings, management issues and the future. The chapters allow the reader to compare the relative importance and interrelationships between ecotourism and other types of tourism in protected areas.

Langholz, J & Brandon, K 2001, 'Ecotourism and privately owned protected areas', in DB Weaver (ed.), *Encyclopedia of Ecotourism*, **CABI Publishing, Wallingford, UK, pp. 303–14.** This chapter provides up-to-date information on a relatively unknown aspect of protected areas. Topics include a description of private protected areas and a discussion of relevant issues and problems related to ecotourism.

Lawton, L 2001, 'Ecotourism in public protected areas', in DB Weaver (ed.), *Encyclopedia of Ecotourism*, **CABI, Wallingford, UK, pp. 287–302.** Lawton provides a detailed and critical analysis of the linkages between public protected areas and ecotourism, using examples from throughout the world. The question of compatibility between the two sectors is emphasised.

Lawton, L & Weaver, DB 2001, 'Ecotourism in modified spaces', in DB Weaver (ed.), *Encyclopedia of Ecotourism*, **CABI, Wallingford, UK, pp. 315–26.** This chapter is one of the very few examples of literature that discusses the potential of expanding ecotourism into modified spaces, such as farmland, landfill sites and urban areas.

Weaver, D 2005b, 'Mass and urban ecotourism: New manifestations of an old concept', *Tourism Recreation Research* **30(1): 19–26.** This paper explores the various dimensions of urban ecotourism, which range from remnant natural habitat to downtown high rises. The opportunities for developing urban and mass ecotourism are considered.

The challenge of introducing ecotourism

into China's protected area network

Of any major country, China has displayed the fastest growth of its protected area network, which consists almost entirely of two designations, nature reserves and scenic areas. The first of these was established in 1956, and by 2005 the network consisted of more than 2000 entities covering 11.3 per cent of the country's land (Earthtrends 2006). Ninety-seven per cent of these have been created since 1985 (Wildlife Conservation Society 2004), and China now ranks fourth, behind Brazil, USA and Russia, in terms of land area protected (see table 3.2). Of these protected areas, 145 are at least 100 000 hectares in size. From a supply-side perspective, China therefore appears to have an excellent basis for developing its ecotourism potential. From a demand-side perspective, both inbound and domestic tourism have expanded at an equally impressive rate. From just 303 foreign visitors in 1968, China now hosts in excess of 30 million visitors per year, and the number of domestic tourists has grown from almost nothing in the late 1960s to 878 million in 2002 (Weaver & Lawton 2006).

Both the supply and demand parts of the equation, however, reveal deep-seated problems that hinder the growth of a legitimate and viable ecotourism industry. The nature reserves, for example, account for more than 90 per cent of all protected land, but are all designated as category V under the IUCN classification system, which means that they accommodate a high level of human interaction with the natural environment (see table 3.3). Scenic areas all fall under even less restrictive category VI criteria. It has been estimated that more than 10 million people actually lived in China's protected area system in the early 2000s (IUCN 2006). As of 2005, China had no land falling under categories I, II or III (Earthtrends 2006). Additional problems arise from patterns of distribution and size. The western half of the country possesses a relatively small number of very large nature reserves in remote areas with low biodiversity whereas the more ecologically sensitive eastern half of the country contains a very large number of small protected areas. Because they are small and fragmented and because of their low order designation, they lack the critical mass to adequately protect the habitats they are intended to represent. The eastern protected areas are also embedded in one of the world's most densely populated rural landscapes, so that they are exceptionally vulnerable along their borders to environmentally harmful and unavoidable external influences, such as predation from dogs and cats, pesticide drift and competition from

(continued)

invasive weed species (Wildlife Conservation Society 2004). Exacerbating such problems is the isolation of individual protected areas, which are not connected to other protected areas by corridors that facilitate wildlife movement and other essential ecological processes.

Systemic problems in planning and management further hinder the ability of China's protected areas to function effectively as habitat sanctuaries and hence as viable ecotourism venues. At least eight national government agencies hold direct responsibility for different protected areas, including the State Forestry Administration (which accounts for the majority), the State Environmental Protection Administration, the Ministry of Agriculture, the Ministry of Water Conservation, the Ministry of Construction, the Ministry of Geology and Mineral Resources, the Ministry of Land Resources and the State Oceanic Administration. Not only is there no coordination in the protected area system but also, for many of these federal agencies, environmental protection is a low priority or even a hindrance to their core mandate of resource extraction or physical development. Another problem is that funding for the system is inadequate, and there is no separate account in budgeting systems to support basic management and operational functions. To the extent that funding is available, it is typically allocated to the construction of new infrastructure in a handful of high-profile entities, which have been targeted because of their potential for generating tourism revenues.

There is also no formal career path for ecologically based protected area management, with directors tending to be appointed from the ranks of local civil servants with no background in ecology or planning. Among staff, morale is often low, staffing is inadequate and technical capabilities are below Western standards. As a result, there is lax enforcement of the weak environmental regulations that do exist, and inappropriate activities, such as captive breeding, predator control and the introduction of alien plant and animal species, are often deliberately practised, as in many other developing countries. Even in parks where 'ecotourism' is supposedly featured, there is a tendency to cater to the 'lowest common denominator' of (mainly domestic) visitors by using loudspeakers, wildlife feeding demonstrations, caged animals and fairground-type amusement facilities to generate revenue, most of which accrues to the tour operators who bring groups into the protected areas (Wildlife Conservation Society 2004).

According to Nianyong and Zhuge (2001), part of the problem is that the protected area system has grown so rapidly that even a more committed government would not have been able to confer an appropriate level of management and planning support. However, commitment to the environment at all levels of government has tended to lag far behind its fixation with rapid economic development, so that protected area status is no guarantee that an area will actually be preserved. Evidence of this is provided by Liu et al. (2001), who found that the fragmentation and degradation of natural habitat in Wolong Nature Reserve in Sichuan province accelerated following its declaration in 1975, even as it emerged as a major tourist attraction because of its giant pandas.

As with the park system, tourism growth has occurred at a level far beyond the capacity of the government to manage its consequences in a sustainable manner. However, tourism is regarded as a major engine to fuel further economic growth, and hence growing problems of litter, noise and water and air pollution in China's nature reserves seem to be regarded as an acceptable price to pay for the short-term economic benefits of mass tourism in those areas (Nianyong & Zhuge 2001). Unfortunately, very little of the so-called ecotourism that occurs in China's protected areas therefore actually meets the qualifying criteria, despite such rhetoric as the declaration of 1999 as the national year of ecotourism. Before any serious attempt can be made to implement a legitimate ecotourism sector, it will be necessary first to reform the protected area system so that a basic level of ecological integrity is assured. This must include the enforcement of existing environmental regulations, the creation of category I and II parks, the establishment of buffer zones and corridors, implementation of more reliable and greater funding resources, master planning for individual parks and the recognition of professional standards in the park management field (Wildlife Conservation Society 2004).

Questions

1 (a) What factors hinder the development of soft and hard ecotourism in China's protected area system?
  (b) Given limited resources, which two factors should be rectified first?
  (c) What should be done to correct these two factors?

2 (a) Why does there appear to be little conformity between the way domestic tourists behave in China's nature reserves and the 'East Asian model of ecotourism' described in 'Practitioner's perspective: An East Asian model of ecotourism?' (chapter 2)?
  (b) What could be done, if anything, to increase the likelihood that such a model becomes normative in these protected areas?

4 Ecological *impact*

LEARNING OBJECTIVES

After reading this chapter, you should be able to:

■ discuss the problems of misrepresentation and legitimacy that are associated with ecotourism

■ explain the potential direct and indirect ecological benefits and costs that can result from ecotourism

■ critically assess the circumstances under which ecological benefits and costs are likely to occur, including the influence of hard and soft ecotourism

■ describe strategies that can be implemented to minimise the ecological costs and maximise the ecological benefits of ecotourism.

4.1 INTRODUCTION

Soft ecotourism (i.e. most ecotourism) is confined to a limited area in a relatively small number of public and private protected areas, whereas hard ecotourism is widely dispersed both in and among protected areas but involves a much smaller number of participants. A primary challenge for managers is to ensure that ecotourism, whether concentrated (soft) or dispersed (hard), does not compromise the ecological integrity of protected areas and other ecotourism venues. Ecotourism is not supposed to have negative ecological consequences, but these may occur inadvertently given that there is still much uncertainty as to what constitutes 'sustainable' practice (section 1.4.4). Ecotourism is also widely assumed to have many positive ecological consequences. This chapter presents the potential ecological benefits (section 4.3) and costs (section 4.4) of ecotourism. First, however, section 4.2 discusses the misrepresentation of ecotourism, since many negative and some positive effects associated with tourism are incorrectly attributed to ecotourism. Section 4.5 concludes the main body of the chapter by discussing impact management strategies that attempt to maximise the benefits and minimise the costs of ecotourism.

4.2 MISREPRESENTATION OF ECOTOURISM

When assessing the impact of ecotourism, a distinction must be made between products and activities that satisfy core criteria (see chapter 1) and those that deliberately or inadvertently misrepresent the term. In the latter case, misrepresentation is often a matter of not understanding the true nature of ecotourism and/or confusion with related terms, such as nature-based, wildlife, sustainable and adventure tourism. Deliberate misrepresentation, in contrast, occurs when ecotourism is used as a form of **greenwashing** (Laufer 2003). Many companies assume that 'green sells', and therefore the label 'ecotourism' may be appropriated as a marketing ploy to convey a misleading image of environmental responsibility. Unfortunately, deliberate misrepresentation is commonplace, given the current lack of effective accreditation schemes that are familiar to the public (see chapter 6), the public's lack of familiarity with ecotourism criteria and the absence of any legal restrictions that govern the use of terms such as 'ecotourism'. Duffy (2002) cites examples of ecotourism greenwashing in Belize, which is competing with Costa Rica to become the major Central American 'ecotourism' destination. One involves an 'eco-resort' where swimming and contact with dolphins is a key attraction. Such misrepresentation fosters cynicism and negatively affects the reputation of genuine ecotourism products, contributing to a situation in the early 21st century where the credibility and legitimacy of ecotourism have yet to be fully established (Fennell & Weaver 2005). Another form of greenwashing is when one or two genuinely sustainable and highly visible eco-products are made available to the public by a company that is otherwise operating in an unsustainable manner, an increasingly common scenario as corporations become more globalised and more vertically and horizontally integrated (see chapter 6).

The question of misrepresentation is relevant to the following discussion of impact, since numerous negative consequences that are ascribed to ecotourism actually pertain to other forms of tourism. If taken into account, this chapter would need to cover the environmental, sociocultural and economic consequences of tourism in general. These have already been addressed elsewhere and includes concerns about ecological degradation, congestion, stress on infrastructure, cultural commodification, sexual exploitation, crime, seasonality, revenue leakage and the undermining of agriculture (e.g. Kelly & Nankervis 2001, Wall & Mathieson 2005, Weaver & Lawton 2006). Instead, this chapter focuses on the positive and negative ramifications of products that satisfy core ecotourism criteria. Positive outcomes when seen from this perspective are usually deliberate whereas negative outcomes are mostly inadvertent. Wall (1997) makes a relevant comment in contending that ecotourism, like any agent of modernisation, inevitably instigates change, and there is always the chance that these changes will have negative and unforeseen consequences. As stated in chapter 1, the litmus test for ecotourism therefore is the sincere attempt to manage the activity sustainably within best practice parameters, including the prompt and effective remediation of any negative impact that is identified.

4.3 ECOLOGICAL BENEFITS

The potential direct and indirect ecological benefits discussed in this chapter are outlined in figure 4.1.

DIRECT BENEFITS	INDIRECT BENEFITS
• Incentive to protect natural environments • Incentive to rehabilitate modified environments • Provide funds to manage and expand protected areas • Ecotourists assist with habitat maintenance and enhancement • Ecotourists serve as environmental watchdogs	• Exposure to ecotourism fosters environmentalism • Areas protected for ecotourism provide environmental benefits

■ **Figure 4.1**
Potential ecological benefits of ecotourism

■ 4.3.1 Direct *benefits*

Incentive to protect natural environments

Relatively undisturbed habitat is being destroyed and degraded at a pace that far exceeds the growth in space occupied by protected areas (see section 3.2.1). Two associated factors — population growth and poverty — are declining in many parts of the world, but this will not have any short or medium-term effect in arresting this destruction for at least two reasons. First, youthful populations in the less-developed world (due to recent high fertility) and increasing life expectancies ensure that world population will continue to increase by around 50 million per year over several decades despite continuing fertility declines and increased mortality from AIDS. Demographers now predict that the global population will stabilise at between 8 and 12 billion by 2050, compared with about 6 billion in the early 2000s (World Resources Institute 2005). Second, as these populations grow more prosperous, per capita consumption of natural resources will increase and gradually approach the high levels already evident in more-developed countries such as the USA. The association between population growth, economic growth and habitat destruction is well illustrated by such countries as Brazil and Indonesia where governments continue to perceive the settlement and exploitation of their extensive peripheries as necessary to attain national development goals. The same logic also applies in both the historical and the contemporary sense to Australia, Canada and other developed countries with a large resource frontier (Mercer 2000).

In the face of relentless developmental pressures, it is difficult to justify the retention of natural spaces and protected areas on ecological or ethical grounds alone, or even on the basis of long-term, indirect economic benefits derived from erosion control and the maintenance of biodiversity. The decision to retain or convert a natural area often comes down to the raw arithmetic of determining the uses that provide the greatest tangible economic benefits to the greatest number of people (or to the most influential corporations) over the shortest time frame. If intact flora and fauna cannot 'pay their own way', then it is likely that the land will be used to support logging, agriculture and/or mining instead. Neither tourism nor ecotourism in particular have traditionally been seen as serious contenders among the stakeholder groups competing for access to natural environments. This perception, however, is changing with help from the growth of tourism and its nature-based subsector, wherein natural environments and their intact flora and fauna in many destinations are emerging as lucrative tourism resources in their own right. Depending on the destination, either soft or hard ecotourism can potentially provide the critical mass of activity and revenue generation that justifies the retention of an area in its natural or semi-natural state. With the former, this usually occurs through the volume of traffic, whereas hard ecotourism normally fulfils this role through higher visitor fees (see section 4.5.4). Ecotourism-related revenues and employment have been directly linked to government support for such protected areas as the Hol Chan Marine Reserve in Belize and the Parc National des Volcans in Rwanda (Lindberg, Enriquez & Sproule 1996).

Evaluating the relative worth of the natural environment as an ecotourism resource

Support for ecotourism has increased in recent years as a result of studies that demonstrate its financial advantages over other resource competitors (Tisdell & Wilson 2004). Much of this research has been conducted in the big game savannas in sub-Saharan Africa where human pressures on the natural environment have been especially acute. Sherman and Dixon (1991) cite three classic studies from the 1970s, including one by Western and Thresher that valued land supporting big game populations at US$40 per hectare and land supporting grazing at just US$0.80 per hectare. Another study, by Western and Henry, estimated that lions in Kenya's Amboseli National Park were each worth US$27 000 per year as a wildlife viewing resource and an elephant herd was worth US$610 000. The third study, by Thresher, calculated the value of a maned lion as a food and hide source at US$960 to US$1325, as a big game trophy at US$8500 and as a photo safari attraction at US$515 000 over an average life span of 15 years.

Regardless of the variable methodologies employed, these studies consistently identify potential returns from ecotourism that are substantially higher than those obtained from competing uses. Corroborating the trend is a study from the late 1990s showing that cattle ranching in Zimbabwe yielded Z$22–37 per hectare per year whereas wildlife tourism (including hunting and culling) yielded Z$67 per hectare per year. A second study based in South Africa found that tourism (including hunting) would produce a net annual income of R14 130 000 for a wildlife-based ranch, whereas cattle ranching in the same location would produce only R1 300 000 (cited in Lindberg 1998).

Ecotourism can also provide an incentive to protect natural areas even if they are not used directly for ecotourism-related purposes. One case study examined an area in the Philippines that was about to be logged in order to generate expected returns of US$13 million over a ten-year period. These returns, however, would be achieved only by logging in a manner that would entail large amounts of clear-cutting and subsequent erosion. These sediments would damage offshore coral reefs and drastically curtail their use for ecotourism and sustainable fishing. If a logging ban was imposed, tourism and fishing could be expected to generate US$47 million and US$28 million, respectively, for a gain of US$62 million over that same 10-year period (Sherman & Dixon 1991).

Incentive to rehabilitate modified environments

If ecotourism gives value to existing natural habitat, then it is logical to assume that it also provides an incentive to rehabilitate modified land so that such areas will also attract ecotourists. Currently, there are only a few examples of ecotourism-induced restoration (see section 3.5.5). In most cases, environmental enhancement, rather than ecotourism, is the primary motive for undertaking restoration, although this may be done with the implicit understanding that the costs of restoration will be partially or fully offset by future tourism-related revenues.

Provision of funds to manage and expand protected areas

Ecotourism not only plays a growing role in the protection and enhancement of protected area systems but is also an important source of the funds required for their management and expansion. Most higher-order protected areas were not originally established to accommodate large numbers of visitors, and capital and operating revenues were traditionally obtained from government rather than from entry fees or other revenue derived from these visitors. However, protected area authorities are facing major budgetary constraints in most countries (see section 3.3) and are increasingly looking to visitor fees and private sector revenue sources to compensate for government funding cutbacks. Accordingly, it is surprising that many protected area systems still have very low entry fees or, as in some Australian states, such as Queensland, have none at all. Possible reasons include public resistance (i.e. a belief that the public is already paying for the parks through taxes) and the cost of collecting fees.

Nevertheless, the potential for substantial fee increases in some destinations is high, in part because entry and other user fees constitute only a very small proportion of total trip costs for inbound or long-haul domestic visitors. An increase in entry fee from $1 to $5 per vehicle, for example, produces an enormous increase in cumulative revenue for a heavily visited park, but represents a negligible increase to the $2000 vacation costs being incurred by an inbound visitor. In the case of Costa Rica, an excessively low park entry fee (equivalent to US$1.25) was initially raised to an excessively high level (equivalent to US$15) in 1994, then reduced to a compromise level of about US$6 for non-nationals after protests and boycotts from local tour operators (Laarman & Gregersen 1996, Mowforth & Munt 1998). Menkhaus and Lober (1996) suggest that the fee could be raised to US$40 without significantly affecting the intake of soft or hard foreign ecotourists. Willingness to pay such a high fee, however, ultimately depends on whether tourists deem the attraction to be worth the cost and, for some potential visitors, whether they are assured that the fee is allocated to park maintenance and enhancement rather than to general government revenue.

Ecotourist assistance with habitat maintenance and enhancement

Direct environmental benefits derive from the willingness of many ecotourists to assist with habitat maintenance and enhancement through their own actions, a phenomenon that is most apparent among hard ecotourist niche markets, such as volunteers (see section 2.4.1). Similarly, a legacy of activism is evident in the role of the early Australian bushwalking clubs in advocating and working for the establishment of national parks (see section 2.2.3). Contemporary evidence is provided in a study of patrons of Lamington National Park (Australia) ecolodge (Weaver & Lawton 2002), 16 per cent of whom indicated that they like to participate in volunteer work at ecotourism sites. Seventy-six per cent agreed or strongly agreed that they usually do what they can to leave a site in better condition than when they arrived, and 62 per cent were willing to pick up litter left behind by others. These findings indicate strong support for enhancement sustainability and comprehensive ecotourism among 'harder' ecotourist segments (see chapter 1), although it is still unclear to what extent respondent proclamations translate into actual behaviour.

Many ecotourists are also willing to participate indirectly in environmental maintenance through donations. In the above-mentioned Lamington National Park research, more than half of the sampled ecolodge patrons stated that they were willing to give extra money to support protected areas. Tisdell and Wilson (2005) report that 40 per cent of visitors to the Mon Repos Conservation Park in Queensland (Australia) indicated an intention to donate more money to sea turtle conservation as a result of their visit, those actually seeing sea turtles and those describing their visit as 'educational' being more likely to state this intention. Related research demonstrates that many ecotourists act on their willingness to donate. Cadiz and Calumpong (2002), for example, found that donations account for 5.5 per cent of all revenues received by the Apo Island Marine Sanctuary in the Philippines. Hvenegaard and Dearden (1998) report that 58 per cent of birdwatching ecotourists and 50 per cent of general ecotourists in Thailand's Doi Inthanon National Park made donations to conservation causes in the previous year compared with 14 per cent of general visitors, the average amount being about US$70. It is reasonable to speculate that soft ecotourists, otherwise not as aware of volunteer opportunities or possibly less disposed to participate in them, would be more willing to participate indirectly through donations.

Ecotourists as environmental watchdogs

A more activist dimension to the above point is the tendency of some ecotourists to serve as environmental watchdogs or guardians who personally intervene in situations where the environment is perceived to be threatened. Seventy-nine per cent of the Lamington National Park ecolodge sample said that they would not ignore a situation where another visitor was behaving in an irresponsible way. However, it is not clear in what way they were willing to intervene, or whether they actually would intervene if confronted with such a situation. Hard ecotourists, as environmental activists who penetrate into more remote areas, are also credited with exposing and opposing such environmentally controversial activities as clear-cutting in Tasmania (Australia) and British Columbia in Canada (Hutton & Connors 1999). According to Stonehouse and Crosbie (1995), tourists were among the first to publicise and react against the careless deposition of litter from research stations in Antarctica. An example of preemption is provided by Algonquin Provincial Park (Ontario, Canada), where the logging-free zone was increased to 25 per cent in 1974 from a proposed 5 per cent so that wilderness canoeists would not be upset by exposure to logged areas. The environmental benefits of this decision, however, were somewhat offset by the resulting low levels of concern among canoeists over the logging that continues in the remaining three-quarters of the park (Eagles & Martens 1997).

■ 4.3.2 Indirect *benefits*

The indirect environmental benefits of ecotourism include the increased support for environmentalism and protected areas potentially fostered both among tourists and local communities and the environmental benefits derived from protected areas that have been established or are kept in existence because of ecotourism (Weaver 2002c).

Environmentalism fostered by exposure to ecotourism

In addition to encouraging participation in the maintenance and enhancement of specific natural environments, involvement with ecotourism can also foster a broader sense of environmentalism. For example, 82 per cent of respondents in the Lamington National Park study claimed that their participation in ecotourism made them more environmentally conscientious. Similarly, the respondents in the Tangalooma study in Queensland, Australia (Orams 1997), declared that their experience with the dolphins made them more broadly aware of environmental issues. In this case, the elevated level of awareness was associated with an educational program that placed the experience in a context of environmentalism. Lee and Moscardo (2005), in contrast, did not find that visitors to an Australian ecolodge were made any more environmentally conscientious as a result of their visit, although this may be because their levels of awareness were already extremely high due to previous ecotourism experiences. The researchers *did* find that those who participated in or were exposed to the ecolodge's environmental programs displayed especially high biocentric tendencies, some of which may be attributable to that exposure. In another study of Lamington National Park visitors, Beaumont (2001) identified substantial gains in environmental knowledge but no concomitant increase in environmentalist attitudes or behavioural intentions.

Changes in environmental attitude and behaviour can also occur in local communities and among other beneficiaries of ecotourism revenue. Support for local protected areas in Belize, for example, increased substantially between the time of their establishment and the time when community surveys were undertaken in the mid-1990s (see figure 4.2). Critically, there was a large increase in the proportion of residents who attributed their support for protected areas to ecotourism (Lindberg, Enriquez & Sproule 1996). Dramatic increases in support for local parks and wildlife as well as concurrent declines in poaching, deforestation and other unsustainable activities were also reported in the vicinity of protected areas in Rwanda, Niger, Madagascar, Burundi and Nepal once a significant revenue stream from ecotourism had been established to compensate for the loss of resources that could no longer be extracted following the establishment of the parks (Wells & Brandon 1992). In northern Tanzania, a study of three villages similarly found that support for wildlife conservation is directly related to the benefits that village residents obtain from ecotourism (Nelson 2004).

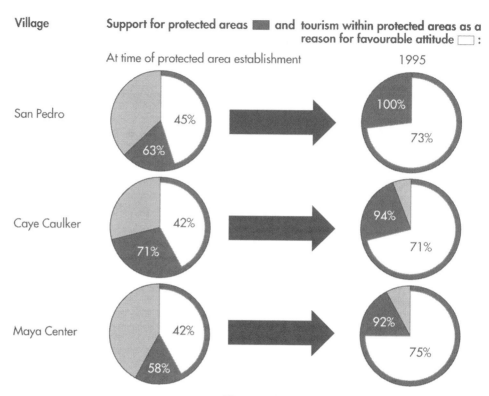

Village   Support for protected areas ■ and tourism within protected areas as a reason for favourable attitude ▢ :

At time of protected area establishment   1995

San Pedro   45%   100%   73%

Caye Caulker   42%   94%   71%

Maya Center   42%   92%   75%

■ **Figure 4.2** *Support for protected areas in Belize*
Source: *adapted from Lindberg, Enriquez & Sproule 1996.*

Areas protected for ecotourism provide environmental benefits

When an area is protected, wholly or partially, for ecotourism, the wider ecological benefits obtained from these protected areas can be considered an indirect environmental benefit of this sector. At the local level, the benefits include watershed protection (e.g. stream-flow regulation, water quality maintenance and minimisation of erosion), maintenance of bio-diversity (e.g. gene pool protection) and regulation of microclimates and other ecological processes.

4.4 ℰCOLOGICAL COSTS

Potential ecological costs associated with ecotourism are listed in figure 4.3.

■ **Figure 4.3**
*Potential
ecological
costs of
ecotourism*

DIRECT COSTS	INDIRECT COSTS
• Impact of building and generation of wastes • Impact of tourist activities (wildlife observation, hiking, introduction of exotic species)	• Effects of induced building • Exposure to less benign forms of tourism • Transit effects • Problems associated with the economic valuation of nature

■ *4.4.1* **Direct** *costs*

Even when all reasonable measures are taken to avoid any negative environmental and sociocultural impact and to correct any negative impact that inadvertently arises from ecotourism, negative consequences can still occur. The activities that directly cause this negative impact can be divided into three categories: building, the generation of wastes and tourist activities. A fourth category, induced building, is discussed later as an indirect cost.

Impact of building and generation of wastes

Although their negative ecological impact can be minimised (see section 4.5.3), direct and deliberate on-site ecological stresses, such as the removal of vegetation, site levelling and water flow disruption, are unavoidably incurred in the building of ecotourism-related facilities, such as ecolodges, viewing platforms, trails, access roads and parking facilities. Potential non-deliberate problems, such as the introduction of weeds and insect pests through non-local building materials and furnishings, are also possible. Following construction, additional ecological costs may be caused by the generation of waste residuals. Sewage and other liquid wastes are particularly problematic if the area is not serviced by waste treatment infrastructure. A high risk of eventual groundwater contamination is associated with the use of septic beds and biological toilets if these are not designed and sited with great care. Other potentially problematic on-site waste residuals include food scraps, exhaust from power generators, leakage of lubricants and other chemicals, wood smoke (Hawkins, Epler Wood & Bittman 1995) and nocturnal light pollution.

Tourist activities

Tourist activities, however well intended, can result in various negative ecological consequences (Liddle 1997). This is in part because of the mobility of tourists, some of whom (mostly hard ecotourists) penetrate deeply into relatively undisturbed areas. Large concentrations of soft ecotourists around interpretation centres, nearby hardened trails and other altered sites can also lead to wildlife stress and the inadvertent introduction and diffusion of exotic species. These concentrations also often attract opportunistic wildlife, such as brush turkeys, lorikeets and rock wallabies in parts of eastern Australia, which as a result may proliferate and upset the local balance of nature.

Each human–wildlife encounter is a unique and unpredictable experience with potential for negative impact, especially given the paradox that ecotourists tend to be most attracted to the rare charismatic megafauna and megaflora that are least able to cope with such attention because of their rarity. To examine inadvertent environmental impact in more detail, tourist activities can be divided into the categories of wildlife observation, hiking and diving, and the introduction of exotic species.

Wildlife observation

Extensive research conducted over several decades indicates that even non-extractive forms of wildlife-based tourism, such as observation, can have negative consequences for the target species (Buckley 2004b, Higginbottom 2004, Krüger 2005, Newsome, Moore & Dowling 2002), and it is possible to include only a small sample of this literature here. With respect to mammals, Buckley (2001) cites a study from the early 1980s which found that the heart rate of dall sheep (a particular type of sheep found in alpine regions) in Alberta, Canada, increases by up to 20 beats per minute upon the approach of hikers. Moreover, elevated stress levels become apparent at a distance of as much as 150 metres. Woodland caribou in the Charlevoix Biosphere Reserve (Quebec, Canada) spend more time standing and being vigilant in the presence of ecotourists during the stressful winter period, at the expense of time spent in vital foraging and relaxing activity (Duchesne, Côté & Barrette 2000). A similar pattern of increased vigilance and reduced feeding time was observed among Asian rhinos in Nepal's Royal Chitwan National Park during elephant-borne ecotourist encounters (Lott & McCoy 1995). Both Lusseau (2003) and Constantine, Brunton and Dennis (2004) found that the resting behaviour and socialising of bottlenose dolphin in New Zealand is disrupted by the presence of sightseeing vessels. Social play among pygmy marmosets (a type of small primate) in the Amazon region of Ecuador is also disrupted by ecotourists (de la Torre, Snowdon & Beharano 2000). In East African protected areas, cheetahs are considered particularly sensitive to viewing by vehicle-based tourists, and hyenas and baboons in some areas have learned to track tourist vehicles to locate and steal cheetah kills (Roe, Leader-Williams & Dalal-Clayton 1997). Proactive adaptation is also evident in British Columbia (Canada) among adult female grizzly bears, which have learned to remain near ecotourists in order to discourage the approach of adult male bears who harass the females and their cubs (Nevin & Gilbert 2005). While increasing the reproductive success of individual female bears, this behaviour may also result in abnormal population increases. Aerial viewing of wildlife can also induce stress, as demonstrated by the reduction in the winter foraging efficiency of bighorn sheep when exposed to overhead helicopter flights in Grand Canyon National Park, USA (Stockwell & Bateman 1991).

Among other types of wildlife, Burger and Gochfeld (1993) found that as many as 95 per cent of boobies (a native bird species) in the Galapagos Islands (Ecuador) fly away when hikers approach within two metres of their nests. This is a common occurrence given that nesting sites are often located near hiking trails. Trumpeter swans at an Alaskan site are significantly disturbed by pedestrians located even several hundred metres from nesting sites (Henson & Grant 1991), while Müllner, Linsenmair and Wikelski (2004) found in Amazonian Ecuador that juvenile hoatzins (a colourful pheasant-like bird) in ecotourist-exposed nests have a lower survival rate than those in non-exposed nests. Jacobson and Lopez (1994) report that tourists disrupt the egg-laying behaviour of sea turtles in Costa Rica's Tortuguero National Park. Stress levels among Magellanic penguins in southern Argentina, in contrast, are not measurably affected by proximity to ecotourists (Fowler 1999). However, as with female grizzly bears in British Columbia, this may simply indicate habituation.

Distance between ecotourists and target wildlife, all else being equal, is probably the main factor influencing stress, increased proximity resulting in increased stress response. The dilemma for ecotourism product managers is that satisfaction levels of ecotourists also tend to increase with increased access to wildlife, so that highly satisfying encounters often occur at the expense of wildlife wellbeing. Management attempts at compromise between these two objectives (i.e. animal wellbeing and ecotourist satisfaction), however, are complicated by factors other than distance that influence any given ecotourist–wildlife encounter. These include such wildlife variables as type of animal, number, activity (e.g. feeding, courting, nesting, resting), distribution and presence of other wildlife species, and location. Additional ecotourist variables include number and distribution of humans perceived by target wildlife, direction and angle of approach, speed of travel, presence of horses or other domestic animals and noise level. Weather conditions (including wind speed and direction) and time of day are other considerations that influence whether a particular encounter between wildlife and ecotourists is ecologically sustainable.

Hiking and diving

Hiking occurs mostly in conjunction with terrestrial wildlife viewing and is associated with such site stresses as erosion, soil compaction and vegetation damage. If severe, these site stresses can induce other effects, such as sedimentation in waterways and vegetation change. According to Marion and Farrell (1998), research indicates that tree damage as well as soil erosion and exposure all display a linear relationship with hiking frequency; that is, the amount of stress increases in pace with the increase in hiking activity (see figure 4.4). Other stresses, however, are characterised by a curvilinear relationship. Organic litter loss, soil compaction and vegetation loss, for example, accelerate rapidly during initial exposure to hikers, but then decelerate as visitor numbers continue to grow — the damage, essentially, is already done. Such findings have important implications for ecotourism managers, since they suggest that ecological costs can be locally significant even when visitor use is minimal.

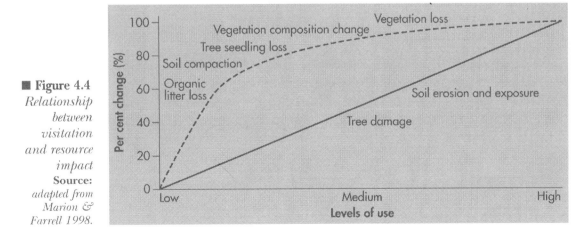

■ **Figure 4.4**
Relationship between visitation and resource impact
Source:
adapted from Marion & Farrell 1998.

In addition to indications of a curvilinear relationship, Buckley (2001) notes the following conclusions from the research carried out to date on the effects of hiking, which further complicate the attainment of ecologically sustainable outcomes:

1. There is still insufficient information to predict or model the impact of different types and levels of hiking in different types of environment.
2. The sensitivity of different ecosystems to the effects of trampling varies enormously.
3. If trampling is heavy enough, death of plant cover and local soil erosion will occur in any ecosystem.
4. If trampling ceases, soil and vegetation will recover to at least some extent, although this may take some time, depending on the ecosystem.
5. Travellers using mountain bikes and horses usually cause far more damage than hikers.
6. In most cases, the direct effects of trampling do not extend beyond the actual track and do not continue to grow if trampling stops.

Resilience to hiking activity therefore varies dramatically and is as yet poorly understood in most ecosystems. However, as described in point 6 above, the area actually affected by such changes may be minuscule compared to the overall size of a given venue and, therefore, these costs may be acceptable when weighed against resulting benefits.

Diving is also associated with ecological stress. Harriott, Davis and Banks (1997), for example, found that recreational divers at four locations off eastern Australia were responsible for a large amount of inadvertent sedimentation and coral breakage, although most of the latter was caused by a small number of inexperienced divers. Zakai and Chadwick-Furman (2002) observed similar effects in Red Sea diving sites in Israel. In the Caribbean, heavily dived sites off Grand Cayman Island (Tratalos & Austin 2001) and Bonaire (Hawkins et al. 1999) have less-than-expected populations of hard and massive coral but greater concentrations of dead and rubble coral. Management challenges associated with diving include the fragility and slow recovery of coral, difficulties in monitoring underwater activities, conflicting external influences such as climate change and maritime traffic (chapter 7), the rapid growth of diving as a recreational activity and a high proportion of inadequately experienced participants (Garrod & Wilson 2003).

Introduction of exotic species
Ecotourist activity can serve as a vehicle for the introduction of alien flora and fauna to relatively undisturbed venues. For example, insect dispersal in the Galapagos Islands (Ecuador) is related to tourist boats, as onboard lighting attracts moths and other flying insects, which are then transported to areas near islands where they are not native (Silberglied 1978). Micro-organism dispersals are even more difficult to control, mountain gorillas in eastern Africa being known to have contracted measles from ecotourists (Wallis & Lee 1999). In Australia, a non-native waterborne pathogen was discovered in a remote rock pool in Lamington National Park, Queensland, five kilometres from the nearest trail head. The only human activity associated with this area is occasional bathing by ecotourists and other visitors, many of

whom are from countries where the pathogen is native. It is assumed that the pathogen was introduced through the faecal matter of these users (Buckley, Clough & Warnken 1998). Almost as confounding is the introduction of exotic plants through seeds lodged in shoe treads, clothing, vehicles and faeces. Vehicles were identified by Lonsdale and Lane (1994) as a source of exotic seed entry in Australia's Kakadu National Park, but low dislodgement and germination rates prompted the researchers to conclude that costly measures to remove seeds before entry are unnecessary.

■ 4.4.2 Indirect *costs*

The potential indirect ecological costs of ecotourism include the effects of induced building, the exposure of venues to less benign forms of tourism, the effects of transit and the risks of placing an economic valuation on nature-based attractions.

Effects of induced building

Induced building refers firstly to physical developments undertaken to support ecotourism, such as housing constructed for employees of an ecolodge, or a road that is widened in response to increased traffic caused by these employees. About a sixth of residents around the Monteverde Cloud Forest Reserve (Costa Rica) in the 1990s, for example, had arrived in the previous five years, largely because of new jobs created by the growing popularity of that private protected area (Honey 1999). Although the reserve itself has maintained a reputation for sustainability, this migration has contributed to unplanned development in adjacent villages and along access roads. A similar 'rural sprawl' effect is evident near Manuel Antonio National Park and other high-visitation Costa Rican protected areas.

The term, secondly, refers to physical development that is otherwise attracted to protected areas and associated recreational opportunities, such as wildlife observation. In both Australia and the USA, **amenity migration** is a growing phenomenon whereby retirees and 'urban refugees' establish primary or second residences in areas of high amenity values, such as coastlines and mountains (Moss 2006). Areas adjacent to high-order protected areas are especially attractive due to the exceptional natural assets of these parks and the high probability that they will remain free from large-scale physical development or purposeful degradation. US national parks such as Great Smoky Mountains, Shenandoah, Yosemite and Yellowstone have experienced this phenomenon on a large scale, as demonstrated by high population growth in adjacent counties. The Australian national park system is also vulnerable due to the large number of entities that are located in mountainous areas near large metropolitan areas. A major rationale for establishing lower-order protected area buffer zones around high-order protected areas is to prevent haphazard encroachment.

Exposure to less benign forms of tourism

When ecotourism is introduced to a remote location, the site becomes vulnerable to the eventual intrusion of less benign forms of tourism. As placed in context by the Butler sequence (see section 1.2.1), hard ecotourists are alternative tourism pioneers who visit the area during the 'exploration' stage and unwittingly induce the 'involvement stage' of increased tourism activity through the publicity they generate and the paths they open up. This in turn can induce intensive tourism development, soft ecotourism-related or otherwise, during the 'development' stage. Minimalist soft ecotourism can subsequently mutate into unsustainable mass tourism. Butler's (1990) description of alternative tourism as a potential 'Trojan Horse' (i.e. an apparent gift that unexpectedly destroys the recipient) is therefore relevant to this discussion. One critical issue is the extent to which protected area and other ecotourism managers really can or wish to maintain activity at a desired level in the face of relentless market forces.

Another possibility is that the site itself remains sustainable but adjacent areas experience unsustainable levels of tourism development. This extends the induced building argument described above to include external landscape changes that are directly related to tourism. Monteverde (Costa Rica) and the Great Smoky Mountains (USA) are again illustrative. Access roads into the former are accommodating an increasing number of unregulated guesthouses, souvenir shops and pseudo-ecotourist attractions, possibly indicating early 'development' stage dynamics. On the Tennessee side of Great Smoky Mountains National Park, the town of Gatlinburg accommodates a sprawl of theme parks, fast food restaurants and factory outlet malls, most of which depend upon the annual in-transit patronage of four million park visitors (Stynes 2002). A second crucial issue for park managers, therefore, is the minimal control that they are able to exert over the external environment, in this case the conventional and informal tourism sectors that capitalise on the success of proximate ecotourism yet serve as a potentially undermining influence (see chapter 7).

Transit effects

Hall and Higham (2005) emphasise the significant contribution to anthropogenic climate change of 'greenhouse gas' emissions from tourist transit activity. This is largely associated with 3S tourists from North America and Europe travelling by air to pleasure periphery destinations, although international ecotourism is also disproportionately implicated due to the long-haul travel required to reach Asian, African and Latin American ecotourist destinations. The contribution of land-based transit is evidenced by Simmons and Becken (2004), who calculate that a typical 22-day 3773 kilometre ecotourism driving circuit in New Zealand releases 430 kg of CO_2. Gössling et al. (2005) reveal a similar impact in estimating that recreational visits to Rocky Mountain National Park (USA) annually produce 1.1 billion kg of CO_2. Gössling (1999) supports a comprehensive ecotourism approach in arguing that fuel consumption should be taken into account when calculating the positive and negative effects of an ecotourism operation or site and refers to this as an example of an **environmental damage cost** (EDC). An even more indirect consideration is whether the ecological costs of manufacturing and maintaining aircraft should also be taken into account.

Problems associated with the economic valuation of nature

The monetary value assigned to natural attractions through ecotourism, as discussed above, is an incentive against the introduction or continuation of unsustainable competing land uses. This process of economic valuation, however, poses its own ecological risks. Ideally, as per comprehensive ecotourism, an entire setting or habitat should be interpreted and experienced as a single interrelated ecosystem (see section 1.4.7), but in reality many ecotourists are only interested in observing specific charismatic megafauna. A cheetah or adult male lion, accordingly, is 'worth' more in the marketplace than a gazelle or hippopotamus. Slime moulds and dung beetles by this logic have no worth, or negative worth despite their critical role in ecosystem maintenance. This anthropocentric approach may encourage managers to realise high levels of visitor satisfaction by giving priority to charismatic species at the top of the monetary hierarchy to the exclusion or suppression of less charismatic species. As with natural resource managers in North America who once 'supported' attractive animals such as elk and deer by reducing wolf (predator) populations, ecological disequilibrium is a probable outcome. A broader ethical question is whether any kind of monetary value *should* be placed on natural phenomena that might be regarded as inherently invaluable.

4.5 IMPACT MANAGEMENT STRATEGIES

The minimisation of the ecological costs of ecotourism, and the maximisation of its benefits, must be a priority for managers and operators of all ecotourism products. As for appropriate strategies, the creation of protected areas is one demonstrable way to increase the probability of positive ecological outcomes, although there have been very few protected areas that have been established specifically to accommodate ecotourism demand. Since the overall role of protected areas has already been examined in chapter 3, the focus in this section is to consider strategies that can be applied not only in existing parks but also to other ecotourism product providers. Considered below are zoning, site hardening and softening, visitation quotas and fees, wildlife viewing and access restrictions, and visitor education. Product accreditation schemes are also relevant but are discussed in chapter 6 because they apply mainly to private sector businesses rather than publicly managed protected areas.

4.5.1 Hard *and soft ecotourism revisited*

With respect to minimising negative impact, the superiority of hard ecotourism was assumed during the era of the adaptancy platform (see section 1.2.1). This assumption, however, does not necessarily stand up to scrutiny.

For example, the critical mass of visitors required to realise incentive and funding effects (section 4.3.1) favours soft ecotourism, as do the visitation economies of scale required to implement sustainable site-hardening strategies. Conversely, hard ecotourists are more likely to invade backstage spaces and to disturb wildlife and spread exotic flora and fauna across a larger area. Moreover, their activities in remote areas are less likely to be monitored or mediated by guides, rangers or other enforcement personnel. Hard ecotourists, however, may also be more likely to participate in 'comprehensive' ecotourism activities that bring about improvements to the environment, while the sheer volume of soft ecotourism, with its 'minimalist' proclivities, increases the probability that it will have a significant inadvertent impact on the natural environment or mutate into unsustainable mass tourism, even if associated experiences are monitored and mediated. Ultimately, potential costs and benefits are associated with both hard and soft ecotourism and, as per the knowledge-based platform, the relevant issue is not which is better but how either can be managed most effectively and what mixture and distribution is most appropriate in any particular protected area or product mix.

Flexible and fixed carrying capacities

Towards this objective of effective management, it is relevant to revisit the issue of the spatial and temporal concentration of tourism in protected areas (see section 3.4.2). Essentially, the 95 per cent of tourists whose activity is confined to 5 per cent of space in a typical heavily visited protected area are mainly soft ecotourists, whereas the 5 per cent of tourists who spend most of their time in the remaining 95 per cent of space incline towards the hard ecotourism pole. In either case, implicit or explicit assumptions are made about the area's **carrying capacity**; that is, the amount of activity that can be accommodated in that site without incurring unsustainable impact (Borrie, McCool & Stankey 1998). Undeveloped areas in protected areas are often maintained as such by managers who assume them to have a fixed carrying capacity (1) by merit of being ecologically sensitive, (2) because the carrying capacity is unknown (i.e. the precautionary principle) or (3) because resources are not available to increase the carrying capacity (Lawton 2001). Under such circumstances, low and dispersed levels of visitation and physical development, below the assumed carrying capacity threshold, are appropriate even if demand is high (see figure 4.5a). In contrast, areas of concentrated tourism-related activity often reflect a management assumption of flexible carrying capacity; that is, that carrying capacity can be continually increased to accommodate increased demand, as long as the visitation curve remains below the escalating carrying capacity threshold (see figure 4.5b). Essentially, the fixed carrying capacity area is usually a bio-centric construct that gives priority to ecological protection (unless it is applied to a heavily visited area where no additional visitation is desired) and thus functions as an internal category Ib area within the IUCN classification system (see section 3.2.2), whatever the actual designation of the protected area as a whole. Flexible carrying capacity areas, in contrast, are more of an anthropocentric construct that seek to accommodate tourist demand, albeit in an ecologically compatible way, within a limited area. Fixed and flexible assumptions about carrying capacity are highly relevant to the subsections that follow.

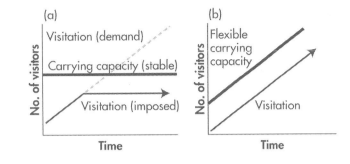

■ **Figure 4.5**
Visitation levels in the context of fixed and fluid carrying capacities

■ 4.5.2 Zoning

Zoning can be defined as 'regulations [that] demarcate specific areas for different types of land uses and the development standards to be applied within each land use zone' (Inskeep 1991, p. 432). As such, these regulations formalise the spaces within a protected area where in varying degrees fixed and flexible carrying capacity assumptions are applied. Some variation of the 95/5 dictum is usually evident. In the proposed master plan for South Africa's iconic Kruger National Park, 'high intensity leisure' and 'medium intensity leisure' zones together account for 2 per cent of the park, whereas at the other pole 'wilderness', 'remote' and 'primitive' zones together occupy 63 per cent (SANP 2006). Mount Kilimanjaro National Park, the tourism icon of Tanzania, along with the surrounding forest reserve, have 'day use' and 'intensive hiking' zones that together account for 3 per cent of the total area, whereas 'wilderness' occupies about 90 per cent and an intermediate category of 'low use hiking' (summit or non-summit bound) applies to 8 per cent (UNEP 2006b).

These various terms are all embodied in the widely applied **recreation opportunity spectrum** (ROS), which recognises protected area zones ranging from 'primitive' (no modification, minimal encounters with other visitors, little active management) through 'semi-primitive', 'roaded natural', 'rural' and 'urban' (major modification, extensive interaction with other visitors, pervasive management) (Eagles & McCool 2002). Ideally, all zones should be designated so that they occupy appropriate environments. Intensive use zones, for example, should be designated in modified or otherwise ecologically less sensitive spaces. Canada's Banff National Park violates this principle insofar as the intensely developed Bow Valley Corridor occupies the rarest, most biodiverse and productive habitat in the park due to its parallel suitability for transportation and physical development (Dearden 2000).

■ *4.5.3* **Site** *hardening and softening*

Site hardening refers here to construction that allows a site's carrying capacity to be increased, as per figure 4.5b. For example, the use of pit toilets may mean that a site can accommodate only a hundred users per week in an ecologically sustainable way. However, the construction of an ablution block may increase that capacity to a thousand users per week. The same logic can be applied to a walking trail paved with cobblestones, as opposed to a dirt track, or the construction of a boardwalk in a wetland, which have the additional advantages of facilitating visitors' comfort and learning. In all cases, an important consideration is to ensure that the enhanced carrying capacity of a particular facility, whether associated with a public protected area or a private business such as an ecolodge, is compatible with other elements of the site or the adjacent environment. A site-hardened trail, for example, may be able to accommodate a thousand walkers per week, but this does not mean that the wildlife or vegetation along the trail is also capable of withstanding this level of exposure. Facility enhancements can backfire if they facilitate access by an inappropriately high number of visitors.

Zones of intensive tourism use provide special opportunities for sophisticated and innovative site-hardening, as illustrated by the South Rim of Grand Canyon National Park (USA), where about 90 per cent of the five million annual visits to the park are concentrated. Its centrepiece is the evolving Canyon View Information Plaza complex, which serves as a gateway to the canyon and efficiently provides orientation, information, interpretation and a wide variety of shops, restaurants and other goods and services. Site-sensitive building standards minimise the environmental impact of the plaza, as does the exclusion of public parking facilities. Day visitors must leave their private vehicles in a parking lot located just outside the park boundary and board a shuttle bus that terminates at the plaza (National Park Service 2006a). In this and similar cases, ecologically sustainable outcomes are further ensured by post-construction **site-softening** measures, such as soil replacement and replanting of native vegetation, that rehabilitate or 'naturalise' the site as much as possible (see 'Practitioner's Perspective: Environmentally friendly building at Kingfisher Bay').

■ *4.5.4* **Sustainable** *design and environmental management systems*

Beyond the strategies of site hardening and site softening, public and private facilities can promote ecological (and to a lesser extent sociocultural) sustainability through the implementation of internal green design principles and environmental management systems. Frequently implemented in ecolodges, these include the use of recycled building materials; energy-efficient windows, lighting and insulation; composting and other recycling systems; cogeneration; and adherence to local vernacular architecture.

Kingfisher Bay Resort opened on Fraser Island (Queensland, Australia) in 1992 and has since been widely lauded as an exemplar of sustainable environmental design and practice. Before construction, a meticulous inventory of the 65-hectare site was undertaken to minimise disruption to the island's biodiversity and hydrology. Much of the complex and its road system were designed around existing mature native trees, and extensive plantings from the resort's own on-site nursery were used to rehabilitate the site after the completion of construction, which relied on non-endangered native timber (Kingfisher Bay 2006). Many of the replanted seedlings had been earlier removed and stored during the construction phase. Heating and cooling by natural convectional currents is facilitated by the architectural design, and a system of carefully sited hardwood boardwalks and woodchip walking trails minimises damage to soil and vegetation from ecotourists. Reinforcing the integration of the complex into the natural surroundings is a building height restriction below the forest canopy and the use of paints that imitate the colour of the native rainforest and dunes. Other measures include an energy efficiency program that employs low-energy bulbs and room key shut-off systems, sewage treatment that uses a self-contained integrated digestion system, and an on-site worm farm that turns organic waste into compost, which is used to fertilise a garden where fresh produce is grown for the resort's restaurant. An environmental code for ecotourists is espoused that discourages inappropriate behaviour towards wildlife and requests that guests apply sunscreen only after swimming, stay on designated tracks and refrain from damaging or removing vegetation.

The plaudits earned by Kingfisher Bay appear overall to be well deserved, although Buckley (2003a) emphasises that negative ecological effects have inevitably been incurred because of the resort's extensive and expanding 'footprint'. He describes the complex as a 'well-landscaped suburb' that essentially functions as a small town with its lodge, docking facilities, self-contained residential villas, swimming pool and other buildings and infrastructure. He questions how the sheer size of Kingfisher Bay and its more recently added villas adhere to the spirit of an ecolodge, and points out that many of the environmental restrictions and practices described above, used heavily to market the resort, were not voluntarily undertaken but were imposed by government because of the resort's special location as an enclave within a World Heritage Site. Also diluting the ecotourism focus is the all-inclusive character of Kingfisher Bay, which offers conventional resort tourist activities, such as beach bathing, fishing, tennis and four-wheel drive tours.

■ 4.5.5 Visitation *quotas and fees*

Zoning and site hardening respectively influence visitation levels in specified areas by defining the activity that is allowed there and providing the facilities to accommodate that level of activity. A potential complementary strategy is to limit the overall number of visitors through the imposition of quotas and user fees. First, the qualifier must be reinforced that absolute visitor numbers and rates of growth on their own are not a reliable indicator of ecological impact. For example, in contrast to such sites as Kingfisher Bay and the Canyon View Information Plaza (see above), three-quarters of all camp sites and 10–30 per cent of all trails in Uganda's Kibale National Park were significantly degraded in 1996, despite an intake of just 5000 visitors, due to the absence of effective site-hardening strategies, non-enforced zoning, poor site selection and inadequate visitor education (Obua & Harding 1997).

Quotas

Quotas are formal restrictions on visitor numbers in a particular area (usually a protected area or a site within a protected area) and over a specified period (often a year, but also seasonally, monthly, weekly, daily or hourly). The Galapagos Islands National Park illustrates an incremental access approach that complements zoning as a means of controlling visitor impact (Weaver 2000b). The Master Plan of 1973 established an annual visitor cap of 12 000, but this was subsequently increased to 25 000 in 1981 and 50 000 in the early 1990s to meet growing ecotourist demand. Concurrently, the number of Intensive and Extensive Visitor Zones (i.e. ecologically less vulnerable zones site-hardened to accommodate tourists) increased from 15 to about 60 to absorb this increase. Fixed carrying capacities in each Intensive Visitor Zone are limited to 12 visitors at any given time and in the Extensive Zone to 90. Occasionally, visitation sites are closed completely to allow for rehabilitation. Despite these precautions and regulations, visitation levels regularly exceeded the quotas, reaching 17 500 in 1980 and 71 500 in 2000 (Taylor, Dyer & Stewart 2003).

User fees

Where formal visitation quotas are not feasible for political or legislative reasons, managers may have the option of implementing a de facto quota through the manipulation of entry and other user fees, the principle being to increase the latter until visitor demand falls below the carrying capacity threshold. This in theory has the advantage of maintaining a high revenue flow without incurring the potentially unsustainable levels of visitation that would otherwise be required to generate this income (Lindberg 1991, Laarman & Gregersen 1996). Curtailment of visitation was not likely to have been the motive of managers in the Costa Rican example described in section 3.4.2, but may be pertinent to such high-fee sites as Mgahinga Gorilla National Park in Uganda, where foreign ecotourists paid a US$175 tracking fee and a US$15 park entry fee in the late 1990s to observe mountain gorillas (Adams & Infield 2003). In this and similar cases, low demand (from about 1500 visitors in 1996–97) is also associated with the high cost of travelling to the site from Europe or North America.

■ 4.5.6 **Wildlife** *viewing and access restrictions*

Given the possible negative impact of wildlife viewing and accessing (see section 4.4.1), it is not surprising that considerable research has been undertaken to identify appropriate modes of ecotourist behaviour. Simple and easily implemented strategies include the suggestion by Jacobsen and Lopez (1994) that the disruption of nesting turtles at Tortuguero National Park (Costa Rica) can be minimised by restricting the use of flashbulbs and avoiding direct contact. At the other extreme, efforts to reduce noise and other interference from scenic overflights in Grand Canyon National Park have entailed highly complex legal negotiations as to aircraft type, flight paths and vertical no-flight buffer zones (see Federal Aviation Administration 2005). Increasingly complicated protocols are also emerging on standards for whale-watching and tourism in Antarctica (see chapter 9). To manage human–bird interactions, Burger, Gochfeld and Niles (1995) suggest that four basic thresholds given below need to be identified:

1. response distance: the distance between bird and human at which the bird makes a visible or measurable response
2. flushing distance: the distance at which the bird leaves its nest or feeding site
3. approach distance: the distance up to which the bird can be approached head-on without disturbance
4. tolerance distance: the distance at which a person can tangentially pass a bird without disturbance.

Because any kind of direct human contact with wildlife may trigger a significant stress response, the Ecology Centre at the Redberry Lake Pelican Project in Saskatchewan (Canada) uses webcams as the primary means of exposing ecotourists to remote pelican colonies (personal observation). It is unclear, however, whether tourists are satisfied with such experiences when they could be just as easily be realised from one's home through 'virtual ecotourism'.

■ 4.5.7 **Visitor** *education*

Carrying capacities can be increased through education that positively influences visitor behaviour. A hundred visitors who have been sensitised to behaving in an environmentally appropriate manner on site (i.e. being quiet, staying on a path and not touching the vegetation or harassing wildlife) will have less impact on a site, all else being equal, than 50 visitors who lack this sensitivity. Managers, however, still face the challenge of conveying appropriate behavioural messages to visitors in a non-dictatorial and friendly way that actually influences visitors' actions (see section 1.4.3 and below).

Codes of conduct

Beyond the incorporation of behavioural education in product interpretation, **codes of conduct** are one popular means of disseminating messages about appropriate behaviour. Although not specifically directed towards ecotourists, the Worldwide Fund for Nature's Code of Conduct for Arctic

Tourists (WWF 2006a) provides a good example of a comprehensive code that incorporates all facets of the visitor experience (see figure 4.6). Notably, wildlife viewing is the topic of just one of 41 recommendations. Advantages of such codes include their simplicity, comprehensiveness and, in most cases, prestigious sponsorship. However, they are also criticised for being voluntary (i.e. entailing recommendations rather than regulations) and self-regulated, and lacking in specific directives. For example, tourists are told not to approach wildlife too closely, but it is left up to the discretion of tourists to determine when they have approached too closely and are not told this distance with regard to major kinds of Arctic wildlife that they are likely to encounter (Weaver 2006).

■ **Figure 4.6**
WWF Code
of Conduct
for Arctic
Tourists

Code of Conduct for Arctic Tourists

1 Make Tourism and Conservation Compatible
- The money you spend on your trip helps determine the development and direction of Arctic tourism. Use your money to support reputable, conservation-minded tour operators and suppliers.
- Get any necessary permits before visiting nature reserves or other protected areas. Leave these areas as you found them and do not disturb the wildlife there.
- Find out about and follow the laws and regulations that protect wildlife in the areas you will visit, and follow them. Learn about the endangered species in these areas, and avoid hunting and fishing of these species, or buying products made from them.
- Your feedback makes a difference. If a tour, tourist service, or supplier was environmentally sensitive and informative, or if it could have been better, tell the owner or operator.
- Become a member of Arctic conservation organisations, and support Arctic conservation projects.

2 Support the Preservation of Wilderness and Biodiversity
- Learn about efforts to conserve Arctic wildlife and habitat, and support them by, for example, giving money, doing volunteer work, educating others on conservation or lobbying governments and business.
- The large undisturbed wilderness areas of the Arctic are a unique environmental resource. Oppose development that fragments these areas or that may disrupt wildlife populations and ecosystems.
- Visit parks and nature reserves. Visitor demand and tourist expenditures support existing protected areas and can lead to the protection of additional nature areas.

(continued)

3 Use Natural Resources in a Sustainable Way

- Walk or use skis, kayaks, boats, dogsleds or other non-motorised means of transportation as much as possible to avoid noise pollution and minimise terrain damage. In particular, minimise use of snow scooters, especially where the snow cover is thin.
- View and photograph wildlife from a distance and remember that in the optimal wildlife viewing experience, the animal never knew you were there. Suppress the natural temptation to move too close and respect signs of distress such as alarm calls, distraction displays, laid-back ears, and raised hair.
- Where laws permit hunting and fishing, obtain the necessary permits, follow all rules, and take only what you require. Fish and hunt only where it is biologically sustainable, and in a manner that does not disrupt local communities.
- Undeveloped natural areas are a resource too — leave them the way that you found them so that others can enjoy them. Don't collect specimens unless it is allowed or you have a permit to do so. Use minimum impact camping techniques, and use existing campsites and trails rather than creating new ones.
- If you travel with a tour, ensure that your tour operator briefs you properly beforehand on the area to be visited, and on what you should do to minimise damage to the site.

4 Minimise Consumption, Waste and Pollution

- Your choice of lodging and products and how much you consume makes a difference. Choose biodegradable or recyclable products and products with minimal packaging.
- Use recycling facilities where available. If you travel with a tour, choose a tour operator who recycles.
- Limit energy use, including your use of heat and warm water.
- Leave as little trace as possible of your visit and take your garbage with you.
- Choose transportation with the least environmental impact — avoid the use of fossil fuels and motorised transport.
- Choose lodgings that have effective waste treatment systems, that recycle, that are energy efficient, and, where possible, that use environmentally friendly energy sources such as solar energy or hydro-electric power.

5 Respect Local Cultures

- Learn about the culture and customs of the areas you will visit before you go.
- Respect the rights of Arctic residents. You are most likely to be accepted and welcomed if you travel with an open mind, learn about local culture and traditions, and respect local customs and etiquette.

(continued)

- If you are not travelling with a tour, let the community you will visit know that you are coming. Supplies are sometimes scarce in the Arctic, so be prepared to bring your own.
- Ask permission before you photograph people or enter their property or living spaces.

6 Respect Historic and Scientific Sites

- Respect historic sites and markets, and do not take any souvenirs. Even structures and sites that look abandoned may be protected by law or valued by local people.
- Keep out of abandoned military installations.
- Respect the work of scientists by arranging your visits to scientific installations beforehand, and by leaving work sites undisturbed.

7 Arctic Communities Should Benefit from Tourism

- The money you spend as a tourist can contribute to the economic survival of the communities you visit.
- Buy local, and choose tour companies, excursions, and suppliers that are locally-owned and that employ local people.
- Buy locally-made products and handicrafts.
- Choose accommodations owned, built, and staffed by local people whenever available.

8 Choose Tours With Trained, Professional Staff

- Select a reputable tour operator who employs trained staff, preferably with Arctic experience.
- Choose a tour operator with staff-client ratio of 15 clients or less per staff member for land-based tours, and 20 passengers or less per staff member for cruises.

9 Make Your Trip an Opportunity to Learn About the Arctic

- Learn about the Arctic environment, particularly in the areas you will visit, before you go. Make your trip an opportunity to learn about conservation in general and Arctic conservation in particular.
- If you travel with a tour, choose one that provides information about the Arctic environment, Arctic conservation, and ways to support Arctic conservation efforts.
- Choose tours and excursions that provide specific information about the climate, species, habitats, local peoples and cultures, and appropriate behaviour in the area you will visit.

10 Follow Safety Rules

- Polar bears, walrus, and muskox are all potentially dangerous and must always be treated with respect. Ensure that you or your group carries guns or other scaring devices in polar bear areas.
- Sled dogs are working animals. Don't feed or caress them. Dogs and Arctic foxes may also carry rabies.

(continued)

- Hiking over ice and glaciers demands specific skills in use of ropes, crampons, ice axes, and other safety equipment. Trained guides should be employed.
- If you go on a trip alone or with others, be sure that local authorities know about your itinerary.
- Be aware of weather conditions, and be prepared for weather that changes suddenly from pleasant to dangerous. Avoid becoming too cold, tired, or wet.
- Basic equipment, even for short excursions, includes warm clothes, sturdy footwear, gloves, a hat, and windproof outer garments. A map, emergency rations such as chocolate, and a basic first aid kit are also essential.

Persuasion

Whether through interpretation or codes of conduct, ecotourists must be persuaded to adhere to the conveyed message. It is alleged that hard ecotourists already possess a high level of environmentalist tendencies that predispose them to behave in accordance with codes of conduct, but this cannot be assumed. In any event, most ecotourists follow a soft trajectory and are likely to require some degree of persuasion, which is a complex process that involves at least six stages and therefore a high potential for target erosion between the message and the action (Petty, McMichael & Brannon 1992): exposure; absorption and reception; interpretation and integration; and action, discussed below.

Exposure
Exposure considers the extent to which the messages are exposed to actual and potential visitors and is therefore largely a matter of effective media dissemination and visitor interception. Additional considerations include whether the exposure is pre-visit, during the visit or, more rarely, post-visit.

Absorption and reception
Absorption describes the proportion of those exposed who actually see, read and/or hear the target message. Relevant considerations include the use of techniques (e.g. bright colours, flashing lights, provocative images, loud noises) that maximise absorption. Reception considers whether the message enters the memory and makes more than a momentary impression on the recipient.

Interpretation and integration
Interpretation is the process through which recipients make sense of a message and form an opinion about it, while integration considers whether the message makes a long-term impression on their values and attitudes.

Action
Finally, those who reach the integration stage can either (a) choose to act in accordance with the message, (b) choose not to act at all, or (c) act in a way that contradicts the message. The latter scenario is demonstrated by local residents who deliberately harm wildlife after being excluded from carrying

out traditional activities in a protected area (see chapter 5) or by vandals seeking to defy authority.

The probability of translating behavioural messages into appropriate visitor action is increased to the extent that five types of factor can be successfully manipulated (Petty, McMichael & Brannon 1992). *Channel factors* consider how the message is delivered. The WWF Code is not widely disseminated among potential or actual Arctic tourists, and hence it experiences massive erosion during the exposure stage. In contrast, almost all visitors to the South Rim area of Grand Canyon National Park are intercepted at the plaza and exposed to selected messages whether they want to be or not. Park managers also place messages on billboards along major access highways. *Source factors* are concerned with who delivers the message and what kind of power they exert in doing so. The WWF exhibits a high level of legitimacy power because of its reputation, but this may be irrelevant given the high level of erosion at the exposure stage. Park rangers who act as uniformed interpreters display legitimacy as well as coercion and expert power, thereby reducing the erosion factor. Referent power is illustrated by the use of a messenger who has celebrity appeal among a target audience. *Message factors* include whether the message is conveyed rationally or emotionally, formally or in the vernacular and so on. Finally, *receiver factors* consider the characteristics of the target audience while *situational factors* describe the actual idiosyncratic circumstances that occur when a message is being delivered. Even the most dedicated ecotourist, for example, might behave inappropriately if the weather is inclement or they become ill.

Ultimately, the capacity to persuade tourists to act responsibly is but one strategy among many that must be employed in order to achieve ecologically sustainable outcomes in ecotourism destinations (see 'In the Field: Reducing the negative impact of ecotourism on shore birds in New Jersey').

IN THE FIELD
Reducing the negative impact of ecotourism on shore birds in New Jersey

Delaware Bay, on the mid-Atlantic coast of the USA, is a major ecotourist destination for two or three weeks each late May and early June when more than a million shorebirds migrate through the area. It also offers a unique scientific case study of ecotourism impact and how it has been affected by a series of management decisions over a 20-year period. During 1982, 1987, 1992 and again in 2002, the researchers (Burger et al. 2004) undertook detailed observations of birdwatcher activity and its effects on shorebirds at nine locations. They found that foraging behaviour was disrupted throughout the study period by the presence of humans (i.e. the birds did not habituate to the proximity of humans), who caused them in a majority of cases to fly away and not return to that same location. In 1982, disturbance by birders was minimal despite the absence of management controls, since they accounted for only 2 per cent of the humans on the beach. However, by 1987, birders accounted for 30 per cent of all disturbances. Restrictive signs were placed by government and conservation organisations on beaches where shorebirds concentrated, but no enforcement was undertaken. Birder disturbances increased to 44 per cent by 1992, despite the added construction of a viewing platform at one of the most popular viewing beaches. Again, no enforcement was provided. In 2002, a dramatic reversal occurred with birders accounting for no disturbances at all. The researchers attribute this to the successful implementation of the New Jersey Endangered and Nongame Species Program by the state government and the New Jersey Audubon Society, which resulted in more effective signage, restricted access provisions, additional viewing platforms and patrols by officers empowered to issue summonses for infractions.

Management also recognised the need to simultaneously control non-ecotourist human disturbances. During all four periods, the single largest group of beach users in the study area consisted of walkers, whose unleashed dogs were a major disruptive factor. By the early 2000s, education and enforcement initiatives resulted in a minimal negative impact from this group as well. A second critical non-ecotourism measure was a ban on the harvesting of horseshoe crabs, a major food source of the shorebirds. With disturbance of the shorebirds now at a minimum, the Delaware Bay case study demonstrates clearly the positive conservation and recreational outcomes that can be obtained through sound government intervention and partnerships with environmental organisations.

4.6 $\int$UMMARY

When assessing the ecological impact of ecotourism, a distinction should be made between genuine ecotourism and tourism that deliberately or naively claims to be ecotourism but does not meet the associated criteria. The impact of genuine ecotourism can be both positive and negative, the latter being mostly unintended. A major ecological benefit of ecotourism is its potential role in providing incentives for preserving and restoring natural environments by putting a monetary value on natural attractions. The sector can also provide funds for the maintenance and enhancement of natural areas, and ecotourists contribute additionally through their actions and donations. By giving financial value to natural areas, ecotourism can also foster pro-environmental values among local residents and reinforce such values among ecotourists and other participants. The financial dimension would seem to favour soft ecotourism because of its volume, whereas the action or donation aspect may favour hard ecotourists with their higher environmentalist tendencies. Ecological costs are associated with building and the generation of wastes, although these are often localised and offset by the revenues they generate. Ecotourist activities are more problematic given the uncertainties associated with the consequences of wildlife observation, the effects of hiking and diving, and the danger of introducing exotic species. Hard ecotourists are implicated in many of these consequences due to their dispersion into relatively undisturbed areas and the lack of mediation by rangers or other enforcement personnel. Other potential costs include induced development, the unintended opening up of areas to more harmful forms of tourism, transit effects and mismanagement caused by placing variable financial value on specific elements of an ecosystem. All seem more likely to occur in the context of minimalist soft ecotourism.

Management strategies that attempt to minimise the ecological costs and maximise the benefits of ecotourism make implicit or explicit assumptions as to whether a site's carrying capacity for visitors is flexible (favouring soft ecotourism) or fixed (favouring hard ecotourism). Among the options for protected area managers are zoning constraints, site hardening and softening measures, green design principles and environmental management systems and the application of visitor quotas and user fees (i.e. unofficial quotas). Negative ecological impact can also be mitigated through regulations governing wildlife viewing and access and through interpretation and codes of conduct that effectively and persuasively impart messages about appropriate visitor behaviour.

QUESTIONS

1. (a) Why does the term 'ecotourism' provoke a cynical reaction from many people?
   (b) What can the ecotourism industry do to reduce this cynicism?

2. (a) What is meant by the contention that ecotourism potentially provides both a preservation and rehabilitation incentive?
   (b) Under what conditions is this incentive effect most likely to be realised?

3. (a) What single factor is most likely to influence whether a wildlife–ecotourist encounter is ecologically sustainable?
   (b) What other factors must be taken into account when managing these encounters?

4. (a) Why is ecotourism sometimes referred to as a 'Trojan Horse'?
   (b) Under what circumstances is the reference valid, and what can be done to minimise this problem?

5. (a) Broadly speaking, how is the ecological impact presented in this chapter likely to vary between soft and hard ecotourists?
   (b) Can any conclusions therefore be drawn as to the relative desirability of both types of ecotourist?
   (c) What other factors are likely to influence whether the ecological impact of ecotourism is positive or negative?

6 (a) How do the concepts of fixed and flexible carrying capacity relate to hard and soft ecotourism?
(b) How do assumptions about carrying capacity influence the management of ecotourism impact?

7 (a) What are the advantages and disadvantages of codes of conduct as vehicles for visitor education?
(b) How could they be improved?

FURTHER READING

Buckley, R (ed.) 2004b, *Environmental Impacts of Ecotourism,* **CAB International, Wallingford, UK.** Twenty-five chapters in this edited volume focus on the impact of wildlife viewing as well as the transportation and overnight stays required to engage in such activity. A global perspective is adopted, although several chapters focus on Australian case studies.

Hall, CM & Boyd, S (eds) 2005, *Nature-based Tourism in Peripheral Areas: Development or Disaster?* **Channel View, Clevedon, UK.** Ecotourism features prominently in this analysis of the character and impact of nature-based tourism throughout the world. The text is organised by geography, the two main sections respectively being concerned with alpine, forest and subpolar settings, and island, coastal and marine settings.

Higginbottom, K (ed.) 2004, *Wildlife Tourism: Impacts, Management and Planning,* **Common Ground Publishing, Altona, Vic.** Although covering wildlife tourism in general, this edited volume has several chapters that consider the impact of wildlife viewing specifically as well as management techniques for mitigating it.

Krüger, O 2005, 'The role of ecotourism in conservation: Panacea or Pandora's box?', *Biodiversity and Conservation* **14: 579–600.** The author analyses 251 international case studies in ecotourism from the literature in order to identify the factors that give rise to positive or negative ecological impact.

Newsome, D, Moore, S & Dowling, R 2002, *Natural Area Tourism: Ecology, Impacts and Management,* **Channel View, Clevedon, UK.** This excellent volume begins with a section on the ecological perspective, then examines the environmental impact of ecotourism and related forms of activity, visitor planning, management strategies, and interpretation. Global case studies are utilised.

Peering at the penguins
in New Zealand and Australia

Penguins rate very highly as charismatic megafauna, yet they are inaccessible to most people as non-captive wildlife because of their concentration in remote sub-Antarctic and Antarctic ecosystems. Several penguin colonies, however, occur in the southern parts of New Zealand and Australia, leading to the creation of important viewing sites at Sandfly Bay (New Zealand) and the Penguin Parade on Phillip Island (Australia).

The Sandfly Bay site on the Otago Peninsula hosts a small population of rare Hoiho or Yellow-eyed Penguins (*Megadyptes antipodes*) as well as a diverse array of other unusual mammals and birds, including New Zealand fur seals, albatross and New Zealand sea lions. During the early 2000s, two commercial operators provided penguin-viewing tours, but access to the Conservation Estate (a higher-order protected area) that was established to protect the penguins was available to non-paying visitors as well, there being no entry fee to the estate. All visitors must transit through private farmland whose owner has granted a right of way (Shelton & Lübcke 2005). The New Zealand Department of Conservation, which manages the protected area, provides an interpretive panel at the nearest road access point with the permission of the local city council. Other panels in the estate carry similar conservationist and educational messages and are deliberately situated to steer tourists away from the area on the coastline where penguins emerge from the sea, to an observation blind where viewing can be undertaken in a non-disruptive way.

Despite these precautions, conflicts have been reported between paying tour participants, whose guides apparently try to implement a basic code of visitor conduct, and non-paying visitors, whose behaviour and motives is more variable. Shelton and Lübcke (2005) also point out an additional layer of potential conflict between environmentalists who view the penguins as essentially 'sacred' and casual spectators who seek to be entertained by the Charlie Chaplin-like movement of the 'profane' penguins. Another important issue is the inadequacy of viewing facilities that cannot accommodate all spectators, who now number around 20 000 per year. This is important given that penguins who see humans on the beach are more likely to remain at sea (and hence delay chick feeding and incubation) until the humans are gone (Shelton & Lübcke 2005).

A major concern for Sandfly Bay is the disconnection between rapidly growing visitation levels, which are indicative of the early development stage of the destination lifecycle, and the relatively rudimentary state of visitor management and regulation despite the protected area status of the site. Few measures are in place to reduce the probability of human interference in penguin activity, and ecotourists both soft and hard must compete with each other and with local residents and other tourists for access to the site. Negative impact on the penguins is increasing, although Shelton and Lübcke (2005) note that they have survived millennia of catastrophic as well as gradual environmental change and are currently threatened as much or more by feral and native predators as by tourism. Nevertheless, this is no basis for complacency about the potential impact that will arise from continued increases in largely unregulated visitation.

Very different from Sandfly Bay is the Penguin Parade near Melbourne, which hosts a colony of little penguins (*Eudyptula minor*). Although mostly unregulated until the 1960s, human activity at the site is now strictly regulated under a series of five-year management plans implemented and enforced by the Phillip Island Nature Park Board of Management (PINPBM). This board is mandated to protect the penguins and their habitat, to provide opportunities for viewing and interpretation, and to be socially responsible. Significantly, the board is also required to operate the park in a financially viable way.

Evidence suggests that the parade has been successful in both ecological and economic terms. For example, an impressive revenue stream has been generated by visitation levels that exceed 500 000 per year (Phillip Island 2006a), given admission prices set at A$17.40 per adult or A$43.50 for a family of four in 2006. Additional income is generated through the sales of penguin-related paraphernalia, food and other goods at an on-site visitors centre (Phillip Island 2006b). These revenues are returned to the parade, and the nature park more generally, to pay for a diverse and sophisticated array of site management measures, including ongoing scientific research projects; strict limitations on and design of site-hardened areas, such as parking lots and boardwalks; the preservation of most of the site's dunes and vegetation; and rehabilitation of habitat through selective vegetation removal and replanting to improve penguin breeding success. To view the nightly parade (i.e. the return of the penguins from the sea in the evening) a 4000-seat viewing platform and a specialised viewing boardwalk have been constructed, and the taking of photographs is prohibited. An innovative practice is the posting of an educational brochure on the park's website, which can be downloaded in English or 10 other languages (Phillip Island 2006b). Although the platform itself is visually obtrusive, no major negative effects on the penguins are apparent, and their numbers had actually increased by 2006 (Phillip Island 2006a).

Although Harris (2002), accordingly, describes the parade as a good example of win-win soft ecotourism, others are more critical. Head (2000), for example, sees danger in the fact that successful ecological outcomes there seem to depend on the full-scale commodification of the penguin colony. He also regards with ambivalence a strategy that seeks to juxtapose spaces where all traces of contemporary human activity are discouraged to intensively site-hardened spaces where extremely high densities of human activity are both accommodated and encouraged. It is unclear therefore whether Phillip Island provides the most appropriate or feasible developmental model for Sandfly Bay, which remains a highly contested space where the *status quo* of stakeholder conflict and *laissez-faire* management is no longer tolerable.

(continued)

Questions

1 (a) What positive and negative ecological impact is evident at the two sites?

(b) How is the negative impact being reduced in each case, and how could it be further reduced?

2 (a) Does the Penguin Parade provide a realistic model of what the managers of the Sandfly Bay site should aspire to?

(b) Why, or why not?

3 (a) Is it necessary for penguins at the two sites to be treated as a spectacle in order to ensure their protection?

(b) What ethical dilemma, if any, does this spectacle dimension raise for ecotourism?

5

Economic
and sociocultural
impact

LEARNING OBJECTIVES

After reading this chapter, you should be able to:

- describe the potential direct and indirect economic and sociocultural benefits that can be realised by ecotourism destinations

- discuss the potential direct and indirect economic and sociocultural costs that are associated with ecotourism

- indicate how these costs and benefits are likely to vary between hard and soft ecotourism

- assess the geographical and sociocultural circumstances under which community-based ecotourism projects are most likely to be pursued

- identify the factors that increase the probability that community-based ecotourism projects will be successful in generating benefits over the long term for local residents.

It is widely understood that the sustainability criterion of ecotourism includes economic and sociocultural dimensions in addition to the ecological dimension discussed in chapter 4; that is, ecotourism must contribute to the economic, social and cultural wellbeing of communities living close to ecotourism venues, and other legitimate stakeholders, at the same time as it serves to minimise its ecological costs and maximise its ecological benefits. Although ecotourism ideally should also facilitate the wellbeing and satisfaction of visitors, that issue is addressed here only tangentially and is explored further in chapter 6 as part of the discussion of the financial viability of ecotourism-related businesses. The main purpose of chapter 5 is to focus on potential economic and sociocultural costs and benefits of ecotourism, both direct and indirect. Sections 5.2 and 5.3 respectively consider the economic benefits and costs, and section 5.4 discusses the sociocultural benefits and costs. Throughout these sections, the interrelationships among the economic, sociocultural and ecological effects are considered along with the influence of hard and soft ecotourism. Section 5.5 concludes the main body of the chapter by examining the role of community-based ecotourism model as a potential vehicle for maximising the positive economic and sociocultural impact and minimising the associated negative impact. The emphasis in this section is on the factors that contribute to successful outcomes.

5.2 $\mathcal{E}$CONOMIC BENEFITS ....

For many decision-makers, economic factors are more influential than ecological factors in deciding how a particular natural resource should be used. Therefore, beyond the incentive and funding effects described in chapter 4, the ecological benefits of ecotourism often eventuate as a desirable side effect after the economic benefits to people, such as the actual amount of revenue and jobs generated, have first been demonstrated. The direct and indirect economic benefits discussed in the following subsections are outlined in figure 5.1.

■ **Figure 5.1**
Potential economic benefits of ecotourism

DIRECT BENEFITS	INDIRECT BENEFITS
• Generates revenue and employment • Provides economic opportunities for peripheral regions	• High multiplier effect and indirect revenue and employment • Stimulation of mass tourism • Supports cultural and heritage tourism

■ 5.2.1 Direct *benefits*

The direct economic benefits of ecotourism include the generation of revenue and employment and the provision of economic opportunities for remote and peripheral regions.

Generation of revenue and employment

Like all forms of tourism, ecotourism involves visitor expenditures and the creation of employment that is directly related to the sector. To illustrate, international visitors, engaging largely in ecotourism-related activities, spent A$1.644 billion in the Great Barrier Reef Marine Park and its catchment area (i.e. the land where rivers flow towards the reef) during the 2004–05 fiscal year, 40 per cent of which was allocated to hotels, food and beverage, 19 per cent to 'trade' and 15 per cent to transportation. These expenditures, furthermore, generated the equivalent of 13 000 full-time jobs in the catchment area (GBRMPA 2005). The restriction in this example to international visitors is deliberate, since the Australian Government (which manages the marine park) is primarily interested in the generation of new revenue from outside the country rather than the redistribution of revenue from one part of Australia to another by domestic tourists, which does not generate new net wealth for the country as a whole. If assessed just from the perspective of the residents of the catchment area, the direct revenue and employment totals are much greater (A$3.673 billion and the equivalent of 25 000 full-time jobs) due to the additional inclusion of expenditure by *domestic* visitors from other parts of Queensland and the rest of Australia.

Even where the direct revenues are not as substantial as in the above example, ecotourism can still have a significant bearing on the wealth and economic empowerment of local residents (see the case study 'John Gray's Sea Canoe' at the end of this chapter). Kiss (2004) reports that an ecotourism project in Peru during the early 2000s yielded a mean annual income of just US$735 to households in the community. However, this accounted for 27 per cent of all income (other activities together generated US$1995) and therefore represented a substantial and crucial supplement to household revenue. Similarly, 20 per cent of the US$181 000 in commercial expenditure generated by ecotourists in the Apo Island Marine Sanctuary (Philippines) during 1999 went directly to local residents, whose income is otherwise minimal (Cadiz & Calumpong 2002). Tyynelä and Rantala (2004) provide a grassroots illustration of this impact in describing 15 Finnish ecotourists each paying the equivalent of US$15 in cash to local residents for carvings at an ecotourism site in Malawi, this amount being equal to half of the average local monthly income. Significant revenue can also be obtained from revenue-sharing schemes. An example is associated with Bwindi Impenetrable National Park in Uganda, where in 1998–99 US$70 000 of ecotourist-derived park revenue was distributed equally to 19 municipalities bordering the park (Archabald & Naughton-Treves 2001). As with income, ecotourism-related employment can have a major positive effect on small communities even if the number of jobs appears to be small from the perspective of a large destination. For example, an ecotourism project near the Greek villages of Dadia and Lefkimi generated 50 full- and part-time jobs for a community numbering just 1100 residents and supported a Women's Cooperative with 34 members that operates a restaurant and grocery (Svoronou & Holden 2005).

Economic opportunities for peripheral regions

Ecotourism is one of the few service sector activities that can stimulate sustainable economic development in peripheral regions, such as the Australian Outback, the rainforests of Central and South America, northern Thailand and the East African savanna. In economically depressed destinations such as Tasmania (Australia), where the traditional mainstays of logging and mining are declining due to resource depletion, depressed commodity prices and pressure from the environmental lobby, ecotourism is being promoted as a viable development alternative. Much of Tasmania's remaining natural habitat is occupied by World Heritage-designated protected areas, and there was growing interest during the 1990s in the potential of ecotourism — and tourism more generally — to propel the state's economy into an era of post-industrial rejuvenation (Peattie, Hanson & Walker 1999). This had not occurred by the early 2000s, although the Tasmanian Budget Speech of 2006–07 featured a commitment to promote tourism as a 'key economic driver for the State' (Parliament of Tasmania 2006). Similar interest is evident in the Appalachian region of the USA, where ecotourism and other nature-based forms of tourism are supplanting the traditional reliance on mining and logging (Fritsch & Johannsen 2004).

■ 5.2.2 Indirect *benefits*

The indirect economic benefits of ecotourism include the **multiplier effect** (a measure of ongoing indirect economic benefits accruing to a destination through the internal circulation of direct tourist expenditure) and related revenue and employment. In addition, ecotourism stimulates mass tourism and cultural and heritage tourism.

High multiplier effect and indirect revenue and employment

Most calculations of economic benefit in ecotourism research use such techniques as Input/Output (IO) modelling that take into account the indirect and induced consequences of the multiplier effect. Indirect effects occur when a hotel uses tourist expenditures to purchase local food or pay its employees, then when the recipients of this income do the same and so on. Induced effects include the goods and services purchased locally by these employees with their hotel wages (Weaver & Lawton 2006). Resulting employment can similarly be divided into direct, indirect and induced outcomes.

Ecotourism's association with a relatively high multiplier effect is supported by evidence from Lamington National Park, in which almost 80 per cent of respondents from two ecolodges indicated that they try to support the local economy of destinations that they visit (Weaver & Lawton 2002). This effect might be expected to pertain more to exotic ecodestinations in the Third World that need this support and offer an attractive culture to 'consume', but it is also evident in developed countries, such as Australia. In 2004–05, international visitors to the Great Barrier Reef Marine Park and its catchment area generated indirect expenditure of A\$657 million in that area (i.e. a 40 per cent increase to the direct expenditure of A\$1.644 billion — see above) and an additional 4000 full-time equivalent jobs accruing mostly to the finance, property and business services sector, agriculture and trade (GBRMPA 2005). Powell and Chambers (cited in Lindberg 2001) estimated that the A$3.2 million spent annually by 160 000 visitors to Dorrigo National Park (Australia) resulted in A$4 million in regional output, A$1.5 million in regional household income and payments to 71 employees.

Stimulation of mass tourism

An indirect economic benefit of ecotourism derives from the fact that many mass tourists visit particular destinations because of the availability of diversionary wildlife-based attractions. This is illustrated by Kenya, where a majority of inbound tourists from Europe have traditionally selected this destination because of the opportunity it provides to view wildlife (Akama 1996). Yet ecolodges near the most popular protected areas account for only a minuscule proportion of the country's overnight accommodation. Sindiga (1996) explains this apparent discrepancy by describing the typical inbound experience as involving overnight accommodation and concentration of activity in the gateway cities of Nairobi and/or Mombasa as well as one or two safari excursions (usually day only) to nearby protected areas, such as Amboseli, Tsavo or Maasai Mara. These visitors therefore fit the profile of the soft ecotourist. The implication is that Kenya's resort industry indirectly owes its existence to safari-based ecotourism. However, to the extent that Kenya's mass tourism industry shows evidence of ecological unsustainability (Sindiga 2000), this issue can also be regarded as an indirect ecological cost of ecotourism.

Support for cultural and heritage tourism

The logic of the mass tourism–ecotourism linkage also applies to cultural and heritage tourism. These sectors are highly compatible with ecotourism, and ecotourists are therefore likely to support them as value-added supplementary attractions. Ecotourism and cultural/heritage tourism are mutually supportive in many destinations, including the Mayan region of southern Mexico and Central America and the Angkor Wat area of Cambodia. In indigenous communities in Australia, New Zealand, Canada and the USA, the interrelationships are even more pronounced (see section 9.5).

Economic benefits from areas protected for ecotourism

Natural areas that are protected for ecotourism purposes provide economic returns from their environmental benefits. These include the exploitation of biodiversity for pharmaceutical purposes, the sustainable harvesting of seed and other products and the benefits provided by flood control and the maintenance of water supplies (Dixon & Sherman 1990).

5.3 ECONOMIC COSTS

Direct and indirect economic costs associated with ecotourism are listed in figure 5.2 (p. 128).

DIRECT COSTS	INDIRECT COSTS
• Start-up expenses (acquisition of land, establishment of protected areas, superstructure, infrastructure) • Ongoing expenses (maintenance of infrastructure, promotion, wages)	• Revenue uncertainties • Revenue leakage due to imports and non-local participation • Opportunity costs • Damage to crops by wildlife

■ **Figure 5.2**
Potential economic costs of ecotourism

■ 5.3.1 Direct *costs*

The direct economic costs of ecotourism include start-up and ongoing expenses. Unlike other costs discussed in this chapter, these should not be considered as a 'negative impact' since direct financial outlays are a normal and inevitable business expense associated with any ecotourism development. Moreover, they are clearly a benefit to the recipients of these outlays. Negative implications may emerge, however, if the costs are insufficient, excessive, improperly allocated or managed, or if they indicate long-term dependence on donors (see section 5.5). Unfortunately, very few studies rigorously investigate the cost or funding aspects of ecotourism-related developments, despite their critical role in determining the success of such operations. Start-up expenses include the purchase or lease of land and the establishment of infrastructure and such services as interpretation trails, visitor centres and parking facilities. Ongoing expenses include upkeep and maintenance of land and facilities, labour costs and marketing. The size and distribution of these expenses in any given situation depends upon many factors, including orientation towards hard or soft ecotourism (the latter requiring far more facilities and services investment), public or private sector control, the availability of land, the market image of the destination and the size of the operation.

■ 5.3.2 Indirect *costs*

The indirect economic costs of ecotourism include revenue uncertainties that exist because of the high risk factor inherent in tourism, revenue leakages, opportunity costs and damage caused by wildlife.

Revenue uncertainties

Revenue uncertainties in tourism are associated with inherent demand-and-supply-side risks. In the former case, leisure tourism is a discretionary form of expenditure that consumers are likely to curtail during times of economic or social uncertainty. For example, the September 11, 2001 terrorist attacks on New York and Washington, followed by recessionary conditions in the USA, resulted in a 10 per cent decline in the number of inbound visitors to Australia from that country between 2001 and 2003 (Tourism Australia 2002, 2004, 2006). However, domestic or international short-haul travel may be substituted for international long-haul travel, demonstrating that a cost to one destination may be a benefit for another. The question of fashion is also relevant, since it is still unclear whether ecotourism is merely trendy or an indication of fundamental social and cultural change (see chapter 2). Even if it is the latter, specific ecotourism destinations will no doubt fall in and out of fashion in the manner of 3S tourism resorts.

On the supply side, political and social unrest are major risk factors in many parts of the world, especially when tourists or ecotourists in particular are targeted by dissidents and terrorists in areas where government control is nominal. An ecotourism-specific example is Bwindi Impenetrable National Park (see section 5.2.1), where the kidnapping of an ecotourist in 1999 caused an immediate decline in monthly visitation from 700 to about 50 (Archabald & Naughton-Treves 2001). Disease outbreaks and seasonality, respectively, are unpredictable and predictable supply-side factors that can induce substantial fluctuations in visitation to tropical ecotourism destinations (see chapter 7).

Revenue leakage

The magnitude of the multiplier effect is limited by the need to import at least some goods and services, which subsequently induces a **revenue leakage** effect. Despite the alleged tendency of ecotourists to consume local goods, Lindberg (2001) estimates that at least 90 per cent of ecotourism revenue in most local destinations is lost through leakage; that is, only 10 per cent of expenditure is retained to stimulate indirect and induced effects. Only about 6 per cent of expenditure is retained, for example, within local communities near Tortuguero National Park in Costa Rica and the Annapurna Conservation Area in Nepal. The retention is even lower in a whale-watching area on Mexico's Baja Peninsula. This effect is arguably more pronounced in destinations dominated by soft ecotourists, who are seen to prefer familiar goods and services (Weaver & Lawton 2006). Local-scale leakage, in any case, may be considered problematic from a national perspective only if these lost revenues are gained by foreign rather than domestic suppliers, indicating that scale (i.e. whether the assessment is at the local, state or national level) can influence whether a given leakage effect is regarded as a cost or benefit.

Opportunity costs

Income that is foregone by not using an area for a particular purpose is an **opportunity cost**. For example, the revenues gained through exclusive ecotourism use should be weighed against the revenue that would have been obtained if the area had been used instead for agriculture, mining or logging. As discussed above, ecotourism in some areas may constitute a more economically rational long-term use of the natural environment, but this advantageous position cannot always be assumed due to differences in demand from one place to another. In any case, there is an immediate 'opportunity cost' in terms of loggers, farm labourers and miners who lose their jobs and are not always able to find alternative employment in the new ecotourism-based economy.

Damage to crops by wildlife

Indirect economic costs are realised when wildlife that is protected because of its ecotourism value causes damage to community assets such as farmland

and livestock. In the buffer zone around Nanada Devi Biosphere Reserve in India, livestock predation by leopards is a major problem, as is crop damage caused mainly by monkeys and wild boar. Total losses per year incurred by the 10 villages in the study are estimated to be about US$45 000 (Rao et al. 2002). Similarly, villagers adjacent to the Bhadra Tiger Reserve in South India each year lose 5 per cent of their livestock to tigers and other large felines and 11 per cent of their crops to elephants (Madhusudan 2003). In the Great Plains region of North America, many grain farmers complain that migratory waterfowl cause extensive crop damage. The issue to date in North America has focused on the quest for compensation from hunters, but ecotourism will be implicated increasingly as wildlife viewing grows in importance. One relevant challenge will be the apportioning of responsibility for wildlife damage among ecotourists, hunters and protected area managers (see section 7.3). In addition, there is a danger that perceptions of inadequate compensation will generate negative social and environmental costs by fostering landowner antipathy towards wildlife as well as tourists, as has occurred in both of the Indian case studies cited above.

5.4 SOCIOCULTURAL IMPACT

A holistic perspective on ecotourism must advocate sociocultural as well as ecological sustainability (section 1.4.4). This can be argued on a purely ethical basis, but also on the more pragmatic assumption that satisfied local communities provide the support for ecotourism that allows environmental benefits to be realised as well (sections 4.3 and 5.5). The direct and indirect sociocultural impact of ecotourism discussed in this section are outlined in figure 5.3.

■ **Figure 5.3**
Potential sociocultural benefits of ecotourism

DIRECT AND INDIRECT BENEFITS

- Fosters community stability and wellbeing through economic benefits and local participation
- Aesthetic and spiritual benefits and enjoyment for residents and tourists
- Accessible to a broad spectrum of the population

■ 5.4.1 Direct *and indirect benefits*

Ecotourism revenue and employment (see section 5.2.1) fosters community stability and wellbeing, especially if these are accompanied by a high degree of local control. Such empowerment can also have important psychological benefits insofar as it confirms an ability to be more financially independent and allows local residents to present their culture and surroundings to appreciative visitors. This impulse is particularly important in indigenous communities where ecotourism involvement contributes to the reassertion of traditional rights (see section 9.5). In addition, just as areas protected for ecotourism provide indirect environmental and economic benefits, so too do they provide indirect social benefits through the enjoyment experienced by local residents and other visitors. Social benefits also derive from the fact that soft ecotourism is accessible to virtually anyone since it does not require special skills or equipment, can be relatively inexpensive and can be tailored to accommodate individuals with substantial physical and mental limitations. Frequently, the ecotourism experience is associated with a high aesthetic or spiritual component for individual participants. In the Lamington National Park study (Weaver & Lawton 2002), 50 per cent of respondents indicated that they had had ecotourism experiences that were intensely spiritual in nature.

■ 5.4.2 Direct *costs*

However well intended, ecotourism can incur direct sociocultural costs through its intrusiveness, its imposition of alien value systems, the erosion of local control, the displacement of people through the creation of protected areas and the disruption of local social relationships (see figure 5.4).

DIRECT COSTS	INDIRECT COSTS
• Cultural and social intrusion • Imposes an elite alien value system • Erosion of local control (employment of foreign experts, in-migration of job seekers) • Local inequalities and internecine disputes	• Potential for local resentment or antagonism • Tourist opposition to aspects of local culture and lifestyle (e.g. hunting, slash/burn agriculture)

■ **Figure 5.4**
Potential sociocultural costs of ecotourism

Cultural and social intrusion

Host societies cope with tourism by formally or informally differentiating between **backstage** space where local culture is retained for unselfconscious consumption within the community and **frontstage** space where an adapted version of local culture and behaviour is self-consciously provided for tourist consumption (MacCannell 1976). Hard ecotourists in particular may intrude for long periods into the backstage of local communities, thereby creating the potential for social and cultural disruption. This is sometimes evident, for example, in ecotourism involving volunteers residing for a long period in a local village, especially when these tourists are motivated primarily by egotistical considerations (Wearing 2001). Local communities and ecotourism operators may induce or exacerbate this effect by promoting the 'authenticity' of the destination as an attraction and by integrating ecotourism accommodation and other services into the community in a way that merges or confuses frontstage and backstage spaces.

Imposition of an elite alien value system

Despite its alleged preference for sociocultural sustainability through community empowerment (see section 5.5), ecotourism is fundamentally based on an elitist Western or Eurocentric value system that is often imposed on destinations under the assumption that ecotourism is the mode of tourism development preferred by local residents and best for them. This sub-conscious form of imperialism, or what Cater (2006) refers to as 'cultural hegemony', is abetted more overtly by the flow of relatively wealthy ecotourists from the developed countries to the less-developed countries, by the extensive involvement in ecotourism there of entrepreneurs and aid agencies from the developed world and by the dominance in the literature of academics from Australia, New Zealand, Canada, the UK and the USA. Ecotourism therefore appears to be a form of neocolonialism that entails a high degree of dependency on the wealthy countries for funding, markets, capital, skills and knowledge (see section 5.5).

Marketing reinforces this Eurocentric dominance when it emphasises travel to 'remote' and 'unspoiled' destinations where 'primitive' cultures with their 'traditional' and 'authentic' lifestyle eagerly wait to be 'discovered' by the intrepid white tourist–explorer. Ecotourism advocates who express a bias for 'unspoiled' cultures and natural environments seem to suggest that these destinations should not attempt to attain the levels of economic development that relatively wealthy and highly educated eco-tourists enjoy in their own home regions. Cynical observers such as Wheeller (1994) contend that the average ecotourist is nothing more than an 'ego-tourist' who travels more to enhance their own status and self-awareness than to engage in any genuine dialogue between equals with local residents. For such tourists, every new destination is another trophy that adds to the display.

Erosion of local control

Ecotourism can facilitate and/or erode local control depending on how it evolves. The community-based model discussed in section 5.5 is based on the principle of long-term local empowerment, but high levels of local participation to achieve this objective may be offset by continued dependency on outside aid and skills as the community becomes increasingly embedded in the world economy. Whether this is ultimately a good or bad development for local communities in peripheral areas is a matter of interpretation and a highly political issue. The disadvantages of dependency, for example, may be offset by improvements in material wellbeing and opportunity, which again in turn can lead to cultural erosion, out-migration and health problems associated with 'modern' lifestyles. Local control can also be eroded by the influx of internal migrants that often follows the emergence of mass ecotourism in such places as Monteverde in Costa Rica (section 4.4.2).

Local inequalities and internecine disputes

It is a truism that the costs and benefits of ecotourism (as with all other forms of tourism) are never equally distributed within a destination and that resentment can result when certain groups or individuals perceive that they are bearing too many costs or not deriving enough benefits. Timothy and White (1999) report that intra-community harmony was disrupted in a remote part of Belize when a group of villagers established a successful ecolodge and other villagers promptly opened a competing facility. In New Zealand, many non-Maori in Kaikoura resent the perceived preference given to Maori in operating highly successful whale-watching tours (see the case study 'Whale-watching and Maori empowerment in Kaikoura, New Zealand' at the end of chapter 9). Even the prospect of an ecotourism development can be contentious, as when a proposal in the Gambia was indefinitely postponed after rival families began to fight over who would manage the facility once it was opened (Jones 2005). In some cases, ecotourism can serve to reinforce the power of the local elite, which has a competitive advantage over other members of the community because of its existing wealth and influence. The negative social implications of such a situation, however, may not be apparent to outside observers, who are pleased that the operation is 'locally controlled'.

■ 5.4.3 Indirect *sociocultural costs*

The effects described in section 5.4.2 can lead to a sense of antagonism towards ecotourists or other non-local ecotourism stakeholders, and there are also circumstances under which tourists may become resentful of local residents (see figure 5.4).

Potential for local resentment or antagonism

Local antipathy towards ecotourism and ecotourists, at least among some residents, can occur in conjunction with resentment over the loss of homes and resources to protected areas or perceptions of inadequate compensation for these losses. Although this issue is usually associated with the establishment of public protected areas, the growing trend towards private sector parks is a concern since these may be even more restrictive in providing access to local residents. Resentment or antagonism towards ecotourists is also likely to result from the aforementioned inequity in the distribution of costs and benefits within the local community (see section 5.5). In either case, a major implication for destinations is that negative attitudes and actions directed towards tourists can lead to bad publicity and subsequent economic costs because of reduced visitation (see section 5.3.2). It is not clear, however, whether this is a significant issue, given the lack of empirical research into this issue.

Tourist opposition to aspects of local culture and lifestyle

Conflict and negative publicity can occur if there is incompatibility between local lifestyles and the expectations and values of ecotourists — a likely scenario given the biocentric and idealistic Eurocentric attitudes held by many of the latter. By way of illustration, an interesting incident occurred during a three-week Arctic ecotourism expedition in northern Canada, when Inuit guides killed five polar bears to feed their sled dogs after supplies unexpectedly ran low. Complaints by the ecotourists and subsequent publicity led to a 'crisis of legitimacy' for the hitherto respected company, which defended the actions of the guides as being consistent with local cultural norms (Lawrence, Wickins & Phillips 1997).

COMMUNITY-BASED ECOTOURISM

As a response to the criticisms of conventional mass tourism by supporters of the cautionary platform, and especially as a result of the popularisation of sustainable development in the early 1990s, community-based models of tourism are now widely advocated as a way of achieving the objective of sociocultural sustainability (Beeton 2006, Jones 2005, Kiss 2004, Murphy 1985, Scheyvens 1999, Singh, Timothy & Dowling 2003). **Community-based ecotourism**, more specifically, has been defined as a 'form of ecotourism where the local community has substantial control over, and involvement in, its development and management, and a major proportion of the benefits remain with the community' (WWF 2001, p. 2). The two main components of this definition — meaningful involvement and benefit — require further comment.

Although economic empowerment (i.e. improvements to the residents' quality of life through the equitable distribution of income derived from ecotourism) is the implied benefit, Scheyvens (1999) proposes that psychological empowerment (e.g. self-esteem and confidence), social empowerment (e.g. community cohesion and mobilisation) and political empowerment (e.g. a representative and responsive political system) additionally need to be taken into account when assessing benefits in a holistic way, although they may be harder to quantify and evaluate. To this list could also be added cultural empowerment, which is the desire and capacity of local residents to practise their culture on an equal footing with external cultural influences. All five of these interrelated dimensions, notably, can also be regarded as precedents that help to determine whether or not a particular ecotourism initiative is socioculturally sustainable, in which case the benefit is to have them reinforced or at least maintained through ecotourism. With regard to the second main component of community involvement, all of the following should be included:

- influence over decisions to initiate, terminate, expand or contract ecotourism projects and initiatives
- right to be consulted and to provide input at every stage of development and ongoing operation
- preferred access to direct and indirect employment arising from ecotourism projects
- participation (full or partial) in ownership and management, including voting representation in relevant committees or organisations.

Whatever the specific issues of benefits and involvement, the community-based ecotourism concept has been widely adopted in the ecotourism literature, as indicated by the explicit community focus in six of the nine definitions quoted in table 1.1.

In the field, Kiss (2004) notes that a community-based ecotourism component was included in 105 projects supported by USAID (the major US government agency that disburses foreign aid) in the late 1990s, representing more than US$2.5 billion in funding, and in 32 of the 55 projects undertaken by the World Bank between 1988 and 2003 to support African protected areas. Geographically, community-based ecotourism initiatives are found mainly in sub-Saharan Africa and tropical Latin America, as well as to a lesser extent in South-East Asia and peripheral, mainly indigenous communities in such developed countries as Canada, USA, Australia and New Zealand. This skewed pattern, among other factors, is attributable to the urgent developmental needs of these areas, proximity to protected areas and communal lands possessing high ecotourism potential, the resultant decision by major funding organisations such as USAID and the World Bank to focus aid disbursements on these areas (given that almost all such projects at least initially depend on external funding), the lack of a private sector business environment with the capacity to initiate and operate ecotourism projects, and robust local community dynamics.

■ 5.5.1 Rationale

There are several pragmatic reasons for advocating a community-based approach to ecotourism, beyond the core assertion that a high degree of local involvement is an effective way to realise community empowerment and other positive sociocultural outcomes. First, in the context of sustainability, local communities in theory have the most to lose from engaging in unsustainable activities and the most to gain from operating in a sustainable manner (Wearing & Neil 1999). A site that is rehabilitated and cleaned to attract ecotourists, for example, also provides an aesthetic and recreational benefit to local residents. They therefore have a particularly strong incentive to work to make a given tourism initiative successful over the long term. As demonstrated by actions sometimes taken against wildlife, local residents are also in a strong position to sabotage tourism activities perceived to be inimical to their interests (see section 5.4.3). Unfriendliness or hostility towards tourists is another way in which tourism can be undermined (Beeton 2006).

A second consideration is that local residents provide authenticity and value to the ecotourism experience through their intimate knowledge and **sense of place** of the local environment. This may result in enlivened and personalised interpretation imbued with deep and privileged knowledge. Moreover, on the basis of this long experience in a particular place, local residents are often better positioned than outside 'experts' to judge whether particular modes of product development or tourist behaviour are ecologically or socioculturally sustainable.

Third, involvement of an entire local community in a tourism project may gain improved economies of scale as compared to engagement by a single family or small business, and generates a wider array of locally originated goods and services that serves to increase the multiplier effect and reduce leakages.

■ *5.5.2* **Factors** *underlying success*

While the WWF definition of community-based ecotourism provided above implies that a participating population will reap benefits, the literature actually indicates a high rate of long-term failure for such initiatives. For example, of 37 small-scale community projects in Asia funded by the NGO Biodiversity Conservation Network (BCN) (most of which had an ecotourism component) just 7 were profitable, whereas 4 produced no revenue, 3 had minimal revenue, 13 covered only their variable costs and 10 covered both fixed and variable costs (Salafsky et al. 2001). Unfortunately, no studies to date have systematically investigated the factors that contribute to the successful implementation of community-based tourism or ecotourism. However, an analysis of the extensive literature on this topic, as elaborated below, reveals a number of threads common to successful initiatives, including a clear definition of the target 'community', strong and popularly supported leadership, control over and access to land, broad-based participation, effective partnerships, skill and capacity acquisition, creating and sustaining tourist demand, maintaining quality, reinvestment and being the appropriate size. The order in which these factors are presented is roughly sequential.

Clear definition

Any community-based ecotourism initiative should begin with a clear understanding of which individuals comprise the 'community' that will have privileged access to participation, funding and the dissemination of any benefits that are generated. Yet this issue is almost always ignored or taken for granted in the literature, giving rise to the potential for conflict and confusion. In isolated settlements where the geographical, cultural and social boundaries between a particular group of people and everyone else are clearly defined, this may not be so problematic, and it helps to explain why funding agencies tend to favour such settlements (see above). However, in almost every other situation, the issue can be extremely complicated and contentious, thereby increasing the likelihood of conflict and ultimate failure (Medina 2005).

The question of who has the right to make this definitional decision is an important consideration. According to the logic of the community-based approach, such a declaration should come from the people themselves. However, unless the community boundaries are unambiguous, self-declaration can be a self-serving act on the part of a clique within the wider local population. The opposite approach, whereby the funding agency exercises sole control over community definition, is also problematic because it reflects a philosophy of dependency and is more likely to lead to decisions that mirror agency agendas and biases rather than the situation on the ground. A compromise therefore is required which takes into account the mandate and fiduciary responsibilities of the funding source as well as the legitimate interests of all local residents through a process of negotiation and a thorough investigation of the sociological landscape. Problems addressed at this scoping stage may be thus averted during implementation.

Nevertheless, even with the best of intentions, it is probable that conflict will arise from several sources. Many definitions of community focus on the people who reside permanently in a particular area, but to what extent should the interests of non-resident property holders, temporary or seasonal residents, and members of a traditional community who now reside elsewhere (and may be several generations geographically removed from the area) also be taken into account in decisions regarding participation and the disbursement of benefits? Such issues are relevant to Australia's Aboriginal community, approximately one in three of whom resides in large cities but for the most part retain familial and other connections with relatively remote communities that have latent ecotourism potential (ABS 2006).

Equally confounding is the issue of newcomers, many or most of whom may have been attracted to the area by the new ecotourism activity, and most of whom probably do not have any familial or cultural ties with the existing community. These may not be issues if the ecotourism project involves no external funding or does not generate benefits, but in all likelihood the array of stakeholders claiming to be part of the privileged 'community' will expand to the degree that it successfully attracts funding and produces a significant revenue stream and other tangible benefits.

Because of the difficulties in defining 'community', and because even a clearly defined community is usually characterised by factionalism and inequality (see section 5.4.2), it may be preferable to focus instead on the more inclusive and socially neutral term 'local residents' when describing the population on which any given ecotourism initiative is focused.

Strong and widely supported leadership

Explicitly or implicitly, the literature notes the importance of strong and popularly supported local leadership in successful community-based ecotourism initiatives, both as a prerequisite to and during implementation (see 'Practitioner's Perspective: Leadership as a factor in successful community-based ecotourism') (Vincent & Thompson 2002, Yaman & Mohd 2004). As described here and in this case study, strong leadership is a core factor that defends community access to resources, negotiates favourable and productive partnerships, encourages and facilitates broad-based participation and so on.

Perhaps the most difficult issue here when assessing sociocultural sustainability is reconciling effectiveness with the factors that engender strong leadership, which in traditional societies may include undemocratic hereditary or clan entitlements and an authoritarian leadership style. Should it be an issue for funding agencies if such a mode of leadership is present but popularly supported because it has a record of ensuring that sufficient benefits are disseminated? And if not, should this be considered socioculturally sustainable in the context of the core criteria of ecotourism?

Leadership as a factor in successful community-based ecotourism

The Maasai village of Ololosokwan in northern Tanzania, adjacent to Serengeti and Maasai Mara game parks, provides a successful example of community-based ecotourism. It is all the more remarkable given that this success has followed a period of alienation and disempowerment caused by the loss of traditional lands when the parks were established and the questionable acquisition of much of their remaining communal land by tourism speculators. A critical factor in the turnaround was relentless political pressure by community leaders to have much of their traditional land returned and their subsequent ability in 1999 to negotiate a lucrative revenue-sharing deal with the South African ecotourism company that had purchased the land from the speculators (Nelson 2004). This deal provided for a US$25 000 annual rent, indexed at 5 per cent per year, for access to 10 000 hectares of restored communal land, a bed-night fee payable to the village council of US$3.15 per ecotourist staying at the company's ecolodge, and landing fees for charter flights bringing ecotourists to the site. The community also built its own simple campground, earning US$18 066 per year from a US$20 per tourist fee per night and a US$10 entry fee. Almost entirely because of this combined tourism income, village revenues increased from an average of US$2500 per year in 1995–97 to around US$56 000 in 2003. These funds are subject to village by-laws, which assure that they are invested in beneficial projects such as schools, dispensaries and infrastructure, local game wardens to safeguard wildlife and individual grants for healthcare and school tuition. By-laws also require quarterly reporting of fund allocation by the village council to the village assembly and regular outside auditing. The success of Ololosokwan is in large part owed to excellent and ethical community leadership that has enabled the villagers to regain lost lands and to resist efforts by the district council to capture the company concessions paid to the village council and by the central government to exercise more control over local tourism through big game hunting concessions, which it had unilaterally granted to foreign interests on vast tracts of communal land. A major contributing factor, however, is the opportune proximity of the village to some of the best game-viewing parks and habitat in all Africa, thereby conferring on the community ecotourism resources in which outside companies are willing to invest much effort and money in return for access.

Control over and access to land

As illustrated by the Ololosokwan community in Tanzania, having other ingredients in place provides no assurance of successful outcomes if the community in question lacks access to communal lands or adjacent protected areas that provide natural resources for ecotourism. In the Bay Islands of Honduras, choice communal lands are being acquired rapidly by foreign investors for tourism and ecotourism purposes due to the lack of collective use rules and protocols, infighting, weak leadership and community dilution caused by the influx of mainlanders seeking work in this rapidly developing tourist destination (Moreno 2005). Similarly, communities in the former 'homelands' of South Africa are impeded from participating in ecotourism by policies that hold communal land in trust under the federal government, which means that it cannot be used as security to obtain loans, and acts as a deterrent to private investors who insist on secure land tenure arrangements (Viljoen & Naicker 2000).

In all such situations, it is critical to emphasise that the land in question must have attractions capable of sustaining a viable ecotourism sector. This is clearly the case at Ololosokwan and in the South African settlement of Mavhulani, which owes its status as one of the very few examples of successful ecotourism in the former African 'homelands' largely to its proximity to Kruger National Park (Viljoen & Naicker 2000).

Broad-based participation

In the literature, broad-based participation is widely cited both as a factor underlying success and a parameter of success, being perhaps second only to a sustained and significant revenue stream as the most cited indicator of sustainable community-based ecotourism. As a *prerequisite*, it is argued that broad-based participation brings to the table a diverse range of skills and capabilities, encourages synergy, dissuades internal competition and internecine disputes, creates a strong united front against external competition and opposition, and fosters a sense of cooperation and harmony that facilitates the smooth operation of all aspects of the ecotourism project and elevates visitor satisfaction (see 'In the Field: The role of positive social capital'). It is cited as a critical factor related to success in the BCN-funded initiatives in Asia examined by Salafsky et al. (2001) (see section 5.5.2). As an *indicator* of success, broad-based involvement embodies the principles of economic, psychological, social and political empowerment of local people described above (Mowforth & Munt 1998, Scheyvens 1999, Wahab & Pigram 1997).

Communal impulses in some traditional peripheral populations are such that broad-based participation and reasonably equitable distribution of benefits are taken-for-granted outcomes of ecotourism or similar initiatives. However, in most cases, a community is not a homogeneous entity but rather a 'community of communities' containing diverse and often conflicting interests, attitudes, beliefs, power asymmetries and circumstances. The potential for conflict is therefore always high and, as stated earlier, likely to be realised when a set of possible or actual benefits becomes apparent. One of the main reasons given for the success of the South African ecotourism project at Mavhulani (above) was a rule that forced broad-based and equitable involvement by prohibiting tribal laws and rankings from being applied at the site (Viljoen & Naicker 2000).

Successful community-based ecotourism is associated with positive social capital, which may be defined as the cooperative internal networks and impulses that allow common goals to be achieved collectively through the shared norms, trust and reciprocity that these networks cultivate (Ecclestone & Field 2003). In contrast, common goals are impeded by, or are never identified in the first place because of, negative social capital, which encompasses internal relationships that foster suspicion, division and infighting. As reported by Jones (2005), the village of Tumani Tenda in the West African country of the Gambia illustrates the benefits of ecotourism that can result from positive social capital. Specifically, community efforts led to the construction of a 13-room 'eco-camp' that employs 15 local volunteers and accommodated about 200 tourists in 2001. Field research in the village indicated a high level of positive 'structural social capital'; that is, roles, precedents and associations that dictate what people actually *do* (Harpham, Grant & Thomas 2002). Collective action, for example, is a non-negotiable founding principle of the village, and every adult is expected to perform a certain amount of unpaid communal labour each year, often through a variety of formal associations that have been formed to address specific needs, including the development of ecotourism. Other collective action associations in the village have had success in suppressing bush fires, gathering resources from the nearby woodland and dissuading villagers from illegally cutting down trees in communal woodlands. The association responsible for ecotourism has been able to leverage its success to attract additional material resources from several outside agencies, which in turn further reinforced positive social capital by demonstrating the tangible benefits of the communal approach.

A more ambiguous picture is painted in terms of the village's 'cognitive social capital', which refers to interpersonal values, attitudes, beliefs and perceptions; that is, the way people actually *feel*. All interviewed villagers stated that they could trust everyone else in the village, and all considered themselves to be equal members of the community. These results were attributed to the high level of contact villagers maintained through the associations and a high-quality school system that encouraged trustworthiness and gave villagers the capability to keep track of internal lending and borrowing. However, there was considerable latent resentment over the fact that power within the associations was focused on two dominant founding families who did not hold themselves accountable for the way ecotourism funds were allocated. Other villagers were reluctant to challenge these families out of a desire to preserve good internal community relationships and because significant benefits were widely obtained within the community. Jones (2005) cautions that the positive social capital in this situation could be quickly dissipated if the current leadership is eventually replaced by weaker leaders who maintain their unaccountability and power but are less committed to communal solidarity and are less successful in ensuring that benefits from ecotourism and other activities are equitably distributed.

Partnerships

Support for partnerships is instilled in planning models to the point of cliché, yet the emphasis is a valid one given the importance of external relationship building in all successful examples of community-based ecotourism (Fuller, Buultjens & Cummings 2005). The most obvious parameter of this is the need for resource-strapped communities to obtain funding by attracting the attention of relevant agencies, which can include bilateral donors (e.g. AusAid, USAID), multilateral donors (e.g. UNEP [United Nations Environment Programme]), development banks (e.g. World Bank, IMF), corporate philanthropy (British Airways, Shell), big international NGOs (or BINGOS) (e.g. Conservation International, the Nature Conservancy), and international foundations (e.g. Ford Foundation, MacArthur Foundation) (Heher 2003). National governments are another potential source of funds, although in cash-strapped, less-developed countries this role is more likely to focus around mediating and facilitating the building of relationships between the community and potential foreign or domestic donors and enablers. In the case of the Bay Islands cited above, local residents traditionally maintained a bad relationship with the Honduras government, which as a result had no compunction in taking the side of foreign investors who sought access to resource-rich communal lands (Moreno 2005).

Protected area managers are another strategically important partner, given the paramount role of protected areas in providing suitable ecotourism venues (see chapter 3). Their cooperation is vital in order to give ecotourists access to those venues and to facilitate the negotiation of lucrative entry fee revenue-sharing arrangements that provide substantial revenues at minimal or no cost to community members (Archabald & Naughton-Treves 2001). Protected area managers who trust local residents are also more likely to allow reasonable access for purposes of carrying out traditional gathering activities in a sustainable way and to favour these residents for employment in the park.

A fourth major partner is the private sector, which Heher (2003) regards as a grossly and unfairly neglected stakeholder because of funding agencies' longstanding reservations about their motives and modes of operation. This argument holds that private businesses are well positioned to contribute operational competencies, capital and connections with the international tourism distribution system. They can also sensitise potential visitors to aspects of the local culture that may cause culture shock or dismay. Another reason why the South African ecotourism initiative at Mavhulani has been successful was the trust that was built between the community and the private investor, who learned all about the culture and traditions of the local people and took these into account in all aspects of project design and in relationships with workers and so on (Viljoen & Naicker 2000).

Skill and capacity acquisition

Tourism is an extremely complex sector and is therefore regarded by Kiss (2004) as an inappropriate entry-level activity for communities with few business competencies, even when they possess local skills and knowledge that confer competitive advantage through their ability to convey a destination's unique sense of place and authentic culture to visitors. Competence in such basic business skills as bookkeeping and monitoring inventories, for example, was associated with success in the Asian community enterprises analysed by Salafsky et al. (2001). Conveyance of these skills therefore should be a priority of funding agencies during the earliest capacity-building stages of ecotourism projects.

Creating and sustaining demand

Decisions to pursue or fund an ecotourism project often come from a belief that this sector is massive and rapidly expanding (see section 2.5.1) and that success is therefore virtually assured. The soft ecotourists who account for most ecotourism activity, however, are highly unlikely to know about or patronise remotely located community-based facilities, leaving only a small (and not necessarily rapidly growing) number of hard ecotourists in the real market pool. Moreover, because these hard ecotourists tend to reside thousands of kilometres from the site, successfully linking supply with demand is a very complex undertaking that requires connections to the global tourism distribution system and sophisticated marketing skills seldom possessed by remote local communities. According to Timothy and White (1999), a lack of marketing skills and connections may be acceptable if the objective is to keep the initiative small-scale, in which case the objectives of the project managers could be met by establishing a strong partnership with a single overseas sponsor that would undertake most of the publicity, marketing and booking for trips to that site, possibly relying on its own membership to provide a sustained market base. Repeat visitation could be encouraged by involving visitors in such enhancement sustainability activities as tree-planting, trail maintenance and community volunteering, which help to establish a personal bond between the visitor and the site.

Maintaining quality

Tourism is a service sector in which intangibility, inseparability, variability and perishability are factors that must be understood in order to successfully market and manage the destination product and produce high levels of guest satisfaction (Weaver & Lawton 2006). Community-based ecotourism managers, however, seldom negotiate these factors in a satisfactory way (Heher 2003), leading to major problems with quality control that can result in low visitor satisfaction. Even hard ecotourists wishing to experience the 'authentic' local culture will probably grow intolerant of inconsistent food quality, indifferent service, the absence of basic goods, guides with poor foreign language skills, unsanitary accommodation, or unpredictable meal times. Dissatisfied guests will not only absent themselves from the repeat market pool but will also generate negative word-of-mouth publicity that will reduce the likelihood of a sustained flow of visitors. Heher (2003) argues that joint ventures with experienced private businesses is an especially effective way of introducing and maintaining quality standards appropriate for higher-income visitors from the more-developed countries.

Reinvestment

The promise of economic benefits that appreciably improve quality of life is a major reason for a materially impoverished local community to pursue ecotourism. If and when revenues do come available, it is therefore extremely difficult to persuade community members that the distribution of benefits should be deferred or limited so that the revenue can be reinvested in the project to make it more viable and competitive over the long term. This is an especially important consideration given that external funding usually has term limits (to avoid long-term dependency) and is provided on the understanding that the project will become self-sustaining by the end of that term (Kiss 2004). Hence, funding agencies expect reinvestment of revenues whereas community leaders may be more focused on converting those revenues into direct or indirect distributed benefits in order to maintain popular support for the project and for themselves. Failure to reinvest is cited as a major factor in the lack of success in the study of community-based projects in Asia cited above (Salafsky et al. 2001).

Being the right size

Given the scale and limited capacities of most remote communities and the challenges involved in attracting and maintaining a visitor flow, it is advisable for community-based ecotourism projects to be small, at least initially. The precepts of alternative tourism (see figure 1.1), in general, are appropriate, bearing in mind that projects should be small enough for them not to exceed local environmental and sociocultural carrying capacities but large enough to justify outside funding and investment and to provide meaningful economic returns to the community (Heher 2003). Viljoen and Naicker (2000), as a general principle, recommend that expectations should be kept low so that there is no major economic downturn or community backlash if overly optimistic or unrealistic predictions are not met.

■ 5.5.3 Communities *in more-developed regions*

As mentioned above, the community-based ecotourism literature focuses almost exclusively on less-developed countries or resource peripheries in developed countries where needs are great, high-quality attractions are available and existing entrepreneurial capacities are low. This does not mean, however, that such activities cannot be pursued in more unconventional settings, albeit in modified form. Differences that would need to be taken into account in formulating an appropriate strategy for more economically developed settings in such countries as Australia, the USA, Canada and New Zealand and in Western Europe include the following:

- other formal economic activities already in place
- relatively high levels of material wellbeing
- greater proximity to markets
- land base outside protected areas mostly privately owned
- some tourism activity already present
- critical skills and capacities available in the community or nearby
- fewer problems of natural resource degradation (e.g. secondary forest now covers much of the southeastern USA)
- power structures based in part on formal political process are more likely to be unstable and flexible.

These characteristics suggest that the private sector could play a much more prominent role in such situations and that outside funding agencies would be less important. Existing tourism activity offers the opportunity to pursue ecotourism as just one option within a more diversified tourism product, and it is likely that the local community would be more self-selecting in terms of which members opt to become involved. However, this is conjecture, since examples of community-based ecotourism in this context are rare. More prevalent is adherence to principles of public participation that recognise the moral (and often statutory) obligation of government and the private sector to keep residents of affected areas, and interested individuals more generally, apprised of development plans (in tourism as well as in other sectors) and to solicit feedback from those residents (Rowe & Frewer 2000).

5.6 SUMMARY

The economic benefits of ecotourism include the generation of direct revenues and employment, especially for peripheral regions that otherwise have few sustainable economic options. These benefits, furthermore, have the potential to stimulate a high multiplier effect and subsequent indirect and induced revenue and employment, especially if the large volumes of visitation associated with soft ecotourism are present. As a diversionary activity, ecotourism can also stimulate mass tourism in other areas and can reinforce cultural and heritage tourism as complementary add-ons. However, these benefits must be weighed against start-up and ongoing costs, which are higher in soft ecotourism, and by revenue uncertainties that arise because of political and social conflicts as well as other factors, such as seasonality. Revenue leakage is another consideration, as is the damage to farmland and livestock caused by wildlife. If economic benefits are accompanied by a significant degree of local control, ecotourism can promote social stability at a destination. Its egalitarian nature also means that its physical, aesthetic and spiritual benefits are accessible to most people. Potential sociocultural costs include ecotourist intrusions into the local backstage (a problem associated more with hard ecotourism), the imposition of elite alien values and the erosion of local control through modernisation, external control and the arrival of immigrants. Indirectly, these can lead to local animosity towards ecotourism and ecotourists, while tourists can become antagonistic towards locals if the observed lifestyle and actions of the latter are perceived to be incompatible with their own. Community-based ecotourism is a widely touted model for minimising its economic and sociocultural costs while maximising the associated benefits. Implemented mainly in peripheral areas where economic needs, community identities and attraction potential are high but existing skills and capacities are low, community-based ecotourism is more likely to be successful when the target community is well defined, local leadership is strong and broadly supported, there is control over and access to land that sustains ecotourism, participation is broad-based, effective partnerships are in place, business skills and capacities are acquired, an appropriate level of demand is generated and sustained, product quality is maintained, revenues are reinvested in anticipation of funding termination, and the right size of the operation is maintained.

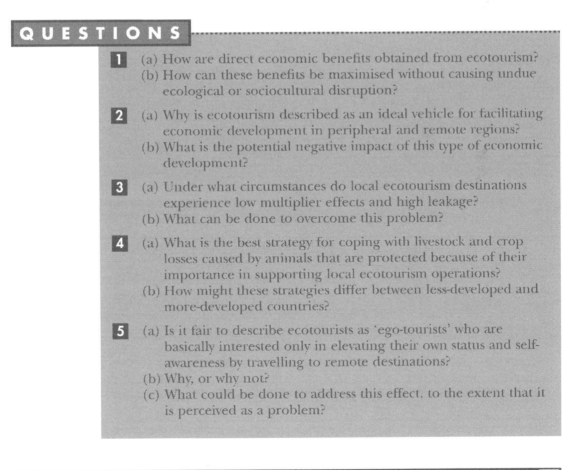

QUESTIONS

1 (a) How are direct economic benefits obtained from ecotourism?
   (b) How can these benefits be maximised without causing undue ecological or sociocultural disruption?

2 (a) Why is ecotourism described as an ideal vehicle for facilitating economic development in peripheral and remote regions?
   (b) What is the potential negative impact of this type of economic development?

3 (a) Under what circumstances do local ecotourism destinations experience low multiplier effects and high leakage?
   (b) What can be done to overcome this problem?

4 (a) What is the best strategy for coping with livestock and crop losses caused by animals that are protected because of their importance in supporting local ecotourism operations?
   (b) How might these strategies differ between less-developed and more-developed countries?

5 (a) Is it fair to describe ecotourists as 'ego-tourists' who are basically interested only in elevating their own status and self-awareness by travelling to remote destinations?
   (b) Why, or why not?
   (c) What could be done to address this effect, to the extent that it is perceived as a problem?

6 (a) Broadly speaking, how is the impact presented in this chapter likely to vary between soft and hard ecotourists?
   (b) Can any conclusions therefore be drawn as to the relative desirability of both types of ecotourist from the perspective of sociocultural sustainability?
   (c) What other factors are likely to influence whether the impact of ecotourism is positive or negative?

7 (a) Why is the community-based model of ecotourism so broadly supported by funding agencies?
   (b) What geographic areas tend to be favoured for such projects by these agencies?
   (c) Why?

8 (a) Which three of the underlying strength factors described in section 5.5 would you regard as having priority over the others if resources were not available to enable them all?
   (b) What is the rationale for your selection?

FURTHER READING

Beeton, S 2006, *Community Development through Tourism,* **CSIRO Publishing, Collingwood, Vic.** Although not explicitly focused on ecotourism, this text covers many aspects of community-based tourism, including strategic planning and marketing. Rural and indigenous contexts are included.

Heher, S 2003, 'Ecotourism investment and development models: Donors, NGOs and private entrepreneurs', www.conservationfinance.org. This unique study critically investigates the funding arrangements for community-based ecotourism projects and considers the comparative strengths and weaknesses of various external funding sources, including multilateral donors and private businesses.

Jones, S 2005, 'Community-based ecotourism: The significance of social capital', *Annals of Tourism Research* **32: 303–24.** Using an African case study, the author shows the importance of social capital in the development and management of a community-based ecotourism initiative.

Lindberg, K 2001, 'Economic impacts', in DB Weaver (ed.), *Encyclopedia of Ecotourism,* **CABI, Wallingford, UK, pp. 363–77.** This chapter examines the direct and indirect economic impact of ecotourism, using empirical evidence gathered in a variety of destinations. Emphasis is placed on the results of input–output modelling.

Singh, S, Timothy, D & Dowling, R (eds) 2003, *Tourism in Destination Communities,* **CABI, Wallingford, UK.** This edited volume includes interesting chapters on power dynamics in local communities, ethics, the challenges of local investment and the role of heritage and identity. Case studies from a variety of international destinations are featured.

John Gray's Sea Canoe
Lessons from Thailand in success and failure

Founded in 1989 by John Gray, an American environmentalist and kayak enthusiast, Sea Canoe is one of the oldest continuously operating ecotourism businesses in South-East Asia and a good illustration of the positive and negative impact of a complex operational environment. Sea Canoe's long tenure and financial success are attributable to a combination of factors, including the charisma, persistence and dedication of the founder, the establishment of good relationships and partnerships with local residents, proximity to unique natural resources and innovative technology that allowed the resource base to be exploited as an ecotourism attraction. The feature in question is the *hong*, or island lagoons in southern Thailand's Phangnga Bay, which are surrounded by limestone cliffs 100 metres high and are accessible only during high tide through cave-like tunnels. Not only are the hongs visually spectacular but also their isolation and inaccessibility has led to the development of unique ecosystems virtually unaffected by human activity. The innovation in question is a special inflatable kayak with a narrow, low profile designed to safely navigate these tunnels so that visitors can enter the lagoons (Buckley 2003a).

Aside from the focus on a unique ecological attraction, the ecotourism credentials of Sea Canoe derive from a policy of consistently limiting visitor numbers (64 per day for all sites and no more than 16 passengers per access vessel in the late 1990s) and exposure to the lagoons (for both environmental and safety reasons) and requiring visitors to discard no wastes or litter. Smoking and drinking were also forbidden. Interviews suggest that customers as well as employees became more environmentally aware as a result of the interpretation offered by Sea Canoe. In addition, the company, which was founded with local partners, has hired 45 to 60 full-time guides and other residents from local villages, who are paid wages that are up to 7.8 times higher than the national per capita average and are supplemented by an array of health and training benefits that are not normally available to workers in Thailand. Notably, most employees have been hired from in the region's traditionally marginalised Malay–Muslim minority, thereby contributing to their economic and psychological empowerment (Kontogeorgopolous 2005). Local residents have been encouraged to purchase shares in the company, and 90 per cent of the company's revenues have allegedly remained in Thailand (Shepherd 2003).

(continued)

Sea Canoe, as a result, has been the recipient of numerous international eco-tourism awards. Brisk market demand is sustained not only by the quality of the attraction but also by the proximity of Phangnga Bay to the island of Phuket, which is one of South-East Asia's primary mass 3S tourism resorts, receiving several million international and domestic visitors each year. The initial intent of Sea Canoe was to book hard ecotourists on multi-day excursions that would include deep exposure to local villages. However, it was decided (correctly in retrospect) that a better cash flow would result from 70-kilometre roundtrip day-only excursions promoted among the mass tourism resorts of nearby Phuket (Shepherd 2003). In general, the financial success of Sea Canoe has been closely linked to the company's ability to forge close relationships with the mass tourism industry (Kontogeorgopolous 2005).

Ironically, the financial success of Sea Canoe was largely responsible for the subsequent negative impact and other problems. The ownership of the islands where the lagoons occur is unclear, and some local residents have long exploited some island resources. Especially important is the presence of a bird species (the swiftlet) whose nests are extremely valuable as a Chinese soup ingredient. These nests are harvested by the Birds Nest Monopoly, which consists of certain local families who keep guards permanently stationed at some cave entrances to discourage other would-be gatherers. Once the profitability of the Sea Canoe operations became known to these families, they demanded payments that Gray refused to make. This led to death threats and the non-fatal shooting of a Thai employee of Sea Canoe.

An arguably greater threat from an ecological perspective has been the proliferation of lower-cost competitors, many of whom use close variants of the Sea Canoe appellation. These businesses use the same caves as Gray, but apparently most do not exercise the same restraints with regard to visitor numbers and behaviour, thereby contributing to the degradation of the caves and deterioration in the quality of the visitor experience. According to Shepherd (2003), entreaties by Sea Canoe to the Tourism Authority of Thailand (TAT) and the Forestry Department to address the situation have been ignored, with authorities preferring to have the sea kayaking businesses deal with the problems themselves. Despite the deteriorating environment and visitor experience, these competitors continue to attract a large customer flow (including a growing number of package tourists from Japan and Korea) by offering high commissions to charter holiday companies focused on the Phuket market and by cooperating with the Birds Nest Monopoly in order to gain privileged access to the best lagoons (Shepherd 2003). Kontogeorgopolous (2005) reports from his field research that many local residents resent the financial success enjoyed by the local employees of the 'foreign' company Sea Canoe and accordingly give their support instead to the Thai-owned competitors who are more likely to hire them.

This changing situation has forced Gray's company to change its name to 'John Gray's Sea Canoe', in order to differentiate itself from less responsible competitors and attract those customers wanting to have their hong experience with the company that won the ecotourism best practice awards. More fundamentally, Gray also decided to become less reliant on the hongs and on Phangnga Bay following the refusal of the Birds Nest Monopoly to allow entry to his kayaks and the shooting of his employee. Since the late 1990s, Sea Canoe has expanded its operations to mangroves and other coastal ecosystems elsewhere in Thailand as well as in Vietnam, Fiji, Philippines and Hawai'i (John Gray's Sea Canoe 2005). Reflecting on his experiences in Phangnga Bay, Gray has expressed regret that his 'discovery' of the lagoons has unleashed a more insidious process of exploitation that could threaten their ecological integrity (Buckley 2003a). However, many local residents, perhaps grudgingly, might argue that Sea Canoe opened the way for many of them to become empowered as tourism entrepreneurs in their own right, either as competitors or employees, allowing them to personally benefit from the growing influx of Asian and other international tourists (Kontogeorgopolous 2005).

Questions

1 (a) From the perspective of the local community in the study area, what have been the advantages and disadvantages of having Sea Canoe controlled primarily by the actions of an expatriate entrepreneur?

  (b) Is community-based ecotourism therefore always the preferred model from the standpoint of local residents?

2 What examples of successful and unsuccessful partnerships and relationship building emerge from this case study?

3 (a) What ecological, sociocultural and economic costs and benefits derive from the fact that the lagoons are located near the major resort destination of Phuket?

  (b) What could be done to minimise these costs and maximise these benefits?

6

Ecotourism
as a business

LEARNING OBJECTIVES

After reading this chapter, you should be able to:

- identify the basic structure and components of the ecotourism industry, including sectors that are mostly specialised or mostly non-specialised

- assess private sector businesses and stakeholder groups that participate in ecotourism businesses

- understand the limitations faced by small ecotourism businesses as well as their potential advantages

- describe the basic activities associated with strategic business planning

- explain how ecotourism is linked to the tourism distribution system through the travel trade

- discuss the status of guidebooks, local tour operators, ecolodges and mediating attractions as small but distinctive and evolving components of the specialised ecotourism industry

- critique the state of quality control within ecotourism, particularly as it pertains to certification-based ecolabels.

$\mathcal{I}$NTRODUCTION ....

Ecotourism in both its hard and soft manifestations is associated with a variety of environmental, economic and sociocultural costs and benefits. However, a premise of this book is that no matter how environmentally and socioculturally sustainable its apparent impact, ecotourism will survive only if it is also sustainable as a business enterprise. Even the most well-supported and ostensibly successful community-based ecotourism projects, for example, eventually experience a termination in external funding and therefore must strive to become financially self-sustaining. This chapter investigates relevant business aspects of ecotourism so that the broader issues of financial viability and the status of ecotourism as an industry can be appreciated. The basic anatomy of the ecotourism industry is described in the first section of this chapter, and this is followed in section 6.3 by a discussion of the major stakeholder groups that participate directly in this sector, with an emphasis on the private sector. The basics of the business planning process that these stakeholders must undertake are presented in section 6.4, which deliberately avoids in-depth coverage of legal, regulatory and other issues that are specific to each destination. Particular business practices such as accounting and pricing are also omitted because of their generic nature and coverage in other publications. Section 6.5 describes and raises issues associated with specific ecotourism industry segments, including guidebooks and supplies, travel agencies, tour operators, ecolodges, protected areas and mediating attractions, such as cableways, submarines and canopy walks. Recognising the link between financial sustainability and the need for the ecotourism industry to attain legitimacy through effective quality control, the final section examines applicable mechanisms such as codes of conduct, awards and certification-based ecolabels.

$\mathcal{S}$TRUCTURE OF THE ECOTOURISM INDUSTRY ....

The ecotourism industry is defined for the purposes of this text as the businesses that directly interact with the ecotourist to facilitate the ecotourism experience from the planning stage through to completion. Segments of this industry occur in the origin, transit and destination regions, and consist of both specialised and non-specialised operations (see figure 6.1). Ecotourist trips within this framework occur through either the formal package circuit or the **FIT** (free and independent travel) circuit. As with 'hard' and 'soft' ecotourist, the distinction between 'specialised' and 'non-specialised' categories is made to facilitate discussion, since many operations combine elements of both. The same holds true for 'formal package' and 'FIT' trips.

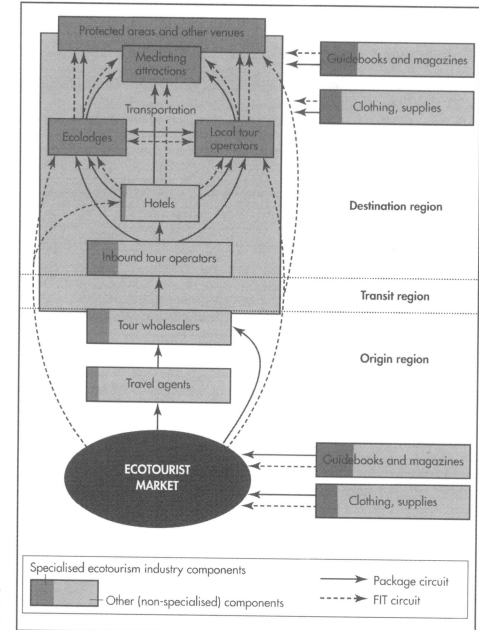

■ *6.2.1* Specialised *and non-specialised operations*

The notion of an 'ecotourism industry' is in some ways a misnomer since only a small proportion of total ecotourism activity takes place in a specialised sector. No hard data is available, so figure 6.1 estimates the portion of ecotourist activity in each industry segment that is specialised and non-specialised. Most guidebooks and magazines purchased by ecotourists, for example, are from the general travel trade, but a small portion is accounted for by specialised publications and a rapidly expanding array of Internet resources (see section 6.5). The same holds true for **travel agencies**, **tour wholesalers** and **inbound tour operators**. In contrast, ecotourist activity related to ecolodges, protected areas and other venues, **mediating attractions** and **local tour operators** is all, or almost all, part of the specialised ecotourism industry. At the other extreme, virtually all transportation (e.g. airlines and transit buses, but not vehicles used by local tour operators) is non-specialised. Most ecotourist nights in hotels occur in urban or resort facilities, and a small proportion, such as those located in or adjacent to national parks, is ecotourism specialised.

An indication of the specialised sector's magnitude in Australia is provided by the membership roster of Ecotourism Australia (see section 8.2.4), the industry's peak national body. In late 2006, this included about 200 mostly private sector operations dominated by tour operators but also representing accommodation and attractions (Ecotourism Australia 2006). The actual number of ecotourism operations may be much greater considering that the latter includes only businesses certified by that body, although the status of other businesses alleging to be ecotourism-focused is less clear due to the lack of quality control mechanisms to better ensure that core criteria are satisfied. Even if the actual figure is closer to a thousand, this appears nowhere near sufficient to satisfy the demand for ecotourism just from international visitors, approximately 2 per cent of whom are estimated to be oriented towards hard ecotourism and 30 per cent towards soft ecotourism (see section 2.5). The discrepancy is explained by allocation of most ecotourist trip expenditures to non-specialised segments such as transportation, tour wholesalers, inbound tour operators and hotels, as illustrated in figure 6.1. For soft ecotourists in particular, direct expenditure in the specialised ecotourism industry is a minuscule or non-existent proportion of total trip costs (see section 6.3.1).

■ 6.2.2 Formal *package and FIT travel*

A substantial proportion of ecotourism activity, particularly in the arena of international travel, proceeds along the formal package tour trajectory. This involves mediation by travel agents, tour wholesalers and inbound tour operators before the use of accommodation, local tour operators and attractions in the destination arranged by these mediators. Soft ecotourists are most likely to travel on a formal package basis, whereas hard ecotourists are more likely to select the alternative of the FIT circuit, which circumvents travel agents, tour wholesalers and inbound tour operators for at least part of the trip experience. While FIT ecotourists cannot avoid the formal transportation sector (even the most hard-core ecotourist travelling from Australia to Alaska will travel with a major airline), they are more likely to take regular, scheduled flights rather than charter flights. From a quality control perspective, a consideration that is particularly important in less-developed countries is the extensive informal sector (including, for example, unlicensed taxis, vendors, guides and guesthouses) that supports the FIT market.

*B*USINESS PARTICIPANTS

The four major stakeholder groups that participate directly in the business aspects of ecotourism are the private sector, local communities, non-government organisations (NGOs) and the public sector. Multiple stakeholder arrangements are the norm rather than the exception, which can be illustrated by a community-based ecotourism project that involves funding from an overseas aid agency, a joint venture with a private sector ecolodge and tour operator, and revenue-sharing agreement with the managers of an adjacent public protected area. Such situations of course add complexity to the single-stakeholder perspectives outlined in the subsections below, which take into consideration the participation of stakeholder groups in the non-specialised sector but emphasise the specialised ecotourism industry.

■ 6.3.1 Private *sector*

In non-indigenous settings in Australia and other more-developed countries, the specialised and non-specialised ecotourism industry is associated mainly with the private sector, as befits the capitalist, individualistic ethos that dominates these societies. The main difference between specialised and non-specialised private businesses, aside from the degree of focus on ecotourism, is a matter of scale. Specialised private sector ecotourism operations tend to be small businesses often run by owner-operators. As with the small business sector in general (Getz & Carlsen 2005), this sector is characterised by its volatility, with a high number entering and leaving the industry each year. Hence, there is a particularly high disparity in the ecotourism sector between the romantic ideals of establishing such a business and the hard realities of the business world that affect ecotourism as much as any sector.

Reasons for the high rate of failure among small private businesses

The factors that contribute to the high failure rate among small, private sector ecotourism businesses have been analysed by McKercher (1998, 2001) and are similar to those experienced by small private tourism businesses more generally (Getz & Carlsen 2005). These include a preponderance of owners and operators with narrow, specialised skills (e.g. as a marine biologist or outdoor guide) and little or no prior knowledge about running a business. Many of these same operators become involved for emotional or lifestyle reasons that frequently conflict with the need to make a profit. Others are ignorant about the nature of the tourism distribution system or make the mistake of confusing participation in ecotourism and visitation levels to protected areas (i.e. apparent market demand) with the much smaller real market demand for specialised ecotourism products. The failure to match supply with demand can also result from seasonality, which is evident in ecotourism mainstays such as spring and autumn bird migrations, autumn tree colours, animal mating rituals and spring wild-flower displays. In addition, sites may become inaccessible during the rainy season or intolerable during times of extreme heat (as in Australia's Northern Territory) or extreme cold (as in northern Canada). Access to ecotourism settings can also be a problem, with a trip potentially requiring several means of conveyance and becoming a lengthy process. An additional factor is the relative lack of barriers faced by someone wishing to start a local tour operation. Hence, one reason why many local tour operators are struggling and disillusioned is that many people decide to become local tour operators with little more than a four-wheel drive vehicle and a guidebook.

McKercher (1998, 2001) identified the above problems mainly in the context of local tour operators, yet these problems also apply to other segments of the specialised ecotourism industry and are associated in large part with inadequate economies of scale (Silva & McDill 2004). Small privately owned businesses have a restricted client base (partly because they have trouble attracting the attention of volume-focused intermediaries with the tourism distribution system, such as travel agents and tour wholesalers), incur high fixed costs per client, have limited financial reserves to cope with emergencies and are more likely to vary in product quality and to experience frustration when attempting to navigate bureaucracy or receive government aid (see 'Practitioner's Perspective: Barriers to small business success as perceived by entrepreneurs and government'). They also have limited ability to obtain finance, lack the resources to conduct or access research into crucial areas such as market segmentation (see section 2.3) and have greater difficulty in implementing sophisticated technology that will better ensure an outcome of environmental sustainability. Inadequate economies of scale also hinder operators from obtaining the best volume-based discounts on the purchase of inputs, reduce their ability to respond quickly to uncertainties and limit the possibility of diverting customers to alternative products if demand should decline for the core product or the latter becomes unavailable. A small local tour operation that is dependent on a particular protected area can be ruined if the manager of that area decides to unilaterally restrict access to a popular trail or raise operator permit and entry fees. A large tour operator, in contrast, is better positioned to divert clients to other protected areas. As well, a large ecolodge or tour operator is more likely to include and control its own ecotourism setting. For those business operators whose concept of ecotourism relates to alternative tourism (see section 1.5.6), it is often found that the ideal of a small-scale operation presents many hindrances to business success, although there are notable exceptions (see Weaver 2002b, pp. 166–7). Catlins Wildlife Trackers, for example, is a small New Zealand-based ecotour operator that has maintained an impressive record of financial success. Underlying factors include an intimate familiarity with the small region of the South Island in which it operates, impressive natural attractions in that region, personal participation by the owners as tour guides, flexible itineraries dictated in part by tourists, and extensive positive publicity gained through a succession of high-profile tourism awards.

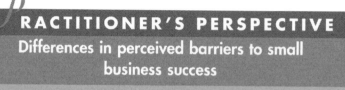

PRACTITIONER'S PERSPECTIVE
Differences in perceived barriers to small business success

Government attempts to assist small ecotourism businesses are often impeded by differing perceptions as to what barriers account for the latter's high rate of business failure. To investigate this issue, Silva and McDill (2004) conducted key informant interviews with 22 local government officials and 23 ecotourism operators in an ecotourism-rich area along the Pennsylvania–Maryland border in the Appalachian Mountains of the eastern USA. Content analysis of the recorded interview transcripts revealed four main categories of barrier: enterprise barriers, agency barriers and network or host community barriers.

Enterprise barriers are related to the owners themselves and their businesses. The government informants were focused entirely on the legal, financial and marketing problems encountered by operators, stating that the latter often underestimated costs, failed to anticipate the tax burden and failed to remain up to date with payroll paperwork. The operators were similarly focused, but perceived that they had overcome these problems and were impeded instead by problems of unanticipated costs associated with equipment failure and maintenance, competition and lack of an innovative capacity. About a third of the owners also cited problems of not having the right kind of personality or adequate business knowledge, or of being susceptible to burn-out due to overwork.

With regard to *agency* barriers, almost all of the government interviewees were concerned that inadequate planning and regulations specific to ecotourism were in place in the region. This was associated with a tendency to regard the sector as risky, seasonal and low-paying and therefore not meriting the priority attention of local or state agencies. In contrast, only about a third of the operators regarded this as a problem and generally did not regard seasonality as a barrier. Only two or three informants on each side saw shortcomings with the government programs (e.g. educational resources and financial incentives) available to assist ecotourism operators, although those who did cite these as a barrier complained that the initiatives were not sufficiently specific to ecotourism.

These two categories accounted for about three-quarters of all the barriers. In contrast, relatively few *network* or *host community* barriers were cited by either group. The former include problems of communication among stakeholders and the inadequate building of mutually beneficial partnerships, while the latter include inadequate infrastructure, unattractive natural resources and unfriendly local residents. The researchers suggest that all stakeholder groups need to focus on building relationships so that they can understand the perceptions of other stakeholder groups and accordingly take collective action to facilitate the successful operation of small ecotourism businesses.

Advantages

There are also advantages associated with operating a small business, such as the Catlins example, including low overhead costs, greater flexibility and the availability of specialised government programs. Family-owned businesses are further assisted by the possibility of free labour from relatives, while locally owned businesses often have an intimate knowledge of place that provides authenticity and enhances the visitor experience, leading to the possibility of positive word-of-mouth promotion that partially compensates for weak ties with the tourism distribution system.

Corporatisation trends

Not all specialised private sector ecotourism businesses are small. As noted in subsequent sections, there is a growing trend towards larger-scale corporate participation, some of which reflects strategies of vertical and horizontal integration (Weaver & Lawton 2006). The acquisition of Australian ecolodges by the multinational corporation GPT is an illustration of this (see section 6.5.4). Other private sector companies such as Lindblad Expeditions, which operates high-end cruise ship tours to hard ecotourism destinations such as Antarctica and the Galapagos Islands, were initially small but expanded as a consequence of their success. Still others, such as the one involved with Skyrail, a cableway in northern Queensland, was formed at a scale commensurate with the ambitious project they undertook.

Large businesses such as these are becoming more visible and prevalent in the ecotourism sector, lending credence both to the theory of paradigm synthesis and to speculation that the dominant paradigm is selectively appropriating non-contradictory elements of the green paradigm that prolong its own dominance (see section 2.2). At a less theoretical level, many corporations become involved in ecotourism simply because they appreciate the potential business opportunities offered by the growth of green consumerism and the soft ecotourism market in particular. Large size (i.e. economy of scale), moreover, confers many advantages to these ecotourism companies, including:

- possession of numerous and diverse skills and competencies
- enhanced capacity to innovate
- access to capital or borrowing potential to undertake large-scale projects, such as cableways and private protected areas
- familiarity with and participation in the tourism distribution system
- control over backward and forward linkages (e.g. a large inbound tour operator also owns a travel agency and an ecolodge)
- ability to divert clients to a range of other tourism products if problems are experienced in any particular location, or during the off-season of that location
- lower fixed costs per client and cheaper bulk purchase costs.

Weaver (2006) emphasises how these economies of scale facilitate the pursuit of sustainable practices. Diverse skills and competencies, for example, can include such specialised positions as environmental manager and community liaison officer, while enhanced capacity to innovate could involve such initiatives as solar power or energy co-generation. High volumes of input and output, furthermore, may make recycling and use reduction highly profitable while allowing environmentally conscientious corporations to require that their suppliers meet stipulated 'green' standards.

■ 6.3.2 Communities, *NGOs and the public sector*

As discussed in section 5.5, community-based ecotourism is a model that prevails in peripheral regions and among indigenous people. Distinctive characteristics that are relevant to business include a high level of dependency upon external funding, isolation from markets, rudimentary or non-existent business competencies, and decision-making that is influenced by communal impulses as well as hierarchical power structures based on culture and clan associations. Community-based operations also experience a high rate of failure, although this is often delayed or masked by term-defined external funding and other support. Although environmental NGOs are best known from an ecotourism perspective for the funding and other support they provide to communities, such bodies also participate directly through their involvement in the formation and operation of private protected areas (see section 3.3) and in the provision of mainly non-profit, outbound travel programs (see section 6.5.3). Direct public sector participation in the business of ecotourism is associated with socialist and centrally governed countries, such as China, Vietnam, Laos and Cuba. In other countries, the public sector is associated more with the management of public protected areas and with playing a supportive and regulatory role to the private sector and local communities. Direct business participation by government is usually confined to the provision of certain commercial services and facilities in public protected areas, although even this is being increasingly transferred to the private sector (see section 3.3.1).

6.4 BUSINESS PLANNING

As discussed above, the enthusiasm about ecotourism that is expressed in much of the literature is not matched by the real world track record of the specialised ecotourism industry. A major shortcoming noted by McKercher and Robbins (1998) is the lack of skill associated with business planning. Strategic business planning is an internal management tool whereby a company (or a destination) analyses and synthesises relevant information in order to assess its current position, set its goals and identify the best way of achieving these goals. A scenario-based approach is usually recommended to allow for the complexities and uncertainties that are inherent in the business environment. The preparation of a comprehensive business plan should be one of the first tasks for anyone thinking about entering the ecotourism industry. By forcing the prospective operator to contemplate all of the relevant realities and discarding nonviable options before any significant costs are incurred, the probability of business failure can be reduced by 60 per cent or more, according to McKercher (2001). Once established, a company should carry out business planning on an ongoing basis.

There is no specific model for preparing a strategic business plan. Four publications on ecotourism business planning were consulted for this book (Beeton 1998, McKercher 1998, Patterson 2001, Tourism Queensland 1999), and each provides a different planning template (see figure 6.2, p. 160). Yet, when analysed, these plans reveal five common elements (see below). The differences occur mainly in the order in which these elements are presented. For example, the marketing component precedes the **SWOT analysis** (assessment of an operation's strengths, weaknesses, opportunities and threats) in the Tourism Queensland Plan whereas the others reverse the order. The Australian Tourism Operators Network (ATON) plan (McKercher 1998) and the plan offered by Beeton (1998) both include an intermediary stage between the SWOT analysis and the marketing plan stages. The only common pattern is commencement with the mission statement and objectives and the placement of the financial analysis in the stages following the SWOT analysis. This lack of consistency suggests that strict sequencing is not crucial. The reason for this is the feedback system, which influences all elements of strategic planning. For example, one may begin with a particular set of objectives, but these may have to be altered once the SWOT analysis has been completed. Effective strategic planning, therefore, is a flexible process in which any element of the plan can be revisited and revised periodically as warranted by changing circumstances and knowledge.

■ 6.4.1 Mission *statement and objectives*

Business plans typically begin with a broad mission statement that describes the essence of the business, its fundamental purpose or *raison d'être* (reason for being) and its vision for the future. For an operation oriented towards comprehensive ecotourism, these statements might amalgamate a vision of ecological enhancement with the desire to provide memorable and transformative customer experiences. Goals and objectives are then stated that indicate how the mission statement will be realised. Goals are usually general (for example 'to be the leader in the whale-watching industry in Australia') whereas objectives cover specific and quantifiable areas, such as sales, profits, client satisfaction, industry recognition, market positioning and achieving specified sustainability indicator targets. The Tourism Queensland template suggests a five-year framework for achieving goals. Beeton (1998) recommends the inclusion of contingency plans that indicate a course of action to be taken if the objectives are not met by the end of the planning period.

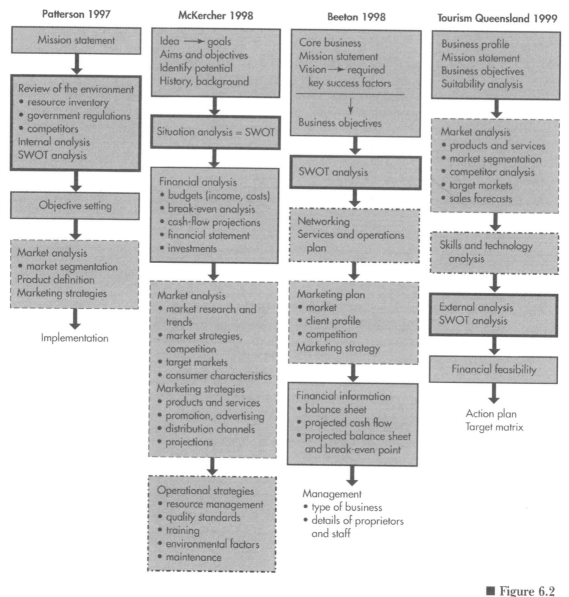

Patterson 1997

Mission statement

Review of the environment
• resource inventory
• government regulations
• competitors
Internal analysis
SWOT analysis

Objective setting

Market analysis
• market segmentation
Product definition
Marketing strategies

Implementation

McKercher 1998

Idea ⟶ goals
Aims and objectives
Identify potential
History, background

Situation analysis = SWOT

Financial analysis
• budgets (income, costs)
• break-even analysis
• cash-flow projections
• financial statement
• investments

Market analysis
• market research and trends
• market strategies, competition
• target markets
• consumer characteristics
Marketing strategies
• products and services
• promotion, advertising
• distribution channels
• projections

Operational strategies
• resource management
• quality standards
• training
• environmental factors
• maintenance

Beeton 1998

Core business
Mission statement
Vision ⟶ required key success factors

Business objectives

SWOT analysis

Networking
Services and operations plan

Marketing plan
• market
• client profile
• competition
Marketing strategy

Financial information
• balance sheet
• projected cash flow
• projected balance sheet and break-even point

Management
• type of business
• details of proprietors and staff

Tourism Queensland 1999

Business profile
Mission statement
Business objectives
Suitability analysis

Market analysis
• products and services
• market segmentation
• competitor analysis
• target markets
• sales forecasts

Skills and technology analysis

External analysis
SWOT analysis

Financial feasibility

Action plan
Target matrix

■ **Figure 6.2**
Ecotourism-related business plans

■ *6.4.2* Situation analysis

All four plans recognise the SWOT analysis as the best technique for assessing the situation of the proposed or existing business. Strengths and weaknesses refer to the internal characteristics of the operation. For example, a property may possess a large koala population (a strength of the business), but its employees may have no formal training in the interpretation of koalas (a weakness of the business). Opportunities and threats refer to the external environment. Inbound tourists, for example, may be eager to see koalas in their natural habitat (an outside opportunity), but the koalas may suffer from chlamydia, a venereal disease common to the species, and a nearby property may already be developing a koala-focused guided tour (outside threats). These opportunities and threats can be external to ecotourism, as discussed in chapter 7. Several of the templates recommend that the SWOT analysis be accompanied by strategies or comments about how to overcome weaknesses and threats while capitalising on strengths and opportunities. For example, the threat of a neighbouring competitor may be converted into an opportunity if it leads to a partnership or forces the owner to develop a superior product. Because the SWOT analysis provides a realistic assessment of the actual and potential advantages and disadvantages of the business, McKercher (1998) argues that this is the most important component of the strategic business plan.

■ 6.4.3 Marketing

Marketing is defined by Weaver and Lawton 2006 (p. 203) as involving:

> ■ ... the interaction and interrelationships among consumers and producers of goods and services, through which ideas, products, services and values are created and exchanged for the mutual benefit of both groups. ■

Hence, 'marketing' is an umbrella term that encompasses not just the promotional and advertising functions commonly associated with the word but also market segmentation (see section 2.4), new product testing, obtaining customer feedback, assessing competing products, pricing decisions and determining distribution channels and methods. The business plans in figure 6.2 all include a marketing component that is typically divided between a market analysis and a marketing strategy that responds to this analysis. According to McKercher (1998), strategic marketing forces a business to define the products it chooses to offer and not offer, the markets it chooses to target and not target and the competitors it chooses to compete with and avoid. He further describes marketing as an overriding managerial philosophy that tries to match consumer needs and preferences with relevant goods and services, and suggests that the failure to identify relevant markets and target them effectively is a major cause of business failure.

The generic literature on marketing is enormous, and it will suffice here to add only selected observations that are relevant to ecotourism. In the first instance, the ideal of carrying out a thorough, sophisticated market analysis and marketing strategy is impeded in most operations by small scale. For example, the market segmentation study in Lamington National Park (Weaver & Lawton 2002), which identified the softer, harder and structured ecotourist segments (see section 2.4), was completed at a cost of $22 000, a prohibitive sum for most small businesses. Moreover, this did not include the salary of the chief investigator or the use of subsidised university resources, nor did it involve any actual formulation of a marketing strategy for the two participating ecolodges. For most operators, the most feasible, but still difficult, alternative is to access research that is already available in the public realm.

The same logic applies to promotional activities. Small businesses can 'piggyback' on campaigns organised and funded primarily by public tourism authorities or industry organisations, if these exist for the destination. Hence, networking with these organisations can result in the underwriting of marketing costs, as recognised in the business plan template of Beeton (1998). Networking can also assist in marketing the destination in which the business operates, which is the primary geographic reference point of many ecotourists, thus allowing the business to focus on the promotion of the unique products that it offers in that destination. For example, a hypothetical ecotour operator in Tasmania can rely on the state government and regional tourism authorities to promote the state's 'World Heritage Wilderness Rainforests', allowing the operator to focus on promoting the company's status as the only business to incorporate terrestrial and marine experiences in the same package.

A major decision for small operators is whether to distribute directly or transfer this responsibility to the tourism distribution system (see section 6.5). The latter option is attractive since the costs are borne by the trade in exchange for a commission — if nothing is sold, the operator incurs no costs. However, many operators do not want to pay commissions to retail travel agents, tour wholesalers or inbound tour operators, or rely on these intermediaries to promote their product. Other operators cannot adequately assess this issue because they lack knowledge about the distribution system (see section 6.3.1).

■ 6.4.4 **Financial** *analysis and operational strategies*

The realm of financial analysis encompasses the 'nuts and bolts' costing and pricing skills that are essential to the success of a business, yet are generally inadequate in most small private sector and community-based ecotourism businesses. Components include the calculation of budgets, break-even analyses, cash flow projections, financial statements, inventorying, pricing and investments. Operational strategies include resource management, quality standards (see section 6.6), training of staff, licensing, legalities and other matters that involve the day-to-day operation of the business. According to McKercher (1998), operational strategies are an element of the business plan that should focus on ethical considerations and their implementation. Yet ironically, it is in this detailed accounting that the manager is most likely to lose track of or disregard essential sustainability principles that may complicate the accounting process.

The following sections examine the components of the ecotourism industry that are depicted in figure 6.1. Both the specialised and non-specialised components are included, although the emphasis is on the former. Transportation is excluded due to the lack of a specialised ecotourism component.

■ 6.5.1 Guidebooks

Guidebooks are aspects of an ecotourism business that is seldom included in discussions of the ecotourism industry. Yet they are interesting and important from several perspectives. First, the sector is spatially dispersed, since they can be obtained in both the origin and the destination regions. Second, while the literature stresses that tourism is a service and focuses on the distinctive attributes and relevance of marketing services, guidebooks are tangible commercial products that require a different set of marketing and management strategies. Third, they are a critical information source of product interpretation that influence the travel patterns of ecotourists and thus serve as a 'gateway' into the ecotourism system. The Lamington National Park survey (Weaver & Lawton 2002), for example, found that guidebooks were the third most popular source of information for ecolodge patrons after word of mouth and brochures. Thirty-two per cent of ecolodge patrons indicated that they frequently used them as an information source, and another 53 per cent reported occasional use. Similarly, they generate consumer expectations and provide publicity and promotion for particular attractions and businesses. Depending on how favourable or critical the commentary, well-written guidebooks can significantly influence the success of ecotourism destinations and businesses.

For a major ecotourism destination such as Australia, dozens of standard guidebooks now explicitly or implicitly incorporate an ecotourism component (e.g. the Lonely Planet series). In addition, a number of specialised low-run ecotourism guidebooks were published during the 1990s (e.g. *Stepping Lightly on Australia* by LaPlanche, 1995), although these appear to have been supplanted during the early 2000s by web-based resources. The most popular of these is planeta.com, which started out as a Latin America–focused online newsletter in the mid-1990s and has since evolved into a major global ecotourism guidebook and blog that allows members to provide real-time comments on any number of relevant destinations, products and issues.

■ 6.5.2 Travel agencies

Until recently, ecotourism had a low profile among travel agencies, which are the component of the tourism distribution system that has the most direct contact with consumers, notwithstanding growing competition from cybermediaries such as Travelocity and Expedia (Goeldner & Ritchie

2006). Travel agents have little incentive to work with small businesses of varying quality that accommodate a low intake of clients and are not well integrated into the travel distribution system. However, as more large companies become engaged with ecotourism, the involvement of travel agencies is increasing. Established travel agency chains are now featuring ecotourism-related tour operators and accommodation that offer acceptable levels of service, reputation and client intake. The Australian chain Harvey World Travel, for example, promotes the coaching safari packages of Scenic Tours and the Fraser Island whale-watching packages of Kingfisher Bay Resort.

■ 6.5.3 Tour wholesalers and operators

A tour operator is defined by Beaver (2005, p. 308) as 'a person or organization combining several elements of travel arrangements and offering them as a product for sale at a single price. Typically, tour operators arrange and sell the products known as package holidays and inclusive tours.' The major components of these packages are transportation, insurance, accommodation and access to attractions and guided tours. Higgins (2001) makes a distinction between outbound tour operators (tour wholesalers), inbound tour operators and local tour operators, and observes that an ecotourist may use any combination of these or circumvent this element of the tourism distribution system altogether by using the informal FIT circuit (see figure 6.1).

Tour wholesalers

Tour wholesalers are located in origin regions (see figure 6.1) and generally are large companies that make contracts with airlines, arrange travel schedules, coordinate marketing and sales, organise groups and liaise with individual clients (Higgins 2001). By purchasing in bulk at discounted prices, tour wholesalers offer package tours at substantially lower prices than those paid by travellers making the same arrangements themselves (Goeldner & Ritchie 2006). Volume purchasing also allows tour wholesalers to be selective with respect to suppliers and influential in facilitating the sustainability of the tourism and hospitality industry if they elect to prefer 'green' suppliers. They may also be vertically or horizontally integrated through the ownership and/or inclusion of travel agencies, inbound and local tour operations, ecolodges or attractions. Member-based environmental NGOs such as the Nature Conservancy (TNC) and Conservation International (CI) essentially serve as specialised integrated tour wholesalers through their member travel programs (e.g. the International Trips Program of TNC), which are often linked to destination products that they control or support.

Inbound tour operators

Inbound tour operators, often located in major urban areas and/or gateways in destination countries, typically market their services to tour wholesalers, prepare client itineraries, select local businesses, plan programs, hire staff and pay applicable fees. Accordingly, they are a hinge component that links the destination-based components of the industry with the local ecotourism destination and is instrumental in determining the participants at either end of this system. Higgins (2001) argues that the marketing decisions of inbound tour operators will depend on the ownership structure of the inbound operation, which can include transnational branch offices, transnational franchises, subsidiaries of a tour wholesaler, expatriate-owned corporations, joint ventures, subsidiaries of national corporations, nationally owned independents, or cooperatives.

Local tour operators

Local tour operations are 'coalface' businesses that mediate directly between the ecotourist and the environmental attraction. Although tour wholesalers and inbound tour operations tend to consist of relatively large businesses, local tour operators are usually small private-sector businesses, or often community-based enterprises in less-developed countries and indigenous territories. Particularly in the latter case, local tour operations may be integrated with providers of accommodation, food, private protected areas and other services. In developed countries, the businesses may exist solely to operate tours, leaving other arrangements to the client, or they may subcontract or work with other small businesses or public protected areas that supply these services. Relatively little is known about local tour operators, although research in the mid-1990s by Cotterill (1996) revealed that the average private ecotourism operation in Australia at that time had four or fewer employees, operated mainly day tours to between one and three natural areas and remained in business for about 10 years. Local tour operators have a high profile in the Australian ecotourism industry, accounting for about 60 per cent of the membership of Ecotourism Australia (see section 8.2.4).

The ambivalent relationship between local tour operators and other local ecotourism businesses on one hand, and the wider travel trade on the other, influences much of the impact described in chapters 4 and 5. Integration into these larger networks, for example, can lead to dependency and product standardisation and to revenue leakage caused by the payment of commissions. However, these in turn may be compensated for by greater revenues and employment from higher numbers of clients and to increased professionalism as local businesses are forced to meet higher product standards.

■ 6.5.4 Accommodation

Ecolodges are a high-profile symbol of ecotourism but account for only a small portion of ecotourist visitor-nights in most countries. Conventional hotels, as demonstrated by the experience of European tourists visiting Kenya (see section 5.2.2), are the 'base camp' for most ecotourists and increasingly provide or arrange access for their clients to nearby protected areas. The potential synergies between ecotourism and conventional hotels as well as other facets of mass tourism are considered further in chapter 7.

Ecolodges

There is confusion over the meaning of the term **ecolodge**. Russell, Bottrill and Meredith (1995, p. x) define it as a 'nature-dependent tourist lodge that meets the philosophy and principles of ecotourism'. However, other sources define an ecolodge less by the activities of its patrons and more by its adherence to the principles of environmental (and possibly sociocultural) sustainability. By this criterion, a small or medium-sized facility catering strictly for hunters, business retreats or adventure tourists could qualify. Prototype ecolodges under the first definition, such as Stanley Selengut's Maho Bay (US Virgin Islands), opened in the late 1980s. Over the following decade, an image of the ecolodge stereotype has emerged: relatively small, private sector ownership, tending towards the luxury end of the market, architecturally imbued with the local sense of place, proximate to a relatively undisturbed high-order protected area, sensitively sited to complement its natural surroundings, and operated in an environmentally sensitive way in which green design (see section 4.5.4) is pervasive. As such, they appear to be especially well suited to the 'structured ecotourist' market (see section 2.4.1). They also deviate substantially in some respects from the prototype accommodation offered by community-based initiatives, which tend to be simple, low-cost and collectively owned. It is debatable therefore whether these should also be classified as 'ecolodges'. For the purposes of this discussion they are not regarded as such.

A fundamental characteristic of an ecolodge is that it must complement its natural and cultural surroundings. Depending on this context, an extremely diverse array of building and design options is possible, as described by Gardner (2001) (see figure 6.3). Structures can range from contemporary to ancient, permanent to temporary, centralised to dispersed and rustic to luxurious. According to a survey conducted by the Ecotourism Society in the late 1990s, ecolodges tend to begin as small structures that evolve over time as resources and market conditions allow (Mehta 1999). Given the obligation of being environmentally sustainable, site and design considerations are especially important. Gardner (2001) includes among these considerations climate (diurnal and seasonal temperature variations; wind; cloud cover; angle of sun amount and frequency of precipitation), site (aspect, slope, bedrock, vegetation, hydrology) and locality (access to resources and services, context, tourism appeal, location of other tourism facilities, landscape features). Whatever these peculiarities, the design of ecolodges must also result in accommodation that is comfortable, since the majority of ecotourists (e.g. the soft and structured ecotourists) will expect a degree of comfort as part of the overall vacation experience.

No definitive survey has yet been undertaken to calculate the actual number of accommodation facilities worldwide that can be classified as 'ecolodges' according to the criteria described above. However, a perusal of the literature as well as relevant web resources and other sources suggests that a figure of a thousand is probably overly generous and that a figure of 300 to 500 is more likely. This inventory can potentially accommodate only a minuscule proportion of the global ecotourism market in any given year, once again demonstrating the importance in ecotourism of the non-specialised tourism sector.

Vernacular building types	*Indigenous structures* Grass huts, mud structures, caves, elevated halls, house boats, reed platforms and buildings, yurts (i.e. Mongolian circular tents), tree platforms, ice houses, teepees, cliff dwellings, stick houses
Historical building types	*Developed vernacular* Colonial architecture, residentially derived styles, commercially developed styles, military architecture, ecclesiastical architecture, monuments, industrial building, palaces and great homes
Contemporary structures	*Prefabricated structures* Masonry, glass-fibre, reinforced concrete, rigid tents, inflatable structures *Traditional tourism* Cottage colonies, inns, guesthouses, homes
Portable and low-impact structures	Rigid tents, collapsible tents, elevated huts, inflatable structures, vehicles, jungle hammocks

■ **Figure 6.3**
Ecotourism building types
Source:
Gardner 2001.

Trends

Ecolodges are a trend in the accommodation sector, and the **ecolodge chain** is a trend in the ecolodge sector related to the corporatisation and increased integration of ecotourism into the tourism distribution system. High-profile examples include the network of luxury safari lodges being developed in Africa and elsewhere by the South African-based Conservation Corporation of Africa (Buckley 2003a). In Australia, the GPT Group controls a significant and growing portion of the country's ecolodges (see 'In the Field: GPT Group and ecolodge ownership concentration in Australia'). Another trend involves integrated mega-resorts, which are a standard feature of conventional mass tourism but, according to Higgins (2001), are now also evident in ecotourism through the appearance of the **ecoresort complex**. Like conventional integrated resorts, ecoresort complexes offer a comprehensive package of experiences, facilities and services at a single location, sometimes in its own private protected area.

Whether such large-scale facilities can rely just on ecotourism, however, is questionable given the experience of Couran Cove Resort, located near the Gold Coast (Australia) on South Stradbroke Island. It was originally developed as a specialised ecotourism facility but was diversified in 1999 after management decided that the ecotourism image was too narrow to sustain a 300-room facility and implied a rusticity that did not reflect the luxurious nature of its product. Couran Cove Resort is now marketed as an all-purpose, environmentally friendly resort that incorporates ecotourism into a product spectrum that also includes sport and fitness, business meetings and conferences, and beach-based activity. A similar profile pertains as well to Kingfisher Bay Resort (see 'Practitioner's Perspective: Environmentally friendly building at Kingfisher Bay' in chapter 4).

Founded in 1971, Sydney-based GPT is one of the largest property groups in Australia, with assets in excess of A$11 billion in 2006. Its holdings include retail and office properties as well as industrial parks, urban communities and hotels (GPT 2006). The 'hotel/tourism portfolio', specifically, includes a major downtown hotel in Sydney and 17 upscale rural lodges operated by Voyages, its hotel management business arm. It is a deliberate strategy of the company to acquire luxury ecolodges and other facilities that appeal to the high-end ecotourism market. Accordingly, it acquired Cape Tribulation Resorts in Far North Queensland in 2002 and El Questro (Kimberley) in 2005. However, by far the most aggressive foray into this niche market was the acquisition of P&O Resorts in 2004, which added five Great Barrier Reef island properties, including the iconic Heron Island and Lizard Island resorts. Other well-known properties under the Voyages umbrella include Silky Oaks Lodge and Ferntree Rainforest Lodge in northern Queensland and Cradle Mountain Lodge in Tasmania (Voyages 2006).

The 800 rooms owned by GPT through Voyages in late 2006 represents a significant and growing portion of the Australian ecolodge sector, and it is worthwhile to speculate on the positive and negative consequences of this concentration from a sustainability perspective. On one hand, most of the properties have advanced certification status through Ecotourism Australia's EcoCertification program, and the parent company alleges to be actively pursuing a policy of corporate social responsibility. For example, in 2004 it established a Corporate Responsibility Steering Group to implement relevant practices across all property portfolios and related support services. Affiliated activities during 2005 included the expansion and formalisation of community outreach initiatives, identifying and monitoring environmental performance indicators, and responding to state and federal environmental legislation (e.g. the federal government's Energy Efficiency Opportunities legislation). Many awards have been received in recognition of these efforts. On the other hand, the core GPT strategy is still squarely focused 'on generating superior returns from investment in real estate and related investments', and main security holders are associated with such financial giants as Westpac, JP Morgan and ANZ, whose level of 'green' commitment is unclear.

■ 6.5.5 Mediating *attractions*

'Mediating attractions' refers to built structures or devices that allow ecotourists to visit normally inaccessible natural attractions through means that are attractive or novel in their own right. These devices may be wholly or partially located in protected areas, and they may be further classified as fixed or mobile. Cableways and canopy walkways are the main examples of fixed mediating attractions. The 420-metre-long Tree Top Walk in Walpole-Nornalup National Park (Western Australia), for example, hosted more than 1 300 000 visitors between 1996 and August 2003 (CALM 2004). Although this example is government-owned, the investment associated with such projects often requires corporate involvement. The use of high-order public protected areas to accommodate privately owned fixed infrastructure is a controversial issue, as demonstrated by the ultimately unsuccessful attempts by private investors to construct the Naturelink cableway to move large numbers of tourists from the Gold Coast through Springbrook National Park to the Springbrook plateau (Weaver 2001b). Less controversial in this regard has been the Skyrail facility in northern Queensland (Weaver 2001b, pp. 127–9) and the submarine tours offered by Atlantis in Hawaii and other destinations, which are also one of the best examples of a mobile mediating attraction.

6.6 QUALITY CONTROL

Quality control has been a central issue for the ecotourism industry since the mid-1990s. In part, this interest reflects the maturing of a fast-growing industry that is moving towards consensus on its core attributes (see chapter 1) and is producing best practice prototypes that allow appropriate benchmarks to be established. This can be said for any emergent sector; however, in ecotourism additional considerations are relevant. Quality control in ecotourism relates not only to satisfying the ecotourist market but also to conducting business in an environmentally and socio-culturally sustainable way that goes beyond what is required by government regulation. For most industries, this is simply desirable, but in ecotourism it is a core imperative (see section 2.3.1). The credibility of ecotourism is therefore at stake because of the innate difficulties in fulfilling these expectations (especially among the small business operators that dominate the industry) and because of the unethical behaviour and 'greenwashing' that characterises so much of what parades under the ecotourism banner (see section 4.2).

Quality control is a means through which ecotourism can attain legitimacy with 'green' consumer markets, environmental NGOs, local communities, government and other stakeholder groups. Related mechanisms are positioned along a spectrum that ranges from the weak and informal to the strong and formal, movement towards the latter indicating increased professionalism and credibility (Black & Crabtree 2007). The following subsections discuss codes of conduct at the weaker end of the spectrum, certification-based ecolabels at the stronger end and awards as an intermediate mechanism.

6.6.1 Codes of conduct

Codes of conduct were discussed in section 4.5.7 in the context of visitor education. As a mechanism for influencing the behaviour of private sector businesses, they became popular throughout the tourism industry during the early 1990s in conjunction with the emergence of the 'sustainable development' model. As with tourist codes, industry codes are criticised as mechanisms that are emasculated by their emphasis on voluntary adherence, self-regulation, non-existent penalties and lack of specific directives or timelines. Moreover, because the costs of writing and displaying a code of conduct are extremely low, they potentially represent an effective vehicle for corporate greenwashing (see section 4.2). The counter-argument is that they offer business a low-risk and non-threatening means of engaging with sustainability, provide generic guidelines that apply to all aspects of a business and morally obligate the sponsoring business or organisation to follow the code. In addition, a major incentive for voluntary adherence and effective self-regulation is the belief that the government will intervene more aggressively as a regulatory agent if the industry is found to be greenwashing.

A good example of an apparently effective voluntary code of conduct for ecotourism is provided by the International Association of Antarctica Tour Operators (IAATO 2006a), which lists procedures that should be followed by organisers and operators before, during and after their trip to Antarctica. The destination portion of this code is depicted in figure 6.4 (opposite), and further discussion is provided in section 8.4.1. Stonehouse (2001) claims that the code has succeeded in modifying the behaviour of Antarctic operators and tourists. However, a broader discussion on the codes described above is speculative since research on the influence of such codes is lacking.

6.6.2 Certification-based ecolabels

Font (2001, p. 3) defines **ecolabels** as 'methods to standardize the promotion of environmental claims by following compliance to set criteria, generally based on third party, impartial verification'. As a vehicle for making ecotourism credible, the crucial aspects here are standard criteria that presumably reflect ecologically and socioculturally sustainable best practice, and verification from a qualified outside auditor that the product in question meets these criteria and thus merits **certification**, or formal confirmation of this status through the relevant ecolabel (Black & Crabtree 2007). Ideally, the ecolabel granting certification should itself be subject to a process of third party scrutiny for the sake of its own credibility, through which it gains **accreditation**, or approval to continue certifying qualifying products and businesses. A useful analogy — and one that the ecotourism industry should aspire to emulate — is the medical student who gains sufficient university grades and credit to be certified as a general practitioner by the University of Queensland's School of Medicine, which in turn is accredited to do so by the Australian Medical Association.

WHEN IN THE ANTARCTIC TREATY AREA, ORGANISERS AND OPERATORS SHOULD:

1. Comply with all requirements of the Antarctic Treaty system, and relevant national laws, and ensure that visitors are aware of requirements that are relevant to them.

2. Reconfirm arrangements to visit stations 24–72 hours before their arrival and ensure that visitors are aware of any conditions or restrictions established by the station.

3. Ensure that visitors are supervised by a sufficient number of guides who have adequate experience and training in Antarctic conditions and knowledge of the Antarctic Treaty system requirements.

4. Monitor environmental impacts of their activities, if appropriate, and advise the competent national authorities of the appropriate Party or Parties of any adverse or cumulative impacts resulting from an activity, which were not foreseen by their environmental impact assessment.

5. Operate ships, yachts, small boats, aircraft, hovercraft, and all other means of transport safely and according to appropriate procedures, including those set out in the Antarctic Flight Information Manual (AFIM).

6. Dispose of waste materials in accordance with Annex III and IV of the Protocol. These annexes prohibit, among other things, the discharge of plastics, oil and noxious substances into the Antarctic Treaty Area; regulate the discharge of sewage and food waste; and require the removal of most wastes from the area.

7. Cooperate fully with observers designated by Consultative Parties to conduct inspections of stations, ships, aircraft and equipment under Article VII of the Antarctic Treaty, and those to be designated under Article 14 of the Environmental Protocol.

8. Cooperate in monitoring programs undertaken in accordance with Article 3(2)(d) of the Protocol.

9. Maintain a careful and complete record of their activities conducted.

■ Figure 6.4
IAATO Code of Conduct: Activities within Antarctica
Source: *IAATO 2006a.*

Ultimately, it is hoped that a tourist market that is increasingly conscientious about environmental and social issues will give their business to certified ecotourism providers, thereby conferring the latter with a competitive advantage over businesses that are not certified. Evidence that this is already an important consideration among ecotourists is provided by the survey of guests at two certified ecolodges adjacent to Lamington National Park (Weaver & Lawton 2002), in which 91 per cent of respondents agreed or strongly agreed that ecotourism operations should be subject to effective certification and monitoring procedures. It is additionally critical that government and other stakeholders offer incentives for operators to become certified. A proactive example is provided by Australia, where the authorities of the Great Barrier Reef Marine Park offer an extended 15-year permit to operators who attain certification under the country's EcoCertification Program, as opposed to a usual period of around six years (GBRMPA 2007a) (see overleaf).

According to Black and Ham (2005), 10 elements are essential for a certification-based ecolabel:

- a credible, committed and well-resourced ecolabel sponsor
- provision of tangible benefits to potential recipients and effective communication of these benefits to the latter
- affordable and reasonable fees for application, certification, recertification and annual renewal, graded to reflect different certification options (e.g. basic, advanced)
- a range of assessment options (e.g. in person, video, written and so on)
- a sufficient network of qualified third party verifiers or assessors to make recommendations about certification
- administrative structures and processes that are simple and user-friendly for applicants, assessors and certifiers
- an accompanying code of conduct that reflects the ecolabel agency's principles and goals
- a stipulated timeframe and set of criteria for eligibility to apply to be certified and recertified
- business planning that incorporates marketing and implementation
- an ecolabel title and logo that are attractive and easily recognisable.

A more prosaic assessment is provided by Buckley (2002), who argues that effective ecolabels must have sufficient 'guts' — that is, substantive standards that positively distinguish certified from uncertified products — and 'teeth' — that is, the capacity to ensure that only qualified products are awarded and allowed to use the ecolabel.

Australia's EcoCertification Program

Australia, through the self-funded **EcoCertification Program**, is widely regarded as the world leader in ecotourism product certification. Introduced in 1996 as the National Ecotourism Accreditation Program or NEAP, the EcoCertification Program is managed by an internal committee of Ecotourism Australia, the national industry peak body (see section 8.2.4). As of late 2006, certification was provided at the regular and advanced levels for ecotourism accommodation, attractions and tours, the focus being on specific products of companies rather than the companies themselves. To encourage a broader ethos of sustainability, a 'nature tourism' category of certification is also provided (Ecotourism Australia 2006). The application procedure is based on self-assessment of various criteria as listed in the application document (see below) and supported by two qualified referees. According to Ecotourism Australia (2006), credibility is maintained by:

1. requiring that at least one of the referees is a manager of a protected area
2. encouraging feedback from the purchasers of certified product experiences
3. undertaking at least one on-site audit on all applicable criteria during the period of certification, and
4. reassessing certification criteria every three years in order to maintain industry best practice standards.

Applicable fees depend on the size of the nominating company. For example, as of late 2006, application and annual fees of A$200 and A$220 respectively were applied for companies with a turnover of less than A$100 000 and A$730 and A$940 respectively for companies with a turnover of more than $10 million. Certified products are allowed to display the relevant logos (see figure 6.5), which are becoming increasingly visible in the promotional material of major Australian wholesalers, such as Sunlover Holidays.

■ **Figure 6.5**
*EcoCertification
logos*
Source:
*www.ecotourism.
org.au.*

The self-assessment procedure is based on 10 criteria and their associated principles. Certification under the 'nature tourism' category requires fulfilment of only the first six (see table 6.1). Ecotourism and Advanced Ecotourism certification additionally requires meeting standards associated with learning, contributions to conservation (which suggests comprehensive ecotourism) and sociocultural sustainability as manifested in working with local cultures and including cultural sensitivity in product interpretation. For each criterion, the application document includes a greater or lesser number of subcriteria that must be fulfilled. For example, criterion number 2 — business ethics — simply requires the applicant to sign off on a code of conduct that is provided in the document. In contrast, criterion number 6 — environmental sustainability — includes 31 core criteria, many of which are applicable to all applicants (e.g. environmental planning and impact assessment; operational environmental management; location; visual impact, biodiversity conservation; lighting; water supply and conservation; wastewater; noise; air quality; waste minimisation and management; energy use and minimisation (transport); minimal disturbance to wildlife and so on), and others that apply only to particular sectors (e.g. construction methods and materials; site disturbance, landscaping and rehabilitation; drainage, soil and water management; energy use and minimisation for buildings; caving behaviour). Each criterion, in turn, has up to 15 statements to assess for basic certification and often as many more for advanced certification. This criterion alone occupies 67 pages of the application document's third edition.

■ **Table 6.1** *EcoCertification eligibility criteria and principles*

CRITERIA	NATURE TOURISM	ECOTOURISM AND ADVANCED ECOTOURISM
1. Business management and operational planning: *Sound business management and operational procedures are integral to the delivery of economic sustainability, which, together with environmental and social sustainability, provide the basis for a 'triple bottom line approach'.*	✓	✓
2. Business ethics: *The business and all its personnel adopt and follow ethical business practices.*	✓	✓
3. Responsible marketing: *Marketing is accurate and leads to realistic expectations.*	✓	✓
4. Customer satisfaction: *Nature tourism and ecotourism consistently meets customer expectations.*	✓	✓
5. Natural area focus: *Nature tourism and ecotourism focuses on directly and personally experiencing nature.*	✓	✓
6. Environmental sustainability: *Nature tourism and ecotourism represent best practice for environmentally sustainable tourism.*	✓	✓
7. Interpretation and education: *Ecotourism provides opportunities to experience nature in ways that lead to greater understanding, appreciation and enjoyment.*		✓
8. Contribution to conservation: *Ecotourism positively contributes to the conservation of natural areas.*		✓
9. Working with local communities: *Ecotourism provides constructive ongoing contributions to local communities.*		✓
10. Cultural respect and sensitivity: *Ecotourism is sensitive to the value of interpretation and involves different cultures, particularly indigenous culture.*		✓

Source: *Ecotourism Australia 2003, 'Eco Certification program application document — third edition', pp. 10–11, www.ecotourism.org.au.*

Limitations

The EcoCertification Program is an evolving quality control mechanism that presumably will continue to be modified as shortcomings are revealed and redressed. Areas of concern at present include the possibility that an otherwise unsustainable company can receive advanced accreditation on the basis of having a particular product certified. Although it is stipulated that the program logo can be used only in conjunction with that product, its appearance could mislead consumers into believing that it pertains to the entire company (see the case study 'Do ecotour operators promote their certified products? Evidence from Australia' at the end of this chapter). It can also be argued that the three logos are insufficiently differentiated. The 'nature tourism' category, although an admirable attempt to certify nature-based products in general, can also be criticised as a half-measure that could theoretically certify culturally insensitive products that happen to meet the required environmental standards. Accordingly, the resemblance of the nature tourism logo to the two ecotourism logos is even more of a concern.

Procedurally, the fact that the initial application process is completed by the applicant and refereed by individuals nominated by the applicant could result in misleading submissions that attain certification and are not exposed until the **auditing** process, which provides a 21-day advance 'warning' to operators. There are also concerns about the specific indicators, almost none of which require adherence to measurable standards. To cite just one example, item 1.15 — energy use and minimisation (buildings) — under criterion number 6 (environmental management), includes the measure 'roofs and walls are insulated'. The applicant ticks this box if applicable and is supposed to provide details in the space provided lower on the page. However, nowhere does the document indicate the acceptable standard of insulation, or whether *all* roofs and walls must be insulated. It is impractical to monitor other indicators, such as the disposal of human wastes in the wilderness or not letting engines run when a vehicle is not moving. When a major infraction is uncovered in the auditing process that leads to suspension (an intermediate step to decertification), the operator is not required to dispose of existing promotional material that displays the EcoCertification logo.

Extensions

Two recent initiatives extend the EcoCertification Program. First, Ecotourism Australia has developed the **EcoGuide Australia Certification Program** to recognise nature and ecotour guides who provide an 'authentic and professional' experience for clients. Individuals with approved guiding qualifications and at least 12 months work experience are eligible to apply for Certified Guide status by working through the questions provided in a self-assessment workbook, then sending this to Ecotourism Australia along with supporting evidence and an application fee. Workplace assessment is a follow-up requirement which documents that the applicant possesses the appropriate skills (Black & Ham 2005).

The second initiative is the **International Ecotourism Standard**, which is an evolving variant of the EcoCertification Program that is intended for global use. As of late 2006, Ecotourism Australia was piloting the standard in partnership with the CRC (Cooperative Research Centre) Sustainable Tourism (an Australian organisation working towards the implementation of sustainable tourism) and Green Globe, an international ecolabel whose criteria are selectively incorporated into the standard (Ecotourism Australia 2006). A growing concern is that resource-strapped communities and small businesses, especially in less-developed countries, will be disadvantaged relative to large companies in obtaining and maintaining their certification credentials.

■ 6.6.3 Awards

In so far as they involve supposedly neutral bodies that confer logos and other recognition to products that meet presumably high standards of environmentally and/or socioculturally sustainable practice, ecotourism awards are similar to ecolabels. However, they differ in (a) being available only to one or two of the products or businesses that qualify, (b) usually having prize money attached, (c) being sponsored by high-profile organisations and corporations, (d) normally being based on outside nominations and (e) involving high-profile awarding ceremonies (Weaver 2006). No research is available to confirm whether possession of an award actually indicates superior performance on the part of the awardee or confers competitive advantage. High-profile sponsors include *Condé Nast Traveler* (a luxury travel magazine), SKAL International (an international association of tourism and travel professionals founded in 1934), *Islands* (a niche travel magazine), Japan's Ministry of the Environment, the government of Queensland, and a partnership between British Airways and the WTTC (World Travel and Tourism Council).

6.7 ∫UMMARY

The ecotourism industry includes a minority of specialised sectors concentrated in the destination, as well as 'mainstream' sectors that facilitate ecotourism travel and organisation in the origin and transit regions. Most ecotourists travel through the formal distribution system, although the FIT circuit is an option for many hard ecotourists. The private sector dominates the ecotourism industry in the more-developed countries, but the corporatisation trend demonstrates the inherent shortcomings of small businesses, which largely pertain to inadequate economies of scale and failure of entrepreneurs to scope the 'real' demand for specialised ecotourism products. Among all business participants, strategic business planning is a necessary but neglected practice that entails the formulation of mission statements, situation (or SWOT) analyses, marketing strategies, financial analyses and operational strategies.

Each segment of the ecotourism industry has its own distinctive characteristics. Guidebooks are a little researched but influential component, and are being rapidly supplanted by Internet resources. Conventional travel agencies and tour operators account for most ecotourism-related package experiences, although NGOs are emerging as an important sponsor of outbound eco-trips. Ecolodges are a specialised high-profile element of ecotourism even though they account for a minor proportion of all ecotourist visitor-nights. However, this may change as corporate-controlled ecolodge chains and ecoresort complexes become more prevalent. Mediating attractions such as cableways, canopy walkways and submarines are acquiring a profile in some destinations. For all components of the ecotourism industry, quality control is an important issue in the context of attaining credibility through increased levels of professionalism. Codes of conduct are a basic form of quality control, but certification is indicative of greater sophistication. In this regard Australia has taken a leading role through the Eco-Certification program, which still has significant limitations. Awards are an intermediate and high-profile category of quality control that often involves sponsors from government and private corporations.

QUESTIONS

1. (a) How much of the world's ecotourism activity occurs through the specialised ecotourism industry?
   (b) Why?

2. (a) Why do small, privately owned ecotourism businesses have a high failure rate?
   (b) What measures could be taken to increase the success rate of such businesses?

3. (a) What are the positive and negative consequences of the corporatisation trend for ecotourism?
   (b) How does this affect economic, ecological and sociocultural sustainability?

4. (a) Why is the SWOT analysis such an important component of business planning?
   (b) How can the same factor be both a threat and an opportunity for an ecotourism business?

5. (a) What advantages and disadvantages are likely to be experienced by small ecolodges and local tour operators that interact or do not interact with the tourism distribution system?
   (b) How does the ownership structure of these intermediaries influence these consequences?

6 (a) What are the strengths and weaknesses of codes of conduct as an industry quality control mechanism?
(b) What role, if any, should codes of conduct play in certification-based ecolabels?

7 (a) Why is Australia's EcoCertification Program regarded as global best practice?
(b) What are the limitations of this program?
(c) How could these limitations be overcome?

8 (a) Why are awards described as an intermediate form of quality control?
(b) What measures could be taken to strengthen awards as a quality control mechanism?

FURTHER READING

Black, R & Crabtree, A (eds) 2007, *Quality Control and Certification in Ecotourism,* **CABI, Wallingford, UK.** This important edited volume is the first to be devoted to the issue of quality control in ecotourism and has a particular focus on certification-based mechanisms. Theoretical and practical perspectives are provided by a variety of experts from academia, government and the non-profit sector.

Black, R & Ham, S 2005, 'Improving the quality of tour guiding: Towards a model for tour guide certification', *Journal of Ecotourism* **4: 178–95.** In addition to chronicling the development of the EcoGuide Certification Program, this article provides background about the certification and eco-labelling process more generally.

Ecotourism Australia 2003, 'Eco Certification program application document — third edition', pp. 10–11, www.ecotourism.org.au. The EcoCertification Program application document represents the state of the art in certification-based ecolabelling, and hence it provides students with an excellent opportunity to assess and critique the self-assessment process and to appreciate the range of indicator variables that the sponsors deem to constitute environmentally and socioculturally sustainable practice.

McKercher, B 1998, *The Business of Nature-Based Tourism,* **Hospitality Press, Elsternwick, Vic.** McKercher provides one of the best and practical guides for actual and potential operators of small nature-based and ecotourism businesses, and it is still relevant. Topics include business planning, marketing, legalities, costing and pricing, and product development. The text is written from an Australian perspective.

Patterson, C 2001, *The Business of Ecotourism: The Complete Guide for Nature and Culture-Based Tourism Operations,* **2nd edn, Explorer's Guide Publishing, Rhinelander, WI.** Now in its second edition, Patterson's book offers useful guidelines for running a successful ecotourism business and provides a valuable template for engaging in business planning.

Do ecotour operators promote *their certified products?* *Evidence from Australia*

For ecotourism business operators and small business owners in particular, gaining Advanced Ecotourism status under the EcoCertification Program for one or more of their products requires a substantial investment in time and money. It is therefore logical that such a status would be prominently featured in the promotional efforts of these businesses, assuming that the effort to certify is made to gain a competitive advantage in the market over non-certified competitors. In contemporary marketing, the Internet has emerged as an increasingly important promotional vehicle for ecotourism and other tourism business owners. For example, almost two-thirds of American adults were reported to have used the Internet to plan their leisure travel in 2004, compared with more than half in 2002 (Lai & Shafer 2005). It is therefore additionally logical to expect that certification credentials would be prominently featured on the websites of these businesses. To investigate this proposition, the websites of 57 Australian tour companies having at least one Advanced Ecotourism certified product were examined in late 2006 (obtained from Ecotourism Australia 2006). Excluded from the study were ecotourism-related accommodation providers such as Kingfisher Bay Resort that also offered certified ecotours. Geographically, Queensland was the best represented host state with 34 tour operators, followed by South Australia (7), Victoria (5), Western Australia (4), New South Wales (3), Northern Territory (2), Tasmania (1) and the ACT (1).

The results of this analysis were unexpected in terms of the degree to which the Advanced Ecotourism certification status of selected products was *not* featured in the company websites. Selected as the standard for high-profile display is (a) the appearance of the relevant logo (see figure 6.5) on the home page of the website with (b) an indication of which product(s) the logo is affiliated with and (c1) a clickable link from the logo to the Ecotourism Australia website and/ or to a detailed explanation of the Advanced Ecotourism certification and how the products meet the relevant standards. The latter was designated with a subscript to allow for option (c2), which is the provision of any kind of non-detailed textual information about the certification. As depicted in table 6.2, only five of the 57 targeted websites met all three substantive criteria (i.e. (a), (b) and (c1)) (line i). In contrast, 12 sites (or 21 per cent) provided absolutely no graphic images or mention of the company's advanced certification credentials (line ix). The remaining 40 sites fulfilled various combinations of the criteria. For example, 6 sites displayed the logo on the front page and clearly linked the logo to the

(continued)

relevant product(s), but provided only cursory textual support (line ii). Eleven more provided the logo and referred it to the product, but did not provide any textual elaboration at all (line iii). Seven sites provided nothing more than the logo on the home page (line vi). Another 7 sites made only passing reference to the certification in the context of applicable products (line vii).

■ **Table 6.2** *Tour operators with Advanced Ecotourism certified products: website adherence to selected criteria*

		CRITERIA			
		(a)	(b)	(c1)	(c2)
Line	Number of operators (n = 57)	Logo appears on home page of website	Logo on home page is clearly linked to applicable products	Detailed information provided, or link to Ecotourism Australia website	Minimal textual information only and no link to Ecotourism Austalia website
i	5	+	+	+	n/a
ii	6	+	+	–	+
iii	11	+	+	–	–
iv	3	+	–	+	n/a
v	3	+	–	–	+
vi	7	+	–	–	–
vii	7	–	+	–	+
viii	3	–	–	–	+
ix	12	–	–	–	–
+	57	35	29	8	19
–	0	22	28	49	30[1]

[1] *Indicates the number not adhering to either criterion c1 or c2; that is, having no textual information at all.*

When examined from the perspective of individual criteria rather than combinations of criteria, several disturbing characteristics emerge. First, 22 sites failed to display the logo on a home page location where it is most likely to be noticed by consumers. However, 17 sites altogether (or 30 per cent) provided no logo on either the home page or on any internal page of the website, despite the fact that a logo serves as the most visible evidence of the special status that the ecolabel confers. Even more disturbing is the fact that three sites displayed the defunct logo used by the NEAP (Weaver 2001b, p. 159), raising to 20 (or 35 per cent) the number of businesses that displayed an incorrect logo or no logo at all. Second, the websites are roughly equally divided between those where the logos are clearly linked to the applicable products and those where the link is unclear. In some cases, the link was by default because the product and the company were synonymous. Third, only eight sites provided Internet readers with detailed information about the EcoCertification program, in most cases through a hotlink to Ecotourism Australia. At best, only two or three sites provided any kind of useful information as to how, in specific terms, the certified product met the standards of Advanced Ecotourism certification. Thirty sites, a majority, provided no textual information at all or any link to the detailed information contained in the Ecotourism Australia website.

These findings have numerous implications for the target ecotour operators, their customers, Ecotourism Australia and the ecotourism industry more generally. With regard to the operators, why are so few of them capitalising on their status as the possessors of Advanced Ecotourism-certified products? If it is argued that the owners do not think the logo has recognition value among consumers, then one is left pondering why certification was pursued in the first place. One possibility is that operators do not yet regard the Internet as a significant marketing tool. Another possibility is that tour operators rely mainly on clients knowledgable enough to access their company's website from the Ecotourism Australia website, at which point the status of the company is already known by these customers. This, however, does not facilitate recruitment of new customers who find out about certification from accessing the company website directly.

Since a major goal of Ecotourism Australia presumably is to improve its brand recognition, this organisation should consider making adherence to criteria (a) and (c1) mandatory for all companies having products with advanced certified products. Adherence to criterion (b) is already required but obviously not well enforced. Companies not clearly affiliating the certification with the relevant products may be doing so out of ignorance, unclear boundaries between products and companies, outdated information on the Ecotourism Australia website or carelessness, but one cannot also rule out deliberate greenwashing. For whichever reason, it is incumbent upon Ecotourism Australia to enforce this policy more rigorously, in the interests of gaining credibility for the organisation and for the ecotourism industry more generally.

Questions

1 (a) What problems do the results in table 6.2 create for consumers wishing to locate and purchase ecotours that meet rigorous standards of environmental best practice?
   (b) How can these problems be overcome?

2 What reasons might account for the fact that a significant portion of the target tour operators do not prominently display their EcoCertification credentials or provide details about them?

External *environments*

After reading this chapter, you should be able to:

- understand and assess the increasing integration and convergence that is occurring between ecotourism and conventional mass tourism

- evaluate the potential positive and negative relationships that can exist between ecotourism and recreational hunting and fishing

- discuss the effect that agricultural expansion and contraction has had and will have on the growth of ecotourism in both the more-developed and the less-developed regions

- assess the actual and potential impact of forestry, mining, non-recreational hunting and fishing, the military and urbanisation on ecotourism

- understand the extent to which ecotourism development is assisted or constrained by government policies and actions

- describe the unpredictable and unstable aspects of natural systems that can affect ecotourism

- employ evaluative criteria to assess the impact of external opportunities and threats on operations so that appropriate actions can be taken.

7.1 INTRODUCTION

Ecological and sociocultural sustainability as well as financial viability are critical outcomes for the ecotourism industry, and it is through business planning that the chances of achieving these objectives are maximised. As part of this process, managers must assess the external opportunities and threats faced by their operation. At a company or destination level this includes consideration of other ecotourism companies or destinations as potential competitors or partners. The emphasis of this chapter, however, is on systems and forces that are external to ecotourism. The ecotourism literature often discounts or ignores the influence of these external environments even though they may greatly influence the capacity of a site or destination to accommodate a viable ecotourism sector. This is partly due to the perception that the ecotourism operator or sector is powerless to influence these forces. The first section in this chapter (section 7.2) examines the relationship between ecotourism and conventional mass tourism as well as recreational hunting and fishing. Section 7.3 considers other economic sectors, including agriculture, forestry, mining and non-recreational fishing and hunting. This section also discusses the influence of the military and urbanisation. Public policy issues that are not directly related to ecotourism, including politics and administration, security, infrastructure, dependency, fiscal policy and financial incentives, are discussed in section 7.4. This is followed by an examination of physical environmental factors, such as earthquakes, volcanoes, climate, disease and the introduction of exotic flora and fauna (section 7.5). Public protected areas, considered separately in chapter 3, may also be regarded as an external environment, although one that is becoming more integrated into the ecotourism industry.

7.2 OTHER FORMS OF TOURISM

Ecotourism, in its soft manifestation, very often occurs as a form of mass tourism (see section 1.5.7). The intention here is to reconsider the relationship between ecotourism and other forms of mass tourism, aspects of which have been raised in previous chapters. Recreational hunting and fishing are also considered as external environments.

■ 7.2.1 Conventional *mass tourism*

Supporters of the cautionary and adaptancy platforms tend to regard the relationship between ecotourism and conventional mass tourism as a mutually exclusive one based on confrontation and competition, but a strong case can be made that the relationship can move more towards cooperation and synergy, provided that the conventional mass tourism is practised in a sustainable manner. For example, as discussed in section 5.2.2, ecotourism stimulates tourism in such 3S destinations as the coast of Kenya and confers competitive advantage to those beach resorts by adding a safari component to the package tour. The benefit for ecotourism is the provision of visitor economies of scale that enhance the ecological incentive effect (see section 4.3.1) and increase the profitability of some specialised ecotourism businesses. This symbiosis is also evident in Australian beach resorts, including the Gold Coast, where marketers have employed such slogans as 'the green behind the gold' to promote the juxtaposition of the intensively built 3S coastline with the heavily forested hinterland. Even the cruise ship industry, widely regarded as the epitome of conventional mass 3S tourism, is increasingly involved in offering ecotourism-based shore excursions (see 'Practitioner's perspective: Ecotourism and cruise ships').

PRACTITIONER'S PERSPECTIVE

Ecotourism and cruise ships

Cruising is one of the most corporatised and rapidly growing sectors of the conventional mass tourism industry (Dowling 2006). The ship itself is the focus of the cruising phenomenon, but shore excursions are an essential component that provides cruise lines with opportunities to diversify the passenger experience and generate additional revenue due to the fact that excursions are not usually included in the 'all-inclusive' cost of a cruise. Traditionally, shore excursions are associated with brief visits to the central business districts of major ports, where passengers indulge in such activities as duty-free and souvenir shopping. However, it is also common to book longer trips that take passengers into the interior of the destination, thus providing even more of a contrast to the 3S experience of the ship. These experiences often have an ecotourism component.

An analysis by Johnson (2006) of 205 Caribbean shore excursions offered by a leading cruise line during the 2003–04 cruise season showed that 21.5 per cent were focused on wildlife observation and another 24.6 per cent were 'landscape and seascape' tours that incorporated some nature observation and learning. The majority of these were clearly soft ecotourism-oriented in that they involved relatively large groups of participants who were conveyed by air-conditioned buses or vans to well-visited 'natural' sites, where various services and facilities were available and minimal physical exertion was required. Many of the tours were mediated by expert local or cruise line guides, but participants effectively remain within the cruise ship-controlled 'bubble'. Also noted were a smaller but still substantial number of tours catering to hard ecotourists, most of which included a strong message of environmental advocacy. Johnson (2006) notes that such destinations as Jamaica and Dominica are developing high-quality natural attractions, such as trails, wildlife sanctuaries and river excursions, that meet high standards of environmental and sociocultural sustainability, and that much of this is specifically in response to growing demand from the cruise lines. However, concerns remain about the willingness of the latter to maintain a long-term commitment to such sites and the emissions and congestion associated with the big vehicles that transport passengers to those sites. More certain is that the large cruise lines will continue to offer a diverse and growing range of ecotourism-based shore excursions in order to expand their market base beyond the stereotypical leisure traveller who dominates the sector.

Symbiosis in many ways is giving way to convergence. This is evident, for example, in the facilitation of much ecotourism activity through the same travel agencies, guidebooks and tour operators that mediate conventional mass tourism experiences (see chapter 6). The involvement of the Sydney-based GPT Group in adding ecolodges to its hotel portfolio illustrates how hotel chains increasingly are also directly involved with ecotourism. Convergence is also demonstrated by the fact that the beach resort and the ecotourism product in such destinations as Kenya and the Gold Coast rely on essentially the same customers. Efforts by the conventional mass tourism industry to become more ecologically and socioculturally sustainable through industry-wide ecolabels, such as Green Globe (see section 2.3.2), are likely to accelerate this trend, eventually leading to the need to reconsider whether conventional mass tourism can be regarded as an external environment.

■ 7.2.2 Recreational *hunting*

There is a stronger case for identifying recreational hunting as an external environment to ecotourism given the apparent contradiction between the viewing and extracting of natural attractions. Moreover, the potential for conflict appears high because hunting often occurs in the same environments frequented by ecotourists (e.g. lower-order protected areas), targets many of the same species valued by ecotourists (e.g. moose and elephants) and can have a disruptive environmental impact (e.g. noise and lead pollution). Yet it becomes apparent when examining global patterns of recreational hunting that, first, there is no single model that describes the relationship between ecotourism and hunting and, second, the relationship is not necessarily contradictory.

A multiple models approach

North America

The relationship between ecotourism and hunting in North America is characterised by ambivalence. In part, this reflects the importance of multiple-use national forests and other lower-order protected areas as venues for large amounts of hunting as well as ecotourism. However, in addition, the tactics of the powerful hunting lobby (e.g. the National Rifle Association and Safari Club International) are becoming increasingly aggressive in response to perceived challenges and the trend of declining participation in hunting, which may or may not be associated with the purported paradigm shift. Between 1991 and 2001, the number of American adults who participated in hunting declined by 7 per cent whereas the adult population overall increased by 12 per cent (US Department of the Interior 2002). This decline appears superficially to favour ecotourism, but the situation is complicated by the fact that pro-hunting NGOs are a major force in the preservation of North American wetland habitats that harbour game birds and other wildlife that are also attractive to ecotourists. For example, conservation easements (i.e. restrictions on property development in exchange for payment or tax concessions to the landowner) arranged by Ducks Unlimited with private owners have resulted in the legal protection of about 200 000 acres of prime wildlife habitat in the USA as of 2004 (Ducks Unlimited 2005).

Australia and New Zealand

The situation in Australia and New Zealand differs from North America in that not only has participation in recreational hunting or 'shooting' increased but also attitudes towards hunting among non-hunters are apparently not as acrimonious. Franklin (1996) attributes this greater tolerance to the late 20th century 'Australianisation' of hunting, which placed the focus on shooting feral animals, such as pigs, rabbits and cats, that destroy native habitat and wildlife. Only a few non-endangered native animals, such as kangaroo, are targeted and, although hunting them is opposed by many environmentalists, it is rationalised as a culling process that is necessary to control unnatural population increases. The former mode of hunting, in any case, can be regarded as an activity that assists ecotourism. In addition, as in North America, NGOs such as Wetland Care Australia (the Australian counterpart to Ducks Unlimited) are involved in wetlands preservation. Despite such complementary relationships, the participation in hunting among ecotourists appears to be negligible. For example, only 2 per cent of respondents to the Lamington National Park survey of ecolodge patrons reported that hunting is somewhat or very important to them as a recreational pursuit (Weaver & Lawton 2002).

Southern and Eastern Africa

Another model is evident in the savanna of southern and eastern Africa, which was the domain of the big game trophy hunter during the era of European colonialism and for some decades afterwards. The introduction of ecotourism in the 1970s, along with anti-poaching measures and the stigmatisation of hunting as an imperialist pursuit, led to the decline of big game trophy hunting in much of Africa. However, trophy hunting has re-emerged in some areas as an important specialised tourism sector. Attention has focused particularly on Zimbabwe's Communal Areas Management Plan for Indigenous Resources (CAMPFIRE), which allows local communities to earn income from wildlife on communal lands as part of a sustainable tourism framework. Big game hunting accounts for most of this activity (Child 2006). Its alleged success as an incentive to protect local wildlife populations has resulted in similar initiatives in other African countries.

Many environmentalists, however, are concerned with the ethics of big game hunting. They also fear that its expansion will lead to unsustainable kill rates, increased poaching (as such commodities as ivory are once again legalised in part, ironically, to curtail poaching) and the expansion in the number of wildlife species that can be hunted. In response to such concerns, most African countries have adopted policies that minimise conflict by segregating hunters from ecotourists. For example, National Parks in Tanzania (IUCN category II) prohibit hunting whereas Game Controlled Areas (IUCN category VI) are reserved exclusively for big game hunting.

Rogue hunting

A final model concerns destinations where unregulated sport hunting is carried out with little or no intervention from government. This 'rogue hunting', often directed at rare and endangered species, is evident in some of the Central Asian and Caucasian republics of the former Soviet Union, which have weak conservation strategies but are stable enough to attract high-spending big game hunters. Such activity often occurs within public protected areas and is threatening the population viability of several wildlife species, such as the snow leopard.

■ 7.2.3 Recreational fishing

Recreational fishing has not generated the same controversy as hunting in part because anglers and ecotourists do not as often use the same environments. Furthermore, a substantial proportion of angling is 'catch and release'. This perhaps helps to explain why 30 per cent of the Lamington National Park survey respondents identified angling as being somewhat or very important as a personal recreational activity (Weaver & Lawton 2002). However, as with hunting, there are different models of recreational fishing. Spearfishing, which is perhaps more appropriately described as a form of hunting, can deplete target species and cause fish to become wary, thereby reducing opportunities for recreational diving. In contrast, advocates of billfish angling (e.g. swordfish and marlin) have argued that their sector is a form of ecotourism (Holland, Ditton & Graefe 1998). Supporters cite the similarities in motivation and behaviour between billfish anglers and ecotourists: the fact that almost all such activity is carried out on a catch-and-release basis, and the contributions that the industry is making to conservation.

7.3 OTHER RESOURCE STAKEHOLDERS

External sectors other than tourism rely on the natural resources used by ecotourists. But whereas ecotourism occurs in relatively undisturbed natural settings, these other sectors produce wealth by disrupting and altering these same settings. This disruption negatively affects the eco-tourism experience because ecotourism depends on the on-site 'consump-tion' of nature-based experiences (i.e. the production and consumption of experiences is simultaneous). However, the same is not true for the consumption of goods produced by these other sectors, since consumption *follows* production and occurs off site (Cohen 2001). Thus, ecotourists are disturbed by the nearby sound of chainsaws, but the buyers of the wooden cabinet ultimately derived from that activity are not, given their spatial and temporal separation from the production process. Other resource users, moreover, have an incentive to degrade natural environments, at least in the short term (e.g. by clear-cutting instead of selective cutting), since this reduces production costs and increases profits. In addition they can substitute new areas of supply once a site has become unprofitable due to degradation. Most of the activities discussed below (e.g. agriculture, forestry and logging, mining, non-recreational hunting and non-recreational fishing) belong to the primary or extractive sector. Military activities are an exception, being loosely related to the tertiary or service sector. Urbanisation and exurbanisation are also discussed in this section because of their large-scale spatial impact in areas that are strategically important to ecotourism.

■ 7.3.1 Agriculture

Agricultural expansion is a major factor underlying the destruction and degradation of natural habitat, and its impact is demonstrated by the fact that most remaining natural habitat occurs in such biomes (ecological communities extending over large areas) as icecaps, tundra, boreal forest, wetlands and desert, which are inhospitable to agriculture. Farming and grazing, in a broader sense, threaten the future viability of ecotourism in most other biomes, despite the potential of agricultural land to accommodate ecotourism (see section 3.5.1) and the incentive value that ecotourism has in preserving natural habitat. However, the threat is not equally distributed, and a basic distinction can be made between the less developed and more developed regions.

Less-developed regions

Large-scale clearance of natural habitat for agriculture now occurs mainly in the less-developed world and especially in rainforest and savanna ecosystems with high ecotourism potential. Brazil and Indonesia are high-profile examples, both having had policies that encouraged colonisation, agricultural expansion, mining and water impoundment in frontier regions. In Brazil's Amazon basin, deforestation is estimated to have occurred at a rate of 1.98 million hectares per year between 1978 and 1989, then slowed to 1.38 million hectares between 1990 and 1994 before accelerating to 1.9 million hectares from 1995 to 2000 (Laurance, Albernaz & Da Costa 2001). Agriculture-related agents include both small-scale peasant farmers and owners of large ranches and plantations. Habitat degeneration is more subtle in areas of shifting cultivation where the cycle of forest regeneration described in section 3.5.1 is shortened due to population pressures.

The proportion of land occupied by forests and other natural habitats, primarily due to agricultural pressures, declined dramatically during the 20th century in almost all less-developed countries, thereby impeding their ability to accommodate ecotourism. This problem extends to such high-profile destinations as Costa Rica, where natural habitat is effectively confined to the protected area system (World Resources Institute 2005). In low-profile countries like Ethiopia, prospects for developing ecotourism are seriously constrained by high deforestation rates. In this case, high-canopy forests have decreased from 16 per cent of the land area to just 2.7 per cent in the early 1990s (Bekele 2001). Extensive protected area systems in many less-developed countries (see table 3.1) should in theory provide core eco-tourism settings that are immune to agricultural expansion. However, as discussed in chapter 3, many of these areas consist of 'paper parks' subject to *de facto* agricultural intrusions due to corruption, inadequate funding for policing, overpopulation and the inability of local ecotourism industries to demonstrate their potential to generate significant revenue from these protected area systems.

The clearance of land for agriculture often results in an indirect negative impact on remaining natural areas, thereby further inhibiting the development of ecotourism and degrading visitor experience at existing sites. This was illustrated in South-East Asia during the late 1990s and early 2000s by the periodic smoke blankets generated by farming-related forest fires in Indonesian Borneo and Sumatra. Other effects include the introduction of exotic flora and fauna, pesticide dispersal and accumulation, sedimentation, microclimatic change and the killing of wildlife (see sections 7.3.4 and 7.3.5). At the macro level, climate change due to the greenhouse effect is associated in part with agriculture (see section 7.6.2). Although agricultural expansion in the less-developed world is often discussed as a barrier to the potential development of ecotourism, there are documented situations where established ecotourism operations are negatively affected. For example, in the Amazon region of southern Peru, the viability of ecolodges was threatened in the mid-1990s by the intrusion of colonists who were given land title in adjacent forests by a sympathetic national government (Yu, Hendrickson & Castillo 1997).

More-developed regions

There is no large-scale agricultural settlement in the developed world comparable to that which is occurring in Brazil or Indonesia. However, Australia is one country in which relatively extensive areas of natural habitat are still being converted to farmland (Rolfe 2002). This is especially true for Queensland, where the conversion of 'scrub' to pasture and other agricultural uses has actually accelerated from an average of 425 000 hectares per year between 1997 and 1999 to 577 000 hectares between 1999 and

2001 (Queensland Department of Natural Resources and Mines 2003). By 2003–04, this had declined to a still unsustainable 483 000 hectares (Queensland Department of Natural Resources and Mines 2006). Moreover, in areas of Australia already used for agriculture, the potential for accommodating ecotourism is hindered by widespread and increasing problems of wind and water erosion, dryland and irrigation salinity, soil structure decline, soil acidification and chemical contamination of soil and water. It is estimated that farming and grazing together are responsible for the extinction of 78 Australian plant species compared with nine species from all other causes (Mercer 2000). Limited rehabilitation is occurring through the National Landcare Programme, which includes measures to plant trees and re-establish native vegetation on peripheral agricultural land (Commonwealth of Australia 2006).

In most of the developed world, the agricultural frontier is either stable or contracting. Stable agricultural landscapes, as discussed in chapter 3, provide substantial opportunities for ecotourism. However, these opportunities are threatened by encroachment on remnant natural habitat as farmers attempt to cope with the cost/price squeeze by increasing production. Contracting frontiers are found along the urban/rural fringe and in areas of marginal productivity. A historical example of contraction is the New England area of the USA where abandonment commenced in the early 1800s as more productive lands to the west became available. States like Connecticut and Massachusetts, once deforested, are now dominated by mature secondary forests offering high-quality ecotourism opportunities, notwithstanding the removal of some of these forests to accommodate urban development. Southeastern states such as South Carolina and Georgia, where natural habitat was almost entirely displaced to make way for cotton plantations and other agriculture, are now mostly occupied by wildlife-sustaining forest land despite rapid population growth. Another contemporary example is Saskatchewan (Canada), where farmland is being abandoned on a large scale in the northern portion of the mixed farming belt. Since the contraction of agriculture is not being replaced by the intrusion of other primary industries, such as forestry, this area has a high potential to become dominated by tourism and by ecotourism in particular (Weaver 1997).

Ecotourists, farmers and hunters

The interaction between ecotourism and other sectors is a complex process involving various external environments and interactions among the latter. This is illustrated by a hypothetical set of scenarios arising from the interrelationships between ecotourists, farmers and hunters on a working farm in a woodland or grassland setting. Each party has its own interests and preferences as to how wildlife on this property should be utilised (see figure 7.1, lines A, B, C). However, only the land-owning farmer usually has the ability to act directly on these preferences (hence the solid line at A but broken lines at B and C). The relationship between farmers and wildlife (trajectory A) is ambivalent and can range from the perception that wild animals are destructive vermin (= desire to eradicate) to a feeling of deep appreciation and stewardship (= desire to preserve), depending on the species. These attitudes influence the willingness of the farmer to accommodate hunters and/or ecotourists.

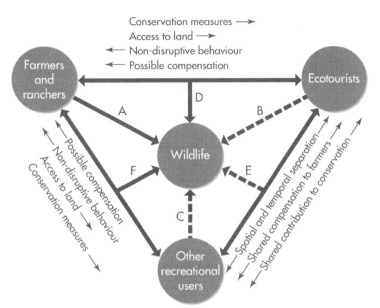

■ Figure 7.1
Stakeholder/
wildlife
dynamics on
a farm

The link between agriculture and recreational hunting (line F) is well established in such countries as the USA, where 77 per cent of farmers reported in the mid-1990s that they provided access to hunters, in many cases to control 'pests', such as groundhogs and crows (Conover 1998). An equally high proportion of farmers and ranchers reported that they took measures to support wildlife on their property. These measures include remnant wildlife habitat such as hedgerows and woodlots, taking wildlife welfare into consideration when applying fertilisers and pesticides, maintaining feeding stations or leaving stubble in fields for wildlife, and acquiring conservation easements on portions of farm properties. In return, hunters are expected to behave responsibly and may be required to provide the farmer with direct or indirect compensation for this access and/or for the damage caused by wildlife. The relationship between farmers and ecotourists (line D) is not well understood, although this is likely to be similar to the relationship between farmers and hunters in terms of compensation expectations. The third bilateral relationship is between ecotourists and other recreational users, such as hunters (line E). As discussed earlier, these relations have a high potential for competition and conflict, especially if both groups attempt to gain exclusive access to a farmer's land. However, there is scope for cooperation between the two groups through strategies of separation in time and space, shared compensation to the farmer and contributions to conservation measures on the farmer's property, all of which could be facilitated by representative organisations and government (see 'In the field: Lobbying for open fields in the USA').

For many Americans, access to private farmland and woodland for recreational purposes is an essential national value based on an unwritten social contract between outdoor enthusiasts and landowners. Such access, however, is diminishing for a variety of reasons. Dominant among these is urban sprawl, which is replacing suitable wildlife habitat near cities with subdivisions, roads and commercial development. Farmland in the 'urban shadow' is also being purchased by urban commuters, who do not want hunters trespassing on or otherwise disrupting or endangering their new 'rural retreats'. An added issue for all landowners is concern over litigation if a hunter or fisher should be injured or injures someone while present on their property. To arrest and reverse this problem of declining access, a bipartisan coalition in the Senate and House of Representatives introduced a bill in 2005 that would provide landowners with modest financial payments through the Department of Agriculture (averaging US$2.50 per hectare) and limited liability protection in exchange for providing recreational access and improving the capacity of their land to serve as wildlife habitat. It is hoped that these financial payments might also assist financially struggling farmers to remain on their land as commercial farmers rather than sell their land to developers (Theodore Roosevelt Conservation Partnership 2006).

Known popularly as the 'Open Fields' bill, this legislation is focused on access for hunters and fishers, but it also accommodates other recreational access. Specifically, it calls for 'public access on private farm, ranch, and forest land, through such activities as hunting, fishing, *bird watching*, and *related outdoor activities* [author's italics]'. Wildlife observation, birdwatching and other ecotourism-related activities are especially suitable because of their minimal liability implications and lesser levels of disruption to landowners. The possibility that birdwatchers and other ecotourists will take advantage of this proposed program is increased by the inclusion of the Sierra Club, a powerful organisation focused on non-extractive conservation, among the 50 or so major outdoor recreation and conservation NGOs that are lobbying to have the bill passed. However, the fact that all the other NGOs are extraction-focused suggests that hunters and fishers will prevail in any disputes that should arise between ecotourists and extractive users.

■ 7.3.2 Forestry *and logging*

Forestry, like hunting, is an extractive activity that appears to be incompatible with ecotourism. Yet both sectors depend upon sustainable management of the resource base for their continued viability, and this constitutes the basis for a potentially compatible relationship. In many areas, however, 'forestry' (i.e. the scientific management of forest resources) is not practised, and it is more appropriate to refer simply to 'logging'. Indonesia is again illustrative as it has enormous reserves of virgin rainforest that are being rapidly depleted due to mismanagement. Attempts to rectify the problem are hampered by the government's preoccupation with higher priority political and economic problems, the escalating breakdown of law and order in certain regions, and the tacit or overt complicity of military and political officials. Furthermore, the government simply cannot contend with the hundreds of thousands of individual loggers who are spontaneously and informally contributing to the problem (Jepson et al. 2001).

The prospect that virtually all old-growth forest in Indonesia will soon disappear is not unreasonable given the unsustainable logging that has already depleted large tracts of forest in South-East Asia, West Africa and elsewhere. It is not always possible to distinguish between timber production and agriculture as causes of this destruction. Opportunistic colonists, for example, may follow logging roads to establish small farms in deforested or forested areas. Often, native forests are cleared to establish fast-growing but biologically impoverished pine or eucalyptus plantations that offer little ecotourism potential (UNEP 2006a). Concerns have been raised over unsustainable large-scale logging projects in such countries as the Solomon Islands and Papua New Guinea, which are regarded as potential ecotourism powerhouses because of their biodiversity and large tracts of relatively undisturbed rainforest. Through desperation, corruption and/or the collapse of social order, governments in such countries are opening enormous areas to logging by transnational corporations even though they lack the means to ensure that these concessions are implemented in a sustainable way (see the case study 'Impediments to ecotourism in Australia's "arc of instability"' at the end of this chapter).

The developed world

The situation is not as dire in the developed countries, where sustainable forestry is more widely practised and governments are better able to police the exploitation of forest resources. Integrated forest use involving the successful accommodation of multiple stakeholders is a long-established practice in Europe. It has been estimated, for example, that 90 per cent of Germany's forests simultaneously provide timber production, ecological maintenance and a variety of recreational activities, including ecotourism, in a sustainable way (Font & Tribe 2000). Lower-order publicly protected wooded areas in North America, such as the US National Forests, are managed with a similar objective, as are some private protected areas (Che 2006).

Controversy surrounds two practices in particular. One is the logging of remnant old-growth forest located outside existing high-order protected areas. In northern California (USA), the charismatic megaflora in question is the redwood. In Western Australia the logging of old-growth jarrah and karri forests has similarly generated conflict between environmentalists and loggers. In response, the state government has embarked on a program to protect large areas of native forest while leaving 42 per cent of all jarrah and karri forests available for timber harvesting (Conservation Commission of Western Australia 2004). Similar conflicts have occurred in the Canadian province of British Columbia, where government is attempting to strike a balance between environmentalists and loggers as to how much primary forest will be made available for logging in the region to be occupied by the proposed 6.4 million hectare Great Bear Rainforest Preserve (British Columbia 2006).

The second issue encountered widely in the more-developed countries is clear-felling or clear-cutting, which is perceived either as a rapacious destruction of the forest or as an efficient means of harvesting and facilitating subsequent replanting or natural regeneration. In Australia, plantations of native tree species are being established as one way of simul- taneously accommodating the needs of ecotourism and the forestry industry in a sustainable way. Nevertheless, some ecologists and environ- mentalists argue that sustainable secondary forests are no substitute for complex old-growth ecosystems.

■ 7.3.3 Mining

As an environment external to ecotourism, mining can be divided into marine and terrestrial operations, recognising that extraction carried out on land can have an impact on offshore waters and vice versa. 'Marine mining' refers particularly to offshore oil and gas drilling and the associated processes of exploration and transportation. Within Australia's Exclusive Economic Zone (EEZ), exploration permits encompass large portions of the Great Barrier Reef, Ningaloo Marine Park and the Great Australian Bight off South Australia. The latter area is one of the most important nursing grounds of the southern right whale, an endangered species. The exploration process is potentially damaging to cetaceans given the risk of collisions with large vessels and the underwater noise pollution caused by seismic testing. Additional problems during the extraction phase include oil spills and pollution (Webster 2003).

Terrestrial mining

Strip mining is a major land-based threat to ecotourism due to its spatially extensive nature, as demonstrated by the large areas cleared for coalmining in the Appalachian region of the USA. In Western Australia, bauxite mining destroyed 6000 hectares of jarrah forest during the latter part of the 20th century (Mercer 2000). Pit or shaft mining does not directly affect such a large area, but may have significant indirect effects through the careless disposal of mine tailings and stream contamination and through related induced effects, such as settlement and road construction. The Jabiluka uranium mine in Kakadu National Park (Australia) is a well-publicised focal point of the conflicts between pit mining interests, indigenous Australians and environmentalists (Banerjee 2000). At the other end of the extractive continuum is small-scale and usually illegal, goldmining, which is causing significant environmental degradation in many remote parts of Suriname and other rainforest destinations (Heemskirk 2002).

■ 7.3.4 Non-recreational *hunting*

Some forms of non-recreational hunting constitute a serious threat to wild-life and hence to ecotourism as well. The most glaring example is poaching that targets endangered species for body parts, delicacies and animal collections. Target animals include rhinoceros (for dagger handles from the horn), elephant (for ivory), tiger and bear (for delicacies, aphrodisiacs and potions). Orangutans and gorillas are captured for animal collections in a manner that often requires the killing of mother animals. Needless to say, these inherently unethical practices pay no attention to sustainability, and resource-starved or corrupt governments in the less-developed world and the former Soviet Union appear unable to reduce poaching levels. The insidiousness of the problem is illustrated by the Virunga Mountains of east-central Africa, where the resumption of mountain gorilla poaching in 2002 after a 17-year period of inactivity quickly led to the death or disappearance of 10 individuals, representing 3 per cent of the site's entire population (WWF 2002). A related problem, although not necessarily illegal, is the increasing popularity of 'bushmeat' in parts of sub-Saharan Africa. Capitalising on logging roads that penetrate the rainforest, bushmeat hunters are killing gorillas and chimpanzees at a rate that will lead to the extinction of these species within the next few decades (Brashares et al. 2004). Traditional subsistence hunting carried out by indigenous people is usually no threat to local wildlife populations, but the exposure of ecotourists to such practices can generate cross-cultural conflict (see section 5.4.3).

The exploitation of wildlife as a basic food source is understandable, although it too can be unsustainable if carried out excessively or if rare species are involved. The same applies to the hunting and killing of wildlife that is regarded as a nuisance because of perceived threats to humans, domestic livestock or crops. Tigers and wolves that prey on livestock are two examples of this threat, although, more commonly, wild animals are killed because they compete for scarce resources with domestic livestock. Traditionally, wild animals have been regarded as a pest by nomadic herders and other users of grazing land in the savannas of sub-Saharan Africa, which is a matter of concern considering that a substantial portion of wildlife in this region is found outside the protected area system. As discussed in chapter 4, ecotourism can potentially discourage such practices because of its incentive effect, although in reality this has occurred to date in only a limited number of destinations in the less-developed world where sufficient revenue-sharing payments are deemed by local residents to compensate for damage by wildlife.

■ 7.3.5 Non-recreational *fishing*

Commercial fishing has a relatively limited direct effect on ecotourism since most target species do not have any status as an ecotourism attraction. Important indirect effects include the depletion of fish species that are food sources for various ecotourism-related marine animals and the inadvertent killing of these species through entanglement in drift nets and other fishing practices. The major direct threats include whaling and the exploitation of reef fish.

Whaling and reef fishing

Whaling is a dormant external factor in most countries, including Australia and New Zealand. Although only a few countries, such as Norway and Japan, maintain residual whaling for ostensible research purposes, a concern for ecotourism and the environmental movement is efforts by these and other countries to resurrect the commercial whaling industry in response to the alleged recovery of cetacean populations (see section 8.2), as Iceland did in late 2006 (Nikolov 2006). Also of concern are continuing efforts orchestrated by Japan to defeat proposals for a whale sanctuary throughout much of the South Pacific (see section 3.2.3).

The harvesting of coral reef fish is a lower-profile but equally serious issue. One manifestation of this sector that is common in some less-developed countries is 'dynamite fishing', which uses explosions to render fish unconscious after which they can be easily netted. It has the residual effect of destroying coral, killing large quantities of non-targeted marine animals and contributing to water pollution. Other non-recreational fishing activities include the collection of live reef species for the aquarium trade or seafood restaurants. A favoured target of the latter is the charismatic Napoleon wrasse, a large and inquisitive reef fish that is a favourite of divers as well as a delicacy in East Asia, and one that is not protected by catch limits in Australian waters or elsewhere. These and other reef fish are commonly captured by using cyanide sprays that, like dynamite, also result in coral destruction and water pollution (NMFS 2004).

The argument for replacing these practices with ecotourism is compelling in theoretical terms. However, as with unsustainable logging and farming, much of the problem is attributable to desperation as individuals seek to survive in the short term by whatever means necessary. For them, the prospect of ecotourism or other tourism income is a remote and unfamiliar possibility.

■ 7.3.6 Military

In most countries, a portion of territory is reserved for military use. Ecotourists and other civilians are normally prohibited from entering such spaces, which moreover may be damaged or rendered unsafe by military activity. The military is a privileged external environment in that it is often given priority in the 'national interest' to areas that are off limits to extractive stakeholders. The Australian military, for example, conducts military exercises that cause local damage to the Great Barrier Reef through bombing practice and to adjacent beaches through landing exercises (GBRMPA 2007b).

It may be argued that the global landscape became 'over-militarised' between 1940 and 1990 due to World War II and its Cold War aftermath. With the collapse of the Soviet Union in the early 1990s, some of this space has been rendered obsolete and was converted to civilian use as part of the so-called 'peace dividend'. The Daniel's Head ecoresort on Bermuda is one example of a conversion directly related to ecotourism

(Gardner 2001). More broadly, Butler and Baum (1999) speculated on the ecotourism potential of defunct NATO bases in the North Atlantic, which encompass and provide ready access to relatively undisturbed natural landscapes. It is unclear, however, whether any of these have actually been converted for this use in any substantive way, especially given increased geopolitical instability in the era following the terrorist attacks of September 11, 2001 in the USA.

◼ 7.3.7 Urbanisation *and exurbanisation*

Intuitively, urbanisation does not seem threatening to ecotourism in sparsely populated countries, such as Australia and Canada. However, all major urban areas in Australia are located in ecosystems of high biodiversity and biological productivity that accommodate significant ecotourism activity. Second, Australian cities are sprawling, low-density entities that occupy an enormous amount of space compared with European and Asian urban areas. Third, the major urban areas are all bordered by much larger exurban hinterlands that combine elements of the urban and rural landscape. They include, for example, people who want a large-lot rural lifestyle and lower rates but who also commute to the city for employment and most of their shopping (Weaver 2005c).

Whereas urbanisation has the pervasive effect of replacing forests and farms with housing and other urban land uses, exurbanisation is a more subtle process of invasion. Typically, forests and other open spaces are gradually fragmented through the haphazard encroachment of individual houses and estates, road improvements and exurban land uses, such as rubbish tips, racetracks and airports. Threats to wildlife include domestic animals, increased traffic, casual and recreational use of bushland and, most importantly, alteration and loss of habitat. A counter-argument, however, is that exurbanites (many of them professionals recently relocated from the city) constitute a well-mobilised opposition group to industrial farming and other negative environmental activity.

7.4 PUBLIC POLICY

Government is a critical external environment for ecotourism, as demonstrated by the central role of public protected area settings (see chapter 3). However, the impact of government and public policy extends far beyond this one component and any other direct participation in the industry. According to Parker (2001, p. 509), 'ecotourism is an activity carried on within a set of social and physical conditions that are heavily influenced by governmental decision making'. This decision-making process, in turn, is influenced by prevalent ideologies, budgets, international trends and the relative lobbying skills of ecotourism stakeholders and the external sectors described above. A model proposed by Parker (2001) will be used in this section to discuss the influence of the public sector on ecotourism (see figure 7.2). At one end of a spectrum, policies involving security, politics and administration operate at a macro level. Micro-level policies, towards the other end of the continuum, involve such areas as infrastructure, fiscal policy and financial incentives where the goals and scope — and subsequent influence on ecotourism — are more restricted. The macro issues mainly involve the national government, whereas micro issues can additionally involve state and municipal governments.

■ **Figure 7.2**
The range of public impact on ecotourism
Source:
Parker 2001.

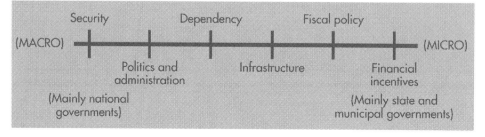

■ *7.4.1* Security

The maintenance of stability and control over all parts of their territory is a core responsibility of national governments and one that has a major influence on the viability of the tourism and ecotourism industries, given the aversion of most tourists to high levels of risk. Governments must therefore do all in their power to protect tourists from physical violence. Most threatening are situations where an entire country is experiencing a civil war or is engaged in warfare with an external enemy. In many countries, ecotourism is threatened by security concerns and instability at the local or regional level. The abduction of an ecotourist in Uganda's Bwindi National Park, and its disruptive effects on that sector, has already been described in section 5.3.2.

Other regional ecotourism destinations that involve a high security risk include the border region between Thailand and Myanmar (due to drug operations and separatist ethnic groups), much of Peru and Colombia (guerrilla movements), Nepal (Maoist guerrillas), parts of the Solomon Islands and Papua New Guinea (see the case study 'Impediments to ecotourism in Australia's "arc of instability"' at the end of this chapter), and Indian Kashmir, the southern Philippines, southern Thailand and eastern Sabah in Malaysia (Islamic insurrectionists in all four cases) (Price 2003). More unusual are situations of instability brought about by official government action. These include the Zimbabwean government policy since the late 1990s of expropriating white-owned commercial farms and of tacitly supporting the occupation of these properties, which has contributed to political instability and large decreases in visitation to ecotourism destinations, such as Victoria Falls.

■ *7.4.2* **Politics** *and administration*

The development of ecotourism is strongly influenced by the overall attitude of the national government towards visitor access, especially where the domestic ecotourist market is small and incapable of compensating for decreases in the inbound flow. At one extreme, isolationist North Korea prohibits access to all but a handful of inbound tourists each year while the Kingdom of Bhutan limits its intake in line with what it perceives to be ecologically and culturally sustainable (see section 9.3.2). The Sultanate of Brunei in South-East Asia has also traditionally placed a low priority on tourism, although concern over the eventual exhaustion of its oil reserves has prompted the government to become more proactive (Brunei Tourism 2006). In rare instances, ecotourism is hindered in origin regions by government restrictions. Perhaps the best-known example is the US government's prohibition on travel by its citizens to Cuba, which reflects long-standing hostility between the two governments. Any relaxation of these restrictions would presumably provide a major stimulus for the development of ecotourism as well as tourism more generally on this Caribbean island.

Government attitudes to tourism

Attitudes towards tourism affect the way that government organises its tourism-related responsibilities. There is no substantive engagement with tourism at the federal level in the USA, while countries such as Australia usually place tourism as a branch of a multisectored ministry. As of late 2006, tourism in Australia was incorporated into the Industry, Tourism and Resources portfolio after having previously been included under the Department of Industry, Science and Resources. Within this portfolio, Tourism Australia was established in 2004 as an umbrella agency that amalgamated the Australian Tourist Commission (international marketing), See Australia (domestic marketing), the Bureau of Tourism Research and the Tourism Forecasting Council (Tourism Australia 2006). These designations are more than bureaucratic artefacts, since they indicate the priority given to a sector and affect the influence and access to funds that the sector can expect. Hence, tourism is now better positioned to compete internally for resources before competing against interests represented by other ministries. The same logic applies to protected areas, which, in such countries as Ecuador, Indonesia and Tanzania, are situated within a ministry of agriculture or forestry.

Government support for ecotourism in Australia

The Australian government has been generally supportive of ecotourism and was instrumental in launching such innovations as the **National Ecotourism Strategy** (NES) (see section 8.4.1) and the NEAP (see section 6.6.2). Although the latter (now the EcoCertification Program) is industry managed and funded, the federal tourism portfolio provided vital seed funding to cover a feasibility study, development of criteria and a pilot study (Allcock 1999). Tangible evidence of government support in the NES was apparent in its allocation of A$10 million towards ecotourism development during the period from 1994 to 1998 through a competitive grants scheme (see section 8.4.1). The federal government also released such influential publications as *Best Practice Ecotourism: A Guide to Energy and Waste Minimisation* (ONT 1997a) and *Ecotourism Education*, a guide to ecotourism-related courses and training programs (ONT 1997b), as part of its efforts to develop the ecotourism sector. It is extremely significant in this context that Tourism Australia has a statutory obligation to help foster sustainability in all facets of Australian tourism (Tourism Australia 2006). At the subnational level, some Australian states, such as Queensland and Western Australia, also support ecotourism. The government of Queensland, for example, has released its own ecotourism strategy (see section 8.4.3) and a business development kit that includes the business planning template discussed in section 6.4.

Ideology and environmental attitudes

The overall political and environmental ideology of a government has a significant direct and indirect impact on ecotourism. For example, the anthropocentric conservatism of the 1980s, symbolised by the Reagan and Thatcher governments, allowed traditional extractive sectors such as forestry and mining to attain an ascendant status. Presumably, the election of a 'green' government would have the opposite effect. In Australia, successive conservative governments in Queensland account for the continuation of widespread habitat clearance and the relatively small portion of land with protected area status. More directly, politics and ideology are evident in the ecotourism industry since federal start-up support in the 1990s was apparently related more to the stimulation of economic development in 'bush' constituencies than to its environmental benefits (Allcock 1999). This also helps to account for the government's concomitant support for small ecotourism businesses.

Elsewhere, pro-environmental policies conducive to ecotourism include a ban on commercial logging in Thailand and legislation in Bhutan that requires 60 per cent of the country to be maintained as forest cover in perpetuity (Penjore & Rapten 2004). Even in pro-development Brazil, the federal government is decelerating its colonisation initiatives due to their expense and disappointing outcomes in the Amazon region. Whether these policy directives have an influence on ecotourism, however, depends on a variety of factors, including the control exercised by the national government and the relationship between the national government and the country's subnational jurisdictions. In the former case, Indonesia is an example of an increasingly ineffectual national government. In the latter case, the power of the national government in Australia and Canada is mitigated by the extensive powers granted to the states or provinces under the federal system of government.

Bilateral and multilateral initiatives

Patterns of inbound visitation are affected by the relationships between countries. This principle can be extended to the willingness of countries to engage in mutually beneficial bilateral and multilateral initiatives that affect ecotourism. The 'Yellowstone to Yukon' (Y2Y 2006) corridor through the USA and Canada is an incipient example that involves more than 200 NGOs working together to manage the corridor as a single functioning ecosystem. A multilateral effort with major implications for cross-border cooperation in ecotourism is the Great Limpopo Transfrontier Park, which involves adjacent high-order protected areas in South Africa, Zimbabwe and Mozambique (see section 10.6.1).

■ *7.4.3* **Dependency**

'Dependency' refers to the *de facto* control that a country exercises over another country, or a national government over states or provinces, through its economic and fiscal dominance. The decisions made by the government of a dependent entity are constrained by the wishes of the government in the dominant entity, just as the empowerment of local residents in community-based ecotourism initiatives is curtailed by conditions that outside funding agencies choose to impose (see section 5.5). Many Latin American governments, for example, prefer policies that require tourism and other businesses to be controlled by their own citizens, but US threats of trade retaliation and aid withdrawal force these governments to permit investment and land ownership by US interests. A more indirect dependency is evident in the effects that one country's fiscal policies can have on another country's tourism sector (see section 7.4.5).

■ *7.4.4* **Infrastructure**

Ecotourism, like all forms of tourism, is dependent on airports, roads and other public infrastructure. However, the ecotourism industry rarely has any influence over their establishment, and rarely do governments undertake these projects with the specific goal of promoting ecotourism. More likely, roads and other infrastructure are constructed to facilitate agricultural colonisation, logging and mining, thereby both increasing access and posing a threat to ecotourism. The best contemporary illustration of this effect is the Brazilian government's longstanding policy of building a road network in its Amazonian frontier to facilitate agricultural expansion, colonisation and border security (Carvalho et al. 2002).

■ *7.4.5* **Fiscal** *policy*

There are several ways in which fiscal policy can directly or indirectly affect ecotourism. Particularly relevant are government decisions regarding entry fees into protected areas. For many years, governments in such countries as Costa Rica and Ecuador diverted entry fees into general treasury revenues (see chapter 3). If these funds were instead reinvested in the protected area system, this could have an extremely beneficial effect on the ability of the parks to accommodate ecotourism in a sustainable way. Taxation is another area of fiscal relevance, since such measures as the imposition of a 10 per cent GST (Goods and Services Tax) in Australia on most aspects of tourism can negatively affect occupancy and visitation levels of businesses already contending with low profit margins. More indirectly, federal fiscal policy on interest rates influences the strength of the Australian dollar and subsequent visitation flows to and from Australia. In North America, the number of US visitors to Canada in the early 2000s decreased substantially largely as a consequence of the strong Canadian dollar (Canadian Tourism Commission 2006). At a broader level, the global free trade or 'globalisation' agenda being pursued by the World Trade Organization and other bodies, if implemented, will further erode national sovereignty in all countries and accelerate the internationalisation and corporatisation of ecotourism.

■ 7.4.6 Financial *incentives*

Government financial incentives usually favour large tourism projects and businesses since these are regarded as more effective producers of revenue and jobs. For example, generous tax and other concessions provided by governments in many English-speaking Caribbean islands are structured to benefit large-scale corporate projects rather than small, locally owned ecolodges and guesthouses. However, in such countries as Australia, political considerations also result in the provision of financial and other support to small business owners, especially in rural areas. Other fiscal policies that have a direct or indirect effect on ecotourism include departure and bed taxes.

7.5 PHYSICAL ENVIRONMENTAL FACTORS

Ecotourism is dependent on the natural environment for its attractions, but related natural systems and forces can also be considered external for purposes of discussion. The stability of natural systems is an important consideration for ecotourism, which can make allowances for predictable daily and seasonal variation in environmental conditions. Problems for ecotourism occur when these systems behave in unstable ways that negatively affect venues. This element of unpredictability is considered below in the context of geophysical, meteorological and biophysical systems.

■ 7.5.1 Seismic *activity and volcanism*

Many ecotourism destinations are located along tectonic plate boundary zones that experience frequent seismic activity. Earthquakes, which are unpredictable in terms of location and timing, can damage ecolodges and other structures, destroy access roads and disrupt hiking trails, particularly in mountainous areas that characterise these zones. Tsunamis (earthquake-induced sea waves) pose an added threat in coastal areas, as demonstrated vividly by the disastrous event of 26 December 2004, which killed an estimated 200 000 people in Indonesia, Thailand, Sri Lanka and other countries in the Indian Ocean basin (Weaver & Lawton 2006). Other vulnerable regions where ecotourism is present include Central America, the Andes, the eastern Caribbean, southern Alaska, the African Rift Valley, the Philippines, New Zealand and South Pacific destinations, such as Vanuatu and Papua New Guinea.

Volcanic activity also poses a potential but more spatially identifiable and confined threat in these regions. In the heavily visited Irazú and Poás national parks of Costa Rica, volcanic eruptions periodically disrupt access. From an ecotourism perspective, the most dramatic volcano-related event in recent years was the devastation of Montserrat, a Caribbean island, by the unexpected eruptions of Chance's Peak in the mid-1990s. Ironically, the supposedly extinct volcano and its residual sulphur springs were a major element of Montserrat's considerable potential as an ecotourism destination. Another irony is that the active volcano and the surrounding landscape devastation have themselves become tourist attractions in the wake of the eruption.

■ 7.5.2 Climate

Cyclones are a serious threat to ecotourism and related infrastructure in susceptible parts of the tropics and subtropics, as demonstrated by the impact of Cyclone Larry on the Far North of Queensland in March 2006 (TTNQ 2006). However, like earthquakes and volcanic eruptions, they are a normal episodic phenomenon in these areas and hence also an element of the natural environment that can be included in product interpretation, although their intensity and distribution may be increasing due to climate change (see overleaf). In addition, human-induced changes in the affected landscape, such as tourism development, urbanisation and deforestation, serve to amplify their environmental impact.

Extreme or aberrant weather conditions in some situations also provide opportunities for ecotourism. High volumes of precipitation may cause washouts and make hiking trails impassable, but it also creates impressive waterfalls. Abnormally high rainfall in central Australia during May 2000 resulted in Lake Eyre being filled to 80 per cent of its capacity, an event that occurs only a few times each century. The ecotourism industry responded to this ephemeral opportunity by temporarily altering itineraries to include the Lake Eyre region. A similar element of uncertainty and opportunism occurs in the semi-arid landscapes of south-western Western Australia and Namibia where suitably timed episodes of unusually high precipitation result in exceptional wildflower displays.

Climate change

More ominous is the instability induced by contemporary climate change, which appears to be related mainly to anthropogenic factors, such as agriculture, logging, manufacturing, transportation and urbanisation (McMichael, Woodruff & Hales 2006). The consequences of climate change for ecotourism are potentially severe. Rising and warming sea levels have been implicated in the degeneration and death of coral reefs throughout the world, including the Great Barrier Reef (GBRMPA 2006). Some scientists suggest that coral will adapt through natural selection and colonisation in higher latitudes, but this does not compensate in the shorter term for the current degradation or offer any comfort to reef-dependent destinations. Furthermore, rates of coral die-back and destruction tend to far exceed rates of establishment in new areas.

Adverse effects are not confined to tropical reefs. In theory, warmer seas caused by global warming reduce phytoplankton production to levels that affect krill populations and, subsequently, the viability of baleen whale populations and other cetaceans (Prideaux & Bossley 2000). Polar bear health and reproduction are also being negatively affected by warming sea temperatures as a shorter period of ice cover on Canada's Hudson Bay reduces the amount of time that animals can feed on baby ringed seals, their preferred prey. Average body weight and the number of offspring are both declining as a result and, on the basis of current climate change predictions, it is unlikely that the species will survive (Derocher, Lunn & Stirling 2004).

■ 7.5.3 Disease

Biophysical threats to ecotourism are found in the increased range of serious diseases that can be contracted by ecotourists, especially in the rural areas of tropical and subtropical destinations. Travellers to most tropical rainforest and savanna-based destinations are at risk of contracting malaria (see figure 7.3), and this risk is increasing as mosquitoes develop resistance to existing anti-malarial medications (IAMAT 2006). This has already occurred in the Thailand–Myanmar border region, a popular trekking destination. Other diseases that can be easily contracted in typical ecotourism settings include dengue fever, Japanese encephalitis, typhoid fever and hepatitis as well as more obscure diseases such as South American cutaneous leishmaniasis. Some diseases associated with Africa, such as ebola and monkeypox, may be a result of increased exposure of primate habitats to hunters using logging roads (LeBreton et al. 2006). The African AIDS epidemic is a particularly serious development given the high rates of adult infection that have been reported in the safari destinations of southern and eastern Africa: an estimated 30 per cent of adults in Botswana and 20 per cent in South Africa (see section 10.6.1). Although ecotourists have an extremely low risk of becoming infected, fears about this disease may discourage visitation.

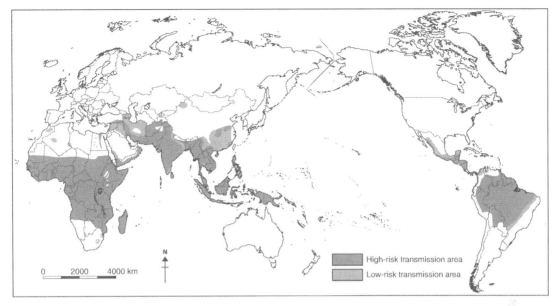

■ **Figure 7.3** *Areas of malaria transmission risk*
Source: *IAMAT 2006.*

■ *7.5.4* Intrusion *of exotic species*

A second major biophysical threat to ecotourism is the deliberate or inadvertent introduction of exotic flora and fauna that can potentially devastate native species. Introduced species have created problems in Kakadu National Park (Australia), where feral water buffalo and pigs have caused significant habitat disruption along with certain introduced South American plants (Low 2002). Park managers are also rightfully concerned about the arrival of the cane toad, which is capable of wreaking environmental havoc in Kakadu if it becomes established there. Another case of severe environmental damage from introduced animals is Macquarie Island, a sub-Antarctic Australian possession where more than 100 000 rabbits are causing destructive landslides and damage to king penguin and albatross colonies by stripping hillsides of their vegetation cover (BBC News 2006).

7.6 ASSESSING EXTERNAL ENVIRONMENTS

Business planning at the destination or enterprise level should assess the threats and opportunities posed by all relevant external environments so that appropriate responses can be made. To facilitate this process, these environments can be evaluated along six continua, as shown overleaf.

- threat $\longleftrightarrow$ opportunity
- formal $\longleftrightarrow$ informal
- major $\longleftrightarrow$ minor
- direct $\longleftrightarrow$ indirect
- ascendant $\longleftrightarrow$ descendant
- immediate $\longleftrightarrow$ gradual

For example, in scenario A, a hypothetical instance of residual logging in old-growth forest by a logging company in a Western Australian lower-order protected area can be perceived as a threat that is formal (legal), major (poses an existential threat to the operation), direct (occurs through direct removal of target charismatic megaflora) and immediate (the damage occurs right when the trees are cut) as well as descendent (about to end due to new regulations). In scenario B, the federal election of the Green Party in Australia is an opportunity that is formal, major, indirect, ascendant (indicates a societal trend) and gradual (policies work their way through government to the field). In scenario C, climate change from the perspective of a tour operator on the Great Barrier Reef is a threat that is informal (the unintended result of collective lifestyle and economic decisions), major (leads to massive dieback of coral), indirect (damage caused to coral by warming waters), ascendant (the problem is getting worse) and gradual (dieback occurs slowly).

The most serious threats are those such as climate change that are major and ascendant as well as harder to control because they are indirect. However, although destinations or businesses can do almost nothing to eliminate such threats, the fact that their effects are revealed gradually allows time to make necessary adjustments, such as relocating operations to cooler waters or focusing on more resistant species. In contrast, such an activity as old-growth logging has immediately dire consequences for individuals of particular species, but may not affect the relevant ecotourism operation over the long term due to the descendant nature of the threat as well as the greater possibilities for the operation or the ecotourism sector more generally to lobby against logging in a particular area, for example on grounds of the threat posed to a water supply or endangered species of mammal. Accordingly, it is extremely important that ecotourism businesses work collectively within relevant interest groups to ensure that their legitimate interests are protected.

7.7 SUMMARY

External environments are critical influences on the development of ecotourism businesses and destinations but tend to be treated in a cursory way in the literature. Conventional mass tourism has traditionally been regarded as one of these external environments, but this perception must be re-examined given the convergence and interdependence that is occurring between the two forms of tourism. Recreational hunting and fishing are more clearly positioned as external environments that can have positive and negative relationships with ecotourism, depending on the model in question. In the primary sector, agriculture has a major impact on the prospects for ecotourism because of its expansion into forest and grassland environments, particularly in less-developed countries. In the developed world, large-scale land clearing is still occurring in Australia, where the problem is one of habitat fragmentation and degradation. In many regions, the contraction of the agricultural frontier has resulted in opportunities for ecotourism. Logging is also having a widespread negative impact on potential ecotourism settings in the less-developed world. Sustainable forestry, in contrast, is common throughout much of the developed world, although old-growth logging and clear-felling are highly publicised practices with negative implications. The influence of non-recreational fishing is focused on whaling activity and with harvesting of reef fish in the vicinity of coral reefs. Mining, non-recreational hunting and the military are other aspects that have local influence on ecotourism potential, while urbanisation and exurbanisation are also influential in highly urbanised countries such as Australia.

Governments, beyond their direct participation in the industry, play an extremely important role in the development of ecotourism. Crucial among these is the maintenance of stability in a region and the imposition of favourable policies and actions. Government ideology, moreover, is a major factor that dictates the nature of these policies as is the lobbying pressure exerted by various resource stakeholders. Less predictable are unstable events within natural systems. Potential geophysical threats in seismically active regions include earthquakes and volcanic eruptions. Cyclones are a major climatic threat in susceptible regions while climate change is a more pervasive danger in coastal and marine areas especially. Enhanced disease risk and fear of disease may become an increasingly dissuasive factor in some regions, and exotic flora and fauna are problematic in others. All ecotourism destinations and businesses should attempt to identify relevant external threats and opportunities so that appropriate actions can be taken. To assist in this process, specific external environments can be profiled using various criteria, including whether they are major or minor, formal or informal, direct or indirect, ascendant or descendant, and immediate or gradual.

1. (a) Is it appropriate to describe conventional mass tourism as an environment external to ecotourism?
   (b) What are the implications of the increasing convergence and integration of ecotourism and conventional mass tourism for ecotourists, small ecotourism businesses and local destination communities?

2. (a) Is ecotourism inherently incompatible with extractive recreational activities, such as hunting and fishing?
   (b) Why or why not?
   (c) Is it reasonable to describe bill fishing and big game hunting as forms of ecotourism?

3. (a) How do the effects of agriculture differ between less-developed and more-developed countries?
   (b) What opportunities do contraction of agricultural frontiers in the more-developed countries offer ecotourism?

4. (a) To what extent are agriculture and logging related as external environments?
   (b) What challenges do these interrelationships pose to the ecotourism sector?

5. (a) Why is the military referred to as a 'privileged external environment' (section 7.3.6)?
   (b) Why has the 'peace dividend' not had the positive effects on ecotourism that some originally predicted?

6. (a) How can the political ideology of a government affect the development of a viable ecotourism industry?
   (b) How would the election of a right-wing federal government most likely be perceived from the perspective of the soft and hard ecotourism sectors respectively, in terms of the criteria outlined in section 7.6?

7. (a) How would the arrival of a major cyclone at a coastal ecotourism site be assessed in terms of the criteria outlined in section 7.6?
   (b) What precautions could an affected operator take in anticipation of a similar disaster in the future?

8. (a) How do biophysical systems negatively affect ecotourism?
   (b) Are these effects becoming more or less serious?
   (c) What can be done by the ecotourism industry to cope with these effects?

FURTHER READING

Font, X & Tribe, J (eds) 2000, *Forest Tourism and Recreation*, **CABI, Wallingford, UK.** This collection of 17 chapters (by various authors) provides a comprehensive overview of issues and case studies from around the world relevant to ecotourism and other forms of recreation in forest settings. The relationship between forests, recreation (ecotourism and other) and logging is addressed in most chapters.

Parker, S 2001, 'The place of ecotourism in public policy and planning', in DB Weaver (ed.), *Encyclopedia of Ecotourism*, **CABI, Wallingford, UK, pp. 509–20.** Parker's chapter is probably the first attempt to describe and model the relationship between public policy and ecotourism. International case studies from the academic literature are used to illustrate the concepts.

Price, S (ed.) 2003, *War and Tropical Forests: Conservation in Areas of Armed Conflict*, **Haworth Press, New York.** Included in this edited collection are case studies from Colombia, Nicaragua, East Africa and Indonesia that effectively illustrate the difficulties of pursuing environmental initiatives in regions beset by chronic civil war and other problems.

Yu, D, Hendrickson, T & Castillo, A 1997, 'Ecotourism and conservation in Amazonian Peru: Short-term and long-term challenges', *Environmental Conservation* **24: 130–8.** Although somewhat dated, this article is unusual in that it provides a detailed case study of a rainforest-based ecotourism operation that was seriously threatened by several external environments, which are still relevant.

Impediments to ecotourism
in Australia's 'arc of instability'

Papua New Guinea (PNG) and the Solomon Islands are two South Pacific countries that have failed to fulfil their enormous ecotourism potential due to a combination of dissuasive external threats. This potential is based on an extraordinary level of biodiversity in a relatively small area. For example, the island of New Guinea (divided about equally between PNG and Indonesia) has as many species of plants and animals as Australia, including most of the world's tree kangaroo and bird of paradise species, although it is just a tenth as large. About two-thirds of these species are endemic; that is, native to nowhere else. New Guinea contains nine of the 142 terrestrial bioregions identified by the Worldwide Fund for Nature (WWF) as global biodiversity 'hotspots', indicating an extremely diverse landscape that ranges from the third largest expanse of continuous high closed-canopy tropical rainforest to alpine glaciers. Seventy per cent of the island is occupied by forests, and the population density is low (12.5/km^2) (WWF 2006b). The Solomons also have a high level of endemism and a low population density (20.1/km^2), as well as a forest cover that similarly occupies about 70 per cent of the country (Mongabay.com 2006). Adding to the ecotourism potential of the two destinations is their location within a few hours flying time from major Australian and East Asian cities.

Despite this potential, ecotourism in both countries is incipient. The Solomons are perhaps best known in this regard for the Rapita Lodge facility in Marovo Lagoon, which was established in 1995 as a community-based project funded by the Japanese Environment Corporation with training provided by the WWF (Buckley 2003a). PNG has several similar projects but is best known for the Kokoda Trail, a hiking path following the supply route used by Australian troops during World War II. Three thousand tourists were expected to hike the trail in 2006. The ecotourism situation reflects the tourism situation more generally in both countries. In the case of PNG, just 70 000 inbound tourists arrived in 2005, of whom only 18 000 were leisure tourists (PNG 2006). In 1995, the last year for which data is available, just 12 000 international tourists visited the Solomons (WTO 2006c).

Lack of accessibility and poorly articulated market image are two factors that help to explain the invisibility of PNG and the Solomons as international tourist and ecotourist destinations. More insidious, however, is the chronic social, economic and ecological instability that is in turn related to deep poverty and the fact that residents of the two countries still tend to identify more with their own tribes than with the nation as a whole. For example, more than 80 per cent of the territory of the Solomons is covered by customary tenure rights and, although this facilitates community-based initiatives, it discourages private sector investors, who insist on the security of their own tenure. It also means that local 'bigmen', or males who have achieved dominance through the accumulation of wealth, have the most decision-making power, whereas government has very little influence in decisions regarding land use (Sofield 2003).

Tenure arrangements explain why PNG and the Solomons are among the countries having the lowest percentage of their territory set aside for public protected areas (see section 3.2). They also account for accelerating rates of unsustainable logging since the late 1980s. In the case of the Solomons, Asia-based logging companies sought access at this time to new timber sources to meet export obligations after the governments of their own countries imposed restrictions on domestic harvesting. These companies overcame existing legal restrictions on logging by negotiating with local bigmen, who were often keen to provide access to customary land in exchange for cash, schools and other benefits not provided by government. These benefits are enormously important given a per capita GDP (adjusted for purchase power parity) of just US$1700 (CIA 2006). By 1994, more than 3 million cubic metres of timber were cut per year, representing about 10 times the estimated sustainable harvest. The national government did take 'paper' action to curtail this abuse, but was reluctant to intervene more forcefully due to resistance from villagers (Calder 1997). The Asian economic recession of the late 1990s reduced this exploitation, but an estimated 1.7 per cent of the forest was subsequently cleared each year between 2000 and 2005. Overall, the percentage of the Solomons covered by forest declined from 90 to 70 per cent between 1990 and 2005 (Mongabay.com 2006). Exacerbating the exploitation of the forests is an extremely high birth rate, which has increased the population from 286 000 in 1986 to 430 000 in 2000 (Sofield 2003) and 553 000 in 2006 (CIA 2006). In PNG, the rate of deforestation has not been as severe, although at least 5 per cent of the forest cover was allegedly lost to logging, mining and agricultural expansion between 1990 and 2000 (Forests Monitor 2001).

Tribal loyalties, poverty and population pressure have also combined to provoke dangerous levels of social instability in the Solomons. Armed warfare erupted in 1999 when residents from the overcrowded island of Malaita purchased former plantation land on Guadalcanal that was regarded as customary land by the locals. Government was basically powerless to prevent this warfare, which induced a mass exodus of Malaitans (Sofield 2003). The Solomons achieved 'failed state' status in the early 2000s due to the combination of tribal warfare, rampant crime, government corruption and widespread environmental degradation. The arrival of an Australian-led multinational security force in 2003 restored order (CIA 2006), but widespread rioting, which destroyed the capital city's Chinatown neighbourhood in April 2006, attested to the precarious nature of this recovery (Spiller 2006).

PNG, with 10 times the population of the Solomons, has not experienced the same degree of sociopolitical disintegration and did experience something of an economic upturn in the early 2000s due to rising commodity prices.

(continued)

However, sociopolitical collapse is not an unreasonable prospect given similar patterns of poverty, rampant population increase, pervasive corruption and persisting tribal loyalties. Of concern is the continuing mass migration of villagers into urban areas such as Port Moresby, which has resulted in high employment (more than 80 per cent in the cities), squatter settlements, increases in violent gang-related crime and inter-ethnic conflict. Moreover, an armed separatist movement on the island of Bougainville is currently quiescent but could reactivate at any time (US Department of State 2006).

Questions

1 What factors provide Papua New Guinea and the Solomon Islands with a potential competitive advantage over other regional ecotourism destinations?

2 (a) What two root factors, aside from lack of accessibility, are primarily responsible for the fact that this ecotourism potential has not yet been realised?

   (b) What actions, if any, could the ecotourism sector in the two countries take to address these root factors?

3 What actions could the ecotourism sector in the two countries take to address the rampant deforestation and inter-tribal warfare that was triggered by these root factors?

8

Organisations
and policies

LEARNING OBJECTIVES

After reading this chapter, you should be able to:

- describe the general characteristics of membership-based ecotourism organisations, including their potential range of functions

- understand the differences between The International Ecotourism Society and Ecotourism Australia and their respective contribution to the global and Australian ecotourism sectors

- assess the geographical and structural challenges faced by these two organisations

- demonstrate the involvement of other NGOs and government agencies in the development of ecotourism

- explain the objectives and accomplishments associated with Australia's National Ecotourism Strategy and the Queensland Ecotourism Plan

- show how ecotourism plans are affected by broader tourism and development plans and policies

- assess the status of Australia as a world leader in ecotourism-related institutional initiatives, such as ecotourism NGOs and plans.

ℐNTRODUCTION

Effective organisations and policies are indicators and facilitators of professionalism. They help the ecotourism sector to attain quality control objectives related to environmental, economic, sociocultural and financial sustainability while offering mechanisms through which the industry can better contend with the multiple external environments discussed in chapter 7. The first section of this chapter focuses on ecotourism-specific organisations and, in particular, The International Ecotourism Society as the primary multilateral organisation and Ecotourism Australia as a country-level leader. The number and distribution of ecotourism organisations is discussed, along with their formation, functions, structure, membership patterns and funding arrangements. Other types of NGO and government organisation are also involved with ecotourism, and they are considered in section 8.3. Ecotourism-related policies and the plans that express these policies are examined in section 8.4. The National Ecotourism Strategy of Australia and the Queensland Ecotourism Plan are featured as examples of ecotourism planning at the national and subnational levels. Finally, section 8.5 outlines the status of ecotourism in policies and plans more broadly related to tourism and other sectors.

ℰCOTOURISM ORGANISATIONS

Ecotourism NGOs can be classified as international, national, state and local, depending on the geographic constituency being represented. The following subsections examine the distribution of such organisations and their formation, function, structure, membership and funding. Subsequently, The International Ecotourism Society and Ecotourism Australia are described and critiqued as the two highest profile ecotourism organisations in the world.

8.2.1 **Number** *and distribution of membership-based organisations*

Halpenny (2001) estimated that 33 membership-based ecotourism organisations were in existence worldwide as of mid-2000. By 2006, this apparently increased to around 50, an estimate that was derived by analysing the 'association' membership category of The International Ecotourism Society, cross-checking the links of the websites of these members and conducting a thorough Google search under the terms 'ecotourism association', 'ecotourism society' and 'ecotourism organisation/ organization' (see table 8.1). This is not necessarily a complete list given that such organisations have proliferated since the late 1990s and information on most is difficult to obtain. For example, several did not yet have an operating website in late 2006 but provided email and/or telephone contacts on other websites. This indicates that they were in the initial stages of mobilisation and organisation at that time. Because table 8.1 is not necessarily inclusive, observations on number and distribution must be made cautiously. It seems clear, however, that national organisations are dominant and that the Asia–Pacific region and the Americas are overrepresented (each has 19 organisations) whereas Europe (with 7 organisations) and Africa (5 organisations) are underrepresented.

■ **Table 8.1** *Membership-based ecotourism organisations in 2006*

ASSOCIATION	COUNTRY	LEVEL
Alaska Wilderness Recreation and Tourism Association (AWRTA)	USA	State
American Ecotourism Association (AEA)	USA	National
Armenian Ecotourism Association	Armenia	National
Asociacion Ecuatoriana de Ecoturismo (ASEC)	Ecuador	National
Asociacion Ecoturismo Guatemala	Guatemala	National
Belize Ecotourism Association (BETA)	Belize	National
Benin Ecotourism Concern	Benin	National
Camara Nacional de Ecoturismo de Costa Rica (CANAECO)	Costa Rica	National
Central Balkan Kalofer Ecotourism Association	Bulgaria	Local
EcoBrasil — Associacao Brasileira de Ecoturismo	Brazil	National
Eco-Nigeria: Ecotourism Association of Nigeria	Nigeria	National
Ecotourism Association of Papua New Guinea	Papua New Guinea	National
Ecotourism Australia	Australia	National
Ecotourism Kenya	Kenya	National
Ecotourism Norway	Norway	National
Ecotourism Society Philippines Foundation	Philippines	National
Ecotourism Society of Sri Lanka	Sri Lanka	National
Ecotourism Society Pakistan	Pakistan	National
Ecotourismo Italia	Italy	National
Estonian Ecotourism Association (ESTECAS)	Estonia	National
Fiji Ecotourism Association	Fiji	National
French Ecotourism Society	France	National

(continued)

ASSOCIATION	COUNTRY	LEVEL
Fundacion Ecoturismo Argentina	Argentina	National
Grand Bahama Island Ecotourism Association	Bahamas	Local
Hawaii Ecotourism Association (HEA)	USA	State
Indonesian Ecotourism Center (Indecon)	Indonesia	National
Japan Ecotourism Society (JES)	Japan	National
Kamchatka Ecotourism Society	Russia	Local
Kunigami Tourism Association	Japan	Local
La Ruta de Sonora Ecotourism Association	USA and Mexico	International
Mesoamerican Ecotourism Alliance	Central America	International
Mexican Association of Adventure Tourism and Ecotourism (AMTAVE)	Mexico	National
Mongolian Ecotourism Society (MES)	Mongolia	National
Marovo Lagoon Ecotourism Association	Solomon Islands	Local
Mount Cameroun Ecotourism Organisation	Cameroon	Local
Murghab Ecotourism Association (META)	Tajikstan	National
Northern NSW Ecotourism Association (NNETA)	Australia	Local
Samoan Ecotourism Network	Samoa	National
Saskatchewan Nature and Ecotourism Association (SNEA)	Canada	State
Sociedad Venezolana de Ecoturismo	Venezuela	National
Socotra Ecotourism Society	Yemen	Local
Sri Lanka Ecotourism Foundation (SLETF)	Sri Lanka	National
Swedish Ecotourism Association	Sweden	National
Taiwan Ecotourism Association (TEA)	Taiwan	National
Thai Ecotourism and Adventure Travel Association	Thailand	National
The International Ecotourism Society (TIES)	USA	Global
The Ontario Ecotourism Society (TOES)	Canada	State
Toledo Ecotourism Association	Belize	Local
Virginia Ecotourism Association (VETA)	USA	State
Zanzibar Ecotourism Association	Tanzania	Local

■ *8.2.2* **Organisational** *characteristics*

Information about the organisational characteristics of ecotourism-related organisations is scarce, partly because of the lack of published research on this topic and partly because of the paucity of information available from the organisations themselves. Nevertheless, tentative observations can be made about their formation, function, membership structure and funding.

Formation

The growth in ecotourism organisations is a reflection of the overall growth in this sector, although according to Halpenny (2001) there are at least three circumstances that individually or in combination trigger their formation. First, some are conceived as a result of ecotourism conferences, which provide the critical mass of stakeholder interaction necessary for identifying common issues and problems and initiating formal institutional measures to address these concerns. The International Ecotourism Society, for example, was formed in 1990 during the International Symposium: Ecotourism and Resource Conservation held in Miami, Florida. The Hawaii Ecotourism Association emerged as an outcome of the 1994 statewide Conference on Ecotourism held in Waikiki.

The second factor is the restructuring and repositioning of existing organisations. An illustration is the Saskatchewan Nature and Ecotourism Association (SNEA), which was previously constituted as the Ecotourism Society of Saskatchewan (ESS) and originally as the Saskatchewan Watchable Wildlife Association (SWWA). In its original guise the organisation was criticised for being too narrowly focused. The initial restructuring positioned it more clearly as an ecotourism organisation while its latest iteration indicates a sphere of interest embracing nature-based tourism more generally.

Some organisations, thirdly, are formed in response to crises and disasters. A disaster-related example is the Alaska Wilderness Recreation and Tourism Association, which was established in response to the *Exxon Valdez* oil tanker spill in 1989. Ecotourism Kenya was originally established as the Ecotourism Society of Kenya (ESOK) in reaction to the perceived crisis of sustainability in Kenya's protected area system. According to Twining-Ward (2005), many of the organisations were formed in the mid-1990s in response to the Rio Earth Summit and its Agenda 21 call to action (see section 2.2.3).

Functions

Most organisations have a mission or vision statement that encapsulates their core mandate and provides a basis for the articulation of strategic objectives. Typically these foundation statements reflect the desire to protect and sustain natural resources while addressing the legitimate interests of operators and other stakeholders. When fully mobilised, a well-supported NGO should carry out the interrelated roles listed overleaf (no priority is intended in the order of citation).

- Provide a forum for a critical mass of ecotourism stakeholders to network, share information, resolve disputes, discuss strategy and work towards a consensus on advocacy efforts; means for fulfilling this role include annual meetings, workshops and seminars, newsletters and interactive websites.
- Identify criteria and standards that will form the basis for the eventual implementation of certification-based quality control standards for at least some categories of organisation membership.
- Develop and contribute to the implementation of ecotourism-related policy and planning by all levels of government as well as NGOs, donor agencies and local communities.
- Conduct and support research on areas such as the impact of ecotourism and markets in order to inform the identification of quality control criteria and standards and the formulation of appropriate planning and policy.
- Expand, promote and market the industry through outreach and education to non-member operators, green consumers, the general public and government.
- Engage in lobbying and advocacy in appropriate government bodies and media so that the ecotourism sector can compete effectively with a single voice against other resource stakeholder groups such as recreational hunting, forestry and mining.
- Assist with the development of appropriate management tools and techniques for ecotourism settings such as protected areas, indigenous territories and local communities.
- Assist in fundraising for community development and biodiversity conservation.

In summary, an effective organisation creates an environment in which member ecotourism operations and the ecotourism industry as a whole (within its geographical area) can become both financially viable and environmentally and socioculturally sustainable. Some of the actions pursued in this environment are internally focused (e.g. forum, quality control standards, research) whereas others are externally oriented (e.g. lobbying, marketing, education, assisting protected area managers and community development). A fundamental advantage of effective organisations is the economies of scale, absent in individual members, that they provide in working towards their strategic objectives.

Structure, membership and funding

Most membership-based ecotourism organisations are non-profit entities controlled by a volunteer board that approves the annual budget, sets the program for the year and reports to members through newsletters and during annual meetings (Twining-Ward 2005). Membership is usually open to any interested party and typically comprises a mixture of individuals from various sectors (e.g. operators, academics, ecotourists, students and government representatives) and such bodies as businesses, government agencies, tertiary educational institutions and NGOs. Separate membership categories are often maintained to accommodate these different types of stakeholder.

Membership dues are by far the most prevalent and important source of operating revenue, and the ability to attract and retain a strong constituency is therefore important not only to fulfil the organisation's various roles through critical mass but also to ensure the organisation's continued existence. In most cases, a scaled fee structure is applied based on ability to pay and the provision of commensurate benefits. For example, students and 'ecotourists' typically pay the lowest fee but in return receive little more than a periodic newsletter and possibly the right to vote for a new board at an annual meeting, which they can usually attend at a discounted cost. Large organisations pay the highest fees and are allowed to display their logo in publications, are given more space in directories and receive other benefits such as exclusive password-protected access to specialised website links. Other sources of funding include government grants (which are often once-only payments intended to initiate organisations), member donations, grants or subsidies from private foundations as well as donor agencies and corporations, and sales of goods and services, such as membership directories and research publications.

■ 8.2.3 The *International Ecotourism Society*

The International Ecotourism Society (TIES) was originally established as The Ecotourism Society (TES) in 1990 to make the sector an effective and financially viable mechanism for contributing to sustainable development and conservation worldwide. As the only global membership organisation focused specifically on ecotourism, TES soon emerged as the main international forum for stakeholders working towards this objective. It is also an important source of information, including publications, and is a body that encourages research, especially on the impact of ecotourism. The mandate and priorities of TIES are reflected in its mission statement, motto and vision statement, which emphasise the promotion of sustainable ecosystems and communities through networking, education and the integration of sustainability principles and practice into the broader tourism industry (see figure 8.1).

■ **Figure 8.1**
TIES mission, motto and vision
Source: *TIES 2006.*

Our Mission:	TIES promotes responsible travel to natural areas that conserves the environment and improves the well-being of local people by:
	■ creating an international network of individuals, institutions and the tourism industry
	■ educating tourists and tourism professionals
	■ influencing the tourism industry, public institutions and donors to integrate the principles of ecotourism into their operations and policies
Our Motto:	Uniting communities, conservation, and sustainable travel.
Our Vision:	To be the global source of knowledge and advocacy uniting communities, conservation, and sustainable travel.

Structure and funding

The core body of TIES is a board of directors limited to 25 members who at each annual meeting elect a five-member executive committee consisting of a chairperson, vice-chairperson, treasurer, secretary and nominating committee chair. Directors are responsible for periodically reviewing the mission statement, approving and monitoring programs and services, selecting and orienting new directors, raising money, approving and monitoring the annual budget and engaging in strategic planning. These activities are facilitated by a committee structure that unites directors with designated TIES staff to address issues in the areas of advocacy campaign; board development; finance; training, education and publications; membership; events; and human resources. To better ensure an active and committed board, directors are required to attend at least one official board meeting per year (at their own expense) and to make a 'personally significant' contribution to the organisation each year, which could include in-kind support.

Funding sources are dominated by annual membership dues, which vary according to TIES's categories and ranged in late 2006 from US$1000 for Sponsors to US$150 for businesses and institutions, US$75 for 'Professionals' and US$35 for 'Travelers'. On the basis of membership rosters at that time, this indicates a membership fee revenue flow of about US$117 000 for 2006. Other income is derived from the sale of publications, consulting, online auctions and participation in training and education programs (TIES 2006). Because it maintains its headquarters in the USA (Washington DC), TIES is not eligible for development agency aid (Epler Wood 1999). However, this also means that TIES is not dependent on government, foundations, companies or any other subsidy-based funding source that might compromise its independence.

Activities

TIES has steadily expanded the range of activities in which it is involved, in large part through strategic partnerships with relevant organisations. For example, ecotourism and sustainable tourism quality control is being pursued in conjunction with the Center on Ecotourism and Sustainable Development (CESD), the Rainforest Alliance and UNEP (United Nations Environment Programme), towards the implementation of global certification standards. Consulting is undertaken in large part through individuals listed in the organisation's Experts Bureau, and TIES offers an online Certificate in Sustainable Tourism Management jointly with George Washington University.

Membership

As of October 2006 TIES had 797 members representing about 90 countries. This represents a substantial decrease from the 1500 members reported for mid-2000. Leading all membership categories was 'Business' (n = 276), followed by 'Professional' (218), 'Traveler' (173), 'Institution' (53), 'Association' (41), 'One-year Sponsor' (30) and 'Three-year Sponsor' (6). In terms of geography, the USA accounted for about half of all members and a third of the board of directors, which raises questions about the actual level of internationalism in the organisation. The issue becomes even more pertinent when the top three membership categories are analysed separately (see figure 8.2). USA-based members accounted for 56 and 63 per cent of all 'Professionals' and 'Travelers' respectively, but only 38 per cent of the Business category. If the more-developed countries (MDCs) are taken as a group, these figures respectively increase to 79, 82 and 57 per cent, thereby corroborating the north/south demand/supply pattern described in section 2.4.2. Reinforcing this is the fact that at least 30 per cent of the USA-based businesses are outbound tour operators or travel agencies explicitly oriented towards destinations in less-developed countries (LDC) and that a significant number of the LDC businesses list US, Australian, Canadian or European owners.

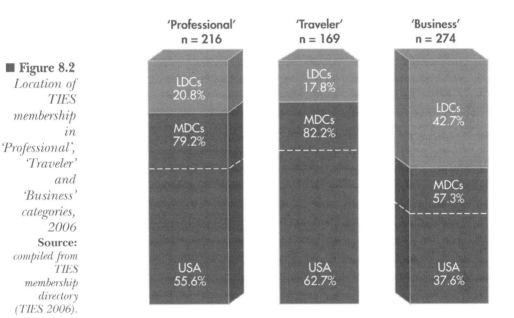

■ **Figure 8.2**
Location of TIES membership in 'Professional', 'Traveler' and 'Business' categories, 2006
Source: *compiled from TIES membership directory (TIES 2006).*

■ 8.2.4 Ecotourism *Australia*

Ecotourism Australia is an incorporated, non-profit organisation established in 1991 as the Ecotourism Association of Australia (EAA) to function as Australia's peak body for the industry. Its vision emphasises the desire 'to be leaders in assisting ecotourism and other committed tourism operations to become environmentally sustainable, economically viable, and socially and culturally responsible' (Ecotourism Australia 2006). The accompanying mission statement reveals how the vision will be implemented through a number of general actions (see figure 8.3). These deviate substantially from the strategic directives of TIES in that the directives of Ecotourism Australia are far more 'businesslike'. Specifically, the first five actions all pertain to improving standards and facilitating the activities of operators while the last three emphasise supply-side sustainability.

Ecotourism Australia's Mission is about growing, consolidating and promoting ecotourism and other committed tourism operations to become more sustainable, through approaches such as:

■ developing and adopting standards for sustainable practices

■ increasing the professionalism of those working within the tourism industry

■ streamlining policies and processes that have in the past complicated operating in protected areas

■ assisting operators to improve the quality of interpretation offered about the places they visit

■ improving positioning and financial viability for operators who adopt sustainable practices

■ contributing to conservation solutions and projects

■ involving and providing benefits to local communities

■ marketing the principles of sustainability to increase awareness across the tourism industry.

■ **Figure 8.3**
Mission statement for the Ecotourism Association of Australia
Source:
Ecotourism Australia 2006.

This difference in emphasis reflects the fact that it is easier to implement specific standards and monitoring procedures in a single country, especially in one that has a rapidly maturing ecotourism industry in which such actions are warranted, feasible and strongly supported across the array of stakeholders. Hence, it is not surprising that the EcoCertification Program (NEAP) is the organisation's flagship project and indisputably its most notable accomplishment to date. The EcoGuide Australia Certification Program, in the early stages of development, is an extension of this pragmatic and proactive approach (see section 6.6.2). In contrast, the global mandate of TIES (as well as its limited resources) gives rise to more general directives that emphasise awareness, training, networking and research. These directives also recognise that most of the organisation's global constituency is far removed from Australia in terms of the level of ecotourism development that has been attained.

Although it is not stated explicitly in the mission statement, support for advocacy is promoted as a benefit of membership. Specifically, an email group and other online resources are provided 'for members lobbying for decisions and initiatives that improve the viability of the ecotourism industry...' (Ecotourism Australia 2006). Other benefits include networking opportunities, the ability to contribute to national and other ecotourism strategies as well as park management plans and education programs, and opportunities to work towards a more effective licensing system for protected areas and to attend training seminars and workshops. Also important is an annual conference, publications in such areas as best practice, and provision of scholarships and grants to support quality research. Structurally, Ecotourism Australia in late 2006 was run by a board of 13 directors who, unlike TIES, are elected directly from the membership. In terms of background, seven board members appeared to be affiliated with state or federal government agencies related to tourism, protected areas and/or the environment, one was a full-time academic and five were affiliated with businesses.

Membership

Table 8.2 shows the structural and geographical distribution of EAA membership in October 2006. The 336 members (table 8.2 omits 10 who are foreign and six who listed no place of residence) represent a decline of 20 per cent from the 421 members listed for mid-2000. Structurally, the Business category is dominant, accounting for 64 per cent of the membership. In this category, local and inbound tour operators constitute the single largest group. Guides certified under the organisation's EcoGuide Australia Program have their own category, which, with 55 members, is the second largest. Several large ecotourism businesses, including the Phillip Island Nature Park and Kingfisher Bay Resort (see the case study 'Peering at the penguins in New Zealand and Australia' in chapter 4), each have a relatively large number of certified guides affiliated with their operations. The Personal and Student categories account respectively for only 10 and 4.7 per cent of all members, while the two public sector categories together account for just 3.1 per cent. The Industry Leaders Forum category is an elite category that is limited to 20 individuals and attracts an annual fee of A$2500. Regionally, Queensland accounted for 44 per cent of the membership, compared with a third in mid-2000. The actual numbers for Queensland have therefore held steady (146 in October 2006 versus 138 in mid-2000) at the expense of steep erosion in the rest of Australia (184 in October 2006 versus 283 in mid-2000 for a decrease of 35 per cent).

■ **Table 8.2** *Ecotourism Australia membership distribution in October 2006*

STATE OR TERRITORY	BUSINESS	ECOGUIDE	PERSONAL	STUDENT	PUBLIC SECTOR (LOCAL)	PUBLIC SECTOR (STATE OR FEDERAL)	INDUSTRY LEADERS FORUM	TOTAL
Queensland	92	33	12	6	1	—	2	146
NSW	36	3	11	1	—	—	—	51
Victoria	20	14	2	6	4	—	—	46
South Australia	23	1	3	—	1	1	—	29
Western Australia	17	3	2	1	—	—	1	24
Northern Territory	9	1	1	—	—	1	—	12
Tasmania	5	—	1	—	—	1	—	7
ACT	3	—	—	1	1	—	—	5
Total	205	55	32	15	7	3	3	320

Source: *collated from Ecotourism Australia 2006.*

■ 8.2.5 **Other** *national organisations*

Information about the other national organisations listed in figure 8.1 is limited. Ecotourism Kenya is notable for its relatively sophisticated website and it 'Eco-rating' certification program, which is a simplified variant of Australia's EcoCertification Program based on an applicant's signed statement of personal confirmation that all responses in a self-assessed questionnaire are accurate (Ecotourism Kenya 2006). The formation of organisations in Japan (in 1998) and Taiwan (in 2002) is an interesting development given that Japan and north-east Asia in general are not regarded outside the region as prominent ecotourism destinations or sources of ecotourists. However, some indication of an 'East Asian' model of ecotourism (see 'Practitioner's perspective: An East Asian model of ecotourism?' in chapter 2) is provided by the extent to which cultural attractions are featured in conjunction with natural sites on the websites of these organisations. An emerging trend is partnerships among national ecotourism organisations. For example, CANAECO, Costa Rica's national ecotourism organisation, worked with TIES in 2006 to sponsor a preparatory international conference to the global ecotourism conference held in Oslo (Norway) in 2007.

■ 8.2.6 **Subnational** *and supranational organisations*

State or provincial ecotourism organisations are most common in such countries as the USA and Canada where (a) the federal political structure confers substantial powers on the states or provinces and (b) no comparable organisation has been established at the nationwide level (the American Ecotourism Association had almost no profile as of late 2006, and its mandate was unclear). In the USA, this may reflect the tradition of non-involvement in tourism at the federal level as well as the inability of any national organisation to effectively represent 50 states and 300 million residents. The lack of state ecotourism organisations in Australia, on the other hand, reflects the small national population, the effectiveness of Ecotourism Australia as a national body and the existence of strong state marketing and administrative tourism agencies. State or provincial organisations in the USA and Canada are generally similar to nationwide bodies with regard to their structure, mandate and roles. The Hawaii Ecotourism Association, for example, has a mission statement ('Protecting Hawaii's unique environment and culture through responsible travel') and nine strategic goals, maintains a relatively sophisticated web site, holds annual meetings, distributes a periodic newsletter and has a diverse membership of operators, academics, government representatives and interested residents (HEA 2006). Local membership-based organisations are distinctive in that their focus is on a geographically and politically limited area, such as the Morovo Lagoon in the Solomon Islands or the Toledo district of Belize. Effectively, they operate as 'hands-on' community-based practitioners who do little in the way of TIES-type functions, such as newsletters, annual meetings, websites, conferences or training. Moreover, because they are mainly based in less-developed countries, these local groups tend to receive substantial assistance from NGOs in wealthier countries.

Supranational organisations are more recent phenomena that differ from a global entity such as TIES by focusing on two or more countries in a particular geographic area. La Ruta de Sonora Ecotourism Association is a bilateral industry initiative between Mexico and the USA that offers tours incorporating attractions and member operators on both sides of the border. The Sonoran Desert serves as an ecological focal point. More geographically ambitious is the Mesoamerican Ecotourism Alliance (MEA), which unites around 20 protected areas and operators in all parts of Central America, including southern Mexico but excluding Costa Rica. MEA is a creation of RARE, a major USA-based environmental NGO that supports grassroots conservation activism throughout the less-developed world (MEA 2006). In other parts of the world, attempts to establish regional supranational ecotourism organisations have been less successful (see 'Practitioner's perspective: Proposal for a Pacific Ecotourism Association').

*P*RACTITIONER'S PERSPECTIVE

Proposal for a Pacific Ecotourism Association

The South Pacific Tourism Organisation (SPTO) is the leading industry advocacy group for the states and dependencies of the South Pacific region. Realising the growing importance of ecotourism to that region, the SPTO in the early 2000s commissioned a consultant to investigate the feasibility of establishing a specialised Pacific Ecotourism Association (PETA) to lead the development of the sector. Representatives from the national organisations of member states were supportive in theory, but had concerns about how such a multilateral entity would be managed and funded, given regional rivalries and lack of financial resources. Representatives from industry were even more sceptical and argued that the alleged ineffectiveness of existing tourism and ecotourism organisations in the region did not augur well for the prospects of such an organisation, which they felt would be dependent on membership fees from the private sector (Twining-Ward 2005).

Although the consultant's research identified such factors as an experienced and committed board, permanent staff and a strategic business plan that would increase the probability of success for such an organisation, it was ultimately determined that these would incur considerable costs but generate little revenue. Instead, the consultant recommended the establishment of a 'Green hub' within the existing SPTO website to provide a forum for exchanging ideas among existing ecotourism organisations and practitioners, developing

(continued)

and sharing guidelines and standards, disseminating statistics and research and publicising good practice ecotourism products to potential visitors. It was felt that such a mechanism was more appropriate for a diverse and resource-scarce region and that there was a potential to generate a small revenue flow based on the provision of one salaried full-time administrator and a revenue flow derived from voluntary sponsors rather than fee-paying members who might be overly demanding in terms of services provided. Fundamentally, this recommendation assumes that the leading regional organisation, SPTO, has a major role to play in the development of the South Pacific ecotourism sector, since the Green hub would rely on its existing infrastructure and be managed by an executive committee consisting of current SPTO board members (Twining-Ward 2005). The proposed name, moreover, suggests a focus on sustainable tourism more generally rather than just ecotourism, thus making it relevant to a larger group of stakeholders.

■ *8.2.7* Discussion

For both TIES and Ecotourism Australia, geographical imbalance is a serious concern, especially given that the respective dominance of the USA and Queensland appears to have increased between 2000 and 2006. This suggests that the designated geographic area of concern for each organisation is not being adequately represented, which can result in the further alienation of stakeholders outside the dominant areas. In the case of TIES, there is the added dimension of dependency and neocolonialism inherent in the aforementioned north/south demand/supply pattern. It is unclear, pending a survey of former members, whether geographic imbalance is a contributing factor to a second major issue, which is the pattern of substantially declining membership. Other possibilities include dissatisfaction with the services offered in exchange for membership fees and/or declining interest in ecotourism among operators and consumers.

Beyond the unstable revenue flow from membership fees, Ecotourism Australia appears to be relying mainly on its best practice EcoCertification and EcoGuide programs, while TIES is pursuing a wider variety of initiatives (e.g. training, consulting and auctions) largely in partnership with relevant organisations, universities and members. Its peripheral involvement with certification through its association with the CESD and other agencies also seems logical given that leadership in the development and/or implementation of credible quality control mechanisms should be a priority of any effective ecotourism organisation. However, this objective could be undermined by the fact that membership for either organisation (except in the case of the EcoGuide category of Ecotourism Australia) is open to anyone willing to pay the applicable annual fee. It is hypothetically possible for unethical interests to appropriate an organisation by 'flooding' it with its own members, then voting at annual meetings to ensure placement of sympathetic individuals on the board. Less dramatically, membership in such organisations can be displayed as a form of greenwashing, thereby potentially bringing discredit to the organisation.

A final observation pertains to the unstable and incipient nature of ecotourism organisations in general. If the quality of a website can be used as one indicator of an organisation's 'state of health', then there is cause for deep concern. Many of the entities listed in table 8.1 apparently do not yet have an Internet presence, and those that do generally provide a poor-quality product with minimal information. As of late 2006, some websites had apparently not been updated for several years. In addition, there was no trace in 2006 of many of the ecotourism organisations listed in 2000. This suggests a high rate of attrition and an even higher rate of effective inactivity that is counter-productive to the evolution of a credible ecotourism sector.

8.3 OTHER ORGANISATIONS INVOLVED WITH ECOTOURISM

Membership-based NGOs specific to ecotourism, such as TIES and Ecotourism Australia, are not the only organisations that directly influence ecotourism. Halpenny (2001) includes NGOs not specifically related to ecotourism and government agencies, as external organisations instrumental in the development of ecotourism. The bodies described below do not constitute an inclusive inventory but rather feature prominent organisations and innovative forms of participation.

■ 8.3.1 NGOs

Environmental NGOs in particular have played a critical role in the development and dissemination of ecotourism, as demonstrated by the involvement of RARE in the creation of the Mesoamerican Ecotourism Association (see section 8.2.6). Others, including Conservation International and the Nature Conservancy in particular, are additionally involved in the ecotourism industry through their membership-focused outbound travel programs and their management of private protected areas (see section 3.3). As part of their broader environmental mandate, such organisations also provide technical and financial support for community and private sector ecotourism-related projects, contributions to research on impact and markets, and support for sustainable development in general. The decision to work in a particular area is dictated in both organisations by the perceived gravity of its environmental problems (see 'In the field: Conservation International and ecotourism').

Conservation International and ecotourism

USA-based Conservation International (CI) is a leading NGO in the area of biodiversity conservation, especially in the less-developed world where the loss of natural habitat is of particular concern to its leadership. Acknowledging the growing importance of the global tourism industry, CI supports the argument that intelligently engaged ecotourism can generate significant revenue for impoverished local communities and thereby provide a strong incentive for local communities to support and protect biodiversity. An Ecotourism Department, accordingly, was established to work with regional programs and partners to integrate ecotourism into local conservation strategies. Biodiversity 'hotspots' (i.e. areas of exceptional but threatened biological richness) are given priority in determining project support. CI's policy in these areas is to support the development of best practice and self-sustaining ecotourism operations through technical assistance, capacity-building and selective funding. Among its accomplishments is the establishment of the successful community-based Chalalán Ecolodge in Bolivia and Wekso Ecolodge in Panama, both pursued in partnership with local indigenous communities. CI was also instrumental in constructing the Kakum National Park Canopy Walkway in Ghana (arguably West Africa's best-known ecotourism attraction) and establishing the Indonesian Ecotourism Network (INDECON) (Conservation International 2006).

A major factor in the success of these initiatives is cooperation with an often complex network of NGO and government partners. For example, CI provided training and advice to local residents for the Caminos Posaderos Andinos project — a 250-kilometre network of hiking trails — in Venezuela, while funding was provided by the European Union, the CODESPA Foundation of Spain, CI Venezuela, the Venezuelan National Parks Institute and several European foundations and companies. In addition, the Programa Andes Tropicales, a local NGO, provides ongoing funding and training for small businesses along the trail network. CI has also partnered with George Washington University in Washington DC to develop the Ecotourism Learning Program, which is designed to empower small-scale operators in less-developed regions (Conservation International 2006).

With regard to the leading tourism-related NGOs, the World Tourism Organization has paid considerable attention to ecotourism and sustainable tourism in general. Ecotourism, for example, is explicitly acknowledged in Article 3(5) of the World Tourism Organization's Global Code of Ethics for Tourism (opposite), which was adopted by the United Nations General Assembly in 2001 as recommended practice for all member countries.

■ Nature tourism and ecotourism are recognized as being particularly conducive to enriching and enhancing the standing of tourism, provided they respect the natural heritage and local populations and are in keeping with the carrying capacity of the sites (World Tourism Organization 2006b). ■

In a move that attracted controversy, the United Nations also expressed its growing involvement in this sector by declaring 2002 as the International Year of Ecotourism (IYE; see the case study 'The International Year of Ecotourism' at the end of this chapter).

■ 8.3.2 Government

In chapter 7 we described how government as an external environment both assists and hinders ecotourism. A major area of assistance has been the preparation of ecotourism plans and strategies, such as the Queensland Ecotourism Plan, and broader tourism and other related initiatives of which ecotourism is explicitly or implicitly a component (see sections 8.4 and 8.5). Often as a result of these plans, governments may also provide funds and other forms of assistance for ecotourism development within or beyond their own jurisdictions. External ecotourism assistance is provided mainly by national governments in the more-developed world through development assistance agencies that distribute funds to projects in the less-developed world. As with aid provided by international environmental NGOs, this assistance is typically implemented through NGOs based in the recipient countries, often at the community level (see section 5.5).

As of 2006, the Australian development assistance agency AusAid was not actively involved with ecotourism (AusAID 2006). In contrast, New Zealand, through NZAID, has supported community-based ecotourism projects since the early 1990s in the South Pacific and Asia under the auspices of its Environment program (NZAID 2006). The external aid program of the Department for International Development (DFID) in the United Kingdom funds ecotourism-related projects, such as the Che Guevara Trail in Bolivia (DFID 2004). The US agency USAID is also active in ecotourism, having identified this area in the mid-1990s as an activity with potential to support environmental conservation in remote areas. Ecotourism, in conjunction with cultural tourism, is a component of integrated conservation programs in priority areas, such as Latin America and the Caribbean (USAID 2006). USAID's emphasis on private sector-focused development suggests that ecotourism assistance, as with any form of foreign aid, is ideologically biased and can be used as an instrument to attain desired foreign policy outcomes.

International governance

In addition to its declaration of 2002 as the International Year of Ecotourism, the United Nations is becoming increasingly active in ecotourism through the international development assistance program of the United Nations Development Programme (UNDP). This specialised agency works in collaboration with recipient NGOs to fund through its Small Grants Programme a diverse range of community-based projects, including some that relate directly to ecotourism (UNDP 2006). Another UN agency that works in the tourism area is the United Nations Committee on Sustainable Development (UNCSD). In 1999, a major meeting was held by the UNCSD to debate the merits of sustainable tourism, and from this event emerged the idea of declaring 2002 as the IYE. In Europe, the European Commission illustrates the multilateral governance that may become more prevalent should regions other than Europe move towards a similar model of political and economic integration. Through the European Travel Commission, which represents the 37 national tourism marketing organisations of Europe, this organisation maintains involvement in ecotourism through its close associations with relevant entities such as TIES and Green Globe (European Travel Commission 2006).

8.4 ECOTOURISM POLICY AND PLANS

A 'policy' is a course of action or inaction that is advocated by a stakeholder (usually used in reference to government) and provides the broad guidelines intended to direct the development of a particular sector in the desired direction. Policy is implemented through the process of 'planning', and the document that articulates this intended process is a 'plan' or 'strategy' (Goeldner & Ritchie 2006). The plan will often include specific actions intended to achieve the broader objectives and ultimately the vision or mission statement. An assessment of the barriers and opportunities that exist in achieving these goals is also usually incorporated. Thus, there are similarities between the planning involved in an ecotourism plan and the business planning that was discussed in section 6.4. There are fundamental differences, however, with respect to the authority that carries out the process (a government or NGO as opposed to a private business operator) and the geographic scope (a destination rather than a single business). Comparisons between the two levels of policy and planning are therefore limited.

Although normally coordinated by government, ecotourism and other tourism plans usually emerge only after an extensive consultative process involving contributions and lobbying from interested stakeholders, including representatives of external environments that may perceive ecotourism as a threat or opportunity (see chapter 5). This is therefore one area where an effective sector lobbying effort, conducted by a well-organised and strong ecotourism organisation, is crucial. Concerted advocacy increases the chances of producing an effective and well-coordinated plan and one that strikes a balance between the interests of the ecotourism sector and those of relevant external environments, such as agriculture, forestry and other forms of tourism.

In addition to contending with the influence of external environments, ecotourism planning (and planning in general) is made more complex by the hierarchical and interrelated nature of plans. A national *ecotourism* plan is meaningful only if it is related to and informed by broader national tourism policy, which is in turn a manifestation of *overall* government policy. However professional the lobbying efforts of tourism and ecotourism interest groups, the prevailing ideology of the government in power ultimately dictates the nature of that policy. A right-wing government with a strong rural constituency, for example, will be guided by its adherence to the basic imperatives of private sector stimulation, which may in turn translate into support for traditional rural industries, such as agriculture and logging.

The national ecotourism plan that emerges from this broader policy arena will in turn influence the nature and effectiveness of state, regional and local ecotourism plans, although this influence will vary between federal states, such as Australia, and unitary states, such as France or New Zealand, where subunits essentially function as municipalities. Any disagreement with plans that are more highly situated in this hierarchy will decrease the likelihood of successful implementation, especially in unitary states. Another difficulty involved in formulating and implementing an ecotourism plan is reaching a compromise within the ecotourism sector itself, since many of the businesses (especially at the regional and local scale) are engaged in an inherently competitive relationship. Yet the effort to formulate an ecotourism plan, at any scale, is vital in providing a focal point around which the sector can mobilise, interact and strategically move towards a desired set of objectives (Fennell, Buckley & Weaver 2001).

■ 8.4.1 National *Ecotourism Strategy (Australia)*

The National Ecotourism Strategy (NES), along with the formation of the Ecotourism Association of Australia (now Ecotourism Australia) (see section 8.2), provides the most important evidence of the institutionalisation of ecotourism in Australia at the national level. As with Ecotourism Australia, the strategy is worth considering in detail not only because of its direct relevance to Australia but also because of its reputation as arguably the best-known example of ecotourism planning and one that has served as a prototype for other jurisdictions. The federal government initiated the NES in 1993 as an overall framework to guide the integrated development and management of the Australian ecotourism industry, committing A$10 million to its implementation. Emerging from an extensive consultative process (see below), the strategy adopted a simple definition of ecotourism that incorporates the core elements discussed in chapter 1. The following vision statement informs subsequent sections of the NES:

> ■ Australia will have an ecologically and culturally sustainable ecotourism industry that will be internationally competitive and domestically viable. Ecotourism in Australia will set an international example for environmental quality and cultural authenticity while realising an appropriate return to the Australian community and conservation of the resource. (CDOT 1994, p. 1.) ■

The NES development sequence

The NES was the product of a lengthy but necessary sequence of stages that allowed interested and relevant parties to contribute (see figure 8.4). For other jurisdictions wanting to develop an ecotourism plan, this sequence provides a useful procedural template. The first stage was the production of an issues paper, which is a short review of relevant issues intended to stimulate discussion at a series of subsequent workshops held in Australian capital cities and other locations. The workshops, attended by interested parties, resulted in outcomes and recommendations for the strategy as well as raising public awareness of the process to encourage further input. For example, those who could not participate in or did not know about the workshops were invited through advertisements in major newspapers to send in written submissions. Together, 149 written submissions and the workshop outcomes informed a draft ecotourism strategy. This was circulated to all those who had participated in the workshops or who had provided written submissions. These recipients sent 103 follow-up responses to the government, which were used to refine the document. Simultaneously, consultations were held with other relevant government agencies at the federal and state levels. The final National Ecotourism Strategy was the culmination of this one-year process (Allcock 1999).

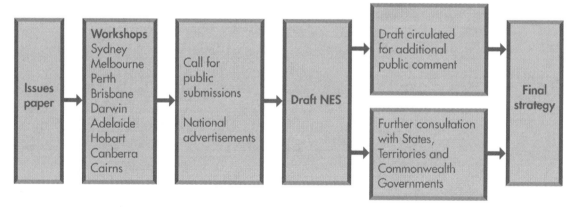

■ **Figure 8.4**

National Ecotourism Strategy development process
Source: *Allcock 1999.*

Structure of the NES

Subsequent to the vision statement and the core component of the National Ecotourism Strategy is a list of 12 relevant ecotourism 'issues', the objectives that emerge from each issue and the actions proposed to achieve these objectives (CDOT 1994, appendix 1). Essentially, the NES advocated the support and promotion of a sustainable and commercially viable ecotourism industry that is integrated with regional planning and natural resource management mechanisms. This industry should use sustainable infrastructure, must be monitored through effective information and education, and should be marketed in an ethical and effective manner. The industry should be subject to rigorous standards and certification procedures, preferably on a self-regulated basis. Finally, ecotourism must involve indigenous Australians in all phases and aspects of ecotourism development and activity and should follow principles of social equity.

The NES identified groups that should take responsibility for implementing each action. In most cases, these involved both industry and government agencies. For example, the data dissemination action listed under the issue of impact monitoring (issue 6) required participation by 'all levels of government, industry, research institutions, natural resource managers' (CDOT 1994, p. 36). Intriguingly, industry or professional associations such as the predecessor of Ecotourism Australia are cited as relevant to only two issues and six specific actions. The two issues (under the standards/accreditation objective) include developing a certification system and exploring the use of a logo to market qualifying ecotourism products. Under the education objective, relevant actions include the development and modification of courses for operators, delivery of education to remote locations, development of educational resources, such as videos and documentaries, and the incorporation of ecotourism education in curricula.

Implementation and assessment

The A$10 million committed by the federal government to the NES was directed towards pilot projects in nine programs over a four-year period from 1993–94 to 1996–97. These programs were undertaken through the National Ecotourism Program (NEP) and included certification, market profiles and research, energy and waste minimisation practices, infrastructure projects, ecotourism education, baseline studies and monitoring, integrated regional planning, business development and conferences and workshops. Tangible outcomes included the high-profile NEAP scheme for industry certification (now the EcoCertification Program — see section 6.6.2), research publications on the nature of ecotourism and ecotourism markets (Blamey & Hatch 1998) and several publications on energy and waste minimisation practices. Other results were a directory of ecotourism educational opportunities in Australia, visitor awareness videos, the development of a community ecotourism planning guide and the construction of boardwalks and signage at ecotourism sites.

The NES is no longer a component of official federal government policy in Australia, but it is still worthy of scrutiny because of its many tangible outcomes, its fostering of collaboration among stakeholders, the high level of concrete government support it received and its apparent success in 'kick-starting' the Australian ecotourism industry. It is also a good example of government response to the problem of market failure; that is, the unwillingness of individual enterprises to engage unilaterally in broader destination planning initiatives because these efforts also benefit their competitors. However, the overall effectiveness of the NES policy has always been hampered by the federal government's limited power to carry out its proposed actions due to the extensive powers vested in state governments in such critical arenas as natural resource management. This is perhaps why a large proportion of the 59 'actions' are qualified by weak and ambiguous verbs such as 'encourage' and 'investigate'.

■ 8.4.2 Other *national policies and plans*

Australia is arguably the world leader in ecotourism policy and institutional-isation, and for the rest of the world it is a question of relative positioning behind the leader (Fennell, Buckley & Weaver 2001). New Zealand, despite its strong reputation as an ecotourism destination and its extensive overseas ecotourism aid, has not yet progressed towards even the early stages of a formal ecotourism plan, although as a unitary state it is better positioned than Australia to implement such a plan. South Pacific states, such as Fiji and Samoa, are similar to Australia in having active ecotourism NGOs and plans (see section 10.2.3). In Asia, Thailand and Malaysia have been simi-larly engaged in planning, but it is unclear whether the resultant plans are substantive.

■ 8.4.3 Subnational *policies and plans*

As with ecotourism organisations, state or provincial ecotourism plans are likely to emerge in such countries as Canada and the USA where no such initiatives exist at the national level. Florida (USA) and Manitoba (Canada) are two of many subnational jurisdictions in this region that have developed ecotourism plans partly in response to federal-level non-involvement (Fennell, Buckley & Weaver 2001). The situation is different in Australia, where ecotourism plans have been formulated by a majority of states as well as by the federal government. In part, this is because cer-tain states had already articulated a formal ecotourism policy before the federal initiative. For example, in 1992 the Victorian government released a policy document that contained a 13-point plan for stimulating eco-tourism (VDCE 1992). Second, perhaps as an admission of its own limi-tations, the federal government through the NES implicitly encouraged the states to formulate their own plans through its support of integrated regional planning. The Queensland Ecotourism Plan (see below), for example, situates national ecotourism principles into the Queensland con-text while the South Australian Ecotourism Strategy 'seeks to complement and build on the National Ecotourism Strategy' (SATC 1995). A third explanation for state involvement is the federal system itself, which del-egates the responsibility for tourism development to the states. Therefore, the formulation of an ecotourism plan by a state government is an affir-mation of this position.

Queensland Ecotourism Plan

The Queensland Ecotourism Plan (QEP) differs fundamentally from the NES in being an 'organic' construct that is currently in its second iteration. The first version covered the period from 1997 to 2002 (QEP1) and was a direct response to the NEP (Queensland 1997) while the second version (QEP2) extends from 2003 to 2008 (Tourism Queensland 2002). Tangible outcomes associated with QEP1 include the development and testing of an ecotourism rapid assessment model (ECORAM), the formulation of regional ecotourism plans in the Whitsunday Islands and Wet Tropics, the publication of the *Ecotrends* newsletter, scholarship funding and the sponsoring of certification workshops. The lead role in both QEP1 and QEP2 has been played by the state tourism marketing body, Tourism Queensland (formerly the Queensland Tourist and Travel Corporation or QTTC). Guiding QEP2 is the following ambitious vision statement:

> ■ Queensland will be the world's leading ecotourism destination with government, industry and the community working in partnership and adopting best practice planning, development, management and marketing. (Tourism Queensland 2002, p. 10.) ■

QEP2 is divided hierarchically into five key objectives and 54 actions (QEP1 had only the first four objectives), which determine how the objectives will be operationalised. Each action, in turn, is allocated to a 0–2 year, 2–5 year or 'ongoing' (0–5 year) implementation schedule. No provision is made in QEP2 for the actual funding of any action, although it is claimed that the accomplishments of QEP1 will be expanded.

Key objective 1: environmental protection and management
Related actions include ensuring the inclusion of ecotourism and the ecotourism industry in protected area strategic planning, facilitating implementation of relevant policies that promote equity and recognise the special status of Aboriginal people, incorporating appropriate marketing strategies for protected areas, developing visitor codes of conduct and promoting sustainability within the broader tourism industry in Queensland. Ecotourism stakeholders are also encouraged to reduce pressure on 'icon sites' by promoting ecotourism in more obscure locations.

Key objective 2: industry development
Actions that facilitate the responsible development of the state ecotourism industry are featured in the second key objective. These include ensuring that ecotourism is highlighted in domestic and international marketing and public education, translating best practice guidelines into tangible actions and ensuring that practitioners have access to these guidelines, establishing regional ecotourism networks, linking ecotourism with cultural attractions and increasing the public profile of EcoCertified products and the scheme itself.

Key objective 3: infrastructure development
The third key objective promotes minimal impact and innovative facility design, provides for safe and reliable visitor access to these facilities, and promotes protected area facilities that meet the expected growth of the industry and adheres to the requirements of internal protected area zones.

Key objective 4: community development
Community development focuses on encouraging the involvement of local residents in all aspects of ecotourism through partnerships and ensuring

that all facets of ecotourism planning and management take into account community needs. The provision of non–English-language interpretation material is also included here.

Key objective 5: research

Actions associated with this new key objective include ensuring that research is relevant to industry as well as to achieving the objectives of ecological, sociocultural and economic sustainability. It should also provide a better understanding of market segmentation and should be used to improve the overall quality and profitability of the ecotourism industry. Other actions include engaging in research that assesses community and visitor attitudes and is disseminated to interested parties in a timely manner.

8.5 ECOTOURISM IN TOURISM AND OTHER STRATEGIES

Ecotourism strategies in some instances emerge from or are informed by the presence of a broader tourism or development plan. Ecotourism is often contained in such plans in other situations, thereby possibly eliminating the need for a specialised ecotourism strategy. The latter scenario is illustrated by Papua New Guinea, where the 'Tourism Sector Review and Master Plan 2007–2017' (PNG 2006) integrates ecotourism both implicitly and explicitly in recognition of the degree to which the boundaries between ecotourism and other tourism products (e.g. cultural tourism) in that country are blurred.

■ 8.5.1 Australian strategies

Australia, in contrast, demonstrates the former scenario. The NES was an outcome of the Labor government-initiated 1992 National Tourism Strategy (NTS), which had as one of its strategic goals the provision for sustainable tourism development through 'responsible planning and management practices consistent with the conservation of our natural and cultural heritage' (CDOT 1994, p. 5). The sustainability component of the NTS, in addition, emerged from the 1991 National Strategy for Ecologically Sustainable Development, which led to the establishment of a tourism working group that drafted the broad tourism document. With a change in government in 1996, right-wing ideology became more explicit in Australian federal tourism policy (see section 7.4.2). The 1998 National Action Plan for Tourism was primarily intended to make the Australian tourism industry more internationally competitive by fostering a favourable economic, regulatory and business environment for operators. It also advocated more effective marketing, improved infrastructure and visitor access to protected areas, and enhanced service skills for workers. The plan proclaimed support for tourism that follows principles of ecologically sustainable development, but this is listed as only the ninth of 11 objectives. Moreover, this is qualified by support for *voluntary* codes of best environmental practice and by the proviso that operators in World Heritage areas should not be faced with unreasonable access and capacity restrictions and should have a certainty of tenure to operate in these areas (DIST 1998).

Succeeding the National Action Plan for Tourism was the Tourism White Paper of 2003, which outlined a 10-year agenda for the industry. In addition to creating Tourism Australia (see section 7.4.2), the White Paper reiterated the importance of sustainability but maintained an emphasis on improving the sector's competitiveness and expanding opportunities for the private sector to invest in public protected areas. As with the previous plan, there is no specific section devoted to ecotourism, although related directives appear to favour soft ecotourism development (Australia 2003).

8.6 SUMMARY

In theory, membership-based ecotourism organisations are important mechanisms for assisting the industry to become more professional as well as more ecologically, socioculturally and financially sustainable. The International Ecotourism Society (TIES) and Ecotourism Australia, respectively, are the most prominent multilateral and country-level examples. Although robust membership profiles are critical to success, both organisations are hampered by memberships that are declining in number and continue to be geographically imbalanced. Otherwise, in keeping with its global mandate, TIES is attempting to expand its revenue base through a growing array of partnership-based educational and consulting initiatives, while Ecotourism Australia has focused more on its domestic certification programs. However, the lack of applicant screening in both organisations raises questions about the ecotourism credentials of non-certified members. A large number of other national, international and subnational ecotourism organisations have been established, but few showed any evidence of being well articulated or effective as of 2006.

International environmental NGOs are involved in ecotourism through their support for community-based projects in environmentally strategic destinations. Ecotourism is also being increasingly recognised by such mainstream organisations as the World Tourism Organization and the United Nations. In government, tourism-related agencies usually take a lead role in the development and implementation of ecotourism policy and planning while some external aid agencies include ecotourism in their overseas development projects. Ecotourism plans usually emerge from an extensive process of consultation and provide coherent objectives and strategies for the advancement of ecotourism in a particular area. Australia in this respect is again regarded as a world leader. At the federal level, the National Ecotourism Strategy articulated issues, objectives and actions for the development of Australian ecotourism and listed the bodies that need to be involved in each action. With substantial federal funding provided between 1993 and 1997, the NES was a critical factor in Australia's emergence as a global ecotourism leader. Other countries have also produced ecotourism plans, but none have achieved a similar profile. Australia is additionally innovative for having effective ecotourism plans implemented at the state level. Queensland, in particular, is noted for the detailed schedule of actions contained in its plan and for accomplishing most of these actions. Ecotourism plans usually reflect broader tourism or development policies and plans. The NES, for example, was the product of a Labor government, but the election of a Coalition government resulted in a more industry-focused ecotourism policy. This suggests support for soft ecotourism but raises questions about the priority placed on environmental and sociocultural sustainability.

QUESTIONS

1 (a) What role can membership-based ecotourism NGOs play in the advancement of the ecotourism sector?
(b) Under what circumstances are they able to fulfil this role?

2 How is an international ecotourism organisation such as TIES different from a national ecotourism organisation such as Ecotourism Australia in terms of membership, structure and functions?

3 (a) What problems are associated with the membership structures of TIES and Ecotourism Australia?
(b) How can these problems be addressed?

4 (a) What is the status of national and subnational ecotourism organisations aside from Ecotourism Australia?
(b) What are the implications of this situation for the global ecotourism industry?

5 (a) In what ways are non-ecotourism NGOs involved with ecotourism?
(b) To what extent is this involvement coordinated with TIES and other ecotourism organisations?

6 (a) Why is it stated that the National Ecotourism Strategy played a crucial role in 'kick-starting' the Australian ecotourism industry?
(b) Should the Australian federal government, like Queensland, maintain an ongoing ecotourism master plan?
(c) Why or why not?

7 (a) What potential difficulties may be encountered in implementing the Queensland ecotourism plan?
(b) How can the state ecotourism industry help to overcome these difficulties?

8 (a) Why is it claimed that current federal government tourism planning in Australia favours soft ecotourism?
(b) What are the positive and negative implications of federal tourism planning for Australia's high-order protected areas?

FURTHER READING

Butcher, J 2006, 'The United Nations International Year of Ecotourism: A critical analysis of development implications', *Progress in Development Studies* 6: 146–56. Butcher critically analyses the International Year of Ecotourism as an example of how MDC-based NGOs can take a patronising attitude towards LDC local communities that may not reflect the actual aspirations or interests of those communities.

Fennell, D, Buckley, R & Weaver, D 2001, 'Ecotourism policy and planning', in DB Weaver (ed.), *Encyclopedia of Ecotourism*, CABI, Wallingford, UK, pp. 463–77. This chapter examines ecotourism-related plans and uses a case study approach to emphasise the differences that exist in philosophy and approach among the world's major regions.

Halpenny, E 2001, 'Ecotourism-related organisations', in DB Weaver (ed.), *Encyclopedia of Ecotourism*, CABI, Wallingford, UK, pp. 479–96. Halpenny provides a systematic examination of NGOs and government organisations involved with ecotourism. This section includes information about The International Ecotourism Society, the main global ecotourism NGO.

Twining-Ward, L 2005, 'Feasibility study for Pacific Ecotourism Association. Draft final report', www.kiribati.spto.org. This consultant's report not only details the study that rejected the proposal to create a multilateral Pacific Ecotourism Association but also discusses the characteristics of other ecotourism organisations studied by the consultant. The case is made for an ecotourism portal in the website of the existing regional tourism association.

The International Year of Ecotourism
A controversial milestone

A milestone in the institutionalisation of ecotourism was the declaration of 2002 as the International Year of Ecotourism (IYE) by the United Nations, which in 1999 asked the World Tourism Organization, with assistance from the United Nations Environment Programme (UNEP), to undertake activities that would help to achieve four objectives, namely:

- increase awareness among consumers, government, the private sector and NGOs of ecotourism's potential for contributing positively both to the conservation of biodiversity and the standard of living of local communities in rural and natural areas
- disseminate mechanisms for planning, managing, regulating and monitoring ecotourism in such a way as to ensure its long-term viability
- promote the exchange of best practice experiences among stakeholders
- promote opportunities for the effective global marketing and promotion of ecotourism destinations and products (Yunis 2003).

In recognition of the special circumstances of each destination and its own preference for small-scale engagement, the World Tourism Organization encouraged national and local-level ecotourism stakeholders to be especially active in pursuing these activities. However, it was the culminating World Ecotourism Summit, held in Quebec City (Canada) during late May 2002, that attracted the greatest publicity and controversy. In conjunction with the above objectives, the summit focused on the issues of planning, product development, monitoring, regulation, marketing and promotion, all in the context of ecologically, socioculturally and economically sustainable development. Special emphasis was given to the participation of local communities and to strategies that would ensure cultural sensitivity and the equitable distribution of benefits. Preparatory to the summit, 18 regional conferences were held to discuss these issues in the specific context of each targeted geographical area, the results of which were then presented in Quebec City (Yunis 2003).

The outcomes of the summit, which attracted more than 1100 delegates from 132 countries, are contained in the 137-page final report. The highlight of this document is the nine-page Quebec Declaration on Ecotourism, which is significant because it sanctions a set of principles and 49 subsequent recommendations that the summit organisers hope will influence the future development of the sector in all parts of the world (World Tourism Organization/UNEP 2002). Of immediate interest is the opening set of principles defining ecotourism and its relationship to sustainability (opposite).

[The participants] recognize that ecotourism embraces the principles of sustainable tourism, concerning the economic, social and environmental impacts of tourism. It also embraces the following specific principles which distinguish it from the wider concept of sustainable tourism:

- Contributes actively to the conservation of natural and cultural heritage
- Includes local and indigenous communities in its planning, development and operation, and contributing to their well-being
- Interprets the natural and cultural heritage of the destination to visitors
- Lends itself better to independent travellers, as well as to organized tours for small size groups. (World Tourism Organization/UNEP 2002, p. 65.)

Notable here is a conception of ecotourism that strongly emphasises the role of local communities as participant and beneficiary and which positions culture as an object of conservation and interpretation along with the local natural environment. Also notable is the emphasis on small tourist groups, which is reinforced in subsequent recommendations by repeated references to the particular suitability of micro, small and medium-sized businesses to ecotourism. These principles are strongly criticised by Butcher (2006), who regards the World Tourism Organization/UNEP conception (and by extension that of such organisations as Conservation International) as an example of 'neopopulist' thinking that supports local empowerment, but only in a context where it is assumed that locals in rural and 'natural' areas prefer their traditional small-scale ways of life over Western-style growth and development. He cites a quote on page 81 of the Final Report, which states: ' . . . participatory processes should be used to educate local people about the value of biological and cultural diversity in ecotourism development, and on how they can both conserve and derive benefits from natural and cultural resources.' Thus, community participation apparently is desirable so long as it conforms to the non-developmentalist ideological agenda of the organisers — an agenda, moreover, that is enforced by implicit threats to terminate funding in cases of non-compliance. Butcher, in essence, sees this model of ecotourism as a vehicle that 'freezes' a culture in some allegedly idealistic traditional setting that generates just enough revenue from hard ecotourists to stave off abject poverty while posing no threat to the area's biodiversity. He states that it 'implicitly denies communities the option of adopting modern ways if they so choose, and only empowers them to have a say in modifying, but never transforming, their relationship to the natural environment' (Butcher 2006, p. 155).

An intriguing aspect of this critique is the extent to which the World Tourism Organization–UNEP position on ecotourism may have been influenced by opposition from a vocal coalition of Third World advocacy NGOs in the two-year period before the summit. In contrast to Butcher, such groups as the Third World Network and the Alliance for Sustainability were concerned that initial UNEP and World Tourism Organisation communiqués were overly uncritical of the ecotourism industry and that the IYE would therefore legitimise the

(continued)

unsustainable Western-style exploitation of unspoiled communities and ecosystems through mass tourism under the guise of 'ecotourism'. A letter sent to the UNEP tourism program coordinator in 2000 and signed by the representatives of 20 organisations (Pleumarom 2001) read in part, ' . . . we oppose the idea that the International Year of Ecotourism serves as an instrument for ecotourism experiments in developing countries, which are likely to cause more harm than good.' The criticism from these groups is strongly neopopulist in its emphasis on preserving traditional lifestyles and local biodiversity; hence, it is reasonable to assume that it not only influenced the deliberations of the summit but also pushed it far enough in this direction to attract condemnation from pro-development (or at least pro-choice) critics such as Butcher. It is interesting to note that both arguments, despite their contrasting assertions as to the model of 'development' that is most appropriate (i.e. remain as far removed from Western-style development as possible, or embrace this model as much as possible), are fundamentally patronising in that their mostly MDC-based proponents presume to know what is best for people in less-developed regions (see section 5.4.2).

Questions

1 (a) Why does Butcher refer to the IYE as an example of the 'neopopulist' perspective?
  (b) Why is he critical of this perspective?

2 (a) How is Butcher's criticism different from and similar to the criticism of such organisations as the Third World Network?
  (b) To what extent should the World Tourism Organization and UNEP take both modes of criticism into account in formulating their own ecotourism policy for less-developed regions?

3 Search ecotourism organisation websites on the Internet to see whether they reveal any evidence that the IYE has had substantive subsequent influence on the ecotourism sector.

9 Selected
environments and
activities

9.1 INTRODUCTION

The parameters of ecotourism discussed in previous chapters, such as impact, markets and the influence of external environments, vary according to the types of activity and environment being considered. The purpose of this chapter is to focus on a selection of special activities and environments that are becoming increasingly important from an ecotourism perspective and require special management because of their distinctive characteristics. The first of these, whale-watching (see section 9.2), is a rapidly growing specialised activity that also occupies its own distinctive environment. Section 9.3 examines the peculiarities of small island states and dependencies as ecotourism destinations, and section 9.4 considers the polar environments of Antarctica and the Arctic. The final section (section 9.5) focuses on territories controlled to a greater or lesser extent by indigenous people and thus is concerned with a special cultural, rather than physical, environment.

9.2 WHALE-WATCHING

As depicted in figure 1.11, whale-watching has emerged as a specialisation within ecotourism that (a) incorporates not just whales but also other types of cetaceans such as dolphins and (b) involves passive observation by land or boat. Activities that involve feeding, swimming or other direct interactions are not normally regarded as examples of ecotourism. The emergence and rapid expansion of whale-watching is an instructive and highly symbolic example of how perceptions of natural phenomena have been redefined by the green paradigm (see section 2.2).

As depicted in figure 9.1, cetaceans were first commercially exploited for their oil and meat at the beginning of the 19th century and, until the middle of the 20th century, this was virtually the sole basis for human interest in the resource. Preservationist motives were first apparent after World War II and rapidly gained momentum in conjunction with the emergent environmental movement and the awareness that commercial whaling was leading to the depletion of cetacean populations around the world. Southern right whales, for example, declined from an estimated pre-exploitation population of 150 000 to 7000 by the end of the 1990s, and blue whales experienced an even more dramatic decline from 220 000 to about a thousand individuals (Gill & Burke 1999).

The steep decline in commercial whaling since the mid-20th century is attributable to the combined impact of declining stocks, pressure from the environmental movement and government measures, both nationally and internationally, to safeguard and restore remaining populations. New Zealand, for example, ended commercial whaling in 1962, and Australia followed in 1978. Australia's Whale Protection Act, passed in 1980, prohibits

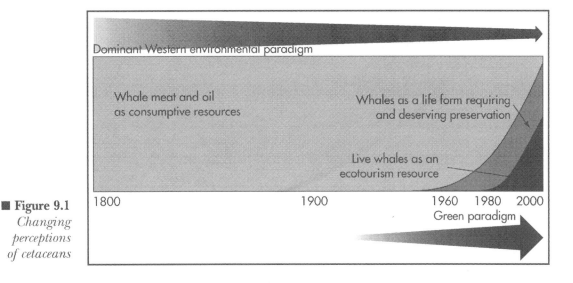

■ **Figure 9.1**
Changing perceptions of cetaceans

the killing or harassment of cetaceans within the country's Exclusive Economic Zone (which extends 200 kilometres offshore) and prohibits Australian citizens from killing or harassing whales anywhere else in the world (Gill & Burke 1999). Both countries actively lobby for the continued banning of commercial whaling through their involvement with such organisations as the International Whaling Commission (IWC), which declared a moratorium on this industry in the mid-1980s. Whaling now persists on a significant scale in only a handful of countries, such as Japan, Norway and Iceland, which carry out their activity under the guise of lethal 'scientific research'. These countries are working to have the moratorium lifted, arguing that the populations of some whale species have recovered sufficiently to sustain a limited commercial whaling industry. Evidence from Tonga, however, indicates that most current international visitors, and whale-watchers in particular, would not visit Tonga in future for any purpose if whale-hunting were reintroduced, suggesting that whale-watching tourism may serve as a disincentive to the resumption of commercial whaling (Orams 2001b).

Organised whale-watching began in southern California during the mid-1950s as the perception of whales as charismatic megafauna became more widespread. However, it did not emerge as a significant commercial sector until the 1980s. In the early part of that decade several hundred thousand individuals participated in commercial whale-watching, mainly in North America. These numbers rose to an estimated 4 million in 30 countries by 1992, 5.4 million participants in 70 countries by 1995, and more than 9 million participants in 87 countries by 1998. In that year, almost 500 communities hosted a whale-watching industry, according to a comprehensive world inventory of the sector prepared by Hoyt (2000). Although more recent estimates are not available, it seems clear in the early years of the 21st century that human interest in cetaceans continues to focus overwhelmingly on whale-watching and preservationist concerns. The influence of residual whaling interests, however, is evident in the success they have had in thwarting the creation of an international South Pacific whale mega-sanctuary (see 'In the Field: Establishing a whale sanctuary in the South Pacific' in chapter 3).

■ 9.2.1 Location

Hoyt (2000) estimates that almost half of the whale-watching industry is still concentrated in the USA, although large and growing sectors are also found in Canada, Mexico, Brazil, Argentina, Spain, Australia, New Zealand and South Africa. Significant sectors have also emerged in the countries where whaling persists, and it remains to be seen whether these whale-watching sectors will be influenced by or will influence the whaling industries. In terms of whale-watching activity, the industry is dominated by boat-based viewing of large whales, such as humpbacks, while viewing of dolphins and small whales accounts for about 15 per cent (Hoyt 2000). Another important factor is duration, environmental conditions dictating whether the sector is seasonal or year-round. Whale-watching along most of the Queensland coast (Australia) is based on migrations and is therefore seasonal. In contrast, the sector in Kaikoura (New Zealand) is year-round due to favourable oceanic conditions (see this chapter's case study 'Whale-watching and Maori empowerment in Kaikoura, New Zealand' on p. 271).

Australia

Commercial whale-watching (including dolphins) in Australia began in Hervey Bay, Queensland, in 1987 and involved around 40 communities from Broome in Western Australia to the Cairns–Port Douglas area of Queensland in the early 2000s (see figure 9.2). Participation increased dramatically from an estimated 700 000 visits in 1998 to 1 600 000 visits in 2003: New South Wales experienced the most rapid increases (37 per cent average annual growth) whereas Western Australia experienced a slight overall decrease of 2 per cent over that period. More dramatic fluctuations are evident at the community level: Hervey Bay declined from about 83 000 visits in 1996 to 66 000 in 2003 whereas Port Stephens (Nelson Bay, NSW) increased from numbers lower than Hervey Bay's to approximately 250 000 during the same period (IFAW 2004). Sydney, similarly, has emerged as a major node of whale-watching activity (see 'In the field: A new Sydney icon?'). Hervey Bay and Port Stephens are both major nodes of boat-based activity while the Head of Bight, in South Australia, is the main commercial location for land-based viewing. Logans Beach at Warrnambool (Victoria) is a major non-commercial, land-based viewing site. Monkey Mia (Western Australia) and Tangalooma (Moreton Island, Queensland) are two distinctive sites where whale-watching is augmented by the observation of bottlenose dolphins under regulated conditions (Gill & Burke 1999).

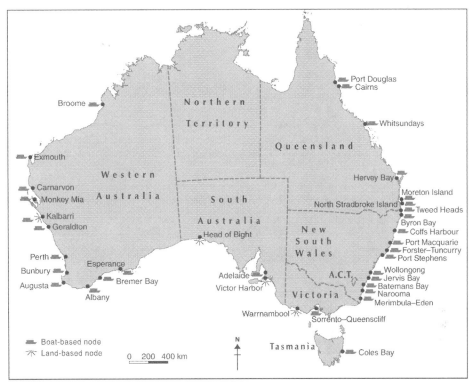

■ **Figure 9.2**

The whale-watching industry in Australia

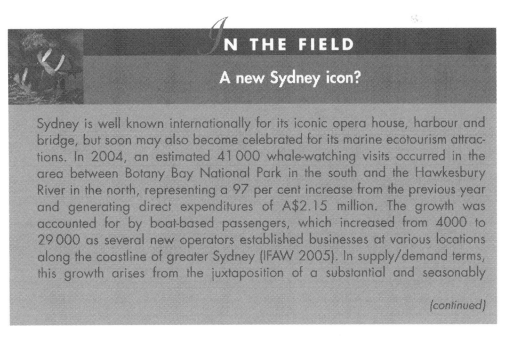

N THE FIELD

A new Sydney icon?

Sydney is well known internationally for its iconic opera house, harbour and bridge, but soon may also become celebrated for its marine ecotourism attractions. In 2004, an estimated 41 000 whale-watching visits occurred in the area between Botany Bay National Park in the south and the Hawkesbury River in the north, representing a 97 per cent increase from the previous year and generating direct expenditures of A$2.15 million. The growth was accounted for by boat-based passengers, which increased from 4000 to 29 000 as several new operators established businesses at various locations along the coastline of greater Sydney (IFAW 2005). In supply/demand terms, this growth arises from the juxtaposition of a substantial and seasonably

(continued)

reliable close-to-shore humpback whale population with an urban area of 4 million residents, which is also Australia's international tourist gateway. As a result, Sydney's whale-watching industry is poised to become one of Australia's best examples of urban ecotourism (see section 3.5.2).

This emerging opportunity, however, is accompanied by significant risks, including the confinement of the viewing season to a nine-week period from late May to the end of July. A second factor is the localised danger posed to migrating cetaceans by heavy shipping traffic, underwater activity and pollutants. The growing traffic in unregulated viewing by recreational vessels is a third consideration, since it provides competition to commercial operators and threatens to increase stress among the whales that they encounter. In general, there is cause for concern in the fact that the whales must pass through an area where there is potential for an exponential increase in the level of interception by whale-watching vessels. If whale-watching is to become another of Sydney's iconic tourist attractions, its development must therefore be accompanied by an agenda of strict regulation, enforcement, monitoring and ongoing research that involves not just the commercial operators but also the shipping industry, producers of land-based marine pollutants and the tourism and recreation industries of Sydney more generally.

■ 9.2.2 Impact

Whale-watching that is practised in an irresponsible manner is not ecotourism. Where it *does* qualify as ecotourism, whale-watching can have a positive environmental, economic and sociocultural impact and complement the efforts of preservationists. However, even responsible whale-watching has the potential to create an inadvertent negative impact, and extensive continued research is necessary to identify these effects so that they can be addressed. An inherent problem in conducting scientific research on whales is the extensive and unstable marine environment that these creatures inhabit — an environment that is often hostile to humans and does not readily lend itself to scientific investigation. Hence, relatively little knowledge is currently available to inform the management of the whale-watching sector.

The continuing rapid growth of whale-watching in Australia and elsewhere is a matter of concern from an environmental perspective. One potential problem is that whales are coming into contact with humans more frequently. As a result, the disruption of underwater communication among whales as a result of boat noise, which is apparently acceptable at low exposure, may eventually become intolerable as the amount of contact increases. A complicating factor is that although whales seem to adjust over time to the presence of humans, research in the New England region of the USA has shown that reactions to boat-based viewing and other human activity vary among individuals and groups of these complex animals (Hoyt 2000). Research based on one particular group of whales therefore is not necessarily a good indicator of impact on other populations or individuals. The susceptibility of cetaceans to hostile external forces is a further confounding factor (see sections 7.3.5 and 7.5.2 and 'In the field: A new Sydney icon?'). All aspects considered, it is not surprising that marine ecologists tend to recommend land-based observation over boat-based operations and to discourage interaction that involves swimming and feeding.

With respect to economic impact, there is no question that whale-watching is now 'big business', direct global revenues having increased from an estimated US$77 million in 1991 to US$300 million in 1998 (the latest year for which statistics are available). Taking the income multiplier effect into account, whale-watching was estimated to generate about US$1.05 billion worldwide in 1998 (Hoyt 2000). Thus, the industry has a strong incentive to ensure its ecological sustainability. However, such indications of revenue-generating potential may also encourage more communities and operators to become involved in this sector and to violate the precautionary principle (i.e. to withhold action if the consequences of that action are unknown) in the interests of profit. For former whaling centres, such as Eden and Byron Bay (New South Wales) and Kaikoura (New Zealand), whale-watching compensates for the economic downturn associated with the demise of whaling and more recent extractive industries, such as fishing and forestry (Mercer 2000) (see the case study 'Whale-watching and Maori empowerment in Kaikoura, New Zealand' at the end of this chapter).

◼ 9.2.3 Management

There is currently no set of international standards that regulates the boat-based, whale-watching industry. Guidelines and regulations, however, have been put forward in Europe (Berrow 2003), Oceania and North America. The National Marine Fisheries Service (NMFS) in the USA recommends simply that boats should not approach within 100 yards (91.4 metres) of gray whales from any direction or move faster than the whales when following them or moving in a parallel direction. Vessels should also do nothing to make the whales change direction, and aircraft should not fly below an altitude of 1000 feet (304.8 metres) when situated within a 100-yard radius of a whale or group of whales. These guidelines emphasise that it is illegal to take any action that disrupts the whales' normal behaviour (NMFS 2006). More detailed guidelines are stipulated in the north-eastern USA, where different protocols apply at different distances. For example, a speed of 13 knots is recommended between 1 and 2 miles (1.61 and 3.22 kilometres) from the whale, 10 knots between half a mile and 1 mile (0.80 and 1.61 kilometres) and 7 knots below half a mile (NOAA 2005). In Australia, whale-watching guidelines from the Queensland Department of the Environment have been put into place in a number of major centres, including Hervey Bay (see figure 9.3). These are similar in principle to the NMFS guidelines but add a 300-metre buffer zone for swimmers, and are enforceable by law.

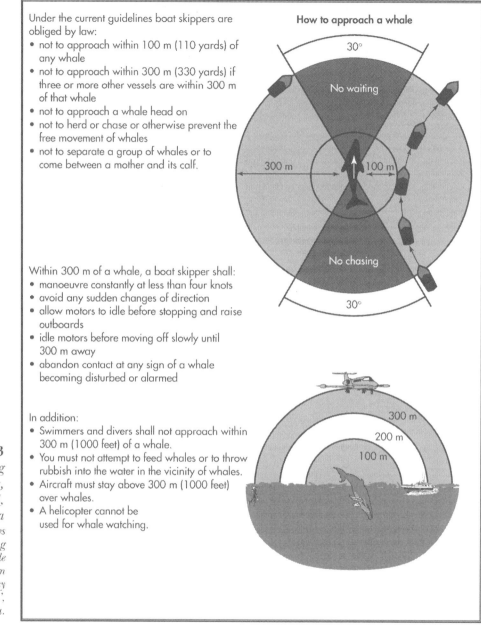

Under the current guidelines boat skippers are obliged by law:
- not to approach within 100 m (110 yards) of any whale
- not to approach within 300 m (330 yards) if three or more other vessels are within 300 m of that whale
- not to approach a whale head on
- not to herd or chase or otherwise prevent the free movement of whales
- not to separate a group of whales or to come between a mother and its calf.

How to approach a whale

30°
No waiting
300 m   100 m
No chasing
30°

Within 300 m of a whale, a boat skipper shall:
- manoeuvre constantly at less than four knots
- avoid any sudden changes of direction
- allow motors to idle before stopping and raise outboards
- idle motors before moving off slowly until 300 m away
- abandon contact at any sign of a whale becoming disturbed or alarmed

In addition:
- Swimmers and divers shall not approach within 300 m (1000 feet) of a whale.
- You must not attempt to feed whales or to throw rubbish into the water in the vicinity of whales.
- Aircraft must stay above 300 m (1000 feet) over whales.
- A helicopter cannot be used for whale watching.

300 m
200 m
100 m

■ **Figure 9.3**
Whale-watching regulations, Queensland, Australia
Source: *'Laws regarding whale watching in Hervey Bay Marine Park',* www.hervey.com.au.

A wider management issue is the extent to which the experience should focus on the core activity of whale-watching (around which the above regulations and guidelines are focused). If the core activity is overemphasised in promotion and regulation, as per an elemental approach towards ecotourism (see section 1.4.2), this may create very high expectations for participants. Operators in turn may feel pressured to provide prolonged close-up experiences to satisfy their clientele and maintain their own financial viability even if this risks interfering with the whales in an unsustainable way. Research carried out at Hervey Bay in the late 1990s showed that proximity to whales was an important parameter of satisfaction to visitors, although operators' adherence to regulations was also highly rated (Muloin 1998). However, research at Tangalooma indicated that proximity to whales is not a major indicator of satisfaction among whale-watchers. Many viewers were highly satisfied even if no cetaceans were sighted as long as other aspects of the entire experience, such as interpretation, weather and boat design, were satisfactory (Orams 2000). According to the principles described in section 1.4.3, this suggests the importance of a comprehensive ecotourism approach; that is, of incorporating the presence of cetaceans into a more thematic and holistic interpretive experience whereby unrealistic and potentially unsustainable expectations are not fostered and viewers can appreciate all aspects of the marine environment inhabited by whales.

9.3 ISLANDS

The physical separation of islands from other landmasses gives rise to special 'insular' considerations that affect the development of ecotourism. These include the presence of endemic species and distinctive ecosystems, isolation and the strong sense of place it fosters, proximity to coastal ecosystems and associated opportunities for marine ecotourism and, in tropical or subtropical settings, the prevalence of 3S tourism.

■ 9.3.1 Endemism *and ecosystem distinctiveness*

Species of flora and fauna are endemic to a specified area if they are found nowhere else in their natural setting. **Endemism** results from the genetic drift that occurs when an area is isolated for a long period from other areas of potential genetic input. Relatively isolated islands and archipelagos, such as Madagascar, the Galapagos and Hawaii, are well known for their endemic flora and fauna (Myers et al. 2000). Madagascar alone has 84 endemic mammal species, 104 of birds and 6500 of plants, the latter representing 80 per cent of its entire flora (World Resources Institute 2005). For ecotourism, the crucial implication is that ecotourists must visit Madagascar if they wish to observe any of these 84 endemic mammals in their native habitat. This monopoly position, however, is significant only if there is a market demand to observe a particular plant or animal. Not all endemics are charismatic, although Madagascar is fortunate to count an array of interesting species, such as lemurs and chameleons, among its native fauna.

Although the biodiversity of Madagascar can be attributed to a period of isolation that has lasted millions of years, the impact of genetic drift can also be experienced in situations where isolation has been of much shorter duration. Rottnest Island, off Perth (Western Australia), is only a few kilometres from the mainland and has been separated by rising sea levels for only about 7000 years. Nevertheless, the island is home to at least two endemic reptiles — the dugite snake and the bobtail lizard — that are regarded as subspecies of their mainland counterparts. Rottnest Island is also a refuge for the quokka, a small marsupial that has become scarce on the adjacent mainland due to habitat degradation and predation by feral animals that are absent from Rottnest. A further distinction of the island's ecosystem is the absence of such common regional flora as banksia, jarrah (a type of eucalypt) and casuarina (she-oak), which have become extirpated (locally extinct) as a result of long-term exposure to wind and salt (Rottnest Island Authority 2006). Visitors to Rottnest Island, through effective interpretation, appreciate a distinctive ecotourism product shaped primarily by the quality of insularity. However, this also means that greater care must be taken to avoid inappropriate modes of tourism activity.

■ 9.3.2 Sense *of place*

The geographical and ecological distinctiveness of islands contribute to a strong sense of place, as does a comparable process of cultural drift that has frequently given rise to unique and attractive human cultures and land-scapes. For potential tourists, sense of place contributes to the romanti-cisation of islands as fascinating and alluring destinations that offer exotic and escapist experiences. This is evident in the exotic and positive images that are conjured by such places as Tahiti, Bali, Bermuda, the Isle of Capri, Norfolk Island, Tristan da Cunha, Aruba, Hawaii and Tasmania. In the field of tourism studies, the popularity of islands as destinations has led to their emergence as a growing focus of specialisation (e.g. Gössling 2003).

Increasingly, ecotourism is advocated by academics and governments as an activity that sustainably promotes understanding of an island's sense of place (Diamantis 2000). Madagascar, Iceland, Dominica, Papua New Guinea, the Falkland Islands, New Zealand and the Solomon Islands are some of the island or archipelagic entities where ecotourism occupies a prominent position in national tourism strategies. In other cases, island components of larger states have deliberately or spontaneously become associated with ecotourism. Examples include Vancouver Island and the Queen Charlottes (Canada), Saaremaa (Estonia), Tasmania, Kangaroo Island, Fraser Island and Rottnest Island (Australia), the Galapagos Islands (Ecuador), Socotra (Yemen), the Andaman and Nicobar Islands (India) and Borneo (Indonesia, Malaysia and Brunei).

■ 9.3.3 SISODs

Small island states or dependencies, or **SISODs**, are a special type of insular environment, being either politically independent (e.g. Dominica and Fiji), or possessing a dependency status separate from their 'mother' country (e.g. Isle of Man, Norfolk Island and French Polynesia). The concept of 'small' is subjective, but 63 states or dependencies could be defined as SISODs in 2006 by merit of having less than 3 million permanent residents and a land area of less than 28 000 km^2. Although these accommodate only 15 million inhabitants or 0.3 per cent of the global population, the 30 independent SISODs account for 16 per cent of all countries, giving the SISODs a disproportionate voice in such forums as the United Nations General Assembly and, as discussed in section 3.2.3, the International Whaling Commission. Further evidence of geopolitical influence is provided by the enormous amount of ocean and sea that is controlled by SISODs through the most recent United Nations Convention on the Law of the Sea, which allocates an Exclusive Economic Zone (EEZ) of 200 kilometres to all coastal states. The South Pacific nation of Kiribati, for example, has a land area of just 717 km^2 but an EEZ of approximately 5 million km^2. Such SISODs, therefore, will continue to play a major role in issues associated with the management of marine ecotourism resources, such as cetaceans and coral reefs.

SISODs are concentrated in the Caribbean, South Pacific and Indian Ocean components of the **pleasure periphery** (Turner & Ash 1975), where much of the world's 3S resort-based mass tourism became established throughout the latter half of the 20th century. Thus, in contrast to their negligible share of resident population, SISODs accommodate approximately 5 per cent of the world's international stayover arrivals and an even greater proportion of the global cruise ship industry. Their dependency on tourism is illustrated by the fact that the latter accounts for at least 15 per cent of GNP in no less than 15 of the 30 independent SISODs (Weaver & Lawton 2006).

Evolution of mass tourism and ecotourism

The development of mass 3S tourism in many pleasure periphery SISODs has important implications for ecotourism that can be discussed in the context of the tourism platforms presented in chapters 1 and 2. Initially, the post-World War II development of mass tourism in SISODs was encouraged by the then-dominant philosophy of the advocacy platform that supported the unconstrained growth of tourism. In the case of small tropical islands facing the prospect of independence, governments tended to regard mass tourism as an especially suitable and viable avenue for economic development in light of inherent natural resource scarcities, dependency on a declining agricultural export sector and economies of scale that were inadequate to support large-scale manufacturing.

During the 1970s, the SISODs of the pleasure periphery became a focal point of the highly politicised criticism directed towards mass tourism by the followers of the cautionary platform, who condemned mass tourism as a new kind of sugar, or pleasure plantation. Such rhetoric aside, it is not surprising that much of the subsequent interest in alternative tourism and ecotourism associated with the adaptancy platform was directed towards small tropical islands. Some SISODS, and especially those that were unsuited for mass tourism or other more conventional modes of economic activity, opted to become specialised in ecotourism and other unconventional pursuits (see 'Practitioner's perspective: Ecotourism in Dominica as paradigm shift or opportunism?'). Similar strategies are evident in St Vincent and the Grenadines and in Samoa, which are both in an early enough stage of tourism development for alternative tourism-related options for future development to be available (Weaver 1998).

For SISODs already dominated by mass tourism, ecotourism during the current knowledge-based platform is being pursued as a complementary add-on. In some cases, relatively undeveloped peripheral islands have been targeted as specialised ecotourism destinations that complement the mass tourism dominant on the main island. Caribbean examples include Tobago (relative to Trinidad), Barbuda (relative to Antigua), Nevis (relative to St Kitts), Little Cayman Island and Cayman Brac (relative to Grand Cayman Island) and the Bahamian Family Islands (relative to Grand Bahama and New Providence Islands). In other cases, mountainous and forested interiors and/or offshore coral reefs are being promoted as ecotourism add-ons located close to coastal resorts or cruise ship ports. In essence, soft ecotourism is emerging as an essential ingredient in the increasingly diverse tourism product of pleasure periphery destinations in the Caribbean, South Pacific and Indian Oceans.

PRACTITIONER'S PERSPECTIVE
Ecotourism in Dominica as paradigm shift or opportunism?

From the 1950s until the early 1970s, the Caribbean island of Dominica unsuccessfully attempted to initiate a mass tourism industry that would reduce the island's dependency on an unstable agricultural sector. Working against these efforts were the lack of white sand beaches, the frequency of cloudy and rainy weather, chronic political instability and mountainous terrain unsuited to the construction of a major international airport. Following the release in the mid-1970s of yet another unrealistic consultant's report advocating mass tourism, the government decided to radically change direction and promote the very same assets that hindered the development of mass tourism. Dominica was subsequently differentiated as the 'Nature Island of the Caribbean', allegedly offering 365 waterfalls, or a different one for each day of the year. The introduction of regulations to promote local ownership of accommodation, and decisions to focus on a decentralised pool of locally supplied guesthouses and to not expand two small airports, all indicate the subsequent pursuit of a deliberate alternative tourism strategy in keeping with the spirit of the emergent green paradigm (Weaver 2004).

A critical analysis of Dominica's economy, however, casts doubt on the government's commitment to deliberate alternative tourism or the green paradigm. As far back as the 1970s, attempts were made by some in power to designate a *laissez-faire* free trade zone in the north of the country that would not be subject to Dominica's laws. The island also acquired a reputation for the mass production of colourful and irrelevant postage stamps intended for collectors rather than postal purposes. More recently, Dominica has been criticised for the sale of its citizenship to individuals willing to pay a designated fee, for tolerating the establishment of online pornographic and gaming sites, for granting strip mining concessions in ecologically sensitive areas to foreign transnational companies, for allowing its cruise ship tourism to expand at an extremely rapid rate and for supporting the pro-whaling bloc in the International Whaling Commission. All these actions suggest an opportunistic openness to innovative if sometimes questionable activities that arise from a small island syndrome of constrained opportunity. Accordingly, it can be argued that its ecotourism product is a similarly opportunistic rather than idealistic pursuit that is unlikely to be supported or protected by government should a more lucrative option become available (Weaver 2004).

9.4 *P*OLAR ENVIRONMENTS

'Polar environments' refer to the high latitude landscapes and seascapes around the North and South Pole that are covered by icecaps, barren rock or tundra. Although the two polar regions of Antarctica and the Arctic share many characteristics, significant physical and cultural differences require that each region be examined on its own merits as an ecotourism venue.

■ 9.4.1 Antarctica

The continent of Antarctica, covering an area of 13 200 000 km^2, is physically, culturally and geopolitically unique. Its primary physical characteristic is the almost total dominance of an icecap that is 5000 metres thick in some locations. Cold temperature extremes and biological impoverishment characterise the icecap, but relatively diverse and locally numerous wildlife populations are found in favourable sites along the interface between the coast and the open water and on the milder Antarctic Peninsula (facetiously described by some as the 'Antarctic Riviera') in particular. Various endemic species of penguin are the charismatic megafauna most popularly associated with Antarctica. Culturally, the continent is unique due to the absence of any indigenous or permanent human population. The meagre cultural landscape consists of about a hundred active scientific bases and a number of abandoned whaling stations and other historical sites, also concentrated along the coast and on the Antarctic Peninsula. Geopolitically, Antarctica is external to the state/dependency system that accounts for the rest of the world's land area. However, seven countries, including Australia, have made formal territorial claims over various and sometimes overlapping sectors of the continent (see figure 9.4).

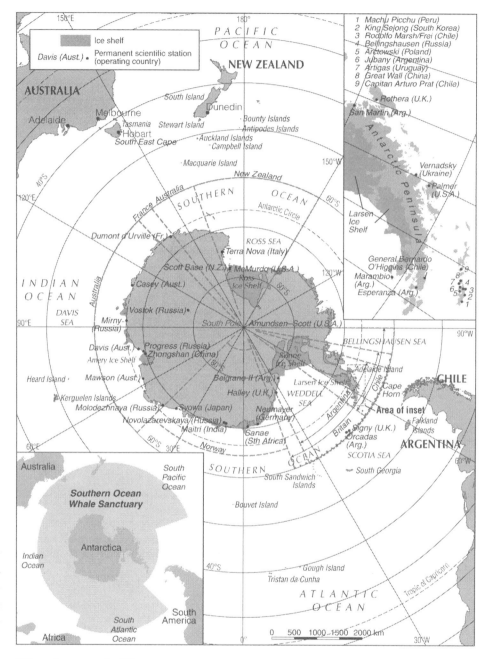

■ Figure 9.4
Antarctica:
claims and
scientific
bases
Source:
Glassner 2004,
p. 468.

The Antarctic Treaty

Virtually all human activity in Antarctica and its adjacent waters is subject to the dictates of the 1959 Antarctic Treaty and subsequent amendments and annexes, known collectively as the Antarctic Treaty System. The system provides freedom of access to all individuals but restricts the types of activity that can be pursued. Included is a ban on nuclear testing, radioactive waste disposal, military activity and mineral exploitation. The treaty also suspends the territorial aspirations of the seven claimant countries in order to reduce the probability of military conflict, the establishment of permanent settlements or other undesirable outcomes related to the projection of national sovereignty. In essence, the treaty maintains Antarctica as a *de facto* international protected area reserved primarily for 'scientific purposes'. Forty-five countries are signatories to the Antarctic Treaty and 28 of these (including Australia and New Zealand) are 'Consultative Parties' that have full voting privileges due to their pursuit of an active research agenda on the continent (SCAR 2006).

Ship-based tourism

Ship-based tourism is the oldest and by far the largest form of recreational activity in Antarctica, having been first recorded in 1958. Tourism ships were visiting on a regular basis by the mid-1960s but cumulatively did not accommodate more than a few hundred visitors per year. The more formalised concept of 'expedition cruising' was introduced in 1966 by the pioneer ecotourism company Lindblad Expeditions. Ship-borne tourists now account for the overwhelming share of Antarctic visitor arrivals, which have increased dramatically during the early years of the 21st century (see figure 9.5). An improbable but significant factor underlying the growing popularity of expedition cruising was the collapse of the Soviet Union in the early 1990s. This external political environment led to the sale of several Russian icebreakers, research vessels and other large ships to Antarctic tour operators. Antarctica-themed movies produced in the mid-2000s have also contributed to popularising the continent. The typical contemporary expedition occurs during the five-month ice-free period from November to March and departs from a gateway port in southern Argentina or Chile. Each trip involves an average of eight landings focused on 50 bases and favourable natural sites on the Antarctic Peninsula. Stops are also made in transit on sub-Antarctic destinations, such as the South Orkneys and the South Shetlands. Landings are made by inflatable rubber craft or, more rarely, by helicopter and involve less than a hundred tourists, who spend about three hours on land (IAATO 2006c).

The case for characterising ship-based tourism in Antarctica as ecotourism is compelling. First, the attractions of Antarctica are overwhelmingly nature-based, given the physical and cultural nature of the destination. Moreover, visits to scientific bases emphasise exposure to activity and research that is related to the natural environment. Second, facilitation of learning is a major component of the expedition product. This is apparent in the visits to the scientific bases, in the provision of expert tour guides and personnel who accompany tourists on the landings and in the on-board availability of libraries, lectures and workshops related to the Antarctic visitation experience. In addition to this learning component, however, it is important to stress that these expeditions represent a form of ecotourism that overlaps with adventure tourism, an element that is often emphasised in marketing material. As well, an ego component is apparent given the exotic allure of Antarctica as the elusive and exclusive seventh continent, which no more than 200 000 humans have ever seen.

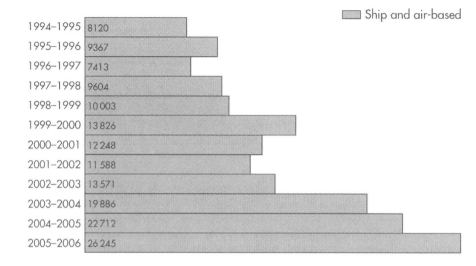

■ **Figure 9.5**
Antarctica
tourists
1984–85 to
2005–06
Source:
compiled from
Hall &
Johnston 1995;
IAATO 2006b.

Ship and air-based

1994–1995	8120
1995–1996	9367
1996–1997	7413
1997–1998	9604
1998–1999	10 003
1999–2000	13 826
2000–2001	12 248
2001–2002	11 588
2002–2003	13 571
2003–2004	19 886
2004–2005	22 712
2005–2006	26 245

Third, Antarctic expedition operators have for the most part demonstrated responsible and sustainable behaviour (Bauer & Dowling 2003). Because of the lack of permanent human inhabitants, issues of cultural and economic sustainability are effectively irrelevant in Antarctica, although the presence of tourists may sometimes interfere with the activities of scientists. The focus, rather, is on environmental sustainability. In this respect, the founding of the International Association of Antarctica Tour Operators (IAATO) is a critical factor. The IAATO is best known for drafting environmental guidelines to govern the behaviour of its members within and in transit to Antarctica (see section 6.6.1). Additional activities include monitoring the activities of treaty signatories with regard to their impact on the tourism industry and serving as a lobby for the Antarctic tourism industry in national and international forums. IAATO bylaws, which full members are pledged to follow, require that ships with landing privileges carry no more than 500 passengers and that no more than a hundred of these are allowed ashore at any one site at any one time (IAATO 2006d). Typically, one expert staff member is provided to accompany and monitor every 15–20 landed visitors (IAATO 2006c). A system is also in place whereby observers from the US National Science Foundation are put aboard selected commercial tour vessels in order to independently verify the sustainability of their activities. Assisting these measures is the fact that ship-borne Antarctic visitors are excursionists who spend their nights and most of their days aboard ship rather than in fragile terrestrial settings.

The demonstrated environmental sustainability of the IAATO membership in the Antarctic is a notable example of apparently effective self-regulation in the ecotourism industry. Moreover, it is significant that this has occurred in the absence of any national regulatory authorities that would normally monitor compliance with environmental laws. Because claimant countries through the Antarctic Treaty have essentially placed their sovereign rights in abeyance, they cannot individually or multilaterally take measures to control tourism. A rare exception is New Zealand's decision to prohibit the entry of tourists into the historic huts of the explorers Shackleton and Scott without being accompanied by a government-appointed warden. These huts are located in the sector claimed by New Zealand (Stonehouse 2001).

The success of the IAATO is owed partly to its exclusive nature (there were only 35 full members as of 2006, compared with 15 in 2000) and to rigorous procedures applied when screening, accepting and monitoring members. As well, and despite their adventure and ego motivations, visitors to Antarctica are generally regarded as conscientious individuals who harbour high expectations about their own behaviour and the practices of expedition operators — a mindset that is constantly reinforced throughout the offshore and onshore expedition experience.

Other forms of tourism

In addition to ship-based cruising expeditions, Antarctica is visited by up to a hundred private yachts per year, a means of conveyance that is very expensive but more flexible in terms of scheduling. As little is known about this form of sea-based tourism, any discussion or analysis regarding its status as a form of ecotourism is premature. However, the absence of any monitoring or regulation of this activity, and its potential for growth, are matters of concern. Another minor form of Antarctic tourism involves the transport of tourists by aeroplane to land, where mountain climbing is the dominant activity. This is clearly affiliated with adventure tourism rather than ecotourism and, although participation is currently minimal, there is a strong possibility that it could also expand to locally unsustainable levels as markets seek ever more novel and remote tourism experiences. Scenic overflights are another aeroplane-based aspect of the tourism sector. They were popular until 1979 when an Air New Zealand DC-10 crashed near Mount Erebus, killing all 257 passengers and crew. They became popular again in the late 1990s, although participants do not have the privilege of being included in Antarctica visitation statistics.

Future of Antarctic tourism and ecotourism

Surprisingly, no explicit or substantive mention was made regarding tourism in the Antarctic Treaty directive until 1994 when the 18th Antarctic Treaty Consultative Meeting finally recognised its legitimacy as an activity potentially compatible with scientific research. It is interesting that tourism was evaluated relative to the anthropocentric concept of 'scientific research' rather than the biocentric concept of environmental sustainability, although the latter was clearly intended as an outcome. In order to ensure this compatibility and facilitate the environmental sustainability of tourism, the meeting also formalised many of the informal operator guidelines and practices of the IAATO by recognising them in the treaty directive. This was not meant to imply that the IAATO's self-regulation was suspect, but rather that Antarctica was vulnerable to less benign tour operators and tourists who might not share the same ideals as the IAATO and who might try to take advantage of the continent's regulatory peculiarities. The growing number of visiting private yachts is one indication of unregulated tourism growth that may become problematic in the future. The subject of tourism is now regularly addressed in annual Antarctic Treaty Consultative Meetings (Antarctic Treaty Consultative Meeting 2006).

With regard to the dramatic growth in tourist arrivals depicted in figure 9.5, it may be pointed out that the 28 246 total for the 2005–06 season is still very low in absolute terms, even considering the concentration of visitation on the Antarctic Peninsula. Nevertheless, some environmentalists advocate the exclusion of tourism from Antarctica, in recognition of its perceived status as a uniquely fragile destination and due to wildlife stress that has been associated with visitation on some over-visited sites. These exclusionists also argue that *any* level of tourist visitation sets a precedent for much larger volumes of visitation in future as the Antarctic tourism industry becomes more articulated. Stonehouse (2001), however, cites the long-held argument that people are less likely to cherish and protect that which they have not or cannot visit. As described in section 4.3.1, Antarctic tourists may also serve as environmental watchdogs and as agents of enhancive sustainability through the collection of litter, participation in scientific research, observation of activities at bases and the provision of donations. Others emphasise that the scale of tourism as a human activity in Antarctica, notwithstanding recent growth, is insignificant in comparison with scientific undertakings. Bauer and Dowling (2003) estimate that tourists account for only 0.5 per cent of Antarctica's human presence in any given year, mainly because scientific personnel remain on the continent for extended periods compared with tourists. The scientific bases are also cited as a demonstrably more significant factor in causing environmental problems, with many having being implicated in such practices as improper waste disposal, fuel leakage, inappropriate runway construction and covert military activity. In 1989, for example, an Argentine supply vessel experienced a hull rupture that resulted in 180 000 gallons of leaked diesel fuel.

While not discounting such incidents, Stonehouse (2001) argues that the Antarctic environment is more dynamic and resilient than is generally realised, being subject to natural processes such as landslides and long-term climate cycles that have a much greater impact on the Antarctic ecosystem than either tourism or scientific research. However, an ominous consideration is the possible impact of accelerated anthropogenic climate change, which has already been implicated by some scientists as a factor in widespread ice melt along parts of the Antarctic coastline. This could emerge as the most important factor in determining the future character of Antarctica as well as Antarctic tourism more specifically.

■ *9.4.2* **The** *Arctic*

Unlike Antarctica, the core Arctic region around the North Pole is occupied by ice-covered water, while the peripheral Arctic is a mainland and archipelagic extension of Eurasia and North America commonly demarcated as the area north of the tree line (which is actually a transition zone). One important consequence of this geographical context is that Arctic temperatures tend to be relatively mild, and a well-defined summer season occurs in all but the most extreme and northerly areas, such as the Greenland icecap and the North Pole itself. In addition, a high proportion of the Arctic landscape is occupied by tundra underlaid by permafrost. These areas have relatively more biodiversity, hosting 50–60 species of flowering plants compared with just two throughout Antarctica (Stonehouse 2001). Dramatic flowering displays are a common feature of the Arctic springtime. In wildlife terms, the polar bear is the symbolic charismatic megafauna of the Arctic.

Indigenous groups such as the Canadian Inuit have occupied the more accessible parts of the Arctic for several thousand years, and issues associated with traditional ownership are therefore especially relevant to this region (see section 9.5). Although a network similar to the Antarctic scientific bases is lacking, the non-indigenous human presence is much more evident than in Antarctica. Included in this cultural landscape are mining towns, administrative settlements, resource exploration sites, a rudimentary road network and military sites, which are largely a vestige of the Cold War. Politically, the entire Arctic is divided into areas of national sovereignty involving Russia, Canada, the USA, Denmark (through Greenland) and Norway, with boundaries converging along lines of longitude on the North Pole. Several geopolitical units, including the Canadian territory of Nunavut, the Danish Dependent Territory of Greenland and the Norwegian Dependent Territory of Svalbard, are located entirely within the Arctic region.

Tourism trends

Unlike Antarctica, the extent of ecotourism in the Arctic is unknown since some countries, including Canada and Russia, do not compile visitor statistics specific to their Arctic regions and do not enumerate 'ecotourists' separately from other types of visitor. However, Stonehouse (2001) speculates that the total tourist visitation figures are much higher than those for Antarctica given the number of operators in the area and its greater accessibility. Other important points of departure from the Antarctic include the lack of strict self-regulation mechanisms, such as those imposed by IAATO, and the need for tourism and ecotourism in particular to coexist with a more complex array of external tourism and non-tourism human forces. For example, Arctic ecotourism, which includes the viewing of polar bears and the northern lights (*aurora borealis*), must share the landscape with big game hunting (including polar bears), adventure tourism and other recreational activities. The presence of indigenous groups, who constitute a majority throughout most of the Arctic, is a major consideration in the development of Arctic ecotourism (see section 9.5).

Also relevant are potential conflicts and synergies that could arise from the exploitation of natural resources and the redefinition of military priorities in the wake of the Cold War. Not only does the Arctic lack any moratorium on resource development comparable to Antarctica but also governments appear increasingly keen to accelerate their exploitation as more accessible resources in the south face depletion. The debate in the USA during the early 2000s over the opening of large Alaskan protected areas to hydrocarbon exploration and mining is a case in point, with the pro-development lobby gaining support from the George Bush presidency and from every increase in the price of crude oil. Increasing the likelihood of further development is the region's small permanent population, which lacks the numbers, organisation and political clout to oppose such developments. Indeed, many Artic residents, both non-indigenous and indigenous, strongly support the continued and accelerated exploitation of the region's natural resources.

The situation with regard to the military is more complex. Tourists were prohibited from military bases during the Cold War for security reasons, but tourism may now provide a rationale for the continued existence of the bases, especially as retaining them may be considered desirable as a way of protecting and projecting national sovereignty. The same logic applies to some obsolete resource settlements.

As in Antarctica, the greatest long-term threat to ecotourism may be the acceleration of climate change, which is expected to have dramatic consequences for the Arctic environment. One example is the weight reduction of polar bears caused by the reduced amount of time spent on ice floes (see section 7.5.2). Another indicator was the extremely rare appearance of open water over the North Pole during 2000. The possibility of an ice-free Northwest Passage is an additional factor that could increase the risk of military confrontation (i.e. between Canada and the USA) as well as water contamination from freighters and other vessels.

9.5 INDIGENOUS TERRITORIES

Any discussion of indigenous territories in the context of ecotourism requires that 'indigenous groups' are defined and their 'territories' demarcated. There is no precise, universally accepted definition of the term 'indigenous', but certain groups clearly qualify because of their long-standing presence in an area before the arrival of newer immigrants. These include Aborigines (Australia), Maori (New Zealand), native Americans or Amerindians (North and South America), Inuit and related people (the Arctic), Saan (southern Africa), Maasai and other pastoral groups (eastern Africa), Ainu (northern Japan), Saami (Scandinavia) and the tribal societies of central India and South-East Asia (Zeppel 2006). In contrast, successive waves of invasion have left such countries such as the United Kingdom and Germany without people who are considered 'indigenous' in the same sense, although some believe that this status should apply to the Celtic people of Western Europe.

The estimated 400 million indigenous people of the world are highly diverse, and caution should be exercised in making any general statements relating these cultures to ecotourism or any other topic. This also holds true for the complex concept of indigenous territoriality. The most obvious and best-known example of the latter are 'third-level' geopolitical units, such as reserves and reservations nested within national (i.e. 'first-level') and subnational (i.e. 'second-level') political structures in such countries as Australia, Brazil, the USA and Canada. For instance, the Hopi Indian Reservation is located in the state of Arizona, which in turn is part of the USA. A second type of indigenous territoriality exists where second-level territories and dependencies are themselves dominated demographically and politically by indigenous groups. Examples include Nunavut and Greenland, both of which have large Inuit majorities. Several Russian autonomous regions (e.g. Buryatia and Yakutia) were established as ethnic 'homelands' for indigenous groups, but these now account for only a minority of their populations due to the arrival of Russian and other non-indigenous settlers.

Interesting indigenous territorial dynamics are also occurring at the 'first' or national level. Bolivia and Peru are Latin American countries with indigenous majorities that are beginning to assert their power nationally, while Papua New Guinea, Vanuatu and the Solomon Islands possess politically dominant indigenous majorities. Fiji and New Caledonia (Kanaky) are unusual in that their indigenous populations are roughly equal to those of more recently arrived groups. Although indigenous groups constitute only a small and racially mixed minority in Australia, New Zealand and Canada, recent trends towards the recognition of traditional ownership rights mean that these groups are involved in many different aspects of decision-making well beyond their officially designated territories. Hence, at least some form of indigenous territoriality can increasingly be seen as extending to all areas of these countries.

■ 9.5.1 Environmental *and cultural considerations*

Indigenous groups are associated with an exceptionally high level of bonding with the environment, often to the extent that culture and the natural environment are effectively inseparable. One implication for ecotourism is the difficulty in divorcing the cultural from the ecological when defining the tourism product base. For example, the Australian trend of incorporating Aboriginal perspectives in the interpretation of such sites as Kakadu and Uluru emphasises that 'natural' environments are the product of long-term interaction with local indigenous populations or their reversion to a natural state after such indigenous activities as burning were halted (Flannery 2002). The slash-and-burn landscapes of traditional Mayan groups in Guatemala and Belize are another illustration of long-term cultural interaction with the natural environment.

Because of these long associations, it is often assumed that indigenous groups are inherently more responsible and knowledgeable than others in using the land and that they can therefore provide the visitor with more authentic interpretation. Moreover, the communal and small-scale character of many indigenous groups suggests an innate compatibility with alternative tourism (see section 1.2.1). Such romantic views, however, can be misplaced. There are numerous situations in which population pressures have led to unsustainable land use practices (as with the Maya) or where the desire to attain economic growth has resulted in the opening of indigenous territories to commercial waste disposal, casinos (as in the USA) or other questionable activities. More frequently, indigenous people and lifestyles are at least superficially identical to the surrounding dominant culture, or they use such tools as rifles and snowmobiles, acquired through acculturation, that expedite traditional activities such as hunting. Given the idealised expectations of those ecotourists who perceive all indigenous people to be instinctive followers of the green paradigm, the encounter with such realities can be a disillusioning experience.

But even without such environmental and social distortions, core cultural values of indigenous people may vary from or be alien to the values and expectations of ecotourists. This is most evident in attitudes towards wildlife, which most indigenous people regard simultaneously as sacred and a means of subsistence. As illustrated by the polar bear incident in northern Canada (see section 5.4.3), ecotourists may react in a negative way to the killing of certain charismatic megafauna by indigenous people, prompting the need for some kind of management response. One option is to introduce strategies that educate and sensitise ecotourists to these practices, as is being pursued in Uluru and Kakadu. Conversely or in conjunction, strategies involving the spatial and temporal separation of ecotourism and native hunting may be implemented, possibly on the basis of backstage/frontstage demarcations (see section 5.4.2). A related issue is the inaccessibility of some indigenous beliefs to ecotourists and other visitors by circumstance or design. Aboriginal people in Australia, for example, may not wish tourists to have access to sensitive religious practices or certain sacred sites, or may attempt to convey culturally specific meanings that cannot be understood or appreciated by some tourists who are subsequently disappointed by the encounter. Such dynamics are apparent at Uluru where many visitors cannot understand or will not heed the opposition among traditional owners to climbing that famous monolith.

If ecotourists often misunderstand indigenous beliefs and behaviour, it is also the case that some less acculturated indigenous people may have difficulty in understanding the Eurocentric concept of ecotourism. According to Mercer (1998), indigenous people often begin with a suspicion of tourism, which at least in its recreational manifestations presupposes a separation of work and play that is alien to many of these cultures. In the past, tourism was also a means through which curious outsiders could glimpse the indigenous culture before it became extinct or, conversely, an excuse to remove them from an area so as not to offend tourists (see section 9.5.3). With respect to ecotourism specifically, it is incomprehensible to many indigenous people that ecotourists will pay large amounts of money just to stare at certain types of plants and animals. This cultural dissonance on both sides, and the concomitant lack of knowledge about running a business, often impedes the ability of indigenous participants to benefit economically and socioculturally from ecotourism. This may help to explain why successful self-sustaining initiatives are rare (see section 5.5). Yet territories controlled by indigenous people often provide ideal ecotourism venues, having often been established in economically marginal but ecologically rich locations that have the potential to generate much-needed revenue from ecotourism (Zeppel 2006).

■ 9.5.2 Political *and social considerations*

The cultural and environmental observations made above must be situated within the contemporary political and social dynamics that are influencing indigenous groups and their territories. Historically, indigenous people have been subject to relentless forces of disempowerment, assimilation and genocide. During the latter part of the 20th century and primarily in developed countries, such as Australia, New Zealand, Canada and the USA, these processes were gradually halted and are now being reversed, providing further indication perhaps of a green paradigm shift (see section 2.2.4). Indigenous identities in these and other countries are being aggressively reasserted along with claims over traditional territories. Reserve lands are often functioning as quasi-independent units, new indigenous territories such as Nunavut are being established, and traditional rights are being reintroduced in lands where these rights have long been extinguished. This **indigenous renaissance**, moreover, is being supported by such bodies as the United Nations, which declared 1995–2004 to be the Decade of the World's Indigenous People and has established a Permanent Forum for Indigenous Issues (UNPFII 2006).

Within their own politically designated territories, this means that indigenous people have the power to incorporate ecotourism and other forms of tourism into their development strategies towards ensuring the protection and appropriate representation of their culture (Hinch 2001, Zeppel 2006). Beyond these areas, indigenous people are increasingly involved in land use decision-making on a countrywide basis through 'co-management' schemes and consultative arrangements that recognise pre-European traditional ownership. These are likely to apply to ecotourism as much as they do to forestry, mining and other activities. In certain cases, the extension of formal land claims over these areas has created an atmosphere of uncertainty that is dissuasive to non-indigenous entrepreneurs and developers. This is illustrated by British Columbia (Canada), where Amerindian groups have made formal (and overlapping) claims to the entire province. Although such actions might initially hinder the development of ecotourism, this sector may benefit in the longer term if the development restrictions associated with the land claims process curtail potentially incompatible activities, such as logging and mining.

Finally, there are various politically motivated reasons for indigenous groups to pursue or encourage ecotourism within their perceived territories, however these are defined. An interpretation program emphasising the indigenous presence in the ecosystem would reinforce land claims by demonstrating to tourists and governments that such lands were not 'empty' before colonisation by outside groups. Such a program, secondly, could also otherwise be mobilised as a propaganda platform to manipulate public opinion among both domestic and inbound tourists. Third, indigenous participation in and control over ecotourism, as for example when 'permission' is given for tourists to visit a particular sacred site, is an exercise in the projection and external acknowledgement of traditional rights (Hinch 2001). A fourth consideration is that the successful operation of an ecotourism sector demonstrates the ability of indigenous people to govern themselves, thereby undermining patronising assertions that pervasive government intervention is necessary to ensure the wellbeing of such groups. Fifth, participation in ecotourism is tangible evidence that indigenous people continue to gainfully utilise their territory, thereby making it difficult for other resource stakeholders to put forward claims on these 'relinquished' or 'underutilised' lands.

These are five emerging dynamics in the context of what Mercer (1998) describes as a collision between two powerful contemporary forces. These are the relentless expansion of tourism and the resurgence of indigenous groups, which may not necessarily welcome this expansion or know-how to effectively manage the sector or its impact. In theory, ecotourism is a benign way for these communities to engage in tourism in a way that reaffirms and facilitates their development as indigenous people.

■ 9.5.3 Protected *areas*

The relationship between indigenous people and protected areas such as national parks, which are the most prominent type of ecotourism venue (see chapter 3), has always been ambivalent. This is in part because the Eurocentric concept of a 'protected area' is alien to indigenous groups. In such countries as Kenya, Canada, the USA and Australia, the formation of protected areas and the subsequent introduction of tourism often contributed to the process of dispossession. For example, Uluru National Park was originally excised from a pre-existing Aboriginal reserve, and Aborigines were purposefully removed from the area so that tourists would not be put off by their presence (Mercer 1998). Indigenous pastoral people in Africa were systematically denied access to traditional grazing lands in the early 20th century as the British established various protected areas in Kenya and Tanganyika (the mainland of modern-day Tanzania) for the benefit of big game trophy hunters (Rutto & Sing'oeie 2004). It is not certain whether such actions were primarily intended to marginalise indigenous communities. However, the formation and management of national parks throughout most of the 20th century was dominated by the Eurocentric view that these parks should encompass economically marginal natural environments from which all human activity (except perhaps tourism) is excluded (Fennell 2003). Traditional indigenous groups, moreover, were disproportionately affected by this process because of their concentration in peripheral areas earmarked for the establishment of parks. Once established, expelled traditional owners were not only denied access but also effectively excluded from any subsequent management decisions.

Attitudes towards the role of indigenous people in national parks began to change during the latter part of the 20th century as part of the indigenous renaissance. Current management practices in such countries as Canada, New Zealand and Australia increasingly recognise the legitimacy of traditional land uses and accommodate these as much as possible in co-management agreements without detracting from other park purposes. In some cases, traditional ownership has been reaffirmed and local indigenous groups have been given a voice in management decisions (Mercer 1998), often affecting certain tourist activities. Institutions and agencies have been established to recognise indigenous interests. For example, the US National Park Service established the American Indian Liaison Office in 1995 to improve relations with indigenous communities and support their participation in park management (National Park Service 2006b). Similarly, indigenous interests in Canadian protected areas were facilitated in 1999 by the establishment within Parks Canada of an Aboriginal Affairs Secretariat, which is mandated to stimulate dialogue, consult with indigenous people in such areas as product interpretation, and identify economic opportunities. The secretariat designated Aboriginal tourism development as a strategic priority for the 2005–06 fiscal year (Parks Canada 2005).

The willingness of some governments to accommodate indigenous interests in protected areas arises from a complex set of motives. Many decisions are taken as part of a genuine desire to rectify past injustices, but many others represent an obligatory — and perhaps begrudging — response to legal decisions that favour indigenous people, such as New Zealand's Treaty of Waitangi. At a macro level, it is interesting to speculate on the status of high-order protected areas as a 'path of least resistance' to which indigenous territorial assertions and empowerment are being diverted at minimal cost to the dominant society. That is, if indigenous aspirations can be satisfied by providing access to national parks, less pressure may be placed on making similar concessions in low-order protected areas and private lands that provide substantial economic returns to the dominant society through farming, forestry, mining and other activity. However, it is not yet clear whether these initiatives in high-order protected areas are more than symbolic. Comprehensive Aboriginal involvement in Australian national parks, for example, is not pervasive but appears instead to be focused on a few high-profile entities, such as Kakadu and Uluru (Central Land Council 2006).

9.6 $\int$ UMMARY

The expansion of commercial whale-watching is an excellent and highly symbolic illustration of changing resource perceptions brought about because of the apparent paradigm shift. Valued for their meat and oil under the dominant Western environmental paradigm, whales are now increasingly valued under the green paradigm as an aesthetic resource. Concerns, however, have been expressed over the rapid growth of the sector and the lack of knowledge about its impact on cetaceans, whose habitat is hostile to concerted scientific investigation. Stringent guidelines and regulations for boat-based whale-watching have been implemented in such important destinations as Australia (and Hervey Bay in particular), although it is advisable, in keeping with a comprehensive ecotourism approach, for the industry to adopt a more holistic approach to the experience so that proximity to whales is not the sole emphasis.

The attractiveness of islands as ecotourism destinations is based mainly on the high incidence of endemism, a strong sense of place and convenient access to marine attractions. Small island states or dependencies (SISODs) in the pleasure periphery are especially important, given the dominance of mass beach-based resort tourism in many such entities. Ecotourism in these destinations is gradually evolving towards a symbiotic relationship with resort tourism, providing diversionary soft ecotourism experiences in such suitable locations as mountainous interiors, coral reefs and less-developed peripheral islands like Tobago and Barbuda. Some SISODs such as Dominica that lack the resource base for mass tourism have opted instead for a strategy based on ecotourism.

Although the polar environments of Antarctica and the Arctic share certain fundamental characteristics, they must be considered separately as ecotourism destinations due to their many physical, cultural and geopolitical differences. Antarctica is an exceptionally isolated destination where the direct presence of humans is restricted to scientific bases and tourism. External to the global system of sovereign states and 'governed' under the highly restrictive protocols of the Antarctic Treaty System, this continent is in effect a massive international protected area in which ecotourism is the 'default' tourism option. Because of its isolation, expedition cruising is the dominant mode of ecotourism. Amendments to the treaty system in the 1990s include the formal recognition of tourism as a legitimate Antarctic activity. Distinctive features of Arctic ecotourism include the need to coexist with a greater array of external environments, including other forms of tourism such as hunting, and non-tourism forces such as mineral exploitation, military activity and accelerated climate change. Important emerging consequences associated with the latter include degradation of polar bear populations and potential geopolitical and environmental conflicts associated with the expansion of ice-free oceanic waters.

Indigenous territories are among the most significant of the cultural environments associated with ecotourism because of the cultural and political renaissance that indigenous people are currently experiencing. An associated issue is the lack of distinction made by many indigenous people between the natural and cultural environments, which blurs or eliminates the boundary between ecotourism and cultural tourism. With respect to financial viability, problems can emerge due to the incompatibility of ecotourist expectations and values with increasingly non-traditional indigenous lifestyles as well as the retention of an extractive attitude towards wildlife. Similarly, indigenous people often have difficulty in conveying their culture to tourists, or even in understanding the motivations that underlie the ecotourism experience. Major implications are also associated with the evolving concept of indigenous territoriality. Long-established reserves often provide excellent venues for ecotourism, but the participation of indigenous people in ecotourism is now extending well beyond these areas. The notion of traditional ownership is being recognised and accommodated in relinquished areas that may cover an entire country. Frequently, ecotourism is being utilised as a means of attaining political goals associated with the assertion of territorial rights. This is especially evident in protected areas, where co-management strategies that incorporate traditional rights and perspectives have been introduced in such countries as Australia and New Zealand. It is not yet clear, however, to what extent this accommodation is more than a token response to the aspirations of indigenous people.

QUESTIONS

1. (a) How does the emergence of a large-scale whale-watching industry reflect the concept of paradigm shift?
   (b) To what extent is the feeding of dolphins consistent with the green paradigm and the ethics of ecotourism?

2. From an ecological, economic and sociocultural perspective, what are the advantages and disadvantages of land-based whale-watching, which is preferred by many marine environmentalists?

3. (a) Why are islands often considered to be excellent locations for ecotourism?
   (b) How does ecotourism fit into the evolving tourism industries of the pleasure periphery SISODs?

4. (a) How do recent developments in Dominica reveal the vulnerability of ecotourism to potentially hostile external environments?
   (b) How can the government of Dominica improve its economic situation without compromising the integrity of its ecotourism product?

5. (a) Are the rapidly increasing visitation levels to Antarctica a matter of ecological concern?
   (b) Why or why not?

6. (a) What are the major differences between sea-based, land-based and air-based ecotourism in Antarctica, in terms of their environmental and sociocultural impact?
   (b) What kind of ecotourist market is likely to be attracted to each of these sectors?

7. What characteristics differentiate indigenous ecotourism from other forms of ecotourism?

FURTHER READING

Bauer, T & Dowling, R 2003, 'Ecotourism policies and issues in Antarctica', in D Fennell & R Dowling (eds), *Ecotourism Policy and Planning*, CABI, Wallingford, UK, pp. 309–29. The authors provide an excellent summary of the status of tourism in Antarctica, including the role of IAATO and the place of tourism in the protocols of the Antarctic Treaty System.

Berrow, S 2003, 'An assessment of the framework, legislation and monitoring required to develop genuinely sustainable whalewatching', in B Garrod & J Wilson (eds), *Marine Ecotourism: Issues and Experiences*, Channel View, Clevedon, UK, pp. 66–78. Berrow focuses critically on the theme of regulation in the context of European whale-watching, citing case studies that range from voluntary codes of conduct to strict licensing regimes.

IFAW 2004, 'From whalers to whale watchers: The growth of whale watching tourism in Australia', www.ifaw.org. This report by the International Fund for Animal Welfare provides the most recent survey-based overview of the Australian whale-watching industry, focusing on the number of participants and revenues generated.

Splettstoesser, J, Landau, D & Headland, R 2004, 'Tourism in the forbidden lands: The Antarctica experience', in T Singh (ed.), *New Horizons in Tourism: Strange Experiences and Stranger Practices*, CABI, Wallingford, UK, pp. 27–36. A good contemporary overview of all main facets of Antarctica tourism is provided in this chapter, the primary author of which has had extensive personal exposure to the region.

Zeppel, H 2006, *Indigenous Ecotourism*, CABI, Wallingford, UK. This volume provides one of the most thorough inventories and analyses of ecotourism involvement on the part of indigenous people in all parts of the world, including Australia and New Zealand, North America and southern Africa.

Whale-watching and Maori empowerment
in Kaikoura, New Zealand

The whale-watching industry in Kaikoura, New Zealand, is an interesting example of the interface between an increasingly lucrative form of marine ecotourism and the assertion of the right of indigenous people to occupy a privileged position in the development of that sector. Cetaceans have long provided the focus for economic activity in the remote Kaikoura region, frequenting the offshore where near-shore deepwater canyons and upwelling caused by the convergence of warm and cold currents generates a favourable year-round environment for whales, mostly male sperm whales and their prey (Orams 2005). European settlers engaged in commercial whaling from the 1830s to the 1920s, but the subsequent decline of this and other primary sector activities caused the region to experience severe economic hardship by the early 1980s. Commercial whale-watching was pioneered in 1988 with the establishment of NatureWatch as a partnership between a local fisherman and an American businessman. During the following year, local Maori, who were especially affected by the recession, established a competing business. In 1991, with assistance from the larger Ngai Tahu tribal unit, the Maori assumed control of NatureWatch and created the now famous WhaleWatch, which has enjoyed a monopoly over the sector ever since (Curtin 2003).

The success of WhaleWatch is revealed in the growth of whale-watchers from just 3500 in 1989 to 60 000 in 1998, accommodated by five vessels owned by the company. The effects of this activity on the local whale population have been researched extensively, and related studies show that there is a biological impact but one that is probably not significant. Specifically, resident whales have apparently become accustomed to whale-watching vessels, which may affect them for about half of the time that they surface during daylight hours. These whales show only slight behavioural modifications in their presence or none at all. In contrast, transient whales are less accustomed to such exposure and exhibit more stress, but are not affected on enough occasions for this exposure to cause significant harm (Orams 2005; Richter, Dawson & Slooten 2006). In keeping with the precautionary principle, WhaleWatch is required to observe rigorous whale-watching regulations, which were introduced by the New Zealand government in 1992 and are enforced by the Department of Conservation. These require, for example, that each vessel make no more than four trips a day and that no more than four vessels be allowed on the water at any given time. The maximum capacity is therefore 16 trips per day, with no

(continued)

more than 50 whale-watchers per trip. One consequence of local research has been the replacement of boat propellers with a water-jet mechanism that produces much less underwater noise (Curtin 2003). Reinforcing such measures is 'deep learning' interpretation that includes broader environmental messages related to climate change, whaling and over-fishing. In addition, the relationship between Maori and the natural environment, and whales in particular, is featured prominently in terms of its alleged ecological sustainability and the essential role that this relationship occupies in the traditional indigenous culture.

Although boat-based whale-watching at Kaikoura appears to be conducted in an ecologically sustainable manner, it has had the ironic consequence of stimulating a broader tourism industry whose consequences are more questionable. Overall visitation numbers increased from an estimated 10 000 in 1989 to 873 000 in 1998, directly supporting around 30 per cent of all local employment and generating NZ$28 million per year in the late 1990s in this town of just 3000 permanent residents. In 2004, visitation exceeded 1.6 million (ICMA 2004). Among local Maori, 70 per cent of employment is directly related to tourism, which has allowed the community to move decisively from a position of relative powerlessness to become a major economic force in the town. Income from whale-watching, moreover, has improved the situation of local Maori through investments in training and education in such areas as horticulture, language, interpretation, forestry, fisheries and social work. Negative effects have included increased social instability, inflation, congestion, especially during the summer season, and increased construction (Curtin 2003). Tourists now engage in a wide variety of more conventional activities, such as shopping, and can view whales from aircraft tours offered by two local companies (Richter, Dawson & Slooten 2006). Accordingly, Orams (2002) argues that although the present tourism product at Kaikoura remains for the moment ecologically sustainable and educational, high growth rates and increased diversification indicate movement towards an ecologically unsustainable, entertainment-focused mass tourism product.

Even more controversial than the growth and change in the tourism product has been the issue of the effective Maori monopoly over local boat-based whale-watching. Many non-Maori believe that they should also have the right to establish similar businesses to take advantage of this 'public' resource, and both the defence of and opposition to this monopoly have become racially and politically charged exercises that have generated tensions between the indigenous and non-indigenous communities. This resentment has led to incidents of sabotage and resistance, including the damaging in 1990 of all eight motors used by Maori vessels and the setting alight of a company bus the following year. At that time a petition was also circulated to ban the company's boats from having berthing privileges in the local harbour (Orams 2002). The monopoly is justified by Maori as part of the 1840 Treaty of Waitangi, which granted them full and exclusive possession of their lands, forests and fisheries and the right to control their 'treasures'; that is, aspects of their environment and culture that have spiritual significance. Local Maori regard the whales as treasures and have consistently rejected and resisted any efforts to grant permits to other operators (Orams 2002). The New Zealand Court of Appeals ruled in favour of the Maori in 1994 and granted a moratorium on new permits, arguing that the monopoly serves to protect their interests. However, the court also sent mixed signals in ruling that conservation values were paramount and that the ruling did not mean that Maori had ownership over whales or the right to harvest them (Simpson 2003).

A recent decision to extend the moratorium on the granting of permits for new whale-watching boats to 2012 has been welcomed by scientists and environmentalists concerned over the ecological impact of expanded whale-watching activity (Richter, Dawson & Slooten 2006). It has also been welcomed by the Maori, but resented by some in the non-indigenous community as continued evidence of an unwarranted place of privilege for Maori in an economically lucrative activity. Thus, the projection of indigenous rights and the subsequent empowerment of indigenous people are a positive impact that have been achieved at the expense of broader social harmony. This politicised context, moreover, cannot be divorced from the environmental impact of the sector. Seen in this light, the willingness of Maori to rigorously observe government regulations and make voluntary changes to the industry when warranted on environmental grounds indicates a conscious attempt to demonstrate a philosophy of responsible stewardship that attracts considerable public and government support.

Questions

1 (a) What ecological and sociocultural threats are posed to the Kaikoura area by the rapid tourism growth that has been induced by the whale-watching industry?
   (b) How can these threats be averted?

2 (a) Is opposition to the Maori monopoly over whale-watching in Kaikoura justified?
   (b) What measures could be taken to address the grievances of non-indigenous opponents without violating the rights of the Maori?

10 Ecotourism
world survey

LEARNING OBJECTIVES

After reading this chapter, you should be able to:

■ outline the overall patterns and status of ecotourism along with associated characteristics and issues in the world's major regions

■ describe inter-regional and intra-regional differences in ecotourism sectors in various parts of the world

■ identify countries that have a relatively high ecotourism profile in their respective regions and describe the factors that underlie this status

■ list world regions that have relatively little ecotourism-related activity and explain why this is the case.

INTRODUCTION

The previous chapters demonstrate that ecotourism is not evenly distributed in terms of its intensity, the types of product and setting available, level of organisation, impact and the external environments that influence its development. This chapter provides a global survey of ecotourism in order to identify dominant regional patterns. Regional coverage is provided for Oceania, Asia, Europe, the Americas and Africa (Antarctica is discussed as a special environment in chapter 9). In each region, countries or subregions with a particularly high or low ecotourism profile are featured so that the differences can be better appreciated and understood.

10.2 OCEANIA

Oceania is divided for discussion purposes into Australia, New Zealand and the islands of the South Pacific, excluding Hawaii (see USA).

10.2.1 Australia

Australia is arguably the world's leading ecotourism country on the basis of an assessment of its ecotourism product and level of sector organisation (Dowling 2002). Iconic and accessible natural sites that have a high international profile include the Great Barrier Reef, the Wet Tropical Rainforests, Fraser Island (the largest sand island in the world) and Kakadu and Uluru national parks. In addition, Australia is home to wildlife that is both endemic and charismatic, such as kangaroo and koala. A large and prosperous domestic ecotourism market is boosted by a high level of participation among inbound visitors, albeit primarily in a form of complementary, soft ecotourism. These patterns are facilitated by the proximity of high-profile natural attractions to major population centres, resorts and international gateways such as the Gold Coast (Lamington National Park), Cairns (Great Barrier Reef and Wet Tropics), Sydney (Blue Mountains) and Melbourne (Phillip Island, Grampians). On the supply side, the network of high-profile and accessible protected areas is complemented by a well-articulated industry the development of which has been stimulated by supportive government schemes such as the National Ecotourism Strategy and the Queensland Ecotourism Plan, Ecotourism Australia (chapter 8) and the EcoCertification and EcoGuide Australia programs (NEAP) (chapter 6).

Geographic patterns

As in any destination, ecotourism opportunities and activities in Australia are not evenly distributed, although they can potentially occur just about anywhere. Figure 10.1 depicts the general pattern. It should be noted that the actual frequency of ecotourism is discontinuous in any designated zone, and similar activities can occur outside a zone, either in an outlying area not generally known for ecotourism or at a low intensity in a large area. For example, not all areas in the 'wildflower' area of Western Australia provide viewing opportunities, while large areas in other states provide relatively minor opportunities to engage in this activity. Similarly, ecotourism (in its soft manifestation) is concentrated in just two small areas of the Great Barrier Reef (off Cairns and the Whitsunday Islands). It is reasonable to assume that small amounts of hard ecotourism occur through all parts of Australia.

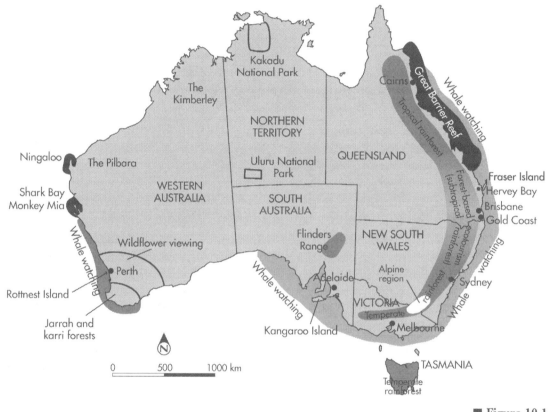

■ **Figure 10.1**
Ecotourism patterns in Australia

The overall pattern indicates a concentration of activity along and off the eastern coastline. This area accounts, in supply and demand terms, for an inordinate share of Australia's high-profile natural attractions, 80 per cent of the domestic population and most inbound visitors. As evident in the distribution of Ecotourism Australia industry members (see table 8.2), Queensland has the highest ecotourism profile of all the states. Its large 3S resort industry and the proximity of that industry to most of Australia's coral reefs and tropical rainforests are important factors that account for this dominance. The Cairns–Port Douglas region and the Whitsundays in particular are notable for the combination of rainforest, reef and 3S resort tourism. In the southern part of coastal Queensland, reef-based ecotourism gives way to activities on barrier sand islands such as Fraser and Moreton, while enclaves of tropical rainforest are replaced by subtropical rainforests. Whale-watching occurs intermittently from Port Douglas to the Gold Coast but is most developed as an industry at Hervey Bay.

Discontinuous subtropical and temperate rainforest and near-rainforest are the main terrestrial ecotourism assets of New South Wales and Victoria. Each of these states also accommodates a significant whale-watching industry. The penguin colonies of Phillip Island, an important Victorian ecotourism attraction, draw more than 500 000 visitors each year, as described by the case study at the end of chapter 4. A small region from Canberra to northern Victoria offers Australia's only semblance of an alpine ecosystem and, for this reason, it has acquired a specialised ecotourism profile. Tasmania is intriguing because of attempts to replace declining extractive activities such as logging with nature-based activities. World Heritage-listed temperate forests, which cover a quarter of the state, are the primary focus of its ecotourism sector, which benefits further from the island's unique biodiversity. Tasmania, for example, is the last refuge for all remaining large predatory marsupials, including the well-known Tasmanian devil. The subdued ecotourism profile of South Australia reflects a relatively small population, a small inbound visitor intake and the presence of only a few high-profile natural attractions, including Kangaroo Island, land-based whale-watching and the Flinders Range.

Ecotourism in Western Australia is well developed in the south-west where whale-watching opportunities, mature karri and jarrah forests and exceptional seasonal wildflower displays are available. Shark Bay and Ningaloo are two important nodes of marine ecotourism along the west coast. The remaining inland and northern regions of Australia comprise the Outback, which occupies a prominent position in the national mythology and geography but does not account for a commensurate share of the ecotourism sector. The major exceptions to this generalisation are Kakadu and Uluru National Parks in the Northern Territory. Activity elsewhere in the Outback is limited by accessibility, although the Pilbara and Kimberley regions of Western Australia have attained a profile as hard ecotourism destinations. Of interest are episodic features such as Lake Eyre during times of water replenishment. Finally, small offshore islands such as Rottnest (section 9.3.1), found along all parts of the Australian coast, are relevant to ecotourism because of the unusual ecosystems fostered by their isolation from the mainland.

Relevant issues

Australia offers the opportunity to assess the performance and prospects of a relatively mature ecotourism sector. Robust visitation rates at major protected areas and other soft ecotourism sites can be seen, on one hand, as an indication of success. However, this is no assurance of either financial or environmental sustainability. Many public protected areas are insufficiently funded to ensure that carrying capacity thresholds remain above growing visitation levels. Yet entry fee policies vary from state to state, with Queensland levying no charge, Tasmania charging entry to all national parks and New South Wales levying entry fees in some national parks only. The willingness of governments to entertain private development proposals in sensitive park areas is further indication of the vulnerability of Australian protected areas. A case in point was the plan in the early 2000s to construct the 'Naturelink' cableway through World Heritage-listed Springbrook National Park in the Gold Coast hinterland (Weaver 2001b, pp. 127–9). Although this plan was ultimately rejected by a State Labor government, a return to conservative rule could resurrect this or similar proposals, which are rationalised as a way of integrating ecotourism with the mass 3S tourism industry. The shift to a right-wing government at the federal level in the mid-1990s appears to have placed the goal of financial sustainability ahead of the ideal of environmental sustainability in terms of the government's involvement with and support for the ecotourism sector.

A related issue is the viability of Australia's specialised ecotourism industry, which is presently dominated by small businesses that should theoretically benefit from a pro-business ideology in government. Although promoted as an ideal, Australian small ecotourism businesses continue to struggle because of their inadequate economies of scale, which can hinder attempts at increased quality control, regulation and professionalism (see chapter 6). The large incomes reportedly earned by such ecotourism destinations as the Great Barrier Reef do not improve this situation, since very little of that income accrues to small specialised ecotourism businesses, which may be misled by estimates of phantom demand. As discussed in chapter 6, ecolodges and other aspects of the Australian ecotourism industry are becoming increasingly corporatised, and the future status of the small business sector in this industry is uncertain.

The maturity of the Australian ecotourism sector also allows opportunities for assessing the trend towards professionalism that is evident in initiatives such as the EcoCertification and EcoGuide programs. Australia is clearly the world leader in ecotourism certification, but matters of concern discussed earlier in this text include declining membership of Ecotourism Australia, the overrepresentation of Queensland in its membership structure, the degree of rigour pertaining to the verification of adherence to EcoCertification criteria and the tendency of certification logos to be associated with entire companies rather than the specific products for which they have been designated. The issue of voting rights for Ecotourism Australia members with no certification credentials is another issue that needs to be addressed.

These internal issues are all likely to be resolved as the industry continues to mature, but certain external factors loom as more serious long-term threats. For example, the Great Barrier Reef, an ecotourism icon, is gravely threatened by the combined forces of climate change and onshore habitat clearance for agriculture, the ecological impact of which may eventually far exceed those induced by mass tourism. The alpine region in the south-east may disappear altogether. Yet the ecotourism industry has little scope for opposing these developments. The continued reassertion of Aboriginal rights provides a further challenge. Co-management schemes in such destinations as Uluru are contributing to a deliberate redefinition of the ecotourism product (e.g. by including an Aboriginal perspective on interpretation and by discouraging certain activities). However, the extent of Aboriginal involvement beyond such controlled public environments will have more unpredictable consequences, especially where land claims or sacred sites are involved.

10.2.2 New *Zealand*

The '100% Pure' overseas marketing campaign aggressively promotes New Zealand as a clean and green destination dominated by outdoor activities (Weaver & Lawton 2006). Enhancing this pristine image is the presence of 1946 types of endemic higher plant species and 76 types of endemic bird, including the iconic kiwi (World Resources Institute 2005). Not unexpectedly, ecotourism-related activities and attractions therefore feature prominently in the visits of some inbound markets (see table 2.1), although, unlike in Australia, there is very little explicit recognition of 'ecotourism' by that name and no specialised institutions or initiatives equivalent to Ecotourism Australia or the EcoCertification Program. Accordingly, Dowling's (2001) reference to New Zealand ecotourism as an 'embryonic' sector that amalgamates with adventure and cultural tourism (e.g. mountain-climbing, Maori and farm attractions) in ACE-type products remains valid. Aside from this lack of institutional articulation, which calls into questions claims of sustainability, other issues include the dominance of struggling small businesses, Maori assertions of traditional property rights, the proliferation of destructive exotic species, such as possum, that threaten the country's biodiversity, and the impact of climate change.

10.2.3 South *Pacific*

Although the discussion of islands in section 9.3 is generally relevant to the South Pacific, an important distinction can be made with respect to ecotourism between Polynesia and Micronesia on the one hand and Melanesia on the other (see figure 10.2). The former subregions are characterised by very small land areas and populations, whereas Melanesia consists of large islands (accounting for 98 per cent of all land in the region) with relatively large populations (84 per cent of the region's population). With high biodiversity and much of their land area still covered by rainforest and other natural habitat, such Melanesian countries as Papua New Guinea, Vanuatu and the Solomon Islands are regarded as potential ecotourism leaders of the future. One reason for their current lack of leadership, ironically, is the absence of a mass tourism industry that would act as a stimulus for the development of complementary soft ecotourism opportunities. In general, the options for such integration in the South Pacific as a whole are limited by the concentration of mass tourism in only a few locations. Eighty per cent of all international stayovers in the region occur in just three destinations: the island of Saipan in the Northern Marianas, Guam and Fiji (Weaver & Lawton 2006). This has, however, allowed such destinations as Samoa to pursue a specialised ecotourism strategy focused on the hard side of the spectrum.

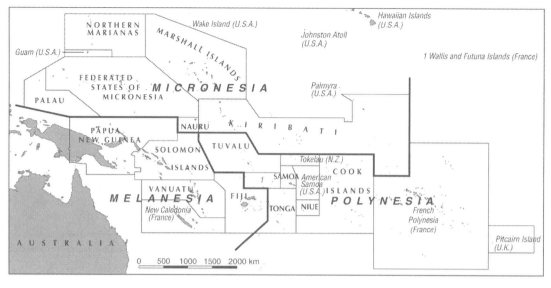

■ **Figure 10.2**
The South Pacific

Fiji, with its combination of mass tourism, proximate village-based eco-tourism and a high level of institutionalisation, has been a leading South Pacific ecotourism destination (Harrison & Brandt 2003). However, Fiji's leadership in ecotourism is threatened by the lack of a strong protected area system (only 0.3 per cent of Fiji is protected) and chronic political instability. These two threats are also present in other parts of Melanesia, as demonstrated by the recent civil war in the Solomon Islands. Environmental degradation associated with rampant logging and mining is also a serious concern in Melanesia, as discussed in the case study at the end of chapter 7, and global warming is a particular threat to low-lying Polynesian and Micronesian SISODs (see section 7.5.2). Unlike New Zealand, virtually all South Pacific destinations recognise ecotourism as a distinct sector. Unlike New Zealand or Australia, domestic ecotourism markets are virtually non-existent, and most initiatives are community-based enterprises funded by development agencies and environmental NGOs based in the developed countries, as per the model described in section 5.5.

10.3 ASIA

Of all the continents, Asia, because of its enormity, is the most variable with respect to climate, physical features and population density, and this gives rise to variability in the tourism and ecotourism sectors. To facilitate analysis of this complex continent, the following outline divides Asia into four subregions: South-East Asia, the Himalayas, South Asia and North-East Asia (see figure 10.3). South-West Asia will be discussed in section 10.7 in affiliation with the Middle East and North Africa. Ecotourism is most closely associated with the first two of these subregions (i.e. South-East Asia and the Himalayas).

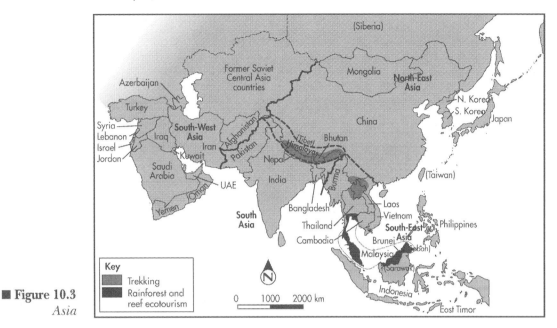

■ Figure 10.3
Asia

■ *10.3.1* **South-East** *Asia*

The high ecotourism profile of South-East Asia owes much to the region's physical geography, which is dominated by insular and peninsular locations that retain a significant cover of tropical rainforest, mangrove and other natural habitat. However, mainly because of human factors, the actual level of ecotourism development varies substantially from country to country. Presently, Thailand and Malaysia are the dominant ecotourism destinations. Both countries contain or are near major international gateways (Bangkok in Thailand, Kuala Lumpur and Singapore relative to Malaysia) and are thus well established as the major recipients of inbound tourists in the region. As two of the most prosperous countries in South-East Asia (only Singapore and Brunei have larger per capita GNPs), Thailand and Malaysia also possess relatively well-developed internal road and air networks that facilitate access by tourists and emergent domestic ecotourist markets to well-developed public protected area networks. Both countries are relatively stable from a political and social perspective and have taken measures to arrest previously unsustainable rates of habitat clearance and to institutionalise ecotourism as an important element in national tourism development policy.

Despite their similarities, Thailand and Malaysia have distinctive patterns of ecotourism product development. In the case of Thailand, two essentially separate ecotourism sectors can be identified. The 'southern' model is a soft 'rainforest and reef' product in which gateways and 3S resorts generate markets for nearby marine and terrestrial protected areas. Examples include Khao Yai National Park near Bangkok and Had Nai Yang National Park near Phuket. The 'northern' model, centred on the city of Chiang Mai, is a mixed soft/hard hybrid trekking product focused on the tribal villages and landscapes of the north-west. Malaysia, by contrast, does not have a trekking industry that is so well defined; its ecotourism is instead mostly oriented to its rainforests and reefs. While important ecotourism opportunities are available in the mountains of peninsular Malaysia (i.e. 'Malaya'), most of the activity and attention is focused on insular Malaysia, which consists of Sarawak and Sabah states on the island of Borneo. Biophysically, these states are advantaged by the presence of superlative natural attractions such as the orangutan, the rafflesia flower (the largest on earth) and the Mulu cave system, all of which can be experienced in accessible and apparently well-managed protected areas.

Indonesia

With its greater landmass and even more impressive endemism and bio-diversity, Indonesia should be at least on a par with Malaysia and Thailand as an ecotourism destination. However, with its array of dissuasive human influences, Indonesia is instead a case study of unrealised potential. Chief among these influences is relentless habitat degradation and destruction (legal and illegal) in most parts of the country and political and social insta-bility in such areas as West Papua, Sulawesi and Aceh (western Sumatra). Environmental destruction routinely extends to Indonesia's protected areas, many of which are classic paper parks that do not adequately fulfil their mandate of environmental preservation. Additional stress is generated by the rapidly increasing numbers of domestic park visitors and their apparent preference for anthropocentric recreational activities that may conflict with ecotourism (Cochrane 2006). Soft ecotourism is most evident as an add-on to 3S resort tourism in Bali (especially in Bali Barat National Park) and in a few protected areas in the mountains of Java within easy driving distance of Jakarta.

Emerging destinations

Indonesia notwithstanding, regional stability and economic growth have cre-ated opportunities for the diffusion of ecotourism-related products in other parts of South-East Asia. In the southern rainforest-and-reef area, Brunei is embarking on concerted efforts to develop its ecotourism potential while Vietnam is opening up some protected areas to accommodate the ecotourism market among its rapidly growing inbound visitor intake. Laos appears to be aggressively marketing itself as an ecotourist destination, although with strong ACE characteristics (Lao National Tourism Administration 2006). Ecotourism is also gaining a foothold in China's Yunnan Province, where pro-tected areas in Xishuangbanna Prefecture are gaining international stature for their biodiversity and tourism potential (JiuXia & JiGang 2006). Oppor-tunities for Myanmar (Burma), in either the rainforest/reef or trekking sectors, are extensive but currently limited by the country's negative image, military rule and instability. For the region of Indochina in general, multi-lateral tourism efforts focused on the Mekong River watershed are intended to accelerate the development of ecotourism and other forms of sustainable tourism in the six participating countries (see the case study 'Developing the regional tourism product in the Mekong River watershed' at the end of this chapter).

■ 10.3.2 Himalayas

Geographically, the Himalayan region contains just one entire country (i.e. Bhutan) but significant portions of four others (China, India, Nepal and Pakistan). This is an area where trekking is well established and therefore can be considered a high mountain extension of the north-west Thailand trekking region (see above). The pattern of trekking development in the Himalayas is mainly the result of geopolitical sensitivities based on long-standing tensions along the disputed China–India and India–Pakistan borders. In recognition of these sensitivities, the governments of all five Himalayan countries have pursued policies of **incremental access**, whereby new areas are gradually opened to tourism development while others are periodically withdrawn as the security and political situation warrants (Weaver & Lawton 2006).

Although tourist access throughout the region has therefore always been subject to uncertainty, Nepal has consistently provided the greatest degree of openness to tourism and consequently has received by far the greatest number of inbound trekkers. Government policies have channelled this flow into three main areas: Annapurna, Khumbu (including Mount Everest) and Langtang, although new areas such as Upper Mustang and Rara are now being added (Nyaupane, Morais & Dowler 2006). Bhutan, in contrast, has maintained an isolationist alternative tourism policy uniquely focused on a minimal visitor intake and strictly regulated itineraries. The Himalayan states of India alternate both spatially and temporally between openness and restriction. For example, the Buddhist Ladakh region of Indian Kashmir was emerging as a major trekking destination in the 1990s, but has now receded due to a renewal of tensions with Pakistan and Kashmiri separatists. Tibet has emerged as a secondary trekking destination as a result of China's own policy of gradually opening its peripheral areas to international tourists.

■ 10.3.3 South *Asia*

Outside the Himalayas, ecotourism has only a limited presence in the South Asian countries of India, Pakistan and Bangladesh, which are characterised by high population densities and highly modified landscapes interspersed with a small number of underfunded and relatively inaccessible protected areas. The low profile of ecotourism is in turn a reflection of the poorly developed inbound tourism industry. These three countries, for example, account for 24 per cent of the world's population but only 0.8 per cent of all inbound stayovers, thereby indicating little immediate or short-term scope for soft ecotourism add-ons to mass tourism (Weaver & Lawton 2006). Among the few high-profile ecotourism destinations is Royal Chitwan National Park in the lowland Terai region of Nepal, famous for its high concentrations of Bengal tiger and rhinoceros.

10.3.4 North-East *Asia*

North-East Asia for discussion purposes consists of China (excluding Yunnan Province — which accords to the South-East Asian patterns — and Tibet but including Taiwan and Hong Kong), the Koreas, Japan and eastern Siberia. At least four distinct patterns of ecotourism are present in this region. First, most of eastern China is similar to South Asia in having very high population densities and highly modified environments. Ecotourism is therefore almost non-existent in these areas, with most inbound tourism occurring in major gateway cities, such as Shanghai and Beijing. The second pattern includes less densely populated areas with some natural habitat in parts of southern and central China that border on heavily populated eastern China. The best-known example of ecotourism in this region is found in the protected areas of Sichuan Province, which provide opportunities to view such charismatic wildlife as the giant panda. As in the Himalayas, protected areas in this sub-region tend to be in low-order categories, as illustrated by the Dinghushan Biosphere Reserve in Guangdong Province, which accommodates a mixture of inbound ecotourists, domestic recreational users and religious pilgrims (see the case study 'The challenge of introducing ecotourism into China's protected area network' in chapter 3).

The third ecotourism pattern is best articulated in Japan, South Korea and Taiwan. Although as densely populated as eastern China, these highly urbanised populations are concentrated in a small area of river valleys and coastal plains, leaving the dominant mountainous areas in a sparsely populated, forested condition. A very large amount of ecotourism appears to occur in these areas, although in an 'East Asian' model that is distinct from the 'Western' model emphasised in this text (see 'Practitioner's perspective: An East Asian model of ecotourism?' in chapter 2). The final and most distinctive pattern includes eastern Siberia and the far north of Chinese Manchuria, which contain extensive wilderness areas that are amenable to hard ecotourism. A developing ecotourism industry is forming around such high-profile such as Lake Baikal in the west and the Kamchatka Peninsula in the east. Threats include continuing industrial and resource development as well as an apparent unwillingness or inability of authorities in Siberia to curtail such destructive activities as rogue hunting (see section 7.2.2). An intriguing possibility is the future emergence of Siberia as a regional recreational hinterland for Japan and Korea.

10.4 EUROPE

For discussion purposes, a useful distinction can be made between Western and Eastern Europe (see figure 10.4). Most of Western Europe possesses a landscape that has been extensively modified by human activity over many centuries. A hybrid product that incorporates nature appreciation along with other recreational activity is therefore dominant and is found especially in lower-order protected areas, such as the IUCN Category V National Parks or Areas of Outstanding Natural Beauty of the United Kingdom and the similarly designated Landscape Protection Areas and Nature Parks of Germany. This product is referred to generically as 'rural tourism' or 'sustainable tourism' without any explicit reference to 'ecotourism' (Björk 2000, Blangy & Vautier 2001). Given this context, it is not surprising that ecotourism in this part of Western Europe lacks specialised institutions comparable to those found in Australia. The three main countries of Scandinavia (Sweden, Norway, Finland) are an exception to this pattern, as is Iceland, by merit of extensive amounts of relatively undisturbed and sparsely inhabited land and the explicit recognition of ecotourism through several national associations and policies. One factor that could stimulate the development of a specialised ecotourism sector in other parts of Western Europe is the restoration of wildlife species long in decline throughout the region (see 'In the Field: The return of the carnivores in Western Europe').

Figure 10.4
Western and Eastern Europe

The return of the carnivores in Western Europe

Large carnivores were almost exterminated in Western Europe during the 18th and 19th centuries, and the recent revitalisation of the 'big four' indigenous predator mammals (bear, lynx, wolf and wolverine) is therefore an interesting phenomenon that has significant implications for the region's ecotourism sector. Healthy wolf packs, for example, are now well established in several parts of Germany, while the region of Abruzzo, Italy, is now marketed to tourists as 'bear and wolf country' (Enserink & Vogel 2006). Four factors account for this comeback. First, public perception of large carnivores has shifted from strongly negative to strongly positive, so that all four species can now be regarded as charismatic megafauna stalked almost exclusively by ecotourists rather than hunters. Second, most Western European countries are engaged in active programs of reintroduction in order to recreate some semblance of the original intact predator/prey relationships. Third, the elimination of physical barriers between Eastern and Western Europe has facilitated the westward migration of individual animals from more stable populations in the east. Finally, rural depopulation and farmland abandonment are widespread phenomena in Western Europe that have opened suitable new habitats for large carnivores.

This re-establishment of carnivore populations, however, is not without controversy. Shepherds in the Pyrenees Mountains of Spain, for example, are among the farming and ranching interests that are vehemently opposed due to the resulting predation on livestock. The typical government response has been to provide monetary compensation to affected individuals, although it is not always possible to confirm that losses were due to wild predators. A second issue is the fear that attacks on humans will increase as carnivore numbers increase and become less fearful of humans as they habituate. Government is trying to address this issue by making yards, farms and villages less hospitable for large predators. Complicating both issues is the migratory tendency of all four species, which makes them harder to track and vastly expands the territory in which problems could arise (Enserink & Vogel 2006). For ecotourists, this similarly means that large carnivores may not be present at any given time in high-order protected areas where they are expected, but may be encountered unexpectedly in other areas.

▪ *10.4.1* **Eastern** *Europe*

The collapse of the Soviet Union and its 'Eastern bloc' alliance in the early 1990s continues to influence the development of ecotourism in Eastern Europe beyond the short-term influx of visitors from Western Europe who were attracted by the novelty effect. For example, although it might be argued that the communist Soviet legacy should facilitate the introduction of community-based ecotourism models in peripheral rural areas, the opposite has occurred due to the desire of many Eastern Europeans to abandon all vestiges of that era. For similar reasons, the regulations and bureaucracy that are implicit in the certification process and in protected area zoning are also rejected or regarded with suspicion and distrust by many in the region. A rapacious and opportunistic form of capitalism, in many cases, has been the vehicle through which post-Soviet economic development has been pursued. Another post-Soviet legacy is the widespread environmental degradation that has resulted from the adherence of communist regimes to longstanding policies of heavy industry development and agricultural intensification. The best-known examples are the Chernobyl nuclear disaster of 1986 (see 'Practitioner's perspective: Chernobyl as ecotourism paradise?' in chapter 3) and the deterioration of the Aral Sea in former Soviet Central Asia. Yet, despite all these precarious circumstances, explicit references to 'ecotourism' are common in many Eastern European countries, and specialised organisations have been established (see table 8.1).

10.5 THE AMERICAS

For discussion purposes, the Americas are divided into six geographical units: the USA, Canada, the Caribbean (confined to its insular component rather than adjacent mainland coasts), Mexico, Central America and South America.

10.5.1 USA

As the world's largest ecotourist market, the USA provides by far the greatest number of international ecotourists and sustains an enormous domestic ecotourism industry. It is therefore ironic that the USA has no federal agency or NGO with responsibility for ecotourism, although the membership structure of The International Ecotourism Society suggests that it can be regarded in some ways as a *de facto* national organisation (see section 8.2). In the absence of a national superstructure, US ecotourism can best be analysed as a mosaic of 50 distinct state models that differ dramatically with regard to the level of recognition and institutionalisation. For example, some states, such as Alaska and Hawaii, explicitly recognise ecotourism whereas other states, including South Carolina and Texas, place an emphasis on 'nature' or 'nature-based tourism' that encompasses an array of outdoor activities, including hunting and fishing.

The lack of official recognition or organisation in a particular state impedes the development of the ecotourism industry as a well-defined and effective lobbying force but, as in New Zealand, does not mean that ecotourism is absent or minor. Activities that more or less meet the criteria outlined in chapter 1 are often included under such terms as 'outdoor recreation', 'outdoor education' or 'nature-based tourism'. In any case, the actual magnitude of ecotourism in any particular state is best gauged by examining visitation patterns to its public protected area network. Private protected areas are still uncommon in the USA despite the country's pervasive capitalist ethos. The national park system (category II under the IUCN classification system) is the ecotourism flagship, supporting an enormous amount of private vehicle-based soft ecotourism in the context of the pattern depicted in figure 3.1.

National Forests are a second major ecotourism venue. Much larger in area than the National Parks, these category VI protected areas accommodate many different types of tourism and recreation as well as potentially incompatible extractive activities, such as logging, grazing and mining. In many cases, National Forests serve as buffer zones for National Parks, such as Mount Rainier (Washington) and Yosemite (California). In some western National Forests, Category 1b wilderness areas have been designated to prohibit all human activities other than those associated with hard ecotourism. Throughout most states, but especially in the east, state parks and state forests are also important ecotourism destinations.

Scenic roadways in the USA are a particularly American phenomenon that capitalise on the national obsession with the private vehicle by providing a strip of well-maintained highway and associated services and activities along a scenic semi-natural corridor that may extend for a thousand kilometres or more. The custom-built Blue Ridge Parkway through the Appalachians and the Natchez Trace National Parkway in the states of Mississippi and Tennessee are the best known examples. Ecotourism-type activities undoubtedly occur along scenic roadways. However, whether these include the actual process of car touring is debatable, given its inherent dependence on the consumption of fossil fuels, the confinement of participants in vehicles and the need for extensive environmental modification to accommodate and sustain vehicular traffic.

The future of ecotourism in the USA will be influenced by changes in the country's ideological direction. The conservative momentum of the 'Reagan Revolution', maintained by the successive presidential victories of the Republican George W. Bush in 2000 and 2004, has been favourable to the extractive industries and to big corporations more generally. Administration resource policy was focused in the early 21st century on opening a broader array of lower- (and some higher-) order protected areas to expanded mining and logging activity, including many category III National Monuments that were established by the Clinton administration in the late 1990s. This is not to say that such developments are entirely unfavourable to ecotourism, since the associated construction of roads would make affected areas more accessible to soft ecotourists in particular. By 2006, there was some indication of a shift in ideological momentum as the centrist Democratic Party gained control over both the Senate and the House of Representatives, thereby seriously impeding the ability of the Republican administration to enable its resource policies. It remains to be seen whether this was an aberration or the first indication of a shift to a more centre-left position that would animate federal government commitment to policies sympathetic to the green paradigm.

■ 10.5.2 Canada

Unlike the USA, the Canadian federal government is involved in eco-tourism at the national and global level, as evidenced by the hosting of the 2002 World Ecotourism Summit in Quebec City. The term 'ecotourism' is used explicitly by the Canadian Tourism Commission, the crown corporation largely involved with international marketing, but usually in conjunction with the term 'adventure tourism' (Fennell 2001). As in the USA, the actual development of ecotourism institutions and products occurs mainly at the provincial level, with several provinces now having ecotourism policies. From a supply perspective, Canada is exceptionally well endowed with open semi-natural spaces, given that 90 per cent of the population is concentrated in the 10 per cent of the country that is close to the border with the USA. A well-developed network of high-order national and provincial parks representing all native ecosystems is the primary venue in which organised soft and hard ecotourism activity is accommodated. Especially intensive in terms of ecotourism volume are 'interface' regions where high-quality semi-natural hinterlands occur close to large urban concentrations. The four most notable examples are Vancouver (relative to the surrounding mountains and coastline), Calgary (the Rocky Mountains), Toronto (Muskoka and Haliburton southern outliers of the Canadian Shield) and Montreal (Laurentian extension of the Appalachian Mountains). However, for the very same proximity-related reasons, ecotourism in these regions is challenged by a variety of external factors, including high and growing visitation levels to protected areas, second home and exurban development, traffic congestion and pollution. In more remote areas of Canada, interaction with indigenous people, as through land claims, community-based participation and co-management schemes, is a major issue that affects the ecotourism sector (see section 9.5), and climate change is an equally compelling issue in Canada's Arctic (see section 9.4.2).

■ 10.5.3 Caribbean

In general, the islands of the Caribbean (see figure 10.5) are more dependent upon the mass 3S tourism industry than their counterparts in the South Pacific (see section 10.2.3). Ecotourism in most of the region is therefore a diversionary add-on closely linked with beach-based resorts and, increasingly, the cruise ship sector. The prevalence of this pattern positions the Caribbean as a test case for investigating the consequences of mass tourism and ecotourism integration.

Critics suggest that ecotourism, with increased growth, will assume the unsustainable characteristics of the dominant tourism mode and hence become no more than unsustainable nature-based mass tourism, as per the Butler sequence (see section 4.4.1). Advocates of this integration, however, believe that exposure to ecotourism can expedite the 'greening' of the conventional tourism industry (see section 2.3) while conferring to ecotourism business acumen and an economic importance that will position the sector as an important resource competitor and stimulus for the expansion of underdeveloped national protected area systems, as per the 'incentive effect' discussed in section 4.3.1. Among individual destinations, Cuba is intriguing because of the rapid but relatively recent growth of its contemporary mass tourism industry. Unlike many mature Caribbean destinations, Cuba has the potential to pursue sustainable mass tourism as well as ecotourism of varying intensity. An important variable, however, will be whether the current socialist decision-making structure is maintained, modified or replaced by a more open capitalist system in the post-Castro era (Winson 2006).

■ **Figure 10.5**
The Caribbean

■ *10.5.4* **Mexico**

Proximity to the US market, a favourable exchange rate and a diversity of natural and cultural attractions are among the primary factors that have transformed Mexico from a relatively minor destination into the seventh largest recipient of inbound stayovers, numbering 22 million in 2005 (World Tourism Organization 2006c). From an ecotourism perspective, this growth has placed an additional strain on a natural environment that has already long been subject to degradation due to 'Third World' problems such as deforestation, land colonisation, poaching, political and social instability, neglect and corruption. Mexico's protected areas cover just 0.6 per cent of the country (Earthtrends 2006) and are mostly 'paper parks' that do not effectively protect biodiversity or accommodate rapidly growing domestic and international visitor numbers in a sustainable way, due to inadequate funding, mismanagement, corruption and other factors.

The experience of the monarch butterfly preserves, encompassing several hundred square kilometres of montane fir forests west of Mexico City, is symbolic of the country's protected area problems. The forests are a winter hibernation area for migrating monarch butterflies, which can achieve a density of 4 million individuals per hectare and have become one of Mexico's iconic ecotourism attractions. Yet aerial photographs and satellite imagery have revealed the clearance of 44 per cent of the host forest between 1970 and 2000, due to encroachment by subsistence farmers and illegal logging by large companies. The establishment of five preserves in 1986 has done little to abate the problem and may have been counterproductive by alienating local people who were officially barred from their traditional extractive practices (Brower et al. 2002). Ecotourism and other forms of tourism are exacerbating the situation by injecting 250 000 visitors into the preserves each year. This is a tenfold increase from 25 000 per year in the mid-1980s, a trend moreover that provides benefits for only a small proportion of surrounding communities (Barkin 2003). To date, there is little evidence of any effective formalisation or mobilisation of the ecotourism sector within Mexican governments or industry to counter these problems.

10.5.5 Central *America*

A major 'pull factor' for Central American ecotourism is the high biodiversity that derives from the region's unique physical setting as a land bridge that combines North and South American ecosystems and acts as a funnel through which many transcontinental migratory waterfowl must pass. Furthermore, several distinct ecosystems can be found within a small area due to the extreme altitudinal variations that occur over short distances. Costa Rica is representative, having 20 'life zones' that harbour 850 bird species, 1260 tree species, 1200 orchid species and at least 361 species of reptile and amphibian (Hall 1985). Counteracting 'push factors' in Central America include high rates of deforestation, a lingering image of political and social instability, susceptibility to natural disasters, and relatively poor accessibility despite favourable spatial proximity to the US market. These positive and negative factors, however, are unevenly distributed, giving rise to an inequitable pattern of ecotourism distribution. In general, Costa Rica and Belize have major, high-profile ecotourism industries whereas Panama, Honduras and Guatemala are emergent. Finally, ecotourism in Nicaragua and El Salvador remains embryonic (see figure 10.6).

Costa Rica

Costa Rica is widely regarded as one of the world's model ecotourism destinations, a status that has been attributed, among other factors, to its political and social stability, well-articulated environmental movement, enlightened leadership and well-developed protected area system. Yet this reputation is not entirely deserved. The protected area system, for example, is often claimed to account for about a quarter of the country, yet it covers only about 9 per cent according to the IUCN (Earthtrends 2006). Most remaining land has been deforested or severely degraded by agricultural expansion and unsustainable logging. Furthermore, as in most destinations, ecotourism is effectively confined to a small area in a few of the more accessible protected areas (see section 3.4) and is dominated by soft ecotourists based in the conventional tourist gateway of San Jose and the 3S-oriented resorts of the Pacific coast. Evidence from such locations as Monteverde and Manuel Antonio reveals a negative impact in and adjacent to some of the more popular protected areas as Costa Rica increasingly assumes the characteristics of a mass tourism destination.

The government has long regarded ecotourism as just one desirable area of tourism concentration alongside conventions, cruise ships and resort tourism (Weaver 1998). However, its longstanding failure to adequately fund its protected area system (which is one reason for the emergence of such high-profile, private protected area destinations as Monteverde and La Selva) is a threat to the viability of future soft and hard ecotourism development. Remedial measures have been taken, including the creation of buffer zones, restoration initiatives (e.g. in Guanacaste National Park) and a restructuring of user fees (see section 4.3.1). However, in the absence of an exceptional effort it is possible that the regional leadership role in ecotourism could pass from Costa Rica to Belize.

■ **Figure 10.6**
Central America

Belize

The ecotourism strengths and opportunities of Belize are impressive and may be outlined as shown opposite, with comparable references to Costa Rica provided in parentheses (Weaver & Schlüter 2001).

- Forests cover 85 per cent of the country (25 per cent)
- Second longest barrier reef in the world is within Belize's EEZ (a few small, relatively inaccessible reefs)
- Population density of 10 persons per square kilometre (72 persons per square kilometre)
- Protected area system covers about 29 per cent of land, as shown in table 3.3 (9 per cent)
- High-profile Mayan ruins and contemporary indigenous communities provide complementary cultural add-ons (a few relatively minor indigenous sites or groups)
- Officially English-speaking (Spanish-speaking)
- Main airport is 1300 kilometres from Miami, positioning Belize as an intervening opportunity relative to Costa Rica (1900 km from Miami).

Like Costa Rica, Belize is the home of several high-profile ecotourism initiatives, including the Community Baboon Sanctuary, the Cockscomb Basin Wildlife Sanctuary and the Toledo Ecotourism Association (Buckley 2003a). Also like Costa Rica, much of the Belize ecotourism product is linked to 3S tourism along the Caribbean coast, a pattern that is likely to be reinforced by the country's small size, which places most ecotourism sites within a relatively easy drive from the coastal resorts. Threats include evidence that the coastal resort product is not always operating or evolving in a sustainable manner, and the degeneration of the barrier reef due to global warming, mass tourism and overfishing (Moreno 2005). This degeneration could have a direct impact on ecotourism through the loss of a primary natural attraction and an indirect effect through the erosion of the mass tourism industry that 'feeds' ecotourism initiatives in the interior.

Emergent destinations

Panama, following Costa Rica and Belize, is the Central American destination showing the most interest in ecotourism. Like those two countries, Panama is deliberately pursuing ecotourism as an adjunct to mass tourism. However, in the absence of a 3S-based resort industry, this linkage is being focused on the Panama Canal and the business-related tourism spawned by Panama City, a major regional finance centre. Accordingly, an unofficial ecotourism corridor is developing along the canal, taking advantage of the need to maintain a well-forested watershed to control silt, the market provided by cruise ships and the availability of repatriated US military bases that can be converted into ecotourism facilities and venues. The ecotourism industries of Guatemala, Honduras and Nicaragua are more embryonic but derive substantial potential from their extensive natural assets. For Guatemala, the presence of the Maya Biosphere Reserve, one of the largest high-order protected areas in Central America, is a major asset (Hearne & Santos 2005), while La Tigra National Park in Honduras has high potential because of its proximity to Tegucigalpa, the capital city (Maldonado & Montagnini 2005). Both Honduras and Nicaragua benefit from the presence of the Miskitia region, the largest semi-wilderness area in Central America.

■ *10.5.6* **South** *America*

The development of ecotourism in South America has been impeded by distance from the major ecotourist-generating markets, the perception of regional political and social instability held by these markets and the lack of well-articulated domestic ecotourism markets. At least four basic patterns of ecotourism can be identified (see figure 10.7).

■ **Figure 10.7**
Ecotourism patterns in South America

Coastal 3S locations

Ecotourism in the South American portion of the 3S-based pleasure periphery is similar to the SISOD/Caribbean model in that the former is closely identified as a diversionary adjunct to nearby mass tourism resorts. Two main subregions can be identified. The Caribbean coastline of Colombia and Venezuela is a functional extension of the Caribbean pleasure periphery, attracting mainly inbound stayovers and cruise ship excursionists who venture from such resort nodes as Santa Marta and La Guara into accessible protected areas in the foothills of the northern Andes. The second subregion is found along the south-eastern coast of Brazil with resort outliers in Uruguay and Argentina. The mass tourism market here is mainly domestic (except for Uruguay), but soft ecotourism opportunities are gradually being made available in such areas as the endangered Atlantic rainforest, which has been reduced to a small fraction of its original extent.

Temperate South America

Ecotourism in the southern countries of South America is most evident in the mountains along the Argentina–Chile border and in the sparsely populated grasslands and coastal areas of Patagonia in southern Argentina. However, in general, the sector is poorly developed due to small international ecotourist markets, weak domestic markets, the low proportion of land occupied by protected areas (Earthtrends 2006) and chronic underfunding of those areas (see 'Practitioner's Perspective: Challenges and opportunities for ecotourism in Uruguay').

PRACTITIONER'S PERSPECTIVE
Challenges and opportunities for ecotourism in Uruguay

The challenges of developing ecotourism in the temperate regions of South America are well illustrated by Uruguay, where farmland and pasture have displaced most of the country's natural habitat, and protected areas account for only 0.2 per cent of the territory (see table 3.2). Moreover, the small protected area network is insufficiently funded to fulfil its dual mandate of protecting the environment while providing high-quality facilities and interpretation for visitors.

However, the country also abounds with opportunity. A network of wetlands and lakes in eastern Uruguay, for example, offers some of the best bird-watching opportunities in South America. Although only a small portion of this area is formally protected under high-order IUCN categories, the larger 200 000 hectare area where these wetlands occur has been designated by UNESCO as the Bañados del Este Biosphere Reserve. As such, innovative and sustainable conservation and recreation practices that incorporate public as well as private land are encouraged under the auspices of PROBIDES (Program for Biodiversity Conservation and Sustainable Development in the Eastern Wetlands), a program that involves the efforts of the federal and municipal governments, the national university and domestic as well as international development and environmental organisations. A very different mode

(continued)

of ecotourism occurs in the vicinity of the beach resort city of Punta del Este, where migrating right whales and large colonies of sea lions can easily be observed. Both the eastern wetlands and the Punta del Este area are serviced by excellent road networks and accommodation, while a system of large rural estates (or 'estancias') offers farm vacation experiences that are suitable for ecotourists.

Uruguay itself is a relatively small country in which any destination can be reached in less than a day's drive from the capital city of Montevideo. More importantly, Uruguay was ranked third out of 146 countries in the 2005 Environmental Sustainability Index, which incorporates such factors as the availability and consumption of natural resources and levels of pollution and crowding (Yale Center for Environmental Law and Policy 2005). For major ecotourist markets such as the USA and Western Europe, low visitation levels are therefore associated more with a lack of market image than a lack of suitable attractions and amenities.

Gateway hinterlands

The third pattern consists of relatively soft ecotourism hinterlands that have developed around major metropolitan areas that (a) function as a gateway for inbound tourists and (b) are the residences for most of the domestic middle- and upper-class individuals who display evidence of ecotourism-type behaviour. Examples include Bogota (Colombia), Quito (Ecuador), Lima (Peru), La Paz (Bolivia) and, at a provincial level, Manaus (Brazil), Santa Cruz (Bolivia) and Iquitos (Peru). As such, these gateways are similar in function to their Central American counterparts of San Jose (Costa Rica), Tegucigalpa (Honduras) and Panama City.

Remote hinterland

The gateway hinterlands gradually give way to less accessible areas that accommodate a harder, overnight, inbound-dominated form of ecotourism. This pattern prevails over most of the rainforest-covered Amazon basin and in the high Andes. These resource frontiers pose many external challenges to ecotourism, including the assertion of indigenous rights, agricultural colonisation, unregulated logging and conversion of rainforest to exotic tree plantations, the 'paper park' syndrome, left-wing insurgencies and the drug trade. Military security is also an issue since the remote hinterland includes all international frontiers in the region. As discussed in section 7.3.1, the direct threat of agricultural colonisation is evidenced by the experience of certain ecolodges in southern Peru.

Guyana, Suriname and French Guiana together provide a special eco-tourism opportunity. None of these three countries has developed a significant tourism industry of any kind but are increasingly turning to tourism as a means of reducing their isolation and diversifying their weak, primary sector-based economies. The case for a specialised ecotourism focus is based on the overwhelming dominance of primary forest cover and the presence of indigenous and 'Bushmen' (descendants of escaped slaves) settlements that could engage in small-scale, community-based initiatives. Guyana already appears to be opting for such a strategy (Fennell, Buckley & Weaver 2001), although the viability of ecotourism in the region must be questioned in light of the threat posed by multinational logging companies, which are attempting to obtain access to large portions of primary forest here and in Suriname.

10.6 SUB-SAHARAN AFRICA

To an extent greater than any other major world region, the development of tourism in sub-Saharan Africa has been impeded by an array of serious shortcomings. Negative market image, widespread corruption, political and social instability, environmental degradation, endemic poverty and poorly developed infrastructure have all contributed to a weak regional tourism industry (Dieke 2000). In turn, these have hindered the development of ecotourism and soft ecotourism in particular, although many parts of sub-Saharan Africa are rich in natural attractions and complementary cultural assets. In the region, ecotourism is best developed in the safari corridor of eastern and southern Africa (see below), while islands here and elsewhere in the region, including Madagascar (Duffy 2006) and Zanzibar (Khatib 2000), are acquiring an ecotourism profile. In contrast, western and central Africa have only isolated and limited examples of ecotourism, including Kakum National Park in Ghana, Korup National Park in Cameroon and the mountain gorilla ecotourism that persists in Rwanda, Uganda and Congo. The countries in western and central Africa are hindered by recurring civil wars (e.g. Rwanda, Liberia, Sierra Leone) and exceptional rates of deforestation, while savannas to the north are relatively impoverished (compared with the east) in terms of wildlife variety and population. Hence, the future potential for ecotourism in these subregions appears limited.

10.6.1 Safari *corridor*

The highest level of sub-Saharan ecotourism is found along a corridor of countries that extends from Kenya to South Africa. The latter two countries are the African leaders in this regard, with the intervening countries — Namibia, Botswana, Zimbabwe, Zambia, Malawi and Tanzania — being somewhat less developed but high in profile relative to other parts of Africa (see figure 10.8). The term **safari corridor** (Weaver 2001b) alludes to the association of ecotourism in this region with safari-style viewing activities in savanna settings that focus on charismatic big game animals such as lion, cheetah, leopard, elephant, giraffe and rhinoceros. Reliance on various types of motorised vehicle is a distinctive characteristic of ecotourism in the corridor, given the distances that must be covered to view wildlife and the dangers involved in such contact (e.g. from the heat and from the animals themselves). Although private protected areas are becoming more popular in this region for a variety of reasons (see section 3.3), ecotourism is still closely identified with such public protected area icons as Amboseli and Maasai Mara (Kenya), Serengeti (Tanzania), Hwange (Zimbabwe) and Kruger (South Africa). In addition to the charismatic megafauna, the popularity of these protected areas is associated with the open savanna settings that virtually guarantee satisfying wildlife-viewing experiences during appropriate times of the year.

■ Figure 10.8
Safari corridor, Africa

As discussed in section 7.2, ecotourism in Kenya is both a major stimulant to the country's 3S mass tourism industry and a form of mass tourism in its own right, given the skewed distribution of soft ecotourism activity. A similar pattern applies to South Africa, although the substantial and mainly 'white' domestic ecotourist market is a distinctive feature of that country's ecotourism sector. A related issue is the identification of ecotourism as a 'white' activity, as symbolised by the retention of the Afrikaaner name 'Kruger' for the famous national park. To counter the possibility that this could generate resentment and opposition from the black community and thus threaten the long-term viability of the sector, the post-apartheid government strongly encourages community participation in rural tourism-related projects (Allen & Brennan 2004).

It is unlikely that any other safari corridor country will challenge the ecotourism dominance of Kenya and South Africa in the foreseeable future. Tanzania has among the most unspoiled and extensive wildlife environments but is impeded by poor infrastructure. However, the proximity of its main natural attractions to Nairobi and to Kenya's own main protected areas offers an excellent opportunity for bilateral product development that capitalises on the strengths of each. Future ecotourism development in Zimbabwe is threatened by political instability associated with the government's expropriation of white-owned farms, while Zambia is spatially remote from either of the corridor anchors (i.e. South Africa or Kenya). Of all the intervening corridor destinations, Botswana and Namibia display the brightest prospects for further ecotourism development. This assessment is based on the presence of the wildlife-rich and mostly unspoiled Okavango Delta, relatively well-developed infrastructure, political and social stability, proximity to South Africa, low population density and the high proportion of territory that is protected. Potential conflicts between ecotourism and big game hunting are evident in both Botswana and Namibia (Novelli, Barnes & Humavindu 2006). Multilateral cooperation in the region is best illustrated by the establishment of the Great Limpopo Transfrontier Park in the area where the borders of South Africa, Zimbabwe and Mozambique coalesce (Doppelfeld 2006).

10.7 MIDDLE EAST AND NORTH AFRICA

The region of the Middle East and North Africa, which extends from Iran to Mauritania, is the least developed of all the world's major regions from an ecotourism perspective. Politically, several countries are dangerous and unstable (e.g. Iraq, Sudan, Algeria and Lebanon) and/or deliberately discourage most types of tourism (e.g. Saudi Arabia). In these, as well as other countries in the region, the lack of ecotourism attractions is also dissuasive. The dominant arid and semi-arid landscapes are almost devoid of protected areas (see table 3.1) and especially ones that are managed to accommodate ecotourism. Such as it is, ecotourism in the region tends to be of a hard variety that intersects with adventure tourism and includes scientific expeditions and individual treks by four-wheel drive or camel. Egypt is among the few regional countries that have made any substantive attempt to develop desert ecotourism opportunities (Weaver 2001c). Mediterranean coastal areas, similarly, have little ecotourism activity due to the aforementioned factors as well as widespread environmental degradation. However, Turkey and Morocco are probably the best developed in this regard, possessing diverse landscapes and relatively well-developed protected area systems as well as a high level of political and social stability.

An examination of global ecotourism patterns demonstrates that the sector is highly differentiated in structure from one region to another as well as highly variable in intensity both between and within regions. Australia is the world's most advanced ecotourism destination in organisational terms, although most activity is focused in populated areas with inbound tourism concentration along the east coast. The capacity of the country's protected areas and small businesses to maintain sustainability is still an open question, while its product and ecoguide certification programs are progressive but still evolving. Elsewhere in Oceania, ecotourism in New Zealand is significant but subsumed under a generic outdoor nature-based product, while significant ecotourism sectors in the South Pacific have been established in only a few destinations, such as Fiji and Samoa. Political instability remains a deterrent throughout that region. The broad Asian pattern includes a 'rainforest and reef' focus in the south-east (especially in southern Thailand and Malaysia) and a 'trekking'-based ACE tourism region that extends from northern Thailand into the Himalayas, where patterns of development are largely dictated by the 'incremental access' policies of national governments. North-east Asia is a rapidly developing ecotourism region with distinctive characteristics, whereas southern Asia has relatively little ecotourism development of any type.

European ecotourism is differentiated between a western and an eastern model. In Western Europe, ecotourism tends to hybridise or coexist with other types of tourism in relatively modified settings and hence is usually included under a broad 'sustainable tourism' banner. The exception is Scandinavia, where large semi-wilderness areas sustain an articulated ecotourism sector. Following the collapse of the Soviet bloc, the western countries of Eastern Europe appear to be gravitating towards the Western European model, although the Soviet legacy of disempowerment and environmental degradation discourages the implementation of community-based ecotourism products in some areas.

In the Americas, the USA has little involvement in ecotourism at the federal level, although a substantial ecotourism sector is accommodated in a well-developed network of national parks, national monuments, national forests and state parks. Federal involvement is more apparent in Canada in conjunction with proactive provincial policies, many of which are focused on the vast wilderness frontier of the 'North'. In the Caribbean, ecotourism usually occurs as a soft, complementary add-on to mass tourism while Central America is notable for the high profile of Costa Rica and Belize. South America is impeded by isolation and negative market images but still displays a complexity of ecotourism patterns ranging from a Caribbean-type soft add-on along parts of the Caribbean and Brazilian coast to a poorly articulated product in the temperate south. The Amazon basin is the core of a large, hard-ecotourism frontier that is interrupted by more-developed gateway hinterlands.

Finally, Africa and the Middle East display the weakest ecotourism sectors, with the exception of a safari corridor that extends from South Africa to Kenya.

1 (a) Why is Australia referred to as the global leader in ecotourism?
   (b) What are the main issues facing the Australian ecotourism sector?
   (c) How should the ecotourism industry respond to these issues?

2 (a) What are the two main ecotourism countries in South-East Asia and Central America, respectively?
   (b) What factors held in common account for the high profile of ecotourism in these countries?

3 (a) In what ways is the ecotourism sector of the Himalayas distinctive?
   (b) What are the prospects for greater multilateral ecotourism cooperation in this subregion?

4 (a) How is Western Europe distinct from eastern Europe with respect to patterns of ecotourism development?
   (b) What are the strengths and weaknesses of the Western European model?

5 (a) How do the USA and Canada compare and differ as ecotourism destinations?
   (b) What are the main ecotourism strengths of each of these two countries?

6 (a) In what way does South America represent the world as a whole in terms of its ecotourism patterns?
   (b) What major challenges face South America's ecotourism sector?

7 (a) Why has ecotourism been able to develop a relatively high profile in Africa's safari corridor?
   (b) How can the future prospects of ecotourism in the safari corridor be enhanced?

8 (a) Why does ecotourism have such a low profile in the Middle East, South-west Asia and North Africa?
   (b) How could this profile be enhanced?

Doppelfeld, M 2006, 'Collaborative stakeholder planning in cross-border regions: The case of the Great Limpopo Transfrontier Park in Southern Africa', in H Wachowiak (ed.), *Tourism and Borders: Contemporary Issues, Policies and International Research,* **Ashgate, Aldershot, UK, pp. 113–38.** The trilateral international protected area spanning South Africa, Zimbabwe and Mozambique is featured as an important example of cross-border cooperation that includes a critical ecotourism component.

Duffy, R 2006, 'Global environmental governance and the politics of ecotourism in Madagascar', *Journal of Ecotourism* **5: 128–44R.** The core of this article is the contention that the pursuit of ecotourism in less-developed destinations such as Madagascar is informed largely by structural changes in global governance that involve networks of powerful environmental organisations and aid agencies.

Harrison, D & Brandt, J 2003, 'Ecotourism in Fiji', in D Harrison (ed.), *Pacific Island Tourism,* **Cognizant Communications, Elmsford, NY, pp. 139–56.** This chapter critically analyses ecotourism in a Pacific Island that in many ways is a microcosm of the wider region. Topics include the relationship with beach-based tourism, chronic political instability and community-based issues, including land tenure.

Weaver, D (ed.) 2001, Section 2: 'A regional survey by continent', *Encyclopedia of Ecotourism,* **CABI, Wallingford, UK, pp. 85–188.** In this section, leading experts describe the patterns and issues associated with ecotourism in sub-Saharan Africa, Anglo-America, Asia, Oceania, Europe and Latin America and the Caribbean.

Winson, A 2006, 'Ecotourism and sustainability in Cuba: Does socialism make a difference?', *Journal of Sustainable Tourism* **14: 6–23.** A critical evaluation of the socialistic model of ecotourism is the focus of this article, as embodied by Cuba. Its strengths and weaknesses and applicability to other destinations are considered.

Developing the regional tourism product
in the Mekong River watershed

The phenomenon of globalisation means that human interactions are increasingly unencumbered by the presence of national boundaries. National governments continue to instinctively protect the prerogatives of sovereignty but, paradoxically, they additionally support policies of globalisation that erode this sovereignty because these policies uphold the national interest by opening the country's goods and services to larger markets and by allowing issues of common concern to be dealt with more effectively at a multilateral level. The European Union is currently the best example of globalisation pursued at the regional scale, but a similar direction is also manifest in such entities as the North American Free Trade Area (NAFTA), the free trade area of southern South America (MERCOSUR) and the Association of South-East Asian Nations (ASEAN). A lesser known regional example is the Greater Mekong Subregion (GMS), which has brought together five countries (Burma, Cambodia, Laos, Thailand and Vietnam) and two provinces or autonomous regions of China (Yunnan and Guangxi) that share the watershed of the Mekong River. The aim of the GMS, which builds on earlier regional initiatives (Tirasatayapitak & Laws 2003), is to fulfil the economic potential of the subregion by strengthening linkages that would expedite intra-regional trade and investment (Sofield 2006).

Tourism has been designated as one of 11 flagship areas of focus in the GMS strategy for the long-term development of the region. The rationale for this, aside from the status of the sector as an important economic sector in all participating countries, is that tourism resources cross or share political boundaries (mountain ranges and rivers, for example) and hence require a regional approach for their effective planning, development and management. Participants hope to develop a distinctive and diverse Mekong tourism brand that will be highly competitive in international tourism markets. During late 2004 and early 2005, representatives from each member country formulated a 10-year strategy for the development of the Mekong regional tourism product, to take effect from 2006 to 2015, which consist of a clear list of constituent programs and projects (Asian Development Bank 2005).

Informing the strategy are several objectives. The first of these is to distribute the benefits of tourism more evenly among the participating countries, in recognition of the fact that Thailand alone in 2005 accounted for 69 per cent of all international visitor arrivals in the region, excluding China (World Tourism

(continued)

Organization 2006). Second, the strategy is intended to reduce poverty throughout the region while empowering women and promoting sustainable development. To achieve these objectives, seven programs have been established:

- marketing and product development
- human resource development
- heritage and social impact management
- pro-poor tourism development
- private sector participation
- facilitation of tourist movements within and to the region
- development of tourism-related infrastructure (Asian Development Bank 2005).

Further examination of the strategy and the specific programs reveals the important role assigned to ecotourism. For example, 10 of the 13 priority 'tourism destination zones' earmarked for marketing and product development are specifically designated as 'nature/adventure-based' or 'culture/nature-based', while the other three are 'marine/river-based' with an emphasis on urban tourism and/or beach resorts. The 10 zones with an explicit nature component encompass relatively remote peripheral regions characterised by sparse human populations, large amounts of relatively undisturbed natural vegetation, a large number of protected areas, a high incidence of poverty and the presence of traditional and indigenous culture groups. The human resource development program includes provisions for the training of professional guides to interpret the natural heritage, while the heritage and social impact management program and infrastructure program advocate the construction of facilities in protected areas that are environmentally sustainable and facilitate high-quality interpretation. These latter two programs — and, even more explicitly, the pro-poor tourism development program — are directly related to the paradigm of sustainability, suggesting that the 10-year strategy is extremely compatible with the development of a comprehensive and credible ecotourism sector in the Mekong region.

The strategy is ambitious and optimistic, but faces numerous challenges. One is the disparate nature of the participants, which range politically from open and capitalist (Thailand) to centrally controlled and socialist (Vietnam, Laos). Burma (or Myanmar), moreover, is widely perceived as a pariah governed by incorrigibly corrupt and secretive military elites who have usually regarded open borders as anathema. In addition, Thailand is by far the most prosperous and tourism-intensive of the members, and it appears to participate on the assumption that its dominant status will not be affected (Tirasatayapitak & Laws 2003). Compounding this geographical diversity is a complex management structure that designates no less than eight layers of administration. For example, leadership and policy guidance is delegated to member ministers of tourism or heads of national tourism organisations, while formulation and implementation of programs and policies is the responsibility of the GMS Tourism Working Group (TWG), which consists of highest-level technical employees of member national tourism organisations. The TWG is assisted by an advisory group of participating international and regional non-governmental organisations. In addition, the Mekong Tourism Coordination Office (MTCO) provides organisational capacity to address issues at the subregional level, and it is assisted in its marketing and product development efforts by a private sector partners group (Asian Development Bank 2005).

The role of the Asian Development Bank in the strategy is also a matter of concern, if loans made to Vietnam, Cambodia and Laos for tourism purposes in late 2002 are any indication. Of 11 subprojects funded by the bank, three involved 'airport improvement', two involved 'access roads' to environmental sites, three involved 'environmental improvement' and two entailed 'river pier development' (Asian Development Bank 2006). This indicates a strong emphasis on infrastructure that may not take into account the capacity of target environments to accommodate this development or the expected hordes of tourists whose entry will be facilitated by its construction. Yet most stakeholders support this emphasis on infrastructure because of its implications for alleviating poverty through access and because of its common role in facilitating development in areas associated with the 10 non-tourism flagship areas of the GMS. Such construction, however, is likely to be undertaken long before relevant staff and administrators are empowered with the tools and skills to ensure that subsequent tourist intakes are managed sustainably. Such concerns are abetted by the above-mentioned existence of a program focused on private sector participation and the establishment of the private sector partners group as an advisory body to the MTCO. Hence, the type of ecotourism that will emerge as a result of the strategy — or whether it will be authentic ecotourism at all — is an issue that has yet to be determined.

Questions

1 (a) What are the advantages of a regional approach to tourism development for the six countries that are participating in the GMS tourism strategy?

   (b) What factors are likely to hinder the successful implementation of this regional approach?

2 (a) On the basis of the information provided above, which kind of ecotourism (i.e. soft or hard) is likely to be favoured in the GMS tourism strategy?

   (b) Why is the focus on the construction of infrastructure regarded as a threat to the development of a genuine ecotourism sector in the subregion?

   (c) How could this threat be minimised?

accreditation: a process whereby an overarching sector body gives approval to an ecolabel or similar entity to certify products that meet stipulated standards. (p. 170)

ACE tourism: an acronym coined by Fennell (1999) that describes hybrids of adventure tourism, cultural tourism and ecotourism. (p. 21)

adaptancy platform: the third of Jafari's four platforms, which builds on the cautionary platform by supporting alternative tourism and ecotourism as small-scale forms of tourism that are deemed more appropriate for most destinations than mass tourism. (p. 4)

adventure tourism: tourism that incorporates an element of risk, higher levels of physical exertion and a need for specialised skills to enable successful participation. The concept is subjective in that perceptions of risk and thresholds of physical exertion vary from person to person. (p. 20)

advocacy platform: the first of Jafari's four platforms, wherein tourism is perceived as an ideal activity that results in little negative impact for destinations. Proponents therefore believe that tourism growth should be encouraged. (p. 3)

Agenda 21: the intersectoral blueprint for sustainable development in the 21st century that emerged from the 1991 Earth Summit in Rio de Janeiro. (p. 35)

alternative tourism: a model of small-scale tourism that is intended to provide a more appropriate alternative to mass tourism. As such, its characteristics are diametrically opposed to unsustainable mass tourism, for example local community-based ownership, high multiplier effect and diverse markets. (p. 4)

amenity migration: permanent or seasonal migrations that involve retirees, 'urban refugees' and other tourists and non-tourists who establish homes in areas such as mountains and coastlines having high amenity values. (p. 103)

anthropocentric: an approach that focuses on the welfare of humans. (p. 14)

artificial reefs: underwater structures that attract various types of marine life. These may be unintentional, as in the case of shipwrecks, or intentional in the case of purpose-built concrete domes or purposely sunk vessels put in place to support fishing and/or recreational diving. (p. 82)

auditing: the process that a business undergoes to identify and confirm benchmarks, provide accreditation with reliability and validity and measure and verify best practice. Audits can be either internal or external; the former usually being a form of preparation for the latter. (p. 175)

backstage: a coping mechanism, whereby an area within a local community is formally or informally designated for the retention of the culture in a non-commercialised form for the community's own use. Tourism is entirely or mostly excluded from such areas, although hard ecotourists may seek access to such areas in order to attain an 'authentic' tourism experience. (p. 131)

benchmark: a given value of some phenomenon against which the performance of an operation or destination can be judged. For example, a benchmark of 2 per cent might be regarded as the desirable standard of growth in visitor intake that a certain ecotourism destination can sustain. (p. 16)

best practice: an industry standard of the most advanced practice with respect to particular criteria, such as the energy-efficient operation of an ecolodge or effective interpretation techniques. Best practice is often used as the standard against which benchmarking is undertaken. (p. 16)

biocentric: an approach that focuses on the welfare of the natural environment. Some argue that a biocentric approach is also ultimately anthropocentric to the extent that the survival of humans depends on the maintenance of a viable natural environment. (p. 14)

buffer zones: areas (usually lower-order protected areas) that are adjacent to a core higher-order protected area and serve as a protective transitional zone or cushion between the core area and unprotected areas. Buffer zones are often regarded as suitable locations for accommodation and other services that might otherwise have to be provided in the more ecologically sensitive higher-order protected area. (p. 70)

bushwalker movement: an early manifestation of the environmental movement in Australia that involved members of largely urban-based walking clubs who lobbied for the creation and expansion of high-order protected areas near large cities. The bushwalkers seem to qualify as ecotourists in all but name. (p. 34)

CAMPFIRE: an acronym for Zimbabwe's Communal Areas Management Programme for Indigenous Resources. CAMPFIRE is widely praised for giving significant control over wildlife resources to local communities, who have earned substantial revenue through tourism and therefore have an incentive to preserve local wildlife populations. However, critics are concerned that most of the resulting revenue has been obtained through big game hunting rather than ecotourism. (p. 74)

carrying capacity: the amount of activity that can be accommodated by a site or destination under its current conditions without incurring an unsustainable impact. Carrying capacity can be environmental, economic or sociocultural. (p. 106)

cautionary platform: the second of Jafari's four platforms, in which tourism is regarded as an activity that almost inevitably leads to a negative environmental, economic and sociocultural impact for destinations in the absence of strict regulations. (p. 3)

celestial ecotourism: activities such as stargazing and northern lights viewing that involve observation of daytime and night-time skies. (p. 24)

certification: formal confirmation from an ecolabel that a specified ecotourism product is found by a qualified third party to meet stipulated standards related to ecological and/or sociocultural best practice. (p. 170)

cetaceans: an order of fish-like mammals that includes charismatic megafauna, such as whales and dolphins. Interest in the cetaceans has given rise to a rapidly growing global whale-watching industry. (p. 24)

charismatic megafauna: varieties of higher wildlife, such as tigers, pandas, koalas, orangutans, polar bears and birds of paradise, that ecotourists consider attractive and/or interesting. Charismatic megafauna are often the focal point of ecotourism destinations. (p. 10)

charismatic megaflora: plants, such as redwood and jarrah trees, that ecotourists consider attractive and/or interesting. (p. 10)

charismatic megaliths: geological formations such as mountains, volcanoes, caves and escarpments that are attractive and/or interesting to some ecotourists. (p. 10)

codes of conduct: itemised lists of recommended behaviour towards achieving sustainability that can apply to operators or tourists. These rudimentary quality control mechanisms are often criticised for their vagueness and self-regulation, but are also supported for providing moral advice to adherents and for providing broad directives to operators in an unthreatening manner. (p. 111)

community-based ecotourism: ecotourism in which substantial control and involvement in development and management is invested in the local community, which is a major recipient of the benefits. (p. 134)

comprehensive ecotourism: ecotourism that is focused on entire ecosystems and encourages deep learning opportunities as well as behaviour transformation. A comprehensive sustainability approach is adopted that seeks to enhance these ecosystems and the environment of the earth in general, as well as the welfare of local communities and humanity as a whole. (p. 17)

consumptive tourism: forms of tourism such as hunting and fishing (except catch-and-release fishing) that extract products from the natural environment. Some critics argue that the term is misleading since all forms of tourism involve the literal and figurative consumption of various products. (p. 23)

cultural tourism: tourism that emphasises contemporary or past cultures or history. (p. 19)

domestic excursionists: tourists who travel to a destination within their usual country of residence, but do not stay overnight in that destination. Each country has its own criteria as to how much and what purposes of travel qualify as tourism. (p. 9)

domestic stayovers: tourists who travel to a destination within their usual country of residence, and remain at least one night in that destination. (p. 9)

dominant Western environmental paradigm: the dominant scientific paradigm with respect to its anthropocentric perception of the relationship between humans and the natural environment. This is based on human/environment separation, human dominance over the environment and the objectification of the natural environment as comprising useful 'resources'. (p. 32)

EcoCertification Program: a best practice certification-based ecolabel (formerly the National Ecotourism Accreditation Program or NEAP) used in Australia to encourage adherence to the criteria of sustainable nature-based tourism and ecotourism. It currently applies to local tour operators, accommodation and attractions, each of which has its own set of best practice criteria. (p. 172)

EcoGuide Australia Certification Program: a certification-based ecolabel developed by Ecotourism Australia to recognise nature and ecotour guides who provide authentic and professional experiences for their clients. (p. 175)

ecolabels: methods that standardise the promotion of environmental claims by corporations or other entities by following compliance to set criteria, usually based on impartial third party verification. (p. 170)

ecolodge: a specialised type of ecotourism accommodation usually located in or near a protected area or other ecotourism venue, and is managed in an environmentally and socioculturally sustainable fashion. Although having a high profile in the ecotourism sector, ecolodges globally account for only a very small proportion of all ecotourist visitor-nights. (p. 166)

ecolodge chain: part of the corporatisation trend in ecotourism; a group of ecolodges owned and operated by the same company. Usually, they are promoted and developed under their own unique brands in order to emphasise their individuality. (p. 167)

ecoresort complex: part of the corporatisation trend in ecotourism; an integrated resort that offers a comprehensive array of services, facilities and attractions, within which ecotourism is a central but not exclusive component. (p. 167)

ecotourism: a form of tourism that fosters learning experiences and appreciation of the natural environment, or some component thereof, within its associated cultural context. It has the appearance, in the context of best practice, of being environmentally and socioculturally sustainable, preferably in a way that enhances the natural and cultural base of the destination and promotes the viability of the operation. (p. 2)

Ecotourism Australia: one of the most advanced examples of a national, membership-based ecotourism organisation. Founded in 1991 as the Ecotourism Association of Australia (EAA), Ecotourism Australia functions as Australia's peak body for the ecotourism industry and is best known for its Eco Certification Program (formerly the Nature and Ecotourism Accreditation Program (NEAP)). (p. 12)

ecotourist: a tourist who participates in ecotourism activities. Ecotourists are commonly segmented into hard and soft ideal types and are found mainly in more developed regions such as North America, Western Europe, Australia and New Zealand. (p. 8)

endemism: the state of being found under natural circumstances only in a particular location, such as an isolated island. For example, koalas and kangaroos are endemic to Australia. Endemism gives a major competitive advantage to ecotourism destinations if the endemic flora or fauna is attractive to ecotourists. (p. 251)

enhancement sustainability: sustainability in which ecotourism and other activities result in net improvements to the quality of the natural environment, as achieved through donations, volunteer activity and so on. In constant capital terms, this involves leaving a greater stock of assets to the next generation. Enhancement sustainability is warranted where the environment is degraded. (p. 15)

environmental damage cost: a term coined by Gössling (1999) to describe indirect environmental costs incurred by an ecotourism operation, such as the greenhouse emissions caused by the aeroplanes and road vehicles conveying ecotourists to an ecolodge. A comprehensive perspective on sustainability suggests that the operation should take measures, such as tree planting, to compensate for these effects. (p. 104)

environmental movement: the increasingly organised and popular trend favouring the protection and enhancement of the natural environment. The emergence and growth of the environmental movement (or environmentalism) parallels and reflects the emergence and growth of the green paradigm. (p. 34)

extractive tourism: an alternative term for consumptive forms of tourism such as hunting and fishing (except for catch-and-release fishing). (p. 24)

FIT: free and independent travel; refers to tourists who prefer spontaneous itineraries, make their own travel arrangements and avoid the packaged formal circuit as much as possible. FIT is associated with hard ecotourists. (p. 151)

frontstage: an area within a local community that is designated formally or informally for the presentation of culture, usually in a commodified format, to tourists. (p. 131)

geotourists: environmentally and socioculturally aware consumers who seek unique and authentic experiences when they travel. (p. 42)

green consumer: a consumer whose behaviour (including purchasing) is influenced by considerations of the environmental implications of their actions. The growth in the non-superficial green consumer market is an indicator of the emergence of the green paradigm. (p. 38)

Green Globe: a membership-based organisation dedicated to the objective of environmental and social sustainability in the global tourism and hospitality industry. Sustainability-related goals, originally monitored through self-regulation, are now being promoted through the implementation of a certification system supported by independent monitoring. (p. 42)

green paradigm: the biocentric environmentalist paradigm that is emerging as a challenge to the dominant Western environmental paradigm. This juxtaposition may indicate a paradigm shift. (p. 35)

green traveller: a green consumer whose environmentally and socially conscientious behaviour is reflected in their travel purchases and patterns. (p. 38)

greenwashing: also known as eco-selling; the process whereby an environmentally unsustainable or suspect product is promoted misleadingly as an environmentally sustainable product. Many tourism products are greenwashed as 'ecotourism'. (p. 91)

hard ecotourist: an ecotourist market segment that is strongly biocentric and characterised as an ideal type by the desire for deep and meaningful interaction with natural settings, minimal services, orientation toward enhancement sustainability, FIT travel, physically and mentally challenging experiences and specialised travel. Hard ecotourists constitute only a very small portion of the ecotourist market. (p. 43)

hard technology: describes large-scale, environmentally destructive forms of technology such as those associated with nuclear energy and modern military hardware. Hard technology is associated with the dominant Western environmental paradigm and the modern era of mass tourism. (p. 36)

ideal type: an ideal model of some phenomenon, useful for discussion purposes, which would occur in the absence of real world distortions. Alternative tourism, mass tourism, hard ecotourism and soft ecotourism are tourism-related phenomena that are often presented as ideal types. (p. 4)

inbound tour operators: businesses within the formal travel distribution system that market their services to tour wholesalers, prepare client itineraries within the destination, select local businesses, plan programs, hire staff and pay applicable fees, such as park entry fees. They are located in the destination region. (p. 153)

incremental access: a process whereby new areas are systematically opened to tourism. Incremental access is government policy in the Himalayan trekking regions of Nepal, Bhutan, India, China and Pakistan, and is motivated by political and sociocultural considerations. (p. 283)

indicators: variables or measures that provide information about the status of some phenomenon with respect to a desired condition, such as sustainability. For example, annual growth rates in visitor intake are commonly regarded as an indicator for tourism sustainability. (p. 16)

indigenous renaissance: the recent reassertion of indigenous identity and rights, especially in more developed countries that originated as British colonies, such as Australia, New Zealand, Canada and the USA. From an ecotourism perspective, this has included the increased participation and empowerment of indigenous people in the management of protected areas and in the ownership and operation of community-based ecotourism destinations. (p. 265)

International Ecotourism Standard: a variation of Australia's EcoCertification Program that is being piloted for global use by a coalition of Ecotourism Australia, CRC Sustainable Tourism, and Green Globe. (p. 176)

international excursionist: a tourist who travels to a destination outside their own usual country of residence and stays less than one night in that destination. (p. 10)

international stayover: a tourist who travels to a destination outside their own usual country of residence and remains at least one night in that destination. (p. 10)

IUCN classification system: a standard classification scheme for protected areas introduced by the World Conservation Union (IUCN). This system differentiates high-order protected areas, which strictly preserve the natural environment, from lower-order protected area categories, which preserve landscapes where culture and the environment exist in a complementary relationship. (p. 66)

knowledge-based platform: the most recent of Jafari's four tourism platforms, which supports a more objective, scientific approach to acquiring tourism knowledge that transcends the ideological biases of the earlier platforms. This platform divorces the scale of tourism from its quality and thereby allows for the possibility of unsustainable alternative tourism and sustainable mass tourism. (p. 6)

leaf-peeping: a commonly applied term for the observation of the autumn change of leaf colour, a seasonally important form of tourism in such northern hemisphere destinations as New England (USA) and south-eastern Canada. (p. 24)

local tour operators: businesses that mediate directly between the ecotourist and the environmental attraction, usually providing tours by 4WD, boat, animal or other conveyance into protected areas. They may exist solely to provide such tours or may additionally offer accommodation, food and other services through subcontracts with other local businesses. Unlike other tour operators and wholesalers, local tour operators are usually small private or community-run operations. (p. 153)

marine protected areas (MPAs): protected areas that comprise mainly sea or ocean, and are managed accordingly. The global network of MPAs is far less developed than its terrestrial counterpart. (p. 70)

market segmentation: the process whereby a market is broken down into discrete market segments so that each segment can be reached through appropriate and effective target marketing. The identification of harder, softer and structured ecotourists by Weaver and Lawton (2001) is an example of ecotourism-related market segmentation. (p. 43)

market segments: subgroups within a market that are distinct insofar as members share certain traits or clusters of traits. (p. 43)

mass tourism: commonly used term for large-scale tourism, implying participation by the mass or bulk of a society's population. The term is usually used in reference to the post-World War II era of exponential tourism growth. (p. 3)

mediating attractions: such devices as cableways, elevated walkways and submarines that allow ecotourists to visit otherwise inaccessible sites and are attractive and/or novel in their own right. They are 'mediating' in the sense that they mediate between the ecotourist and some aspect of the natural environment. (p. 153)

minimalist ecotourism: ecotourism that involves shallow or superficial learning opportunities in conjunction with specific charismatic wildlife, and sustainability objectives that are *status quo*-oriented and focused on a particular site. (p. 17)

multiplier effect: a measure of the ongoing indirect and induced economic benefits that accrue to a destination through the internal circulation of direct tourist expenditures. Ecotourism is often associated with a high multiplier effect, although studies suggest that this is substantially eroded by revenue leakage. (p. 126)

National Ecotourism Strategy (NES): one of the best-known examples of a national ecotourism plan, the NES was inaugurated in 1994 as an overall framework to guide the integrated development and management of the Australian ecotourism sector. The NES consists of 12 relevant issues, objectives that arise from each issue, and a listing of the federal and state bodies and other groups that should take a lead role in carrying out each objective. The NES is apparently no longer part of government tourism policy in Australia. (p. 199)

national park: a high-order, Category II protected area under the IUCN classification system that provides a high level of environmental protection but allows compatible activities such as ecotourism. Zoning is a mechanism usually used to identify areas where various types of activity can or cannot be undertaken. National parks are the highest profile and most popular settings for ecotourism. (p. 66)

nature-based tourism: any type of tourism that relies mainly on attractions directly related to the natural environment. Ecotourism and 3S tourism are both types of nature-based tourism. (p. 18)

NEAT: an acronym coined by Buckley (2000) that describes hybrids of nature-based tourism, ecotourism and adventure tourism. (p. 21)

non-consumptive tourism: tourism activity such as ecotourism and adventure tourism that provides experiences rather than tangible products. The consumptive/non-consumptive dichotomy is criticised by those who believe that all forms of tourism entail elements of 'consumption' and 'non-consumption'. (p. 23)

opportunity cost: income or other benefits that are lost to an area by not using it for purposes other than its present use. As a hypothetical example, $10 000 earned in a year from ecotourism and watershed protection should be weighed against $100 000 that would have been obtained from clearing the area. In this case, the opportunity cost is only short term. (p. 129)

paper parks: protected areas in which applicable regulations are inadequately enforced due to funding constraints, external pressures and/or corruption. Hence, the entity is a park only on paper, and the ability to accommodate ecotourism may be impaired by the presence of activities that harm the natural environment and/or interfere with ecotourists. Paper parks are usually found in less-developed countries in Latin America, Asia and Africa. (p. 62)

paradigm: a model. In its broadest sense, a paradigm is a collective world view or model of how the universe operates. In Kuhn's (1970) terminology, a paradigm is the entire collection of beliefs, values, techniques, and so on shared by the members of a given community. (p. 31)

paradigm shift: the process whereby one paradigm is gradually supplanted by another paradigm that is better able to explain and contend with contradictions and anomalies that emerge in the older paradigm. For example, it appears that the dominant Western environmental paradigm is being replaced by a green paradigm, which advocates a more sustainable way of existing within the natural environment. New paradigms usually incorporate elements of the older paradigm through a process of synthesis. (p. 31)

pleasure periphery: a term coined by Turner and Ash (1975) to describe peripheral areas, including many SISODs, in which 3S tourism emerged as an important economic activity in the decades following World War II. The pleasure periphery was a focal point of the criticism of mass tourism by proponents of the cautionary platform. (p. 253)

protected area: according to the IUCN (1994), an area of land and/or sea especially dedicated to the protection and maintenance of biological diversity, and of natural and associated cultural resources, and managed through legal or other effective means. Protected areas (high-order protected areas, such as national parks, in particular) are the most popular ecotourism setting. (p. 61)

purchase of development rights (PDR) agreements: legally binding arrangements in which a landowner is given a one-time payment in exchange for agreeing to restrict development on their property in perpetuity. This in essence results in the creation of a private protected area in which ecotourism may provide an acceptable means of generating revenue. (p. 73)

recreation opportunity spectrum (ROS): a widely adopted protected area management tool that accommodates zones ranging from 'primitive' to 'urban' wherein the former is based on no modification to the natural environment, minimal contact with other visitors and no active management, whereas the latter is based on extensive modification, contact and management. (p. 107)

restoration ecotourism: an emerging form of ecotourism that emphasises the attraction of environments that are in the process of restoration. The learning experience is therefore focused on such processes as succession and recovery rather than relatively undisturbed natural settings. (p. 83)

revenue leakage: the loss of revenue and subsequent truncation of the multiplier effect in a destination due to profit repatriation and the need to import goods and services. Studies suggest that most revenue from ecotourism in rural destinations is lost through the leakage effect. (p. 129)

sacrificial space: small areas, usually within high order protected areas, that are intensively developed or site hardened to accommodate services and facilities for visitors. They are 'sacrificial' in the sense that their development eliminates the need to carry out similar modifications in other parts of the park. This may, however, be an unwarranted term in areas that are already highly degraded or in which effective restoration is achieved through site softening. (p. 78)

safari corridor: a cluster of sub-Saharan countries extending from South Africa to Kenya where safari-type ecotourism, focused on big-game viewing from special vehicles, is well developed in many protected areas in the savanna ecosystem. It is by far the most important area of ecotourism development in Africa. (p. 297)

sense of place: the consciousness that individuals or communities have of places that are significant to them. Ecotour guides who have a strong sense of place for their sites are better able to convey meanings and associations that add value to the interpretation process. Indigenous people are often described as having a particularly acute sense of place for their own territories. (p. 135)

SISODs: an acronym for small island states or dependencies, which Weaver (1995) defines as insular entities with an area of less than 28 000 km^2 and three million residents. Most of the 63 SISODs are dependent on 3S tourism, and in these situations soft ecotourism complements the dominant tourism sector. However, some SISODs (e.g. Dominica and Samoa) have emerged as specialised ecotourism destinations. (p. 252)

site hardening: measures that increase the carrying capacity of a site or facility. For example, the paving of a hiking trail may result in a tenfold increase in its carrying capacity. However, this new threshold does not necessarily apply to the wildlife that lives alongside the newly paved trail. (p. 22)

site softening: such measures as soil restoration and the replanting of native vegetation that contribute to the restoration of an area following site hardening. (p. 108)

soft ecotourist: an ecotourist market segment that is more anthropocentric in perspective, and prefers short-term and diversionary contact with the natural environment. This preferably occurs in a well-serviced and mediated setting, such as the sacrificial space in a high-order protected area. Soft ecotourists are often the same as mass tourists and constitute the overwhelming majority of the ecotourist market. (p. 44)

soft technology: technology associated with small-scale, environmentally benign activities such as solar-energy generation. Also described as alternative technology, it is associated with the green paradigm and with alternative tourism. (p. 36)

status quo sustainability: sustainability in which ecotourism or other activities maintain the *status quo* (or present state of an area). (p. 15)

structured ecotourists: an ecotourist market segment identified by Weaver and Lawton (2001) that combines characteristics of hard ecotourism (i.e. desire for intense and physically challenging contact with the natural environment) and soft ecotourism (i.e. desire for interpretation and services). (p. 47)

sustainable development: a term popularised by the Brundtland Report in the late 1980s; development that meets the needs of the present generation without compromising the ability of future generations to meet their own needs. (p. 14)

sustainable tourism: tourism that adheres to the principle of sustainable development and to associated criteria of environmental, sociocultural and economic sustainability. (p. 14)

SWOT analysis: a type of situational evaluation or analysis that involves the identification of an operation's or destination's internal strengths and weaknesses as well as its external opportunities and threats. SWOT analysis is a standard component of business planning. (p. 159)

technological utopianism: extreme anthropocentrics who argue that science and technology will provide solutions for all problems faced by humans. (p. 32)

The International Ecotourism Society (TIES): the global membership-based, ecotourism-specialised non-government organisation, originally founded as The Ecotourism Society (TES) in 1990. TIES serves as an international forum for ecotourism stakeholders and an important source of publications and other information. (p. 219)

3S tourism: 'sea, sand and sun' or beach resort tourism. 3S tourism can be included in other types of tourism but is usually associated with mass tourism. (p. 21)

threshold: a value beyond which some phenomenon experiences critical change, often used in conjunction with carrying capacity. For example, under existing conditions, the weekly threshold number of visitor-nights in a hypothetical destination may be 10 000. Any subsequent increase has exceeded the destination's carrying capacity and is unsustainable. (p. 16)

tour wholesalers: businesses within the formal travel distribution system that offer package tours, make contracts with airlines, arrange travel schedules, coordinate marketing and sales, organise groups and liaise with individual clients. Tour wholesalers are usually located in origin regions. (p. 153)

travel agencies: businesses within the formal travel distribution system that provide retail travel services to customers for commission on behalf of other tourism industry sectors, such as airlines and accommodation. Travel agencies are normally located in origin regions. (p. 153)

trekking: a form of ACE tourism that involves travel by foot or animal in a usually mountainous rural region, such as northern Thailand or the Himalayas. (p. 21)

veneer environmentalists: consumers whose stated proclamations and intentions of environmentally friendly behaviour do not translate into purchasing decisions or other behaviour that reflects these sentiments. Environmental priorities are abandoned when another more basic concern, such as health or the economy, arises. Soft ecotourists are considered more prone to veneer environmentalism than hard ecotourists. (p. 40)

volunteer tourism: a form of alternative tourism that encompasses a variety of activities in which the participating tourists receive no financial compensation in return for engaging in organised activities that are environmentally and/or socioculturally beneficial to the host destination. (p. 45)

whale-watching: when carried out in a sustainable manner, a form of ecotourism that involves the viewing of whales and other cetaceans by land, boat or through swimming and other interactions. (p. 24)

wildlife tourism: a subset of nature-based tourism characterised by encounters with non-domestic animals in captive and non-captive settings. (p. 19)

World Heritage Site: a higher-order parallel protected area designation by UNESCO that signifies an area with globally significant natural and/or cultural assets. (p. 64)

zoning: regulations that demarcate certain areas for different land uses, and the standards of development that apply to each of these areas. (p. 107)

Adams, W & Infield, M 2003, 'Who is on the gorilla's payroll? Claims on tourist revenue from a Ugandan national park', *World Development* 31: 177–90.

Akama, J 1999, 'Western environmental and nature-based tourism in Kenya', *Tourism Management* 17: 567–74.

Allcock, A 1999, 'Facilitator or watchdog? Development of government ecotourism policy in Australia', paper presented at the World Ecotourism Conference and Field Seminars, Kota Kinabalu, Sabah, Malaysia, October.

Allcock, A, Jones, B, Lane, S & Grant, J 1994, *National Ecotourism Strategy*, Commonwealth Department of Tourism, Canberra.

Allen, G & Brennan, F 2004, *Tourism in the New South Africa: Social Responsibility and the Tourist Experience*, IB Tauris, London.

Anderson, G & Hussey, P 2000, 'Population aging: A comparison among industrialized countries', *Health Affairs* 19: 191–203.

Angus Reid Global Monitor 2006, 'Environment is top world issue in Australia', www.angus-reid.com.

Antarctic Treaty Consultative Meeting 2006, 'Tourism on the table at Antarctic Treaty Meeting', www.atcm2006.gov.uk.

Archabald, K & Naughton-Treves, L 2001, 'Tourism revenue-sharing around national parks in Western Uganda: Early efforts to identify and reward local communities', *Environmental Conservation* 28: 135–49.

Asian Development Bank 2005, 'The Greater Mekong Subregion Tourism Sector Strategy', www.adb.org.

——2006, 'Mekong Tourism Development Project (Loans 1969, 1970 and 1971)', www.adb.org.

Atlantis Adventure 2006, 'Another Atlantis Adventure', www.atlantisadventures.com.

AusAID 2006, 'Overseas aid', www.ausaid.gov.au.

Australia 2003, 'Tourism White Paper: A medium to long term strategy for tourism', www.industry.gov.au.

Australia and New Zealand 2002, 'A South Pacific Whale Sanctuary: Agenda Paper', www.doc.govt.nz.

Australian Bureau of Statistics 2006, *Year Book Australia, 2004*: Aboriginal and Torres Strait Islander population, www.abs.gov.au.

Banerjee, S 2000, 'Whose land is it anyway? National interest, indigenous stakeholders, and colonial discourses', *Organization & Environment* 13: 3–38.

Barkin, D 2003, 'Alleviating poverty through ecotourism: promises and reality in the monarch butterfly reserve of Mexico', *Environment, Development and Sustainability* 5: 371–82.

Bat Conservation International 2006, 'Viewing bats in Texas — Congress Avenue Bridge', www.batcon.org.

Bauer, T & Dowling, R 2003, 'Ecotourism policies and issues in Antarctica', in D Fennell & R Dowling (eds), *Ecotourism Policy and Planning*, CABI, Wallingford, UK, pp. 309–29.

BBC News 2006, 'Rabbits "destroy" seabird habitat', 24 October, http://news. bbc.co.uk.

Beaumont, N 2001, 'Ecotourism and the conservation ethic: Recruiting the uninitiated or preaching to the converted?', *Journal of Sustainable Tourism* 9: 317–41.

Beaver, A 2005, *A Dictionary of Travel and Tourism Terminology*, 2nd edn, CABI, Wallingford, UK.

Bécherel, L 1999, 'Strategic analysis and strategy formulation', in F Vellas & L Bécherel (eds), *The International Marketing of Travel and Tourism: A Strategic Approach*, Macmillan, Basingstoke, UK, pp. 37–106.

Beeton, S 2006, *Community Development through Tourism*, CSIRO Publishing, Collingwood, Vic.

Bekele, M 2001, 'Country Report — Ethiopia', FAO Forest Outlook Studies in Africa, www.fao.org.

Berrow, S 2003, 'An assessment of the framework, legislation and monitoring required to develop genuinely sustainable whalewatching', in B Garrod & J Wilson (eds), *Marine Ecotourism: Issues and Experiences*, Channel View, Clevedon, UK, pp. 66–78.

Björk, P 2000, 'Ecotourism from a conceptual perspective: An extended definition of a unique tourism form', *International Journal of Tourism Research* 2: 189–202.

Black, R & Crabtree, A (eds) 2007, *Quality Control and Certification in Ecotourism*, CABI, Wallingford, UK.

Black, R & Ham, S 2005, 'Improving the quality of tour guiding: Towards a model for tour guide certification', *Journal of Ecotourism* 4: 178–95.

Blamey, RK 1997, 'Ecotourism: The search for an operational definition', *Journal of Sustainable Tourism* 5: 109–30.

——2001, 'Principles of ecotourism', in DB Weaver (ed.), *Encyclopedia of Ecotourism*, CABI, Wallingford, UK, pp. 5–22.

Blamey, RK & Hatch, D 1998, *Profiles and Motivations of Nature-Based Tourists Visiting Australia*, Occasional Paper No. 25, Bureau of Tourism Research, Canberra.

Blangy, S & Vautier, S 2001, 'Europe', in DB Weaver (ed.), *Encyclopedia of Ecotourism*, CABI, Wallingford, UK, pp. 155–71.

Bonta, M 1997, 'Turning wastewater into wetlands', *Living Bird* 16(4): 22–6.

Boo, E 1990, *Ecotourism: The Potentials and Pitfalls*, vol. 1, World Wildlife Fund, Washington, DC.

Borrie, WT, McCool, SF & Stankey, GH 1998, 'Protected area planning principles and strategies', in K Lindberg, M Epler Wood & D Engeldrum (eds), *Ecotourism: A Guide for Planners and Managers*, vol. 2, Ecotourism Society, North Bennington, VT, pp. 133–54.

Boyd, SW 2000 'Tourism, national parks and sustainability', in RW Butler & SW Boyd (eds), *Tourism and National Parks: Issues and Implications*, John Wiley & Sons, Chichester, UK, pp. 161–86.

Brashares, J, Arcese, P, Sam, M, Coppolillo, P, Sinclair, A & Balmford, A 2004, 'Bushmeat hunting, wildlife declines, and fish supply in West Africa', *Science* 306: 1180–3.

Breiter, M 1996, *Kakadu and the Top End*, Kangaroo Press, Kenthurst, NSW.

British Columbia 2006, 'Province announces a new vision for coastal BC', www2.news.gov.bc.ca.

Broad, S 2003, 'Living the Thai life — a case study of volunteer tourism at the Gibbon Rehabilitation Project, Thailand', *Tourism Recreation Research* 28(3): 63–72.

Brower, L, Castilleja, G, Peralta, A, Lopez-Garcia, J et al. 2002, 'Quantitative changes in forest quality in a principal overwintering area of the Monarch Butterfly in Mexico, 1971–1999', *Conservation Biology* 16: 346–59.

Brunei Tourism 2006, 'Concept statement', www.tourismbrunei.com.

BTR 1998, *Domestic Tourism Monitor 1996–97*, Bureau of Tourism Research, Canberra.

Buckley, R 2000, 'Neat trends: Current issues in nature, eco- and adventure tourism', *International Journal of Tourism Research* 2: 1–8.

——2001, 'The environmental impacts of ecotourism', in DB Weaver (ed.), *Encyclopedia of Ecotourism*, CABI, Wallingford, UK, pp. 379–94.

——2002, 'Tourism ecolabels', *Annals of Tourism Research* 29: 183–208.

——2003a, *Case Studies in Ecotourism*, CABI, Wallingford, UK.

——2003b, 'Environmental inputs and outputs in ecotourism: Geotourism with a positive triple bottom line?', *Journal of Ecotourism* 2: 76–81.

——2004a, 'The effects of World Heritage listing on tourism to Australian national parks', *Journal of Sustainable Tourism* 12: 70–84.

——2006, *Adventure Tourism*, CABI, Wallingford, UK.

——(ed.) 2004b, *Environmental Impacts of Ecotourism*, CAB International, Wallingford, UK.

Buckley, R, Clough, E & Warnken, W 1998, '*Plesiomonas shigelloides* in Australia', *Ambio* 27: 253.

Budowski, G 1976, 'Tourism and environmental conservation: Conflict, coexistence or symbiosis?', *Environmental Conservation* 31(1): 27–31.

Burger, J 2000, 'Landscapes, tourism, and conservation', *Science of the Total Environment* 249: 39–49.

Burger, J & Gochfeld, M 1993, 'Tourism and short-term behavioural responses of nesting masked, red-footed, and blue-footed boobies in the Galapagos', *Environmental Conservation* 20: 255–9.

Burger, J, Gochfeld, M & Niles, L 1995, 'Ecotourism and birds in coastal New Jersey: contrasting responses to birds, tourists, and managers', *Environmental Conservation* 22: 56–65.

Burger, J, Jeitner, C, Clark, K & Niles, L 2004, 'The effect of human activities on migrant shorebirds: Successful adaptive management', *Environmental Conservation* 31: 283–8.

Butcher, J 2006, 'The United Nations International Year of Ecotourism: A critical analysis of development implications', *Progress in Development Studies* 6: 146–56.

Butler, RW 1980, 'The concept of a tourist area cycle of evolution: implications for management of resources', *Canadian Geographer* 24: 5–12.

——1990, 'Alternative tourism: Pious hope or Trojan horse?', *Journal of Travel Research* 28: 40–5.

Butler, RW & Baum, T 1999, 'The tourism potential of the peace dividend', *Journal of Travel Research* 38 (August): 24–9.

Butler, RW & Boyd, SW (eds) 2000, *Tourism and National Parks: Issues and Implications*, John Wiley & Sons, Chichester, UK.

Cadiz, P & Calumpong, H 2002, 'Analysis of revenues from ecotourism in Apo Island, Negros Oriental, Philippines', *Proceedings of the Ninth International Coral Reef Symposium, Bali, 23–27 October 2000*, vol. 2, pp. 771–4.

Calder, J 1997, 'Solomon Islands and deforestation', American University Trade and Environment Database (TED), www.american.edu.

CALM 2004, 'Valley of the Giants fact sheets: Construction of the Tree Top Walk', www.naturebase.net.

Canadian Forestry Service 1973, *Ecotour of the Trans-Canada Highway: Ottawa–North Bay*, Information Canada, Ottawa.

Canadian Tourism Commission 2006, 'Tourism snapshot May 2006', www.canadatourism.com.

Capra, F 1982, *The Turning Point*, Bantam Books, New York.

Carson, R 1962, *Silent Spring*, Houghton Mifflin, Boston.

Carvalho, G, Nepstad, D, McGrath, D, del Carmen Vera Diaz, M, Santilli, M & Barros, A 2002, 'Frontier expansion in the Amazon: Balancing development and sustainability', *Environment* (Washington DC) 44(3): 34–45.

Cater, E 2006, 'Ecotourism as a Western construct', *Journal of Ecotourism* 5: 23–39.

CDOT 1994, *National Ecotourism Strategy*, Commonwealth Department of Tourism, Canberra.

Central Land Council 2006, 'National parks', www.clc.org.au.

Chapman, DM 1995, *Ecotourism in State Forests of New South Wales: Who Visits and Why?* State Forests of New South Wales and University of Sydney, Sydney.

Che, D 2006, 'Developing ecotourism in first world, resource-dependent areas', *Geoforum* 37: 212–6.

Child, B 2006, 'Building the campfire paradigm: Helping villagers protect African wildlife', www.perc.org.

CIA (Central Intelligence Agency) 2006, 'The World Factbook', https://www.cia.gov.

Clarke, J 1997, 'A framework of approaches to sustainable tourism', *Journal of Sustainable Tourism* 5: 224–33.

Cochrane, J 2006, 'Indonesian national parks: Understanding leisure users', *Annals of Tourism Research* 33: 979–97.

Cohen, J 2001, 'Ecotourism in the inter-sectoral context', in DB Weaver (ed.), *Encyclopedia of Ecotourism*, CABI, Wallingford, UK, pp. 497–507.

Commonwealth of Australia 2006, 'Report on Operations of the National Landcare Programme 2002–03 and 2003–04', www.daffa.gov.au.

Conover, M 1998, 'Perceptions of American agricultural producers about wildlife on their farms and ranches', *Wildlife Society Bulletin* 26: 597–604.

Conservation Commission of Western Australia 2004, 'Forest management plan 2004–2013', www.naturebase.com.au.

Conservation International 2006, 'Ecotourism', www.conservation.org.

Constantine, R, Brunton, D & Dennis, T 2004, 'Dolphin-watching tour boats change Bottlenose Dolphin (*Tursiops truncates*) behaviour', *Biological Conservation* 117: 299–307.

Cordell, H, Lewis, B & McDonald, B 1995, 'Long-term outdoor recreation participation trends', in J Thompson, D Lime, B Gartner & W Sames (eds), *Proceedings of the Fourth International Outdoor Recreation and Tourism Trends Symposium and the 1995 National Recreation Resource Planning Conference*, University of Minnesota, St Paul, MN, pp. 35–8.

Cotterill, D 1996, 'Developing a sustainable ecotourism business', in H Richins, J Richardson & A Crabtree (eds), *Taking the Next Steps*, Ecotourism Association of Australia, Brisbane, pp. 135–40.

Curtin, S 2003, 'Whale-watching in Kaikoura: Sustainable destination development?', *Journal of Ecotourism* 2: 173–95.

Cutter, S & Renwick, W 2003, *Exploitation Conservation Preservation: A Geographic Perspective on Natural Resource Use*, 4th edn, John Wiley & Sons, New York.

Davis, D, Banks, S & Davey, G. 1996, 'Aspects of recreational scuba diving in Australia', in G Prosser (ed.), *Tourism and Hospitality Research: Australian and International Perspectives*, Proceedings from the Australian Tourism and Hospitality Research Conference, Bureau of Tourism Research, Canberra, pp. 455–65.

de la Torre, S, Snowdon, C & Beharano, M 2000, 'Effects of human activities on wild pygmy marmosets in Ecuadorian Amazonia', *Biological Conservation* 94: 153–63.

Dearden, P 2000, 'Tourism, national parks and resource conflicts', in RW Butler & SW Boyd (eds), *Tourism and National Parks: Issues and Implications*, John Wiley & Sons, Chichester, UK, pp. 187–202.

Department of Conservation 2000, *Developing Ecotours and Other Interpretive Activity Programs: A Guidebook for Planning, Designing, Promoting and Conducting Ecotourism Activity Programs*, Department of Conservation, Como, Western Australia.

Dernoi, LA 1981, 'Alternative tourism: Towards a new style in north–south relations', *International Journal of Tourism Management* 2: 253–64.

Derocher, A, Lunn, N & Stirling, I 2004, 'Polar bears in a warming climate', *Integrative and Comparative Biology* 44: 163–76.

DFID 2004, 'Success with a capital Che: Bolivian eco-tourism project highly commended', http://www2.dfid.gov.uk.

Diamantis, D 1999, 'The characteristics of UK's ecotourists', *Tourism Recreation Research* 24(2): 99–102.

——2000, 'Ecotourism and sustainability in Mediterranean islands', *Thunderbird International Business Review* 42: 427–43.

Diamantis, D & Ladkin, A 1999a, 'The links between sustainable tourism and ecotourism: A definitional and operational perspective', *Journal of Tourism Studies* 10(2): 35–46.

——1999b, '"Green strategies" in the tourism and hospitality industries', in F Vellas & L Bécherel (eds), *The International Marketing of Travel and Tourism: A Strategic Approach*, Macmillan, Basingstoke, UK, pp. 121–41.

Dieke, P (ed.) 2000, *The Political Economy of Tourism Development in Africa*, Cognizant Communications, New York.

DIST 1998, *Tourism: A Ticket to the 21st Century*, Department of Industry, Science and Tourism, Canberra.

Dixon, J & Sherman, P 1990, *Economics of Protected Areas: A New Look at Benefits and Costs*, Island Press, Washington, DC.

Doppelfeld, M 2006, 'Collaborative stakeholder planning in cross-border regions: The case of the Great Limpopo Transfrontier Park in Southern Africa', in II Wachowiak (ed.), *Tourism and Borders: Contemporary Issues, Policies and International Research*, Ashgate, Aldershot, UK, pp. 113–38.

Dowling, R 2001, 'Oceania (Australia, New Zealand, South Pacific)', in DB Weaver (ed.), *Encyclopedia of Ecotourism*, CABI, Wallingford, UK, pp. 139–54.

——2002, 'Australian ecotourism — leading the way', *Journal of Ecotourism* 1: 89–92.

——(ed.) 2006, *Cruise Ship Tourism*, CABI, Wallingford, UK.

Duchesne, M, Côté, S & Barrette, C 2000, 'Responses of woodland caribou to winter ecotourism in the Charlevoix Biosphere Reserve, Canada', *Biological Conservation* 96, 311–17.

Ducks Unlimited 2005, 'US habitat conservation through land ownership and conservation easements', www.ducks.org.

Duffy, R 2002, *A Trip Too Far: Ecotourism, Politics and Exploitation*, Earthscan, London.

——2006, 'Global environmental governance and the politics of ecotourism in Madagascar', *Journal of Ecotourism* 5: 128–44.

Dunlap, R, Van Liere, K, Mertig, A & Jones, R 2000, 'New trends in measuring environmental attitudes: Measuring endorsement of the new ecological paradigm: A revised NEP scale', *Journal of Social Issues* 56: 425–42.

EAA 2000, 'What is ecotourism?', www.ecotourism.org.au.

Eagles, P & Higgins, B 1998, 'Ecotourism market and industry structure', in K Lindberg, M Epler Wood & D Engeldrum (eds), *Ecotourism: A Guide for Planners and Managers*, vol. 2, Ecotourism Society, North Bennington, VT, pp. 11–43.

Eagles, P & McCool, S 2002, *Tourism in National Parks and Protected Areas: Planning and Management*, CABI, Wallingford, UK.

Eagles, P & Martens, J 1997, 'Wilderness tourism and forestry: The possible dream in Algonquin National Park', *Journal of Applied Recreation Research* 22(1): 40–3.

Earthtrends 2006, 'Protected Areas 2005', http://earthtrends.wri.org.

Ecclestone, K & Field, J 2003, 'Promoting social capital in a "risk society": A new approach to emancipatory learning or new moral authoritarianism?', *British Journal of Sociology of Education* 24: 267–82.

Ecotourism Australia 2003, 'EcoCertification (NEAP Edition III)', www.ecotourism.org.au.

——2006, 'All about Ecotourism Australia', www.ecotourism.org.au.

Ecotourism Kenya 2006, 'ESOK eco-rating scheme: Questionnaire for bronze certification', www.ecotourismkenya.org.

Enserink, M & Vogel, G 2006, 'The carnivore comeback', *Science* 314: 746–49.

Epler Wood, M 1999, 'The Ecotourism Society — An international NGO committed to sustainable development', *Tourism Recreation Research* 24(2): 119–23.

Eubanks, T, Stoll, J & Ditton, R 2004, 'Understanding the diversity of eight birder sub-populations: Socio-demographic characteristics, motivations, expenditures and net benefits', *Journal of Ecotourism* 3: 151–72.

European Travel Commission 2006, 'Ecotourism', www.etc-corporate.org.

Faulkner, B & Russell, R 2003, 'Chaos and complexity in tourism: In search of a new perspective', in E Fredline, L Jago & C Cooper (eds), *Progressing Tourism Research — Bill Faulkner*, Channel View, Clevedon, UK, pp. 205–19.

Federal Aviation Administration 2005, 'Noise limitations for aircraft operations in the vicinity of Grand Canyon National Park: Rule', www.nps.gov.

Fennell, D 1999, *Ecotourism: An Introduction*, Routledge, London.

——2001, 'Anglo-America', in DB Weaver (ed.), *Encyclopedia of Ecotourism*, CABI, Wallingford, UK, pp. 107–22.

——2003, *Ecotourism: An Introduction*, 2nd edn, Routledge, London.

Fennell, D, Buckley, R & Weaver, D 2001, 'Ecotourism policy and planning', in DB Weaver (ed.), *Encyclopedia of Ecotourism*, CABI, Wallingford, UK, pp. 463–77.

Fennell, D & Smale, BJ 1992, 'Ecotourism and natural resource protection: Implications of an alternative form of tourism for host nations', *Tourism Recreation Research* 17(1): 21–32.

Fennell, D & Weaver, D 2005, 'The ecotourium concept and tourism–conservation symbiosis', *Journal of Sustainable Tourism* 13: 373–90.

Flannery, T 2002, *The Future Eaters: An Ecological History of the Australasian Lands and People*, Grove Press, Berkeley, CA.

——2006, *The Weather Makers: How Man is Changing the Climate and What It Means for Life on Earth*, Atlantic Monthly Press, New York.

Font, X 2001, 'Regulating the green message: The players in ecolabelling', in X Font & R Buckley (eds), *Tourism Ecolabelling: Certification and Promotion of Sustainable Management*, CABI, Wallingford, UK, pp. 1–17.

Font, X & Tribe, J 2000, 'Recreation, conservation and timber production: A sustainable relationship?', in X Font & J Tribe (eds), *Forest Tourism and Recreation*, CABI, Wallingford, UK, pp. 1–22.

Forestell, P 1993, 'If Leviathan has a face, does Gaia have a soul? Incorporating environmental education in marine eco-tourism programs', *Ocean and Coastal Management* 20: 267–82.

Forests Monitor 2001, 'Papua New Guinea factsheet', www.forestsmonitor.org.

Fowler, G 1999, 'Behavioral and hormonal responses of Magellanic Penguins (*Spheniscus Magellanicus*) to tourism and nest site visitation', *Biological Conservation* 90: 143–9.

Franklin, A 1996, 'Australian hunting and angling sports and the changing nature of human–animal relations in Australia', *ANZJS* 32 (3):39–56.

Fritsch, A & Johannsen, K 2004, *Ecotourism in Appalachia: Marketing the Mountains*, University Press of Kentucky, Lexington, KY.

Fuller, D, Buultjens, J & Cummings, E 2005, 'Ecotourism and indigenous micro-enterprise formation in northern Australia: Opportunities and constraints', *Tourism Management* 26: 891–904.

Gardner, J 2001, 'Ecotourism accommodations', in DB Weaver (ed.), *Encyclopedia of Ecotourism*, CABI, Wallingford, UK, pp. 525–34.

Garrod, B & Wilson, J (eds) 2003, *Marine Ecotourism: Issues and Experiences*, Channel View, Clevedon, UK.

GBRMPA 2000, 'Great Barrier Reef Marine Park Authority', www.gbrmpa.gov.au.

——2005, 'Measuring the economic and financial value of the Great Barrier Reef Marine Park', www.gbrmpa.gov.au.

——2006, 'Climate change and the Great Barrier Reef', www.gbrmpa.gov.au.

——2007a, 'High standard operations', www.gbrmpa.gov.au.

——2007b, 'Environmental management of Defence activities', www.gbrmpa.gov.au.

Getz, D & Carlsen, J 2005, 'Family business in tourism: State of the art', *Annals of Tourism Research* 32: 237–58.

Gill, P & Burke, C 1999, *Whale Watching in Australian and New Zealand Waters*, Australian Geographic, Terrey Hills, NSW.

Glassner, MI 2004, *Political Geography*, 3rd edn, John Wiley & Sons, New York.

Goeldner, C & Ritchie, J 2006, *Tourism: Principles, Practices, Philosophies*, 10th edn, John Wiley & Sons, Chichester, UK.

Gonsalves, P 1987, 'Alternative tourism: The evolution of a concept and establishment of a network', *Tourism Recreation Research* 12(2): 9–12.

Goodwin, H 1996, 'In pursuit of ecotourism', *Biodiversity and Conservation* 5: 277–91.

Gössling, S 1999, 'Ecotourism: A means to safeguard biodiversity and ecosystem functions?', *Ecological Economics* 29: 303–20.

——(ed.), 2003, *Tourism and Development in Tropical Islands: Political Ecology Perspectives*, Edward Elgar, Cheltenham, UK.

Gössling, S, Peeters, P, Ceron, J-P, Dubois, G, Patterson, T & Richardson, R 2005, 'The eco-efficiency of tourism', *Ecological Economics* 54: 417–34.

GPT 2006, 'About GPT', www.gpt.com.au.

Green, MJ & Paine, J 1997, 'State of the world's protected areas at the end of the twentieth century', paper presented at the IUCN World Commission on Protected Areas Symposium, Albany, WA, Australia, 24–29 November.

Griffin, T & DeLacey, T 2002, 'Green Globe: Sustainability accreditation for tourism', in R Harris, T Griffin & P Williams (eds), *Sustainable Tourism: A Global Perspective*, Butterworth-Heinemann, Oxford, pp. 58–83.

Hall, C 1985, *Costa Rica: A Geographical Interpretation in Historical Perspective*, Westview Press, London.

——1998, 'Historical antecedents on sustainable development: New labels on old bottles?', in CM Hall & A Lew (eds), *Sustainable Tourism: A Geographical Perspective*, Longman, London, pp. 13–24.

Hall, CM & Boyd, S (eds) 2005, *Nature-based Tourism in Peripheral Areas: Development or Disaster?* Channel View, Clevedon, UK.

Hall, CM & Higham, J, (eds) 2005, *Tourism, Recreation and Climate Change*, Channel View, Clevedon, UK.

Hall, CM & Johnston, M (eds) 1995, *Polar Tourism: Tourism in the Arctic and Antarctic Regions*, John Wiley & Sons, New York.

Halpenny, E 2001, 'Ecotourism-related organisations', in DB Weaver (ed.), *Encyclopedia of Ecotourism*, CABI, Wallingford, UK, pp. 479–96.

Halpenny, E & Caissie, L 2003, 'Volunteering on nature conservation projects: Volunteer experience, attitudes and values', *Tourism Recreation Research* 28(3): 25–33.

Harpham, T, Grant, E & Thomas, E 2002, 'Measuring social capital within health surveys: Key issues', *Health Policy and Planning* 17: 106–11.

Harriott, V, Davis, D & Banks, S 1997, 'Recreational diving and its impacts in marine protected areas in eastern Australia', *Ambio* 26: 173–9.

Harris, R 2002, 'The tale of the Little Penguins and the tourists: Making tourism sustainable at Phillip Island Nature Park', in R Harris, T Griffin &

P Williams (eds), *Sustainable Tourism: A Global Perspective*, Butterworth-Heinemann, Oxford, pp. 238–51.

Harrison, D & Brandt, J 2003, 'Ecotourism in Fiji', in D Harrison (ed.), *Pacific Island Tourism*, Cognizant Communications, Elmsford, NY, pp. 139–56.

Harrison, D & Hitchcock, M (eds) 2004, *The Politics of World Heritage: Negotiating Tourism and Conservation*, Channel View, Clevedon, UK.

Hawkins, D, Epler Wood, M & Bittman, S (eds) 1995, *The Ecolodge Sourcebook for Planners and Developers*, Ecotourism Society, North Bennington, VT.

Hawkins, J, Roberts, C, Van 'T Hof, T, De Meyer, K, Tratalos, J & Aldam, C 1999, 'Effects of recreational scuba diving on Caribbean coral and fish communities', *Conservation Biology* 13: 888–97.

Hazeltine, B & Bull, C (eds) 2003, *Field Guide of Appropriate Technology*, Academic Press, London.

HEA 2006, 'Hawaii Ecotourism Association', www.hawaiiecotourism.org.

Head, L 2000, 'Renovating the landscape and packaging the penguin: Culture and nature on Summerland Peninsula, Phillip Island, Victoria, Australia', *Australian Geographical Studies* 38(1): 36–53.

Hearne, R & Santos, C 2005, 'Tourists' and locals' preferences toward ecotourism development in the Maya Biosphere Reserve, Guatemala', *Environment, Development and Sustainability* 7: 303–18.

Heher, S 2003, 'Ecotourism investment and development models: Donors, NGOs and private entrepreneurs', www.conservationfinance.org.

Heemskirk, M 2002, 'Livelihood decision making and environmental degradation: Small-scale gold mining in the Suriname Amazon', *Society and Natural Resources* 15: 327–44.

Henson, P & Grant, T 1991, 'The effects of human disturbance on Trumpeter Swan breeding behavior', *Wildlife Society Bulletin* 19: 248–57.

Higginbottom, K (ed.) 2004, *Wildlife Tourism: Impacts, Management and Planning*, Common Ground, Altona, Vic.

Higgins, B 2001, 'Ecotourism-related tour operators', in DB Weaver (ed.), *Encyclopedia of Ecotourism*, CABI, Wallingford, UK, pp. 535–48.

Hinch, T 2001, 'Indigenous territories', in DB Weaver (ed.), *Encyclopedia of Ecotourism*, CABI, Wallingford, UK, pp. 345–57.

Hirsch, P & Warren, C (eds) 1998, *The Politics of the Environment in Southeast Asia*, Routledge, London.

Holden, A 2003, 'In need of new environmental ethics for tourism?', *Annals of Tourism Research* 30: 94–108.

Holland, S, Ditton, R & Graefe, A 1998, 'An ecotourism perspective on billfish fisheries', *Journal of Sustainable Tourism* 6: 97–116.

Honey, M 1999, *Ecotourism and Sustainable Development: Who Owns Paradise?* Island Press, Washington, DC.

Horwich, R & Lyon, J 1999, 'Rural ecotourism as a conservation tool', in TV Singh & S Singh (eds), *Tourism Development in Critical Environments*, Cognizant Communications, New York.

Hoyt, E 2000, 'Whale watching 2000: Worldwide tourism numbers, expenditures, and expanding socioeconomic benefits', www.ifaw.org.

Hunter, C 1997, 'Sustainable tourism as an adaptive paradigm', *Annals of Tourism Research* 24: 850–67.

Hunter Wetlands Centre 2006, *2005 Annual Report*, Hunter Wetlands Centre, Newcastle, NSW.

Hutton, D & Connors, L 1999, *A History of the Australian Environmental Movement*, Cambridge University Press, Cambridge.

Hvenegaard, G & Dearden, P 1998, 'Ecotourism versus tourism in a Thai national park', *Annals of Tourism Research* 25: 700–20.

IAATO 2006a, 'Guidance for those organising and conducting tourism and non-governmental activities in the Antarctic', www.iaato.org.

——2006b, '1992–2007 Antarctic tourist trends', http://image.zenn.net.

——2006c, 'Scope of Antarctic tourism — a background presentation', www.iaato.org.

——2006d, 'IAATO Bylaws', www.iaato.org.

IAMAT 2006, 'World malaria risk chart', www.iamat.org.

ICMA 2004, 'Green Globe: Kaikoura's path to a sustainable future', www.solgm.co.nz.

IFAW 2004, 'From whalers to whale watchers: The growth of whale watching tourism in Australia', www.ifaw.org.

——2005, 'The growth of whale watching in Sydney 2003–2004', www.ifaw.org.

Inskeep, E 1991, *Tourism Planning: An Integrated and Sustainable Development Approach*, Van Nostrand Reinhold, New York.

IUCN 2003, *2003 United Nations List of Protected Areas*, www.iucn.org.

——2006, 'International experts discuss China's draft protected areas law in Beijing', www.iucn.org.

Jaakson, R 1997, 'Exploring the epistemology of ecotourism', *Journal of Applied Recreational Research* 22(1): 33–47.

Jacobson, S & Lopez, A 1994, 'Biological impacts of ecotourism: Tourists and nesting turtles in Tortuguero National Park, Costa Rica', *Wildlife Society Bulletin* 22: 414–19.

Jafari, J 1989, 'An English language literature review', in J Bystrzanowski (ed.), *Tourism as a Factor of Change: A Sociocultural Study*, Centre for Research and Documentation in Social Sciences, Vienna, pp. 17–60.

——2001, 'The scientification of tourism', in VL Smith & M Brent (eds), *Hosts and Guests Revisited: Tourism Issues of the 21st Century*, Cognizant Communications, New York, pp. 28–41.

Jepson, P, Jarvie, J, MacKinnon, K & Monk, K 2001, 'The end for Indonesia's lowland forests?', *Science* 292: 859–60.

JICA 1994, *The Study on the National Tourism Master Plan in the Republic of Kenya (Interim Report)*, Japan International Cooperation Agency, Nairobi.

JiuXia, S & JiGang, B 2006, 'The community participation model of tourism: An empirical study of Yunnan and Guangxi', *China Tourism Research* 2: 130–45.

John Gray's Sea Canoe 2005, John Gray's Sea Canoe home, www.johngray-seacanoe.com.

Johnson, D 2006, 'Providing ecotourism excursions for cruise passengers', *Journal of Sustainable Tourism* 14: 43–54.

Jones, S 2005, 'Community-based ecotourism: The significance of social capital', *Annals of Tourism Research* 32: 303–24.

Kellert, S 1985, 'Birdwatching in American society', *Leisure Sciences* 7: 343–60.

Kelly, I & Nankervis, T 2001, *Visitor Destinations: An International Perspective*, John Wiley & Sons, Brisbane.

Kerstetter, D, Hou, J-S & Lin, C-H 2004, 'Profiling Taiwanese ecotourists using a behavioral approach', *Tourism Management* 25: 491–8.

Khatib, A 2000, 'Ecotourism in Zanzibar, Tanzania', in P Dieke (ed.), *The Political Economy of Tourism Development in Africa*, New York, Cognizant Communications, pp. 167–80.

Kimmel, J 1999, 'Ecotourism as environmental learning', *Journal of Environmental Education* 30(2), 40–4.

Kingfisher Bay Resort 2006, 'Kingfisher Bay Resort, Fraser Island', www.kingfisherbay.com.

Kiss, A 2004, 'Is community-based ecotourism a good use of biodiversity conservation funds?', *TRENDS in Ecology and Evolution* 19: 232–37, www.for.nau.edu.

Knill, G 1991, 'Towards the green paradigm', *South African Geographical Journal* 73: 53–9.

Knudson, D, Cable, T & Beck, L 1995, *Interpretation of Cultural and Natural Resources*, Venture Publishing, State College, PA.

Kontogeorgopoulos, N 2005, 'Community-based ecotourism in Phuket and Ao Phangnga, Thailand: Partial victories and bittersweet remedies', *Journal of Sustainable Tourism* 13: 4–23.

Kontoleon, A, Swanson, T, Wang, Q, Xuejun, Q & Yang, C 2002, 'Optimal ecotourism: The economic value of the Giant Panda in China', in C Pearce & C Palmer (eds), *Valuing the Environment in Developing Countries: Case Studies*, Edward Elgar, Cheltenham, UK, pp. 206–35.

Krippendorf, J 1984, *The Holiday Makers: Understanding the Impact of Leisure and Travel*, Heinemann, Oxford.

Krüger, O 2005, 'The role of ecotourism in conservation: Panacea or Pandora's box?', *Biodiversity and Conservation* 14: 579–600.

Kuhn, T 1970, *The Structure of Scientific Revolutions*, 2nd edn, University of Chicago Press, Chicago.

Laarman, JG & Durst, PB 1987, Nature Travel and Tropical Forests, FREI Working Paper Series, Southeastern Center for Forest Economics Research, North Carolina State University, Raleigh, NC.

Laarman, JG & Gregersen, HM 1996, 'Pricing policy in nature-based tourism', *Tourism Management* 17: 247–54.

Lai, P-H & Shafer, S 2005, 'Marketing ecotourism through the internet: An evaluation of selected ecolodges in Latin America and the Caribbean', *Journal of Ecotourism* 4: 143–60.

Langholz, J 1996, 'Economics, objectives, and success of private nature reserves in sub-Saharan Africa and Latin America', *Conservation Biology* 10: 271–80.

Langholz, J & Brandon, K 2001, 'Ecotourism and privately owned protected areas', in DB Weaver (ed.), *Encyclopedia of Ecotourism*, CABI, Wallingford, UK, pp. 303–14.

Langholz, J, Lassoie, J, Lee, D & Chapman, D 2000, 'Economic considerations of privately owned parks', *Ecological Economics* 33: 173–83.

Lao National Tourism Administration 2006, 'Ecotourism Laos', www.ecotourismlaos.com.

LaPlanche, S 1995, *Stepping Lightly on Australia: A Traveller's Guide to Ecotourism*, HarperCollins, Sydney.

Laufer, W 2003, 'Social accountability and corporate greenwashing', *Journal of Business Ethics* 43: 253–61.

Laurance, W, Albernaz, A & Da Costa, C 2001, 'Is deforestation accelerating in the Brazilian Amazon?', *Environmental Conservation* 28: 305–11.

Lawrence, T, Wickins, D & Phillips, N 1997, 'Managing legitimacy in ecotourism', *Tourism Management* 18: 307–16.

Lawton, L 2001, 'Ecotourism in public protected areas', in DB Weaver (ed.), *Encyclopedia of Ecotourism*, CABI, Wallingford, UK, pp. 287–302.

Lawton, L & Weaver, DB 2001, 'Ecotourism in modified spaces', in DB Weaver (ed.), *Encyclopedia of Ecotourism*, CABI, Wallingford, UK, pp. 315–26.

LeBreton, M, Prosser, A, Tamoufe, U, Sateren, W, Mpoudi-Ngole, E, Diffo, J, Burke, D & Wolfe, N 2006, 'Patterns of bushmeat hunting and perceptions of disease risk among Central African communities', *Animal Conservation* 9: 357–63.

Lee, W & Moscardo, G 2005, 'Understanding the impact of ecotourism resort experiences on tourists' environmental attitudes and behavioural intentions', *Journal of Sustainable Tourism* 13: 546–65.

Leiserowitz, A, Kates, R & Parris, T 2005, 'Do global attitudes and behaviors support sustainable development?', *Environment* 47(9): 22–38.

Leslie Street Spit 2001, 'Tommy Thompson Park: Important bird area conservation plan', www.ibacanada.com.

Liddle, M 1997, *Recreation Ecology*, Chapman & Hall, London.

Lindberg, K 1991, *Policies for Maximizing Nature Tourism's Ecological and Economic Benefits*, World Resources Institute, Washington, DC.

——1998, 'Economic aspects of ecotourism', in K Lindberg, M Epler Wood & D Engeldrum (eds), *Ecotourism: A Guide for Planners and Managers*, vol. 2, Ecotourism Society, North Bennington, VT.

——2001, 'Economic impacts', in DB Weaver (ed.), *Encyclopedia of Ecotourism*, CABI, Wallingford, UK, pp. 363–77.

Lindberg, K, Enriquez, J & Sproule, K 1996, 'Ecotourism questioned: Case studies from Belize', *Annals of Tourism Research* 23: 543–62.

Lindberg, K & Hawkins, D (eds) 1993, *Ecotourism: A Guide for Planners and Managers*, vol. 1, Ecotourism Society, North Bennington, VT.

Liu, J, Linderman, M, Ouyang, Z, An, L, Yang, D & Zhang, H 2001, 'Ecological degradation in protected areas: The case of Wolong Nature Reserve for Giant Pandas', *Science* 292 (5514): 98–101.

Lott, D & McCoy, M 1995, 'Asian Rhinos *Rinoceros Unicornis* on the run? Impact of tourist visits on one population', *Biological Conservation* 73: 23–6.

Lovelock, J 1979, *Gaia: A New Look at Life on Earth*, Oxford University Press, New York.

Low, T 2002, *Feral Future: The Untold Story of Australia's Exotic Invaders*, University of Chicago Press, Chicago.

Luniak, M 2004, 'Synurbization: Adaptation of animal wildlife to urban development', in W Shaw & L Harris (eds), *Proceedings, 4th International Urban Wildlife Symposium*, Tucson, AZ, pp. 50–5.

Lusseau, D 2003, 'Effects of tour boats on the behavior of Bottlenose Dolphins: Using Markov chains to model anthropogenic impacts', *Conservation Biology* 17: 1785–93.

MacCannell, D 1976, *The Tourist: A New Theory of the Leisure Class*, Schocken Books, New York.

McKercher, B 1998, *The Business of Nature-Based Tourism*, Hospitality Press, Elsternwick, Vic.

——2001, 'The business of ecotourism', in DB Weaver (ed.), *Encyclopedia of Ecotourism*, CABI, Wallingford, UK, pp. 565–77.

McKercher, B & Robbins, B 1998, 'Business development issues affecting nature-based tourism operators in Australia', *Journal of Sustainable Tourism* 6: 173–88.

McMichael, A, Woodruff, R & Hales, S 2006, 'Climate change and human health: Present and future risks', *Lancet* 367: 859–69.

Madhusudan, M 2003, 'Living amidst large wildlife: Livestock and crop depredation by large mammals in the interior villages of Bhadra Tiger Reserve, South India', *Environmental Management* 31: 466–75.

Maldonado, E & Montagnini, F 2005, 'Carrying capacity of La Tigra National Park, Honduras: Can the park be self-sustainable?', *Journal of Sustainable Forestry* 19: 29–48.

Marion, JL & Farrell, TA 1998, 'Managing ecotourism visitation in protected areas', in K Lindberg, M Epler Wood & D Engeldrum (eds), *Ecotourism: A Guide for Planners and Managers*, vol. 2, Ecotourism Society, North Bennington, VT, pp. 155–81.

MEA 2006, 'Mesoamerican Ecotourism Alliance', www.travelwithmea.com.

Meadows, DH, Meadows, DL, Randers, J & Behrens, W 1972, *The Limits to Growth*, 2nd edn, Potomac Associates, Washington DC.

Medina, L 2005, 'Ecotourism and certification: Confronting the principles and pragmatics of socially responsible tourism', *Journal of Sustainable Tourism* 13: 281–95.

Mehta, H 1999, 'International trends in ecolodges', paper presented at the World Ecotourism Conference, Kota Kinabalu, Malaysia, October.

Menkhaus, S & Lober, D 1996, 'International ecotourism and the valuation of tropical rainforests in Costa Rica', *Journal of Environmental Management* 47: 1–10.

Mercer, D 1998, 'The uneasy relationship between tourism and native peoples: The Australian experience', in WF Theobald (ed.), *Global Tourism*, 2nd edn, Butterworth Heinemann, Oxford, pp. 98–128.

——2000, *A Question of Balance: Natural Resources Conflict Issues in Australia*, 3rd edn, Federation Press, Leichhardt, NSW.

Mongabay.com 2006, 'Pacific Islands: Solomon Islands', http://rainforests.mongabay.com.

Moreno, P 2005, 'Ecotourism along the Meso-American Caribbean reef: The impacts of foreign investment', *Human Ecology* 33: 217–44.

MORI 2000, *Attitudes of Package Holiday Makers*, Association of British Travel Agents, London.

Moss, L. (ed.) 2006, *The Amenity Migrants: Seeking and Sustaining Mountains and Their Cultures*, CABI, Wallingford, UK.

Mowforth, M & Munt, I 1998, *Tourism and Sustainability: New Tourism in the Third World*, Routledge, London.

Müllner, A, Linsenmair, K & Wikelski, M 2004, 'Exposure to ecotourism reduces survival and affects stress response in Hoatzin chicks (*Opisthocomus hoazin*)', *Biological Conservation* 118: 549–58.

Muloin, S 1998, 'Wildlife tourism: The psychological benefits of whale watching', *Pacific Tourism Review* 2: 199–213.

Murphy, P 1985, *Tourism: A Community Approach*, Methuen, New York.

Myers, N, Mittermeier, R, Mittermeier, C, da Fonseca, G & Kent, J 2000, 'Biodiversity hotspots for conservation priorities', *Nature* 403: 853–8.

Navarro, J 1998, *Panama National Parks*, Ediciones Balboa, Panama City.

Nelson, F 2004, 'The evolution and impacts of community-based ecotourism in northern Tanzania', International Institute for Environment and Development, www.poptel.org.uk.

Nelson, J 2000, 'Tourism and national parks in North America: An overview', in RW Butler & SW Boyd (eds), *Tourism and National Parks: Issues and Implications*, John Wiley & Sons, Chichester, UK, pp. 303–21.

Nevin, O & Gilbert, B 2005, 'Measuring the cost of risk avoidance in Brown Bears: Further evidence of positive impacts of ecotourism', *Biological Conservation* 123: 453–60.

Newsome, D, Dowling, R & Moore, S 2005, *Wildlife Tourism*, Channel View, Clevedon, UK.

Newsome, D, Moore, S & Dowling, R 2002, *Natural Area Tourism: Ecology, Impacts and Management*, Channel View, Clevedon, UK.

Nianyong, H & Zhuge, R 2001 'Ecotourism in China's nature reserves: Opportunities and challenges', *Journal of Sustainable Tourism* 9: 228–42.

Nikolov, P 2006, 'Iceland resumes commercial whaling', Discovery News Channel, http://dsc.discovery.com.

NMFS 2004, 'Species: Humphead wrasse', www.nmfs.noaa.gov.

——2006, 'Whalewatching guidelines', http://swr.nmfs.noaa.gov.

NOAA 2005, 'Gerry E. Studds Stellwagen Bank National Marine Sanctuary', http://stellwagen.noaa.gov.

Novak, M 1982, *The Spirit of Democratic Capitalism*, Simon & Schuster, New York.

Novelli, M, Barnes, J & Humavindu, M 2006, 'The other side of the ecotourism coin: Consumptive tourism in southern Africa', *Journal of Ecotourism* 5: 62–79.

NPS 2006a, 'Canyon View information plaza', www.nps.gov.

——2006b, 'American Indian Liaison Office', www.cr.nps.gov.

——2006c, 'Park visitation report', www2.nature.nps.gov.

Nyaupane, G, Morais, D & Dowler, L 2006, 'The role of community involvement and number/type of visitors on tourism impacts: A controlled comparison of Annapurna, Nepal and Northwest Yunnan, China', *Tourism Management* 27: 1373–85.

NZAID 2006, 'Environment', www.nzaid.govt.nz.

Obua, J & Harding, D 1997, 'Environmental impact of ecotourism in Kibale National Park, Uganda', *Journal of Sustainable Tourism* 5: 213–23.

ONT 1997a, *Best Practice Ecotourism: A Guide to Energy and Waste Minimisation*, Office of National Tourism, Canberra.

——1997b, *Ecotourism Education*, Office of National Tourism, Canberra.

Orams, M 1997, 'The effectiveness of environmental education: Can we turn tourists into "greenies"?', *Progress in Tourism and Hospitality Research* 3: 295–306.

——1999, *Marine Tourism: Development, Impacts and Management*, Routledge, London.

——2000, 'Tourists getting close to whales: Is it what whale-watching is all about?', *Tourism Management* 21: 561–69.

——2001a, 'Types of ecotourism', in DB Weaver (ed.), *Encyclopedia of Ecotourism*, CABI, Wallingford, UK, pp. 23–36.

——2001b, 'From whale hunting to whale watching in Tonga: A sustainable future?', *Journal of Sustainable Tourism* 9: 128–46.

——2002, 'Marine ecotourism as a potential agent for sustainable development in Kaikoura, New Zealand', *International Journal of Sustainable Development* 5: 338–52.

——2005, 'Dolphins, whales and ecotourism in New Zealand: What are the impacts and how should the industry be managed?', in CM Hall & S Boyd (eds), *Nature-based Tourism in Peripheral Areas: Development or Disaster?* Channel View, Clevedon, UK, pp. 231–45.

Organic Trade Association 2006, 'The OTA 2004 Manufacturer Overview Report', www.ota.com.

Ottman, J 1998, 'Green marketing: Opportunity for innovation', 2nd edn, NTC Business Books, Lincolnwood, IL.

Outdoor Industry Foundation 2005, *Outdoor Recreation Participation Study*, 7th edn, Boulder, CO.

Page, S & Dowling, R 2002, *Ecotourism*, Pearson Education, London.

Palacio, V & McCool, S 1997, 'Identifying ecotourists in Belize through benefit segmentation: A preliminary analysis', *Journal of Sustainable Tourism* 5: 234–43.

Parker, G & Ravenscroft, N 2000, 'Tourism, "national parks" and private lands', in RW Butler & SW Boyd (eds) 2000, *Tourism and National Parks: Issues and Implications*, John Wiley & Sons, Chichester, UK, pp. 95–106.

Parker, S 2001, 'The place of ecotourism in public policy and planning', in DB Weaver (ed.), *Encyclopedia of Ecotourism*, CABI, Wallingford, UK, pp. 509–20.

Parks Canada. 2005, 'Aboriginal Affairs Secretariat', www.pc.gc.ca.

——2006, 'Parks Canada attendance 2000–2001 to 2004–2005', www.pc.gc.ca.

Parks Victoria 2006, 'Visitation statistics', www.parkweb.vic.gov.au.

Parliament of Tasmania 2006, '2006–07 Budget speech: Strong economy. Strong communities', www.premier.tas.gov.au.

Patterson, C 2001, *The Business of Ecotourism: The Complete Guide for Nature and Culture-Based Tourism Operations*, 2nd edn, Explorer's Guide Publishing, Rhinelander, WI.

Pearce, PL & Moscardo, G 1994, 'Final report: Understanding visitor plans for, visitor expectations of and visitor reactions to the Wet Tropics World Heritage Area', unpublished report, James Cook University, Townsville, Qld.

Peattie, K, Hanson, D & Walker, R 1999, *Key Issue in Eco-tourism Development: A Tale of Two Islands*, School of Management Working Paper Series No. 99–03, University of Tasmania, Hobart.

Penjore, D & Rapten, P 2004, 'Trends of forestry policy concerning local participation in Bhutan', www.iges.or.jp.

Petty, R, McMichael, S & Brannon, L 1992, 'The elaboration likelihood model of persuasion', in M Manfredo (ed.), *Influencing Human Behavior: Theory and Applications in Recreation, Tourism, and Natural Resources Management*, Sagamore, New York, pp. 77–101.

Phillip Island 2006a, 'Phillip Island Nature Park management plan 2006–2011: Draft for public comment', http://penguins.org.au.

——2006b, 'Phillip Island Nature Parks Australia', http://penguins.org.au.

Pleumarom, A 2001, 'Do we need the International Year of Ecotourism?', www.mtn.org.

PNG 2006, 'Papua New Guinea tourism sector review and master plan (2007–2017)', www.pngtourism.org.pg.

PollingReport.com 2006, 'Environment', www.pollingreport.com.

Price, S (ed.) 2003, *War and Tropical Forests: Conservation in Areas of Armed Conflict*, Haworth Press, New York.

Prideaux, M & Bossley, M 2000, 'Lethal waters: The assault on our marine mammals', *Habitat Australia* 28(2): 13–20.

Queensland 1997, *Queensland Ecotourism Plan*, Department of Tourism, Small Business and Industry, Brisbane.

Queensland Department of Natural Resources and Mines 2003, *Land Cover Change in Queensland: A Statewide Landcover and Tree Study Reports (SLATS)*, Brisbane.

——2006, *Land Cover Change in Queensland: A Statewide Landcover and Tree Study Reports (SLATS)*, Brisbane.

Queensland Parks and Wildlife Service 2004, 'Principles', www.epa.qld.gov.au.

Rao, K, Maikhuri, R, Nautiyal, S & Saxena, K 2002, 'Crop damage and livestock depredation by wildlife: A case study from Nanda Devi Biosphere Reserve, India', *Journal of Environmental Management* 66: 317–27.

Ray, P & Anderson, S 2000, *The Cultural Creatives: How 50 Million People are Changing the World*, Three Rivers Press, New York.

Reef Ball Foundation 2006, 'Reef Ball Foundation', www.reefball.org.

Richter, C, Dawson, S & Slooten, E 2006, 'Impacts of commercial whale watching on male sperm whales at Kaikoura, New Zealand', *Marine Mammal Science* 22: 46–63.

Roe, D, Leader-Williams, N & Dalal-Clayton, B 1997, *Take Only Photographs, Leave Only Footprints: The Environmental Impacts of Wildlife Tourism*, IIED Wildlife and Development Series No. 10, Environmental Planning Group, International Institute for Environment and Development, London.

Rolfe, J 2002, 'Economics of vegetation clearing in Queensland', *Rangeland Journal* 24: 152–69.

Romeril, M 1985, 'Tourism and the environment: Towards a symbiotic relationship', *International Journal of Environmental Studies* 25: 215–18.

Rottnest Island Authority 2006, 'Experience Rottnest Island', www.rottnestisland.com.

Rowe, G & Frewer, L 2000, 'Public participation methods: A framework for evaluation', *Science, Technology and Human Values* 25: 3–29.

Russell, D, Bottrill, C & Meredith, G 1995, 'International ecolodge survey', in D Hawkins, M Epler Wood & S Bittman (eds), *The Ecolodge Sourcebook for Planners and Developers*, Ecotourism Society, North Bennington, VT, pp. ix–xvii.

Rutto, B & Sing'oeie, K 2004, 'The Endorois and their lost heritage', *Indigenous Affairs* 4(4): 47–50.

Ryan, C, Hughes, K & Chirgwin, S 2000, 'The gaze, spectacle and ecotourism', *Annals of Tourism Research* 27: 148–63.

Salafsky, N, Cauley, H, Balachander, G, Cordes, B, Parks, J, Margoluis, C, Bhatt, S, Encarnacion, C, Russell, D & Margoluis R 2001, 'A systematic test of an enterprise strategy for community-based biodiversity conservation', *Conservation Biology* 17: 1585–95.

Sale, K 1996, *Rebels Against the Future: The Luddites and Their War on the Industrial Revolution*, Addison-Wesley, Sydney.

SANP 2006, 'Park management plan. Kruger National Park. August 2006', www.sanparks.org.

SATC 1995, *Ecotourism: A Natural Strategy for South Australia*, South Australian Tourism Commission, Adelaide.

Scace, RC 1993, 'An ecotourism perspective', in JG Nelson, RW Butler & G Wall (eds), *Tourism and Sustainable Development: Monitoring, Planning, Managing*, University of Waterloo, Waterloo, Canada, pp. 59–82.

Scace, RC, E Grifone & R Usher 1992, *Ecotourism in Canada*, Canadian Environmental Advisory Council, Hull, Canada.

SCAR 2006, 'Scientific Committee on Antarctic Research: Antarctic Treaty', www.scar.org.

Scheyvens, R 1999, 'Ecotourism and the empowerment of local communities', *Tourism Management* 20: 245–49.

Schumacher, E 1973, *Small is Beautiful: A Study of Economics as if People Mattered*, Blond & Briggs, London.

Shackley, M (ed.) 1998, *Visitor Management: Case Studies from World Heritage Sites*, Butterworth-Heinemann, Oxford.

Shelton, E & Lübke, H 2005, 'Penguins as sights, penguins as site: The problematics of contestation', in C Hall & S Boyd (eds), *Nature-based Tourism in Peripheral Areas: Development or Disaster?* Channel View, Clevedon, UK, pp. 218–30.

Shepherd, N 2003, 'How ecotourism can go wrong: The cases of SeaCanoe and Siam Safari, Thailand', in M Lück & T Kirstges (eds), *Global Ecotourism Policies and Case Studies: Perspectives and Constraints*, Channel View, Clevedon, UK, pp. 137–46.

Sherman, P & Dixon, J 1991, 'The economics of nature tourism: Determining if it pays', in T Whelan (ed.), *Nature Tourism: Managing for the Environment*, Island Press, Washington, DC, pp. 89–131.

Silberglied, R 1978, 'Inter-island transport of insects aboard ships in the Galapagos Islands', *Biological Conservation* 13: 273–8.

Silva, G & McDill, M 2004, 'Barriers to ecotourism supplier success: A comparison of agency and business perspectives', *Journal of Sustainable Tourism* 12: 289–305.

Simmons, D & Becken, S 2004, 'The cost of getting there: Impacts of travel to ecotourism destinations', in R Buckley (ed.), *Environmental Impacts of Ecotourism*, CABI, Wallingford, UK, pp. 15–23.

Simpson, K 2003, 'Ecotourism policy and practice in New Zealand's national estate', in D Fennell & R Dowling (eds), *Ecotourism Policy and Planning*, CABI, Wallingford, UK, pp. 255–73.

Sindiga, I 1996, 'Domestic tourism in Kenya', *Annals of Tourism Research* 23: 19–31.

——2000, 'Tourism development in Kenya', in P Dieke (ed.), *The Political Economy of Tourism Development in Africa*, Cognizant Communications, New York, pp. 129–53.

Singh, S, Timothy, D & Dowling, R (eds) 2003, *Tourism in Destination Communities*, CABI, Wallingford, UK.

Social Investment Forum 2006, '2005 report on socially responsible investing trends in the United States', www.socialinvest.org.

Sofield, T 2003, *Empowerment for Sustainable Tourism Development*, Pergamon, London.

——2006, 'Border tourism and border communities: An overview', *Tourism Geographies* 8: 102–21.

Spiller, P 2006, 'Riots highlight Chinese tensions', BBC News, 21 April, http://news.bbc.co.uk.

Splettstoesser, J, Landau, D & Headland, R 2004, 'Tourism in the forbidden lands: The Antarctica experience', in T Singh (ed.), *New Horizons in Tourism: Strange Experiences and Stranger Practices*, CABI, Wallingford, UK, pp. 27–36.

Stewart, W 2006, 'Flowers in hell', *Courier-Mail* (Brisbane, Australia), 11–12 March, pp. 22–5.

Stockwell, C & Bateman, G 1991, 'Conflicts in national parks: A case study of helicopters and Bighorn Sheep time budgets at the Grand Canyon', *Biological Conservation* 56: 317–28.

Stonehouse, B 2001, 'Polar environments (Arctic and Antarctic)', in DB Weaver (ed.), *Encyclopedia of Ecotourism*, CABI, Wallingford, UK, pp. 219–34.

Stonehouse, B & Crosbie, K 1995, 'Tourist impacts and management in the Antarctic peninsula area', in CM Hall & M Johnston (eds), *Polar Tourism: Tourism in the Arctic and Antarctic Regions*, John Wiley & Sons, Chichester, UK, pp. 217–33.

Stynes, D 2002, 'Economic impacts of Great Smoky Mountains National Park visitors on the local region, 1997–2000', National Park Service Social Science Program, http://web4.msue.msu.edu.

Svoronou, E & Holden, A 2005, 'Ecotourism as a tool for nature conservation: The role of WWF Greece in the Dadia–Lefkimi–Soufli Forest Reserve in Greece', *Journal of Sustainable Tourism* 13: 456–67.

Tao, C-H, Eagles, P & Smith, S 2004, 'Profiling Taiwanese ecotourists using a self-definition approach', *Journal of Sustainable Tourism* 12: 149–68.

Taylor, J, Dyer, G & Stewart, M 2003, 'The economics of ecotourism: A Galapagos Islands economy-wide perspective', *Economic Development and Cultural Change* 51: 977–97.

TerraNature 2005, 'The conflict of mineral mining in a nature sanctuary', www.terranature.org.

Theodore Roosevelt Conservation Partnership 2006, 'Voluntary Public Access and Wildlife Habitat Incentive Program Act of 2005 (Senate, May 17, 2005)', www.trcp.org.

TIA 2003, *Geotourism: The New Trend in Travel*, Travel Industry Association of America, Washington DC.

TIES 2006, 'The International Ecotourism Society', www.ecotourism.org.

Timothy, D & White, K 1999, 'Community-based ecotourism development on the periphery of Belize', *Current Issues in Tourism* 2: 226–42.

Tirasatayapitak, A & Laws, E 2003, 'Developing a new multi-nation tourism region: Thai perspectives on the Mekong initiatives', *Asia Pacific Journal of Tourism Research* 8: 48–57.

Tisdell, C & Wilson, C 2001, 'Wildlife-based tourism and increased support for nature conservation financially and otherwise: Evidence from Sea Turtle ecotourism at Mon Repos', *Tourism Economics* 7: 233–49.

——2004, 'Economics of wildlife tourism', in K Higginbottom (ed.), *Wildlife Tourism: Impacts, Management and Planning*, Common Ground, Altona, Vic., pp. 145–63.

——2005, 'Perceived impacts of ecotourism on environmental learning and conservation: Turtle watching as a case study', *Environment, Development and Sustainability* 7: 291–302.

Tourism Australia 2002, 2004, 2006, 'International Visitor Survey'.

—— 2006, 'About us', www.tourism.australia.com.

Tourism Queensland 2000, *Innovation in Interpretation: 30 Case Studies*, Tourism Queensland, Brisbane.

——2002, 'Queensland Ecotourism Plan 2003–2008', www.tq.com.au.

——2006a, 'The US ecotourist market', www.tq.com.au.

——2006b, 'The German ecotourist market', www.tq.com.au.

——2006c, 'The United Kingdom ecotourist market', www.tq.com.au.

Tourism Research Australia 2005, 'Inbound tourism trends. Year ended 30 December 2004', www.tourism.australia.com.

Tourism Research Council New Zealand 2006, 'International visitor survey', www.trcnz.govt.nz.

Tratalos, J & Austin, T 2001, 'Impacts of recreational SCUBA diving on coral communities of the Caribbean island of Grand Cayman', *Biological Conservation* 102: 67–75.

TTNQ 2006, 'TNQ tourism operations update 3', Tourism Tropical North Queensland, http://tourism.australia.com.

Turner, L & Ash, J 1975, *The Golden Hordes: International Tourism and the Pleasure Periphery*, Constable, London.

Twining-Ward, L 2005, 'Feasibility study for Pacific Ecotourism Association. Draft final report', www.kiribati.spto.org.

Tyynelä, T & Rantala, S 2004, 'Linking ecotourism to the future of Lake Malawi National Park', in D Baumgartner (ed.), *Proceedings of Human Dimensions of Family, Farm, and Community Forestry International Symposium, March 29–April 1, 2004*, Washington State University, Pullman, WA, pp. 215–18.

UNDP 2006, 'The GEF Small Grants Programme', http://sgp.undp.org.

UNEP 2006a, 'GEO: Global environment outlook', www.unep.org.

——2006b, 'Protected Areas Programme: World Heritage Sites: Mt Kilimanjaro National Park', www.unep-wcmc.org.

UNPFII 2006, 'UN Permanent Forum on Indigenous Issues', www.un.org.

USAID 2006, 'USAID from the American people', www.usaid.gov.

US Department of the Interior 2002, *2001 National Survey of Fishing, Hunting, and Wildlife-Associated Recreation*, Department of the Interior, Washington, DC.

US Department of State, 'Background notes', www.state.gov.

Valentine, P 1992, 'Nature-based tourism', in CM Hall & B Weiler (eds), *Special Interest Tourism*, Belhaven Press, London, pp. 105–27.

Valentine, P & Birtles, A 2004, 'Wildlife watching', in K Higginbottom (ed.), *Wildlife Tourism: Impacts, Management and Planning*, Common Ground, Altona, Vic., pp. 15–34.

Vaske, J, Donnelly, M, Williams, D & Jonker, S 2001, 'Demographic influences on environmental value orientations and normative beliefs about national forest management', *Society and Natural Resources* 14: 761–76.

VDCE 1992, *Ecotourism: A Natural Strength for Victoria, Australia*, Victorian Department of Conservation and Environment. Melbourne.

Viljoen, J & Naicker, K 2000, 'Nature-based tourism on communal land: The Mavhulani experience', *Development South Africa* 17: 135–48.

Vincent, V & Thompson, W 2002, 'Assessing community support and sustainability for ecotourism development', *Journal of Travel Research* 41: 153–60.

Voyages 2006, 'Voyages hotels and resorts', www.voyages.com.au.

Wahab, S & Pigram, J (eds) 1997, *Tourism, Development and Growth: The Challenge of Sustainability*, Routledge, London.

Wall, G 1997, 'Is ecotourism sustainable?', *Environmental Management* 21: 483–91.

Wall, G & Mathieson, A 2005, *Tourism: Change, Impacts, and Opportunities*, Pearson Education, Upper Saddle River, NJ.

Wall, I 2004, 'Postcard from hell', Guardian Unlimited, online edn, 18 October, http://travel.guardian.co.uk.

Wallis, J & K Lee 1999, 'Primate conservation: The prevention of disease transmission', *International Journal of Primatology* 20: 803–26.

WCED 1987, *Our Common Future*, Oxford University Press, Oxford.

WCPA 2006, 'World database on protected areas', www.unep-wcmc.org.

Wearing, S 2001, *Volunteer Tourism: Experiences that Make a Difference*, CABI, Wallingford, UK.

Wearing, S & Neil, J 1999, *Ecotourism: Impacts, Potentials and Possibilities*, Butterworth-Heinemann, Oxford.

Weaver, D 1997, 'A regional framework for planning ecotourism in Saskatchewan', *Canadian Geographer* 41: 281–93.

——1998, *Ecotourism in the Less Developed World*, CABI, Wallingford, UK.

——2000a, 'A broad context model of destination development scenarios', *Tourism Management* 21: 217–24.

——2000b, 'Tourism and national parks in ecologically vulnerable areas', in RW Butler & SW Boyd (eds), *Tourism and National Parks: Issues and Implications*, John Wiley & Sons, Chichester, UK, pp. 107–24.

——2001a, 'Ecotourism in the context of other tourism types', in DB Weaver (ed.), *Encyclopedia of Ecotourism*, CABI, Wallingford, UK, pp. 73–83.

——2001b, *Ecotourism*, John Wiley & Sons, Brisbane.

——2001c, 'Deserts, grasslands and savannas', in DB Weaver (ed.), *Encyclopedia of Ecotourism*, CABI, Wallingford, UK, pp. 251–63.

——2002a, 'Asian ecotourism: Patterns and themes', *Tourism Geographies* 4: 153–72.

——2002b, 'Hard-core ecotourists in Lamington National Park, Australia', *Journal of Ecotourism* 1: 19–35.

——2002c, 'The evolving concept of ecotourism and its potential impacts', *International Journal of Sustainable Development* 5: 251–64.

——2004, 'Managing ecotourism in the island microstate: The case of Dominica', in D Diamantis (ed.), *Ecotourism: Management and Assessment*, Thomson, London, pp. 151–63.

——2005a, 'Comprehensive and minimalist dimensions of ecotourism', *Annals of Tourism Research* 32: 439–55.

——2005b, 'Mass and urban ecotourism: New manifestations of an old concept', *Tourism Recreation Research* 30(1): 19–26.

——2005c, 'The distinctive dynamics of exurban tourism', *International Journal of Tourism Research* 7: 23–33.

——2006, *Sustainable Tourism: Theory and Practice*, Elsevier Butterworth-Heinemann, Oxford.

Weaver, D & Lawton, L 2002, 'Overnight ecotourist market segmentation in the Gold Coast hinterland of Australia', *Journal of Travel Research* 40: 270–80.

——2006, *Tourism Management*, 3rd edn, John Wiley & Sons, Brisbane.

Weaver, D & Schlüter, R 2001, 'Latin America and the Caribbean', in DB Weaver (ed.), *Encyclopedia of Ecotourism*, CABI, Wallingford, UK, pp. 173–88.

Webster, P 2003, 'Will oil spell trouble for Western Pacific Gray Whales?', *Science* 300: 1365.

Weiler, B & Ham, S 2001, 'Tour guides and interpretation in ecotourism', in DB Weaver (ed.), *Encyclopedia of Ecotourism*, CABI, Wallingford, UK, pp. 549–63.

Weiler, B & Richins, H 1995, 'Extreme, extravagant and elite: A profile of ecotourists on Earthwatch expeditions', *Tourism Recreation Research* 20(1): 29–36.

Wells, M & Brandon, K 1992, *People and Parks: Linking Protected Area Management with Local Communities*, World Bank, Washington DC.

Wheeller, B 1994, 'Egotourism, sustainable tourism and the environment: A symbiotic, symbolic or shambolic relationship', in AV Seaton et al. (eds), *Tourism: State of the Art*, John Wiley & Sons, Chichester, UK, pp. 647–54.

Wight, P 1996, 'North American ecotourists: Market profile and trip characteristics', *Journal of Travel Research* 34(4): 2–10.

——2001, 'Ecotourists: Not a homogeneous market segment', in DB Weaver (ed.), *Encyclopedia of Ecotourism*, CABI, Wallingford, UK, pp. 37–62.

Wildlife Conservation Society 2004, 'Using protected areas to extend economic benefits to rural China', www.chinabiodiversity.com.

Winson, A 2006, 'Ecotourism and sustainability in Cuba: Does socialism make a difference?', *Journal of Sustainable Tourism* 14: 6–23.

World Resources Institute 2005, *A Guide to World Resources 2005: The Wealth of the Poor*, Oxford University Press, Oxford.

Wright, J & Skaggs, R 2002, 'Purchase of development rights and conservation easements: Frequently asked questions', www.cahe.nmsu.edu.

WTO 1997, *Agenda 21 for the Travel and Tourism Industry*, World Tourism Organization, Madrid.

——2001, *Compendium of Tourism Statistics* 1995–1999, 21st edn, World Tourism Organization, Madrid.

——2002, *Ecotourism Market Reports*, World Tourism Organization, Madrid.

——2006a, 'Tourism market trends', 2005 edn, www.unwto.org.

——2006b, 'Global code of ethics for tourism', www.unwto.org.

——2006c, 'Tourism highlights', 2006 edn, www.unwto.org.

WTO/UNEP 2002, 'World Ecotourism Summit (Quebec, Canada, 19–22 May 2002) Final Report', www.uneptie.org.

WTTC 2003, *Blueprint for New Tourism*, World Travel and Trade Council, London.

WWF 2001, 'Guidelines for community-based ecotourism development', www.icrtourism.org.

——2002, 'Resumption of mountain gorilla poaching after 17 years sends shockwaves through conservation circles', www.panda.org.

——2006a, 'Code of Conduct for Arctic Tourists', http://assets.panda.org.

——2006b, 'Welcome to Papua New Guinea', www.wwfpacific.org.fj.

Y2Y 2006, 'Yellowstone to Yukon conservation initiative', www.y2y.net.

Yale Center for Environmental Law and Policy 2005, '2005 Environmental Sustainability Index: Benchmarking national environmental stewardship', www.yale.edu.

Yaman, A & Mohd, A 2004, 'Community-based ecotourism: A new proposition for sustainable development and environmental conservation in Malaysia', *Journal of Applied Science* 4: 583–89.

Young, G 1973, *Tourism: Blessing or Blight?* Penguin, Harmondsworth, UK.

Yu, D, Hendrickson, T & Castillo, A 1997, 'Ecotourism and conservation in Amazonian Peru: Short-term and long-term challenges', *Environmental Conservation* 24: 130–8.

Yunis, E 2003, 'Sustainable tourism: World trends and challenges ahead', in R Buckley, C Pickering & DB Weaver (eds), *Nature-based Tourism, Environment and Land Management*, CABI, Wallingford, UK, pp. 11–16.

Zakai, D & Chadwick-Furman, N 2002, 'Impacts of intensive recreational diving on coral reefs at Eilat, northern Red Sea', *Biological Conservation* 105: 179–87.

Zeppel, H 2006, *Indigenous Ecotourism*, CABI, Wallingford, UK.

INDEX

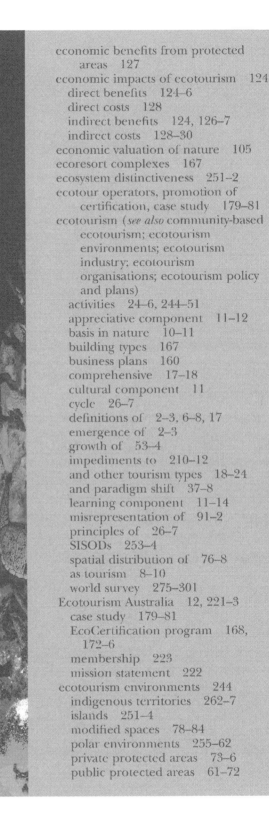

environmental damage 34–5, 104, 260
environmental damage cost (EDC) 104
environmental movement 34–5
environmental paradigm 32–4, 36, 37–8
environmentalism, fostered by ecotourism 97–8
environmentalism-related population clusters 40–1
Eurocentric value system, imposition of 131–2
Europe 320, 284–5
exotic species introduction 102–3, 205
external environments 183–207, 210–12
  assessing 205–6
  impediments to ecotourism 210–12
extractive tourism 24, 25
exurbanisation 197

failure rate, small business 154–6
farmers, interaction with ecotourists and hunters 190–2
fiscal policy 201–2
fishing 187, 195–6
FIT (free and independent travel) 151, 153
forestry and logging 192–4, 211
frontstage space 131
funds to manage and expand protected areas 95

gender and ecotourism 50–1
geographical segmentation 47–50
geotourists 42
Germany, as ecotourist market for Australia, case study 57–9
governments
  and ecotourism development 229–30
  and ecotourism in Australia 199–200
  ideology and environmental attitudes 200
  initiatives 200–1
  and tourism 199–200
GPT Group 168
Gray, John 147–9
green consumers 38–41

Green Globe 42, 176
green paradigm 35–7, 37–8
green travellers 38, 41–3
greenwashing 91–2
guidebooks 163

habitat/species management areas (IUCN category IV) 67, 69–70
hard ecotourism 43–4, 105–6
hard/soft ecotourism spectrum 43, 44, 46–7
hard technology 36
health tourism 25
heritage tourism 127
Hervey Bay Marine Park, whale-watching regulations 249–50
hiking, as ecological cost 101–2
Himalayas, and ecotourism 283
hunters, interaction with ecotourists and farmers 190–2
hunting 185–7, 195
hybrid types of tourism 20–1

ideal types
  of ecotourists 43–5
  of paradigms 36
  of tourism 4–5
impact management strategies 105
  hard and soft ecotourism 105–7
  site hardening and softening 108
  and sustainable design 108–9
  visitation quotas and fees 110
  visitor education 111–17
  whale-watching 249–51
  wildlife viewing and access restrictions 111
  zoning 107
inbound tour operators 153, 164–5
income level and ecotourism 52
incremental access 283
indicators, sustainability 16
indigenous cultures 11, 263–4
indigenous renaissance 265
indigenous territories 262–3
  environmental and cultural considerations 263–4
  political and social considerations 265–6
  protected areas 266–7
indigenous tourism 26
indirect ecological benefits of ecotourism 92, 97–8

Manufactured by Amazon.ca
Bolton, ON